Independence
and
Foreign Policy

Independence
and
Foreign Policy

New Zealand in the World
Since 1935

Malcolm McKinnon

AUCKLAND UNIVERSITY PRESS

First published 1993
Auckland University Press
University of Auckland
Private Bag 92019
Auckland

Typeset by Deadline Typesetting Ltd
Printed by GP Print Ltd

Publication is assisted by the Historical Branch of the Department of
Internal Affairs.

Distributed outside New Zealand by Oxford University Press.

For my parents

Contents

Abbreviations

AB	Airmail Bulletin (Department of External Affairs)
AIBR	*Australasian Insurance and Banking Record*
AJHR	*Appendices to the Journals of the House of Representatives*
AMDA	Anglo-Malayan Defence Agreement
ANU	Australian National University
ANZAM	Australia, New Zealand and Malayan region
ANZUS	Australia, New Zealand and United States security treaty
ASEAN	Association of South East Asian Nations
ASPAC	Asian and Pacific Council
ATL	Alexander Turnbull Library, Wellington
CAFCA	Campaign Against Foreign Control of Aotearoa
CAP	Common Agricultural Policy (of the EEC)
CCEFQ	Cabinet Committee on Economic and Financial Questions
CER	Closer Economic Relations (New Zealand and Australia)
CND	Campaign for Nuclear Disarmament
COTP	Cabinet Committee on Overseas Trade Policy
CPNZ	Communist Party of New Zealand
DEA	Department of External Affairs
EA	External Affairs (National Archives series classification)
EAR	*External Affairs Review*
ECAFE	(United Nations) Economic Commission for Asia and the Far East
EEC	European Economic Community
EP	*Evening Post*
FOL	Federation of Labour
FRUS	*Foreign Relations of the United States*
GATT	General Agreement on Tariffs and Trade
GGNZ	Governor-General of New Zealand
HART	Halt All Racist Tours (organisation)
HST	Harry S Truman Library, Independence, Mo.
IEA	International Energy Agency
IMF	International Monetary Fund
IPR	Institute of Pacific Relations
JCPS	*Journal of Commonwealth Political Studies*
JICH	*Journal of Imperial and Commonwealth History*
JSEAS	*Journal of South East Asian Studies*
LRC	Labour Representation Committee
MERT	Ministry of External Relations and Trade
MFA	Ministry of Foreign Affairs
N	Nash Papers, National Archives, Wellington
NA	National Archives, Wellington

NAC	National Advisory Council (US)
NBR	*National Business Review*
NLF	National Liberation Front (Vietnam)
NRC	National Records Center, Suitland, Md
NZEAR	*New Zealand External Affairs Review*
NZER	T. C. Larkin, ed., *New Zealand's External Relations*
NZERR	*New Zealand External Relations Review*
NZE&T	*New Zealand Economist and Taxpayer*
NZFAR	*New Zealand Foreign Affairs Review*
NZH	*New Zealand Herald*
NZIIA	New Zealand Institute of International Affairs
NZIR	*New Zealand International Review*
NZJH	*New Zealand Journal of History*
NZP	New Zealand Party
NZPD	*New Zealand Parliamentary Debates*
NZRFU	New Zealand Rugby Football Union
NZWA 1945-57	A. D. McIntosh *et al.*, *New Zealand in World Affairs*, v. 1, *1945-1957*
NZWA 1957-72	Malcolm McKinnon, ed., *New Zealand in World Affairs*, v. 2, *1957-1972*
ODT	*Otago Daily Times*
OECD	Organisation for Economic Cooperation and Development
OPEC	Organisation of Petroleum Exporting Countries
PACDAC	Public Advisory Committee on Disarmament and Arms Control
PBEC	Pacific Basin Economic Council
PIIDS	Pacific Islands Industrial Development Scheme
RG	Record Group (US State Department archive classification)
RNZAF	Royal New Zealand Air Force
RNZN	Royal New Zealand Navy
SEA	Secretary of External Affairs
SEATO	South East Asia Treaty Organisation
SFA	Secretary of Foreign Affairs
SIS	Security Intelligence Service
SPARTECA	South Pacific Regional Trade and Cooperation Agreement
SSDA	Secretary of State for Dominion Affairs (UK)
T	Treasury series, National Archives, Wellington
TLS	*Times Literary Supplement*
USAF	United States Air Force
USNA	United States National Archives, Washington DC
VUW	Victoria University of Wellington
WEA	Workers' Educational Association

Preface and acknowledgements

Questions of identity and foreign relations have long been linked in discussion, and my wish to write this book arose partly because I felt that this should not be the case. It did not seem to me that the evolution of identity explained foreign policy, even that it had much to do with it. An analysis of the idea of 'independence' proved to be a much more fertile way of approaching the subject of foreign policy, and it also allowed me to talk more generally about New Zealand's foreign relations over the last five and a half decades.

A number of experiences have shaped my approach to the subject. I became aware of the preoccupations of J. C. Beaglehole and F. L. W. Wood, two scholars often cited in this study, while I was teaching in the History Department at Victoria University, though neither of them had taught me; and also through my involvement with the New Zealand Institute of International Affairs. There is a sense therefore in which I inherited an interest in the issues addressed in the following pages.

Such involvements also exposed me to a world of political assumptions different from those of the world in which I had grown up. In one world it was assumed that one voted National until proven otherwise, in the other it was assumed one voted Labour until proven otherwise. While many studies of New Zealand's culture, including its political culture, have emphasised its homogeneity, I experienced heterogeneity. This in turn meant that in writing this book I would both want, and feel the need, to address ideological issues in foreign policy.

If some experiences made me aware of the extent of division within New Zealand's political culture at any one time, others made me aware of continuities over time. We live in an age when to be physically active, mentally alert and over seventy-five is no great cause for comment. A large number of people now in their seventies and eighties were actively involved in almost all the events recounted in this study, and may be some of its most interested readers. The time period of this book is less than that of my parents' lifetime, even though it traverses two generations (25-30 years) in which there have been two major (1943-45, 1989-91) and two lesser (1953-55, 1969-72) 'revolutions' in international relations. But the outlook and experience of my parents, and many of their generation in New Zealand, have been marked by continuity rather than change, and that continuity has shaped the political culture as a whole.

Some readers may expect a book like this to deal extensively in matters of personality, to reveal the truth about episodes that have not yet fully seen the light of day, and such like. I do not doubt that there are some fascinating—and still untold—stories in the history of New Zealand foreign relations. I am more preoccupied myself with identifying systems and patterns than with revealing secrets and solving mysteries. There are undoubtedly temperamental reasons for this, but I think there are more substantial ones as well—certainly one of the aims of the book is to demonstrate that much in the history of New Zealand foreign relations is clear if we apprehend the underlying patterns.

Writing contemporary history is always tricky, not to say questionable. Although this study covers the period from 1935 to the present, it is not evenly based on archival research. I have done quite a lot of such research for the pre-1970 period, partly in the course of working in the field of external economic relations for my Ph.D., partly in the course of subsequent writing, partly specifically for this book. There is also a considerable thesis and research paper literature for the pre-1970 era. The parts of the book covering the period after 1970—chapters 8 and 12, and parts of chapters 9, 10 and 11—are not based on archive research. They constitute rather a series of extended essays applying the arguments developed in the first two thirds of the book to this later period.

In writing this book I became even more keenly conscious than I had been of the dearth of monographs on New Zealand's post-Second World War history, and in particular on its political history. The number of practising historians in New Zealand is of course small, and the pitfalls of writing contemporary history I have already alluded to, but other reasons have also been influential. The first is the pressure on university teachers to administer and teach—but also to publish. The conflicts engendered by such competing pressures have been reconciled partly through the publication of journal articles and edited collections rather than book-length studies. Secondly, a shift away from political history in historiography generally occurred worldwide, from the 1960s onwards, just when New Zealand had acquired an historical profession which could not be counted on the fingers of both hands. The energies of those historians have largely been directed to other than political history. Thirdly, the idea that New Zealand national history has a progessive, or indeed unified shape to it, be that shape of left or right ideological origin, has fallen out of favour. This has happened partly because of the historiographical shift, but also because of changes in New Zealand's circumstances and in the country's politics. The actions and records of neither the Muldoon government, 1975-84, nor the fourth Labour government, 1984-90, can readily be assimilated into earlier, progressive, interpretations of national history.

A study like this accumulates many debts which can be acknowledged rather than fully repaid. The staffs of National Archives, the Alexander Turnbull Library, the National Library, and the libraries of Victoria University of Wellington and the Department of Internal Affairs were unfailingly courteous and helpful in assisting me with my research and bibliographical enquiries. So also were the staffs of overseas institutions in which I consulted material—National Archives, the National Record Center and the Harry S Truman Library in the United States and the Public Record Office in London. I am indebted in particular to the Trustees of the K. J. Holyoake and J. R. Marshall Papers, both held at the Turnbull Library, for granting me permission to study in those collections, and to the then Secretary of Foreign Affairs, Merwyn Norrish, for providing access to Ministry files. The Commonwealth Fund of New York helped make it possible for me to work in the archives collections in the United States. My employer to 1990, Victoria University of Wellington, gave me the opportunity to take leave which allowed me to do a substantial amount of work on the book over an uninterrupted period. The community of Raglan—Whaingaroa—provided an hospitable environment in which to do this. Sarah Catherall, Ann McLellan and Richard Shires all provided valuable research assistance on different occasions and Sara Knox did that and much more over a longer period. Kristin Downey, Gloria Biggs and Barbara Cleverley in the History Department at Victoria, and Simon Harding, Kathryn Hastings and Philip van Dyk at the Historical Branch were also very helpful. I am very grateful to them all.

Thanks too to Joan McCracken and staff in the Alexander Turnbull Library photographic section, Liz Brooker at the *Evening Post*, Jane Mulryan at the Ministry of External Relations and Trade, and National Archives staff for their assistance in the search for photos.

My former colleagues in the Victoria University History Department and elsewhere in that University, both present and past, and my present colleagues in the Historical Branch, have all been invaluable in providing moral support, encouragement and a sounding board for ideas. I owe a special debt to Mary Boyd, teacher as well as colleague, who patiently and intelligently guided me in my earlier efforts in the field of international relations and on whose students' work I have also been able to draw. My debt to many past years of honours students at Victoria will be evident from the references. Ian McGibbon, Jock Phillips, Roberto Rabel and Kerry Taylor all read early versions of the manuscript right through, a true test of friendship. So also did Brook Barrington, Malcolm Templeton and Graham Fortune at the Ministry of External Relations and Trade. The responses and comments of all these individuals substantially helped improve the book, though needless to say none of them bear any responsibility for its final form. I am also indebted to Ian McGibbon for allowing me to read his manuscript, presently in press, of New Zealand's involvement in the Korean War, and to cite it, to Roberto Rabel for his efforts in locating United States archival material with reference to New Zealand and to Malcolm Templeton for drawing my attention to particular documents and for enlarging in discussion my understanding of New Zealand's external relations in the 1950s in particular. Christine Dann generously provided me with her invaluable collection of material on the peace and related movements in the 1970s and first half of the 1980s and Elsie Locke kindly allowed me to read her equally valuable manuscript on the history of the peace movement. I am also grateful to those who agreed to be interviewed in the course of my research.

Auckland University Press, its Managing Editor, Elizabeth Caffin, and its readers, were a pleasure to work with, not because they were easy on me, but because they were not. If I did not before know the difference between an unpolished manuscript and a book, I do now. I am very grateful for the efforts Elizabeth in particular put in to ensuring that this work was transformed from the one into the other, and for the encouragement she provided on the way.

My biggest single debt, intellectual and personal, is to my brother John, who also read the manuscript through from beginning to end, more than once, and with whom I discussed its argument and interpretations extensively; indeed so extensive was that discussion in both time and character that I now find it difficult at some points to distinguish our respective contributions: at other points I can. His family were very tolerant of this, and I am very grateful to them for that.

My friends—many relatives included—have demonstrated the quality of their friendship over the time this book has been written, some by asking about it, some by not, and some by developing to a fine art the ability to judge when it was better to do one and when the other. I am in all of their debts. It would be invidious to name names, but many—though not by any means all— live and/or work in those inner parts of Wellington City that lie between Tinakori Hill and Mt Victoria, within walking distance of my house and my place of work, luckily for me, perhaps less so for them. My biggest debt of friendship is to Kazuo, and my biggest debt of all is acknowledged elsewhere.

Wellington
June 1992

1. Introduction: independence and foreign policy

The idea of independence is a favoured theme in discussion of New Zealand's foreign relations and the country's place in the world over the last half century and more. It is both the most common and the most valued interpretation. Not only do many accounts stress New Zealand's increasing independence, but most of their authors have also approved of such a development[1]. Critical writing is most often directed at identifying New Zealand's lack of independence, not questioning the validity of the goal.[2]

I do not want to challenge directly the importance of independence in the historical analysis of New Zealand's foreign relations in the present century. Indeed it is precisely because over the last five to six decades so much ink has been spilt in discussing independence that it seems worth standing back and examining the discussion rather than taking 'independence' as a given.

For New Zealand, it is impossible to separate out the notion of independence from the country's status as a part of the British Empire, a 'self-governing colony' since 1856, a 'Dominion' since 1907. The word 'independence' was used in varying ways to identify the relationships of component parts of the Empire to the whole. Four meanings are important for this study. All have been known and understood in New Zealand. Two have been habitually rejected, two as habitually accepted as appropriate. The two rejected meanings were the independence of secessionist nationalism and the

[1] Including, F. L. W. Wood, *New Zealand in the World*. Wellington, 1940; *The New Zealand People At War: Political and External Affairs*. Wellington, 1958; J. C. Beaglehole, a number of shorter pieces including, for example, 'International and Commonwealth Relations' in Horace Belshaw, ed., *New Zealand*. Berkeley, 1947; T. C. Larkin, ed., *New Zealand's External Relations*. Wellington 1962 (hereafter *NZER*); Henderson, J., R. Kennaway and K. Jackson, *Beyond New Zealand*. Auckland, 1980; Colin James, *The Quiet Revolution*. Wellington, 1986; David Lange, *Nuclear Free: The New Zealand Way*. Wellington, 1990. And numerous shorter statements by politicians, diplomats and scholars, many of which have appeared in periodical publications, notably *External Affairs Review* (hereafter *EAR*), subsequently *New Zealand Foreign Affairs Review* (hereafter *NZFAR*), and in occasional publications of the New Zealand Institute of International Affairs (NZIIA) including its journal *New Zealand International Review* (*NZIR*), bi-monthly since 1976.

[2] See particularly the writing in *Tomorrow* (1934-40), *Here and Now* (1949-57), *New Zealand Monthly Review* (1960-) (hereafter *Monthly Review*), and, for economic issues especially, works by W. B. Sutch, Wolfgang Rosenberg and Bruce Jesson.

independence of revolutionary socialism. The two accepted meanings were the independence of interest and the independence of what I call loyal dissent or loyal opposition.

Nationalist, secessionist independence was identified with the assertion by a people of their political distinctiveness from another people and/or state. Characteristically, this independence would have been achieved through struggle, often war: 'We will let our children fight and we ourselves will fight for independence. This is the beginning of the killings. There is no independence movement without victims.'[3] The protagonists of the fight for independence would become national heroes. Independence would become a given of the political culture: those who had supported it would have the advantage, those who for one reason or another wished to promote closer relations with other states or peoples would have to present these goals as compatible with the maintenance of the country's independence. Wars of independence, liberation wars, as they came to be known in more recent times, were familiar landmarks of late eighteenth-, nineteenth- and twentieth-century history. To New Zealanders in the middle decades of this century the most familiar were probably the American War of Independence 1776–83; the Greek rebellion against the Turks in the early nineteenth century; the Italian Risorgimento in the mid nineteenth century; the Irish nationalist movement, culminating in the Easter Rising of 1916; the Afrikaner (South African) war against the British 1899–1902, and the subsequent recovery of Afrikaner political self-determination; the Indian nationalist movement, culminating in Indian independence in 1947.

There is obviously a family relationship between this kind of independence and the independence of revolutionary socialism. But after the Russian Revolution in 1917 nationalist and socialist movements either competed alongside each other in independence struggles or at best maintained uneasy truces and so it is useful to distinguish them. The best known of these socialist revolutions were those in Russia, China, and later, Cuba and Vietnam.

Such independence movements, such nationalisms, were unacceptable in the Empire. Nationalist movements were rebellions against the Crown, movements promoted by disaffected citizens, often journalists, teachers and the like, who aroused the bulk of the population, a population not only quite contented under British rule, it was thought, but believing it preferable to any other because it provided order, stability and progress. These ordinary people, however, were political innocents and easy prey for the nationalists. So neither Parnell in Ireland nor Gandhi in India nor the Jewish nationalists in Palestine met with widespread support from British public opinion. Socialist, or communist, revolution, although no such revolution was carried out against Britain directly, was also unpopular because it attacked capital, including

3   Comment by a Lithuanian, *Dominion*, 5 Aug. 1991.

British capital, and threatened, it was believed, the world order of international democracies.

The New Zealand public, descendants at the time this study opens of migrants from Great Britain or migrants from that country themselves, satisfied for the most part with the social and economic configuration of a community bound by ties of defence and commerce as well as kinship to Britain, rejected these two notions of independence. What then did independence mean to New Zealand, a self-governing colony, then Dominion, in the British Empire or Commonwealth?[4]

New Zealand's own pursuit of independence in international affairs remained resolutely confined to the other two categories. A consideration of them will suggest why.

Firstly, independence could be a form of dissent, a progressive critique of an existing pattern, which did not, however, challenge its underlying structure. This form of independence had its roots in the evolution of the British parliamentary system, the idea of an opposition which was not seditious but loyal, and also in the many strands of dissent, in religion in particular, but also in other areas of British public life. The idea of a moral foreign policy, a frequent phrase in the dissenting lexicon, implied the capacity to reform, to renovate an existing policy. Dissent was attached to, rather than detached from, the British state, believing that it could be renewed, that it could be directed to enlightened purposes. The vigour with which New Zealand—and Australian—Presbyterians lobbied in the 1880s to stop the British government acquiescing in French annexation of the New Hebrides, where Presbyterian missions were active, is a good example.[5] This was dissent, but it was a dissent which ruled out revolution or secession: it involved, if anything, a certain pride in one's position in relation to the rest of the world in general and to Britain in particular. As the official report on the 1895 Colonial Conference in Ottawa observed: 'it may legitimately be asserted that the progressive spirit which marks the legislation of the colonies generally is having the effect of bringing them into a political prominence that invests their proceedings with considerable interest in the eyes of the British public'.[6]

And sometimes even further afield: the young Frenchman, André Siegfried, writing about the political climate of the 1890s and early 1900s, noted in this heyday of Liberal reform 'a certain sense of apostolic mission . . . . Many New Zealanders are honestly convinced that the attention of the whole

---

[4]   For a full discussion of the flavour of New Zealand's attitude to the Empire in the 1920s and early 1930s, see Angus Ross, 'Reluctant Dominion or Dutiful Daughter? New Zealand and the Commonwealth in the Inter-War Years', *Journal of Commonwealth Political Studies*, 10/1 (March 1972), pp. 28–36.

[5]   See John Salmond, 'New Zealand and the New Hebrides' in Peter Munz, ed., *The Feel of Truth*. Wellington, 1969, pp. 113–35; also Raewyn Dalziel. *Julius Vogel. Business Politician*. Auckland, 1986, p. 290.

[6]   *AJHR*, 1895, A.5, p. 2.

world is concentrated upon them, waiting with curiosity and even with anxiety to see what they will say and do next. They have certainly been a little spoilt by being always spoken of as the most *advanced* [*sic*] people in the world . . . .'[7]

The years leading up to the First World War are often identified as a period of growing militarism in British and New Zealand society. While this may be true, it is also important to recall that anti-militarism had a place in the political culture too. This was not just a case of pacifist opposition to conscription; it also played a part in the national self-image. It was the Germans who were militarist, not the British; the Germans and other continentals who had standing armies, not the British, who had ended such a practice in the seventeenth century.[8] Britain's hesitation about joining in the war was partly a reflection of the calculation of its interests; it was also the hesitation of Liberal politicians who had been nurtured in the political tradition of Cobden, Bright and Gladstone, of free trade and universal peace, of suspicion of martial values and arms races. The British population may have been swept by patriotic fervour in 1914, but some of its leaders took the decision for war in sorrow not in anger, resolved in one instance to 'watch the hideous struggle, as I should watch a devastating plague or famine—with a stoic's fortitude'.[9]

The second 'permitted' kind of independence, the vigorous defence of interest, was deeply embedded in British political culture, at least among the political classes. The settlers in the 1840s demonstrated against Colonial Office rule, which they regarded as tyrannical and undemocratic, no better than the Holy Alliance of reactionary European powers, and in securing self-government in 1856 demonstrated what good Englishmen they were. In 1869–70 political New Zealanders of even conservative persuasion were talking—admittedly rather loosely—of leaving the Empire for the United States: 'So again in 1869 [colonists] told each other that the United States gave generous help to frontiersmen struggling with Indians at a time when Britain brutally told New Zealanders to manage the Maoris as best they could.'[10] In this instance though, and certainly in others, dissatisfaction was vented essentially by the process of 'speaking up'. A glance at any history of provincial politics makes the point plainly—and repeatedly. No sooner had a new settlement been established than it claimed the same rights to its own revenue and government that its 'parent' had claimed from the Colonial Office. The colonists were equally vocal about issues outside New Zealand's

---

7   André Siegfried, *Democracy in New Zealand.* 2nd ed., with an introduction by David Hamer, Wellington, 1982, p. 58.
8   At home: the British did have a standing army in India. See also the observations in Paul Baker, *King and Country Call: New Zealanders, Conscription and the Great War.* Auckland, 1988, pp. 12, 15.
9   John Morley, who resigned from the Cabinet on Britain's entering the war, quoted in David Hamer, *John Morley: Liberal Intellectual in Politics.* London, 1968, p. 374.
10   Wood, *NZ in the World*, p. 53.

territorial limits. Angus Ross was able to get good copy from New Zealand press comment on the British government's failure to follow an expansionist, annexationist policy in the Pacific: 'Future generations will not easily forgive the apathy and almost criminal neglect of the British statesmen who are meanly trafficking away every inch of territory which might and should be secured to the British flag.'[11]

As this last quotation suggests, interest in the nineteenth and early twentieth centuries, like dissent, did usually link New Zealand and England. Raewyn Dalziel points out that Vogel was an 'Empire man' in part because the Empire advantaged New Zealand, the colony in which he had found opportunity for himself:

> New Zealand gained security, access to British finance, colonists, and markets . . . . For a politician eager to expand trade, to establish communications with other countries and to improve defence, . . . restrictions [on colonial autonomy] were constantly frustrating. In an attempt to resolve the conflict between colonial status and aspiring nationhood within the imperial framework, Vogel became one of the earliest advocates of imperial federation, a complex solution to the dilemma of New Zealand . . . .[12]

The connections were reinforced by the development of a frozen meat and dairy product trade to England at the end of the century: 'the results of our own enterprise are, in many forms, making a deep impression on the imagination of the British population. New Zealand frozen mutton, cheese and butter are invading the markets of every town and hamlet in Great Britain.'[13] This trade established a partnership with Britain, a dependence on the British market that would last relatively unchallenged for seven decades. It was a powerful buttress of patriotic sentiment:

> . . . sentimental reasons, however, would not be sufficient to determine in any lasting manner the conduct of a people, especially of an Anglo-Saxon people. That is to say, New Zealand also happens to find her interests in the friendship which unites her to England . . . . New Zealanders have been persuaded, up to now, that they have nothing to fear from the mother-country, and that she would on all occasions respect their autonomy and their integrity. In spite of their respect and devotion, it is clear that they would not tolerate the encroachment of the central power on territory which they consider to be their own.[14]

So it needs to be stressed that 'interest' as a form of independence did not necessarily entail 'independence' in the fullest sense of the term. It embodied

11   *ODT*, 30 March 1886, quoted in Angus Ross, *New Zealand Aspirations in the Pacific in the Nineteenth Century*. Oxford, 1964, p. 196.
12   Dalziel, *Vogel*, p. 179.
13   *AJHR*, 1895, A.5, p. 2.
14   Siegfried, pp. 359-60.

rather the notion of 'speaking up' and in theory it could express itself in new forms of 'dependence' if required.

In the case of New Zealand's decision not to join the Australian Federation at the turn of the century, the interest arguments were crucial. Only limited gains could be expected for New Zealand commerce and agriculture from joining the new Federation, at a time when its economic connection with Britain was not just important, but expanding. This was a classic expression of independence of interest, an independence which also expressed itself in the quest for some regulatory underpinnings to the closer economic relations with Britain (for instance, a preferential tariff).[15] It could also be seen, to the habitual fury of the more outward-looking members of the community, in a comfortable, even smug, insularity. As much dissent in the twentieth century was in the tradition of loyal opposition, so interest was rooted in the exigencies of New Zealand's commercial, financial and strategic circumstances. If these changed, then so would the formulation of interest and the pattern of thinking about the country's external relations.

When New Zealand became a Dominion in 1907, the change in status was conferred by the British government. Dominion status is a key phrase in this study. For New Zealanders it embraced both the ideas of independence of interest and values, when necessary, and of loyalty and participation. The wish of the South Africans, the Irish and in different fashion the Canadians to push Dominion status to its limits and beyond was resisted in New Zealand. It was secession in another guise. Writers on early-twentieth-century New Zealand nationalism and identity confirm this. Keith Sinclair in *A Destiny Apart* stressed that 'the achievement of political independence was not an emotional issue. Self-government had been progressively gained in the 1850s and later in the nineteenth century. The British had never sought to encroach on the colony's powers.... The remaining restrictions upon dominion autonomy were not such as to arouse a clarion call for national independence.'[16]

Speaking more specifically about Gallipoli, the New Zealand army's first major engagement in the First World War, Jock Phillips noted that 'there was in 1915 never any real possibility that many New Zealanders would define their nationalism in terms of complete independence of the mother country.'[17]

---

[15] For discussion of New Zealand and Australian Federation see Siegfried, pp. 333–48; F. L. W. Wood, 'Why did New Zealand not join the Australian Commonwealth in 1900–1901?' *NZJH*, 2/2 (Oct. 1968), pp. 115–29; Miles Fairburn, 'New Zealand and Australasian Federation 1883–1901: Another View', *NZJH*, 4/2 (Oct. 1970), pp. 138–59; Wood accords some significance to Seddon's role in keeping New Zealand out; Fairburn places more stress on economic factors, in this respect following Siegfried—'it must never be forgotten that among the Anglo-Saxons, and in particular the Australasians, the arguments from personal interests, that is to say, economic arguments, are the most powerful' (Siegfried, p. 341).

[16] Keith Sinclair, *A Destiny Apart*. Wellington, 1986, p. 103.

[17] Jock Phillips, '75 years Since Gallipoli', in David Green, ed., *Towards 1990*. Wellington, 1990, p. 93.

He defined a spectrum of nationalist sentiment: at one end, none, at the other, complete independence from Britain. He argued that Gallipoli underlined the ruling elite's position at the imperial end of the spectrum, giving its members a 'more assured and confident pride in their special role within the Empire.' The ordinary soldier, he argued, moved more towards the independent end of the spectrum, but never questioned New Zealand's place within the Empire.[18] New Zealand nationalism overlapped with British nationalism.

In the 1920s and 1930s each of the two 'permitted' kinds of independence was associated with one of the main political currents in New Zealand life. Dissent over foreign policy was for the Labour movement part and parcel of dissent over other issues, and was closely connected with the role that Labour parties played in British political systems in the first two-thirds of this century. The New Zealand Labour Party, like others, was still fighting off charges of disloyalty: Labour's rejection of the Communist Party and Communist policies, in particular its rivalry with the Communist Party in the trade union movement, informed its foreign policy as it did other aspects of its political behaviour.

The vigorous assertion of interest, whatever that interest may have been, was second nature to the business and farmer elements that dominated the non-Labour parties, the Coalition of 1931-5, and the National Party from 1936. While the balance of interests on the right favoured close ties with Britain or with the international economy generally, there was no hesitation about vocally expressing New Zealand's interests, or those of particular groups of New Zealanders, for instance, primary producers, when the occasion required it. On security matters, even a 'loyal' Prime Minister like Massey would speak up if he thought New Zealand's interests were threatened: 'On behalf of New Zealand I protest earnestly against the proposal to make Singapore a strong and safe naval station being abandoned, because I believe that as long as Britain holds the supremacy of the sea the Empire will stand, but if Britain loses naval supremacy the Empire may fall . . . .'[19]

In his excellent study of modern nationalism, *Imagined Communities*, Benedict Anderson argued that even in colonies of settlement there was some exclusion from the highest reaches of metropolitan power: 'Anglicised Australians did not serve in Dublin or Manchester, and not even in Ottawa or Cape Town.'[20] In fact they did—Australians, and New Zealanders, took

---

18 Phillips, pp. 96, 100.
19 Quoted in Ian McGibbon, *Blue-Water Rationale: The Naval Defence of New Zealand 1914-1942*. Wellington, 1981, p. 135.
20 Benedict Anderson, *Imagined Communities*. London, 1983, p. 89. Anderson qualifies the point in a footnote, 'to be sure, by late Edwardian times, a few "white colonials" did migrate to London and became Members of Parliament or prominent press lords'. Some New Zealand examples in more recent times: Ralph Grey, b. Wellington 1910, joined Colonial Service 1936, Deputy Governor-General of Nigeria 1957-60; Alexander Ross, b. Northland 1907, Chairman, United Dominions Trust, London 1963-74. See also the list—and revealing entry—of expatriates in A. H. McLintock, ed., *Encyclopaedia of New Zealand*. Wellington, 1966, pp. 573-604.

prominent positions in the City, were recruited to the Colonial Service, the Indian Civil Service and the universities. There was a widespread satisfaction with the relationship. The Statute of Westminster in 1931, which formalised the Dominion's independent status, was disliked, because it offered a kind of independence which these New Zealanders did not need: 'We had all the self-government we wanted. We could choose our fellow citizens and do the other things we wanted to do. We didn't see any need for the Statute of Westminster. We were doing all right without it.'[21]

The idea of 'an independent foreign policy', a leitmotif from the 1930s to 1960s, with elements still surviving in modified form, is, it will be shown, a version of Dominion status, an amalgam of the two permitted kinds of independence. Its persistence is evidence of the persistence of a received pattern in New Zealand's foreign relations, despite all the commentary about change, new departures and turning points. Diplomacy, that is, the conduct of relations among sovereign states with only a limited sense of moral solidarity and no sense of binding obligations, was the world of British foreign relations, foreign relations of the Empire as a whole, not of New Zealand. New Zealand wanted its ambassadors to conduct relations as if they were High Commissioners (envoys accredited to other Commonwealth governments) rather than the other way round. Indeed New Zealand's foreign relations were not foreign—they were external relations, and the department which conducted them was called until 1970 the Department of External Affairs.

New Zealand's conception, not just of its own 'independence' but of the world of international relations generally, did not therefore place relations of power, of coercion, at the centre. The Empire, the Commonwealth, was a realm in which relations of consent dominated, not relations of power. In such a fashion were 'acceptable' and 'unacceptable' independence distinguished. The imperatives of New Zealand's circumstances took its diplomacy beyond the ambit of the Commonwealth but New Zealand politicians, diplomats and commentators hoped nonetheless to replicate the Commonwealth pattern in the new relationships.

While radicalism, secessionism and power politics were frowned on, one kind of nationalism was acceptable, indeed treasured. Nationalism, in the sense of the demarcation drawn between people's attitudes to compatriots and to foreigners and the preference for the former over the latter, was for New Zealanders lodged in their identity as Britons, not as New Zealanders. The assertion of British interests in the international community was moral: Britain was after all a free country, the freest in Europe. 'Britain' and 'principle' were so intertwined in the minds of at least a large section of the British—and of the New Zealand—public, that what seemed like British interests to others looked like principle to the British themselves. France might need Britain, but

21   Carl Berendsen, quoted by Angus Ross in 'Reluctant Dominion', p. 43.

the relationship would be on Britain's terms. Equally, the United States might be an ally, and this was expected to involve American support for British interests. If the Americans faltered, they were accused of being selfish, irresponsible, isolationist. But George Washington's oft-quoted words to the American people at the end of his presidency, words that reverberated down the years as a benchmark of independence in foreign policy, in the United States but also in other countries, would happily have been applied by New Zealanders to Britain and the Empire: 'The great rule of conduct for us in regard to foreign nations is, in extending our commercial relations to have with them as little *political* connection as possible .... Why forego the advantages of [our] peculiar situation? Why quit our own to stand upon foreign ground? Why, by interweaving our destiny with any part of Europe, entangle our peace and prosperity in the toils of European ambition, rivalship, interest, humour, or caprice?'[22]

In one fictional but realistically depicted world, it was

> uphill work for a foreigner, lame or sound, to make his way with the Bleeding Hearts. In the first place, they were vaguely persuaded that every foreigner had a knife about him; in the second, they held it to be a sound constitutional national axiom that he ought to go home to his own country .... In the third place, they had a notion that it was a sort of Divine visitation upon a foreigner that he was not an Englishman, and that all kinds of calamities happened to his country because it did things that England did not, and did not do things that England did.[23]

'I believe', said the M.P. Colonel Hargest in May 1936, 'that while it is essential that we should do our utmost to preserve the ideals of the League of Nations, it is also essential that we should maintain the strength of our Empire ... believing that our Empire will never be the aggressor in international dispute.'[24]

Reformism could also be patriotic. Writing about the ban-the-bomb movement of the 1950s and early 1960s, Richard Taylor notes that the Labour left belief in Britain's moral lead stemmed in part from 'the long tradition of quasi-pacifist internationalism .... and yet this tradition embodied also a moral *nationalism* [sic] ....' Taylor went on to argue that

> The need for Britain to reassert her importance on the world's stage—following her rapid demotion from great power status after 1945—was seen as important on the left as well as the right. Psychologically and politically the desire for Britain to 'lead again' was a powerful motivating force—and on both the Labour left and the New Left there were repeated calls for Britain to lead a new grouping of predominantly Commmonwealth countries in a neutralist third force.[25]

22 Quoted in *The Record of American Diplomacy*. New York, 1957, pp. 86–88.
23 Charles Dickens, *Little Dorrit*. Harmondsworth, 1967, p. 350.
24 *NZPD*, 345, pp. 1159–60 (15 May 1936).
25 Richard Taylor, *Against the Bomb*. Oxford, 1988, pp. 305, 306.

As British nationalism was acceptable, so also were nationalist movements which challenged other European nations. These movements were characteristically seen as assertions of the rights of people to freedom, a freedom which the British people, under their unequalled constitution, without standing army or arbitrary government, had enjoyed for centuries. The record of nineteenth-century history is replete with nationalists who were lionised by the British public—Simon Bolivar, Kossuth from Hungary, Garibaldi and Mazzini; and with English literary figures who identified with these struggles—Byron and the Greeks, Browning, George Eliot and the Italians.

This brings us back to the second theme foreshadowed at the beginning of this introduction —the notion of independence as a process rather than a goal. Our discussion of 'independence' has been analytic not progressive, arguing that ideas of independence have been embedded in the New Zealand political culture for its entire history as colony and Dominion. But many of the discussions of independence that we will consider have a strongly progressive element in them. Their authors see independence as something that has been attained, in their generation, implicitly for the first time.

The fact that independence has been 'achieved' on so many different occasions should make us reflect. The following, in the period under review, have all been instanced on occasion:

1935: the election of the first Labour government, committed to independence in foreign policy;

1939: Governor-General ceases to be a representative of the British government as well as of the Crown; New Zealand makes its own declaration of war;

1940: Britain indicates its inability to protect New Zealand in the event of a Japanese attack in the Pacific;

1943: establishment of the Department of External Affairs;

1945: New Zealand a Charter (foundation) member of the United Nations;

1947: New Zealand passes the Statute of Westminster;

1951: New Zealand signs its first treaty with a foreign power (the United States) without British involvement;

1955: first diplomatic mission in Southeast Asia;

1961: British decision to seek entry to the European Economic Community;

1965: involvement in war without Britain (Vietnam);

1969: decision to deploy military forces in Asia without Britain or United States;

1971: Britain negotiates entry into the EEC;

1972: third Labour government explicitly pursues independence in foreign policy;

1976: Muldoon government's doctrine that New Zealand must take an independent stance in negotiations with 'friends, allies and trading partners';

1984: fourth Labour government adopts anti-nuclear policy against the wishes of the United States and other allies.[26]

What is going on here, apart from amnesia? We can usefully conduct the discussion in terms of two periods with a division in the 1960s. In the first period, independence was associated particularly with a group of scholars and diplomats who believed New Zealand had 'fallen behind' in the matter of independence, had succumbed to a 'mother complex'. The Empire was no longer the all-embracing world it had been before the First World War—the international community had to be taken account of too, as witness the existence of the League of Nations, and New Zealand's interest in the outcome of the conferences on naval disarmament and security in the Pacific in the early 1920s. New Zealand's independence had to be international as well as imperial.[27]

At least some conservative politicians saw this—Downie Stewart was active in the Institute of Pacific Relations; Sir James Allen, Minister of Defence during the First World War, was interested in the League of Nations and President of the New Zealand branch of the IPR on his return to New Zealand in 1927.[28] Internationalism was more widespread on the left. War and its aftermath had focused attention on international issues—would the revolution in Russia last? Would the international socialist movement split between Communists and Social Democrats? Would there be a socialist revolution in Germany? Would the peoples of the colonial Empires revolt? Would Italian Fascism spread elsewhere through Europe? In 1919 the New Zealand Labour Party had been hostile to the League of Nations, seeing it as not much more than a predatory alliance of capitalist victor nations. By 1935 Labour was a strong supporter of the League, seeing it as a means for preserving and/or attaining a more just international order. The amalgamation of Labour's internationalism with its dissenting tradition created a strong expectation of 'new departures' when the party took over the government at the end of 1935.

Over the next generation the implications of these new ideas of independence were fully worked out in New Zealand foreign policy. By 1960 it seemed to many that not only had this process run its course but it had done so successfully: New Zealand's 'independence' in 1960 was incomparably more international than in 1935. Moreover there was a high degree of consensus between the two main traditions, of interest and of dissent. We will assess the

[26] And for earlier examples, see James Cowan, *Travel in New Zealand: The Island Dominion.* Chch, 1926, p. 12; Sinclair, *Destiny Apart*, pp. 25, 74–75, 91.
[27] E. P. Kohn, 'Internationalism, Imperialism and Insecurity: The Effect of the United States on New Zealand's International Outlook in the Early 1920s'. M. A. thesis, VUW, 1991.
[28] H. F. von Haast and G. H. Scholefield, 'New Zealand and the Pacific', *Pacific Affairs*, 3 (1930), p. 1038. See also other articles and comment in *Pacific Affairs* (the journal of the IPR), especially William Downie Stewart, 'New Zealand's Pacific Trade and Tariff', *Pacific Affairs*, 4 (1931), pp. 980–1004.

idea of an independent foreign policy at that time in a special section at the end of Chapter 6.

In the mid 1960s New Zealand fought in Vietnam alongside Australia and the United States but not Britain. A fundamental element in the idea of an independent foreign policy was called into question—that international relations, and in particular New Zealand's involvement in them, should be mediated through the Commonwealth and in close association with Britain. Was New Zealand to become a client state of a militarised American 'empire'? Or was it about to be consigned to oblivion and isolation by Britain's retreat— maybe even by America's?

The questions were asked by different individuals but they had one thing in common—they dealt with what was to most New Zealanders the unpalatable prospect of the country's external relations being dominated by power considerations rather than by the interplay of interest, dissent and shared culture that had characterised the Commonwealth and which New Zealanders hoped to see grow ever stronger in the international community as a whole— not least because in any contest of power, save only with Pacific Island states, they would come off second best.

When we turn to the record of the 1970s and 1980s, however, we do not find a sharp transition from the one formulation of independence to the other. The world of the 1970s was more benign than either right or left feared, and the interplay of interest and dissent continued, albeit against the backdrop of a rather more diffuse set of relationships than New Zealand had possessed before 1960. Further, the notion that New Zealand had progressed to a 'new' independence and maturity at this time has to be treated with care. A nationalism which had previously attached to Britain now attached to New Zealand. New Zealanders showed an 'old' rather than a new maturity.

In 1985 a collision did occur with the United States and other allies which underlined the fact of power as well as cooperation in New Zealand's international relations. It could be argued that the collision took place precisely because New Zealanders did not believe that power was a significant element in the country's relations with friends and allies. Out of that collision came another 'independent foreign policy', one which embodied both the idea that power was crucial, and the idea that it should be ignored.

This book is an analysis and a survey of the history of New Zealand foreign relations rather than a revision of an existing history. But as the discussion on the idea of 'growing up' indicates, there is scope for some revision. Writers on New Zealand foreign relations, in taking a particular approach to the question of independence, have inevitably explored some topics and issues more than others. Much more attention has been paid to the Labour Party's than to the National Party's policies. The business press, in which there is a great deal of comment about foreign relations, has not been explored as extensively as the labour and left-wing press. Labour's internationalism has been explored more than its anti-Communism; the distinctiveness of the New Zealand experience rather than the many parallels to it elsewhere in the world; New Zealand thinking and policies rather than the (most often) British antecedents of or parallels to both, and most generally, and closely connected to the last-mentioned, the immediate rather than the more distant past. One of the goals of the present study is to redress some of these omissions and oversights.

2. Independence and loyalty

The first Labour government has a reputation as the country's first government to pursue an independent foreign policy.[1] This chapter will ask two questions: where do we locate Labour's foreign policy in terms of the analysis of independence presented in the previous chapter? To what extent was Labour's policy a departure from what had gone before?

Labour's challenge

What sort of a government would Labour be? Would it attack capital, would it weaken New Zealand's links with the Empire, with Britain? Such loaded questions were the staple of much conservative rhetoric against Labour, and some of Labour's own rhetoric lent credence to these suggestions. Labour believed in independence. Was this what independence would entail? Some of Labour's leaders during the First World War were remembered for their fiery rhetoric, their opposition to conscription, their welcome for the October Revolution in Russia which brought the Bolsheviks (renamed Communists in 1918) to power. There had been sympathy in the Labour movement for the Irish nationalists. Harry Holland, Labour leader till his death in 1933, was a relentless critic of British imperialism. Labour had initially been critical of the League of Nations as an alliance of victor, capitalist nations.[2] Labour had 'moderated' its rhetoric and its programme since the early 1920s, and Michael Joseph Savage, who succeeded to the leadership on Holland's death in 1933, was of less radical inclinations;[3] but at the time it was elected to government, Labour was still ideologically a party of the left. It was a particular—and radical—vision of world order and justice which prompted the Labour

[1]   See, for instance, many of the papers in *NZER*; Wood, *Political and External Affairs*, ch. 3; A. D. McIntosh, 'The Origins of the Department of External Affairs and the Formulation of an Independent Foreign Policy' in A. D. McIntosh *et al.*, *New Zealand In World Affairs*, v. 1, *1945–1957* (hereafter *NZWA 1945-57*). Wellington, 1977, pp. 9–35; W. David McIntyre, 'Labour Experience in Foreign Policy' in *New Directions in New Zealand Foreign Policy*, ed. Hyam Gold. Auckland, 1985, pp. 27–35; 'Independent Labour line first seen in 1930s', *EP*, 22 Mar. 1985.
[2]   P. J. O'Farrell, *Harry Holland, Militant Socialist*. Canberra, 1964.
[3]   See in particular Robin Oliver, 'Ideology, the Slump and the New Zealand Labour Party: A Study of the Ideology of the NZ Labour Party in the 1930s'. Univ. of Auckland, M.A. thesis, 1981; Bruce Brown, *The Rise of New Zealand Labour*. Wellington, 1962; Barry Gustafson, *From the Cradle to the Grave*. Auckland, 1986; Keith Sinclair, *Walter Nash*. Auckland, 1976.

government to take many of its initiatives in the external sphere: 'whether Britain, or France or Russia do or do not agree with us, the moral righteousness of New Zealand's attitude is not affected in the least'.[4] Labour was therefore different, different in its approach and its concerns, from the Coalition politicians and the editorial writers of the daily press.

In political (as distinct from economic) external relations, the new government's ideological approach and its differences with Britain were especially evident in its responses to the successive international crises of the late 1930s. Labour had become a strong supporter of the League of Nations in the 1920s—the League was seen as an organisation that could banish war and create a more just world. In the later 1920s the world was largely at peace; but in the 1930s conflict had become the norm. Imperial Japan and Nazi Germany had both left the League and presented a far more direct challenge to its idea of world order than had the revolutionary Soviet Union in the 1920s. The latter power, fearful of German resurgence, had joined the League in 1934. Three 'blocs' could be discerned in international relations (although there were still some ties crossing the bloc boundaries)—the western capitalist democracies: France, Britain and the United States; the Fascist/authoritarian powers: Germany, Japan and Italy; and the Soviet Union.[5]

When Italy invaded Ethiopia in 1935 the belief that a strong League would *prevent* a major war was tested, and found wanting by many. The League of Nations Union itself found much of its membership wanted to see it take a stronger stand against aggression, even if this meant a major war became more, rather than less, likely.[6] The new government felt the same way.[7] But the British and French governments were far from settled on sanctions, on a hard-line policy. News leaked of proposals put together by the two Foreign Ministers, Hoare and Laval, which would have amounted to a de facto recognition of Italian predominance in Ethiopia and a considerable territorial cession to Italy. The news brought a tidal wave of protest, but even before that the new Labour government in Wellington had told London that it could not associate itself with the proposals.[8]

France and Britain reverted to the sanctions policy, but it proved ineffectual. By May the Italian conquest was complete: the League decided to end sanctions. The depleted ranks of National M.P.s in Parliament agreed, but the government did not—New Zealand officially acquiesced in their removal but on condition that the League would look at its structure with a

4   Fraser quoted in Ross, 'Reluctant Dominion', p. 40.
5   For an excellent discussion, see Martin Wight, 'The Balance of Power', in *Survey of International Affairs, 1939-1946: The World in March 1939*. Royal Institute of International Affairs, London, 1952, pp. 508-31.
6   See B. M. Attwood, 'Apostles of Peace: the New Zealand League of Nations Union'. Univ. of Auckland, M.A. thesis, 1979, pp. 76-97.
7   The implications of this for its own supporters are discussed below, pp. 28-31.
8   J. D. O'Shea, 'New Zealand and the Italo-Ethiopian Dispute', pp. 30-31. WA-II 21, NA.

view to toughening it.[9] New Zealand presented a lengthy memorandum to the League on the strengthening of its Covenant, including the need for military action to be certain if sanctions were not effective. Bill Jordan, New Zealand's Labour-appointed High Commissioner in London and representative at the League in Geneva, addressed the Assembly: 'the British delegates moved restlessly in their seats as [Jordan] raised one issue after another which Britain would prefer to regard as closed'. But the Committee of 28 set up to address the question, on which New Zealand was represented, adjourned for over a year after four tortuous procedural meetings.[10]

Despite this failure the government did continue to advocate a strong stand by the democratic powers and the League against aggression. This was particularly evident in its response to the Spanish Civil War, in the interventions by the Prime Minister, Michael Joseph Savage, at the Imperial Conference in 1937, and in the response to the war that broke out between China and Japan in the middle of 1937. New Zealand served a two-year term on the Council of the League, 1936–38. In December 1936 Jordan made his first public statement on Spain, supporting the appeal of the Spanish government to the League to recognise the shortcomings of the non-intervention policy, which meant that the Western powers did not help the government but Italy and Germany did help Franco, the rebel leader. Britain was one of the architects of the non-intervention policy: on a number of subsequent occasions New Zealand took a stronger stand on Spain than did Britain.

At the Imperial Conference in May 1937, New Zealand was clearly the Dominion least enamoured of the British government's appeasement policy.[11] Both Walter Nash, the Minister of Finance, who had a long-standing interest in international relations and commitment to the League, and Savage were disappointed to find how little enthusiasm there was for the League at the Conference. The Dominions Secretary, Inskip, rebutted New Zealand's attack on British weakness in the face of aggression, but the New Zealanders were unrepentant. Zetland, Secretary of State for India, said that Savage gave a 'sermon on the immorality of British foreign policy'. While being patronising, the British also made efforts to win the New Zealanders over; but on his return to New Zealand Savage made no secret of his disappointment: 'I expressed the view that mistakes—and grievous mistakes—had in the past been made in the foreign policy of the British Commonwealth.'[12]

9   H. Witheford, 'The Labour Party and War', ii, pp. 7–10. WA-II 21/45c, NA.
10   O'Shea, 'Italo-Ethiopian Dispute', pp. 17, 19; quote is from *EP*, 30 Sept. 1936.
11   Appeasement, the British and French policy of trying to resolve differences with Italy, Germany and Japan without recourse to war, had positive connotations for many including the peace movement. Only after Hitler invaded Prague and liquidated the Czechoslovak Republic in March 1939 was the policy—and the word—widely discredited. For peace movement comments on the justice of some of Italy and Germany's concerns in 1935 see Martin Ceadel, *Pacifism in Britain 1914–1945: The Defining of a Faith.* Oxford, 1980, p. 188.
12   *Dominion*, 29 July 1937; for British at the conference see Ritchie Ovendale, *Appeasement and the English Speaking World—Britain, the United States, the Dominions and the Policy of Appeasement 1937–1939.* Cardiff, 1975, pp. 42–44 (Zetland), 198 (Inskip).

By the time Savage was back, war had broken out in China. In the League Jordan again consistently urged strong action against Japan, with the new British Foreign Secretary, Anthony Eden, emphasising a more cautious approach. At a private meeting of Dominion and British delegates at Geneva Jordan found himself disagreeing with the British representative, who wanted a resolution condemning the bombing of open towns couched in such a way that it gave no offence to the Japanese, although aid would be offered to non-combatant victims. Jordan characterised this as 'refusing to stop a mad gunman but merely following with bandages patching up some of the damage he was doing'. On the motion of Maxim Litvinov, the Soviet Foreign Minister, New Zealand was appointed to a Committee on the war but it achieved little, although Jordan did succeed in having Japan labelled as the aggressor.[13]

Hitler took decisive steps in foreign policy in 1938. The government does not seem to have responded to the Anschluss—enforced union—of Austria with Germany in March. It is hard to believe it could have approved, but Savage told the British Prime Minister, Neville Chamberlain, that the British government was better able to judge what to do. Eden's resignation as Foreign Secretary and the Anglo-Italian rapprochement, a consequence of the Anschluss, did bother Savage. New Zealand refused to agree that League members should be free to recognise the Italian conquest of Ethiopia, one of the by-products of the rapprochement. A question was asked in the House of Commons, while Jordan's statement on this to the League Council provoked a clause in the New Zealand Opposition's amending Address-in-Reply motion—'that the attitude of the Government with regard to foreign affairs is a direct threat to the solidarity of the Empire at a time when a united stand for world peace on a basis of strength and security is more necessary than ever'—and exchanges between Peter Fraser, the Deputy Prime Minister, and Adam Hamilton, the Leader of the Opposition, and later between Walter Nash, the Minister of Finance, and Joseph Gordon Coates, the former conservative Prime Minister, on New Zealand's loyalty to Britain.[14] Nash, for instance, 'was not', he said, 'questioning the good will and desire of Mr Neville Chamberlain . . . to avoid war. But surely we have a right to question the road the the United Kingdom Government is following, if we think it will lead to war and greater trouble.'[15]

[13]   Ovendale, p. 83; N. D. Pratt, 'The New Zealand Government's Attitude to Appeasement Policies'. VUW History Dept. research paper, 1969, p. 20; Gustafson, p. 211; for detailed discussion of the response to the Sino-Japanese War, see I. F. Milner, *New Zealand's Interests and Policies in the Far East*. Vancouver, 1939, pp. 86–114.
[14]   *NZPD*, 251, pp. 124, 132–3 (1 July 1938); pp. 405–14 (12 July 1938). See also J. V. Wilson, 'New Zealand's Participation in International Organisations', in *NZER*, pp. 65–71; P. A. Monteith, 'New Zealand and the Czechoslovak Crisis'. Univ. of Auckland, M. A. thesis, 1980, pp. 32, 37 (latter reference is to House of Commons question in which Dominions Secretary Malcolm McDonald stonewalled 'we have never allowed . . . differences of opinion to divide the British Commonwealth of Nations'); see also below, p. 27.
[15]   *NZPD*, 252, p. 414 (12 July 1938).

Through the European summer of 1938 tension built up over Czechoslovakia and Germany's professed concern for the German-language population in that country. Jordan, as President, opening the League Assembly on 12 September, said that 'if peace were violated then it would not be possible for the violators to count on the neutrality even of the countries which were most remote.'[16] But the government was much more cautious over the German–Czech crisis than over earlier disputes. This was not a proxy conflict like Spain: the great powers were directly involved. The first of Chamberlain's trips to Germany to attempt a peaceful accommodation of German demands took place on 14 September. In a statement issued on 15 September, Savage supported Chamberlain's decision to fly to Germany. The principal burden of Savage's observations was that New Zealand was completely united with Britain and that Chamberlain was trying to avert a war.[17] Chamberlain went to Germany for a second abortive meeting with Hitler on 22 September. The Empire's sole Labour government was not as happy with the direction of British policy as were other British Dominions: Jordan had written to Savage that the Australian and Canadian representatives were 'willing . . . to endorse the policy of the Conservative Party of Britain at every opportunity. . . . Nevertheless I am careful not to say or do anything which may be misunderstood or which may be used against us at any time.'[18] The British Navy was mobilised and war fears peaked. The third and final meeting with Mussolini and Daladier, the French Foreign Minister, as well (but no Czechoslovak or Soviet representative) reached an agreement on 29 September. The Labour government in a cable to Chamberlain 'expressed the hope that the basis of settlement is such as will prove to be a lasting safeguard of world peace, founded on justice and order between nations'.[19] This response was somewhat less fulsome in its praise than the messages received from other Dominions.

The Spanish Civil War ended early in 1939, with Franco's victory. New Zealand was the only Dominion not to recognise the new regime.[20] Angus McLagan, then President of the Federation of Labour, later to become one of the most anti-Communist ministers in the Labour government, welcomed New Zealand nurses home in January 1939, with a comment that as a Labour

16 Quoted in J. W. McKenzie, 'New Zealand and Czechoslovakia'. VUW History Dept research paper, 1969, p. 20. See also Monteith, 'Czechoslovak Crisis', p. 42.
17 Witheford, 'Labour Party and War', ii, p. 74.
18 Quoted in Monteith, 'Czechoslovak Crisis', p. 50; Nicholas Mansergh, *Survey of British Commonwealth Affairs: Problems of External Policy, 1931–1939*. London, 1952, p. 199. See also Fraser, *EP*, 3 Oct. 1938: gratitude to Chamberlain for saving the world from war, quoted in Nancy M. Taylor, *The New Zealand People at War: The Home Front*. Wellington, 1986, p. 16.
19 Thus incidentally pre-empting any need to accede to the British government's request to send a message of support to help with public opinion in Britain: a tricky move for the New Zealand government, Jordan thought, because of its party political implications: Pratt, p. 28.
20 F. O. Wilson, 'New Zealand's Attitude to the Spanish Civil War'. VUW History Dept. research paper, 1969, p. 26.

organisation, the FOL 'could do no other than support the Spanish people in their fight against the Fascist aggressors'.[21] In January Savage proposed the holding of an international economic conference, in the belief that the fundamental causes of international strife were economic. In March he wanted a conference of democratic powers specifically directed at removing the causes of war.[22] In May he sent a message to the British government urging the importance of concluding an agreement with the Soviet Union.[23]

Limits to Labour's challenge: Labour and the left

The attitudes, statements and actions discussed above present a familiar picture of Labour foreign policy—the new party, breaking with the old order, an architect of independence and a standard-bearer of morality in international relations. Countless studies, both of aspects of the period itself and of the broader historical context, place a great deal of emphasis on this view of Labour's first years in office.[24]

It is illuminating to consider Labour's foreign policy not just in terms of its challenges to the accepted ways of doing things but also of the limits the new government itself set to those challenges. One key to understanding this restraint is the nature of the relationship between the Labour government and the left, in particular the Communist Party, but also to some extent those Labour Members of Parliament who on some or most issues were to the left of the Labour leadership—M.P.s like John A. Lee, Arnold Nordmeyer and Dr D. G. McMillan. Although the tensions and conflicts between these different groups in domestic politics is familiar territory, writers on foreign policy have not paid so much attention to them.[25] But they are crucial to understanding the outlook of Labour leaders. Rivalry with the Communist Party went to the very core of Labour Party politics. Weak though the CPNZ might have been, its very existence and persistence posed a standing challenge to the Labour Party's claim to represent working-class interests. It represented to Labour

---

21 *Workers Weekly*, 27 Jan. 1939, quoted in Witheford, 'Labour Party and War', ii, p. 30; see also *Women Today*, Feb. 1939, p. 1.
22 *Standard*, 19 Jan., 23 Mar. 1939, quoted in Witheford, 'Labour Party and War', ii, pp. 91-94; *Women Today*, May 1939, commented that there was confusion about Savage's proposals and what he actually intended by them.
23 Ovendale, p. 272.
24 See the references in n. 1. Note also the many research papers cited in this chapter. A good contemporary example is Milner, pp. 82-85. The most recent more extensive study is Bruce Bennett, *New Zealand's Moral Foreign Policy 1935-1939: The Promotion of Collective Security Through the League of Nations*. Wellington, 1988. It does not have a very systematic discussion of the independent nature of Labour's foreign policy (see pp. 94-95) but the nature of the discussion reinforces the notion of a government taking new departures. Studies like Sinclair's *Nash* and Gustafson, *Cradle to Grave*, do not tackle the issue directly but tend to focus on Labour differences with the British government rather than on other aspects of the relationship.
25 Latterly. Witheford's war history narrative, as will be evident from the references, was invaluable for this discussion. Taylor, *The Home Front*, pays a lot of attention to Communist and left positions on foreign issues, especially in 1939-40.

the danger of fractionalism, of a working-class movement divided and weakened against itself. It was in many ways a more serious threat than the parties of capital, who were after all 'the enemy', on the analogy that civil war is always more dangerous than external war. And while the Communists had no representation in Parliament, they were significant in some trade unions.

Foreign policy was not itself an important arena of Labour/Communist conflict. But in an era when the role of the Soviet Union was critical in international relations, disagreement about foreign policy became a surrogate for conflict on the domestic front. Labour's foreign policy looks different viewed from this perspective, less radical, and more accepting of British policy.

When Germany reoccupied the Rhineland in March 1936, the Communists urged New Zealand to back France and Belgium rather than endorse Britain's more acquiescent stance and the Otago Carpenters' Union at the Labour Party conference protested at New Zealand representation at the Berlin Olympics.[26] In respect of Spain, the government's stance was influenced by the Catholic sympathies of some of its supporters, as well as by its caution about associating its foreign policy too closely with the Communists and the Soviet Union. The New Zealand Medical Aid Committee was formed in November 1936 with trade union, Labour Party branch and CPNZ support but Savage declined to become its President on the grounds that he was going to England.[27] Three nurses about to go to Spain were interrogated by the New Zealand police.[28] At the League of Nations, Jordan was more concerned with the issue of collective security than with political support for the Spanish government as such.[29] Carl Berendsen, who headed the Prime Minister's

[26]   Witheford, 'Labour Party and War', ii, p. 3. This was probably the first time a New Zealand group had called for a sports boycott for international political reasons.

[27]   *Workers Weekly*, 2 April 1937, quoted in Witheford, 'Labour Party and War', ii, p. 30; see also Susan Skudder, ' "Bringing It Home": New Zealand Responses to the Spanish Civil War, 1936–1939'. Univ. of Waikato, Ph.D. thesis, 1986, p. 24: the New Zealand government ignored requests to state publicly its solidarity with the Spanish government; Skudder also notes, pp. 24-25, that particularly for anti-Communist ministers like Robert Semple and Fraser, Communist efforts to use the issue to build up solidarity with the Labour Party were a problem.

[28]   Skudder, pp. 48-50.

[29]   Skudder, p. 20. And see also p. 59, Jordan to Savage: 'while the Government of Spain might have some "objectionable features", you and I are not so much interested in the policy of the government as the fact that it was elected and that it is a member of the League of Nations' (EA1 355/4/2, 23 Sept. 1937). The oft-cited 'blue pencil incident' has its place here: in May 1937, a draft of Jordan's address on Spain's appeal to the Council of the League for the extension of the powers of the non-intervention committee was modified by the British delegation, which included Eden. The incident was reported in a cable from Geneva published in the *EP*, 31 May 1937: it was stated that Jordan intended to invoke Article X of the Covenant. But according to A. D. McIntosh, Jordan had not accepted it as his text and did not intend to. This seems plausible: such an initiative would have been out of keeping with the tenor of Jordan's other contributions over the Spanish issue. See the discussion in Wilson, 'Spanish Civil War', p. 24; O'Shea, 'Spanish Civil War', Appendix III plus attached comments by McIntosh. Skudder, pp. 36-46, discusses *inter alia* a draft speech, found in the Nash Papers, much more radical in tone than the one Jordan delivered.

Department, and had handled all External Affairs matters since 1926, drafted New Zealand's submission on reform of the League Covenant in 1936. Far from being a radical, Berendsen was a Churchillian conservative, crying out for a hard line against the dictators at a time when accommodation was in the air. Berendsen's thinking provides one of the connections between 1930s anti-Fascist collective security and 1950s anti-Communist collective security.[30]

Over the Sino-Japanese war Communists and others on the left pressed for a harder line than the government was prepared to follow. Confronted with Japanese vessels in port at the end of September, many watersiders were reluctant to work them and certainly opposed loading scrap iron. The *Evening Post* said that the watersider action 'expressed a very fine sentiment, but they cannot hope to do what the League of Nations failed to accomplish'.[31] The Auckland Chamber of Commerce was angry with the watersiders for taking the law into their own hands—a familiar cry. The government agreed: 'There is only one body in a position of authority in New Zealand and that is the Government. We are not going to have five or six different organizations standing up and telling us with what different countries we are going to trade.'[32]

After a conference with the watersiders and the FOL, which had recommended to its affiliates a ban on war materials exports to Japan, the Prime Minister announced that it had been agreed that the Japanese ships would be worked. A compromise had been reached. The boycott idea was abandoned and in exchange, on 7 October, the government gazetted an Order-in-Council prohibiting the export of non-precious scrap metal to all countries.[33] The Communist newspaper, the *Workers Weekly*, and also *Women Today*, in the absence of government action, continued to promote a people's boycott.

It was also the Communists and the FOL rather than the government who protested against the von Luckner visit in early 1938.[34] On 18 March 1938 the Council of the FOL stated that 'It is the considered opinion of the Council that the suppression of all working class political and industrial organizations in Nazi Germany . . . have earned for the Nazis the condemnation of the Labour movement of the whole world. It asked von Luckner to debate the virtues of

[30] Ann Trotter, 'Personality in Politics: Sir Carl Berendsen', *NZJH*, 20/2 (Nov. 1986), pp. 142-56.

[31] 29 Sept. 1937 quoted in Kevin Moriarty, 'A Historical Survey of the Foreign Policy of the New Zealand Waterside Workers' Union 1945-1951', VUW History Dept research paper, 1976, p. 5.

[32] *EP*, 19 March 1938, quoted in Witheford, 'Labour Party and War', ii, pp. 54-55.

[33] Witheford, 'Labour Party and War', ii, pp. 32-35; Milner, *NZ and the Far East*, p. 104.

[34] Von Luckner was a German naval officer who commanded a camouflaged raider in the Pacific during the First World War. He was captured and interned in New Zealand in October 1917, making a spectacular, albeit brief, escape in the camp commander's launch, which was then used to capture a larger vessel. In the 1930s he became an internationally popular lecturer but many saw him as a propagandist for Nazism (*New Zealand Yesterdays*. Sydney, 1984, pp. 266-7).

Nazism compared with democracy with a representative of the Federation.'
The statement went on to claim that before leaving Germany, von Luckner
had announced he intended to preach the virtues of Nazism to the whole
world. Von Luckner's response was to argue that the labouring people of
Germany supported Hitler. In the absence of a debate the Federation
suggested to its members that 'a further effective way of replying to von
Luckner's visit is to increase our efforts to raise support for the people of
Spain and China in their fight against Fascism'.[35] A diatribe in *Tomorrow*, 30
March 1938, against Chamberlain's policy, argued in similar vein.[36]

While the government publicly accepted the Munich agreement, it met with
opposition from the Communists: in Auckland a demonstration, which
included banners such as one with the slogan 'Hitler thanked Chamberlain,
why should you?', was stopped by the police.[37] On 1 November, Robert
Semple, the Minister of Works, made a speech in which he was quoted as
saying that the defence of New Zealand could not be neglected while 'mad
dogs like Hitler and Mussolini were running loose'. Both the German and
Italian consuls protested and Savage replied, dissociating the New Zealand
government from Semple's comments and conveying Semple's apologies.[38]
An incident perhaps more revelatory of the mood of the time came a few
weeks later. It was reported in the press in January that a series of radio talks
on international relations, 'History behind the Headlines', by Kenneth
Melvin, advocating a hardline policy towards the Fascist powers, was
suspended, with three of the sessions being cancelled, while another three
were ultimately broadcast in amended form. Censorship continued in
subsequent sessions. The *Standard* printed a statement by Savage, in his
capacity of Minister of Broadcasting, on 2 February: 'I am not going to allow
Mr Melvin or anyone else to broadcast on a Government station his
interpretation of inspired propaganda articles appearing in overseas
newspapers.' The *Workers Weekly* of 29 January was angry that talks on
international affairs continued to be given over the YA stations by L. K.
Munro and G. H. Scholefield. According to the *Workers Weekly*, Melvin
addressed a protest meeting of nearly 3500 people about the isssue in the
Auckland Town Hall on 10 February 1939: nonetheless at the meeting he
accepted Savage's assurances that the assumption of German interference was
incorrect. The CPNZ was committed to a policy of cooperation with Labour:
'We protest at the Government's actions because we are true friends of the
Government, because we are willing to risk abuse and misunderstanding

35 *EP*, March 19, 1938, quoted in Witheford, 'Labour Party and War', ii, pp. 54-55.
36 Taylor, *Home Front*, p. 14. Seamen's Union and *Tomorrow* opposed exclusion on grounds of
freedom of speech. Von Luckner's addresses were very popular, especially in Wellington, where
he received a tremendous ovation.
37 Witheford, 'Labour Party and War', ii, pp. 75-77. See also Monteith, esp. pp. 40-50.
38 Published in *EP*, 11 Nov. 1938, quoted in Witheford, 'Labour Party and War', ii, p. 82.

rather than submit ... to an action that is detrimental to the best interests of the Labour movement ....'[39]

After the fall of Prague to the Germans in March 1939 all the left's energies were directed at securing an Anglo-Russian agreement: the way to avert war was the immediate creation of a pact between Britain, France and the Soviet Union, with the backing of the United States.[40] At the same time, opposition to conscription and war became an increasing preoccupation.

Labour and the Empire

Labour may not then have been radical or far to the left in its foreign policy. Was it nationalist, secessionist and isolationist in the fashion of national movements in some of the other Dominions and in the colonial parts of the Empire and India? Did it want to take New Zealand out of the Empire? This is another key dimension of the issue of independence which needs to be addressed if Labour's policy is to be seen in context. Loyalty was a major preoccupation of the Empire in the 1930s, or perhaps more accurately, it had been in the 1920s. The Statute of Westminster, 1931, which effectively gave all the Dominions independence, had resulted not just from evolution but from the agitation of South Africa, Ireland and Canada. In the case of both Ireland and South Africa, the agitation was driven by nationalist, anti-British sentiment. In Canada, isolationism was more important. Even in Australia, a section of the Labour movement, most often associated with Lang, the erstwhile Premier of New South Wales, was opposed to Australian involvement in foreign wars—a more vigorous version of the anti-militarism found in New Zealand.[41] New Zealand conservatives were apprehensive, or claimed to be apprehensive, about what Labour might do to New Zealand's external relations as well as to its domestic policy. Some believed that given half a chance Labour would sunder the ties of Empire. But this was always unlikely.

Lee and his ally, W. E. Barnard, came closest in the New Zealand political world at this time to meriting a label such as nationalist or isolationist. Lee described himself as a New Zealand nationalist, which was itself unusual in politics in the 1930s. He wanted to insulate the economy and he believed that New Zealand's defence effort should concentrate on New Zealand.[42] Barnard,

[39] Sid Scott in the *Workers Weekly*, 3 Feb. 1939, quoted in D. S. Carter, 'The Attitude of the New Zealand Communist Party to Foreign Affairs, 1930-1941'. Univ. of Auckland, M.Phil. thesis, 1981, p. 46.

[40] Witheford, 'Labour Party and War', ii, p. 26 (second pagination sequence), quoting Gordon Watson (who succeeded Sid Scott as editor in April) in the *Workers Weekly*, 26 May 1939. For more on left enthusiasm for the United States see Ormond Wilson, 'A tourist's notebook' (part ii), *Tomorrow*, 5/16 (7 June 1939), pp. 502-4, in which Wilson compares Roosevelt's anti-Fascism favourably with Chamberlain's, and *Women Today*, June 1939, p. 12.

[41] E. P. Andrews, *Isolationism and Appeasement in Australia 1935-1939*. Canberra, 1970.

[42] Erik Olssen, *John A. Lee*. Dunedin, 1977, pp. 87, 140-1.

who founded the Five Million Club early in 1937 to promote population increase and greater security, had similar views, and left the Labour Party when Lee was expelled from it in 1940. Lee and Barnard justified their stance by reference to circumstances, in particular the danger—and the likelihood—of New Zealand being cut off in the event of war, and the need therefore for more self-reliance. Lee and Barnard were a minority. Lee did have a certain cachet with anti-militarist sentiment because he talked about national defence and not sending men overseas. But how much of an overlap was there, given that Lee's and Barnard's motives were not so much anti-militarist as nationalist?

Did the Labour leadership come close to this nationalist position? Savage was the first Prime Minister to bring to the office a distinct lack of enthusiasm for the British monarchy. According to Gustafson he had firmly opposed the abdication of Edward VIII in 1936, seeing no reason why the King should have to abdicate because he wanted to marry a divorced American. He was reluctant to go to the Coronation of George VI and the concurrent Imperial Conference in May 1937 and wrote back to his niece on one occasion: 'The amount of artificial humbug that one meets with here is astounding . . . If you could have seen me in Westminster Abbey decked out in the uniform of a Privy Councillor you would have wondered if I was the person who in 1893 carried his swag through the Riverina.'[43] It was entirely characteristic that the Opposition should seek to make an issue out of Labour's loyalty when the Imperial Conference was debated at the end of September. Hargest said the Opposition heartily agreed with Savage that it would be very regrettable if anything in New Zealand was done that caused difficulty at the heart of the Empire but then wondered whether he and other delegates might not on occasion 'have expressed a little more loyalty to the Empire'.[44]

The habitual form of words of the New Zealand response to any British proposal had been that 'New Zealand is content to be bound by the determination of His Majesty's Government in London.'[45] Labour's ideology did foster an independent outlook on New Zealand's Dominion status. Labour wanted to be able to transform New Zealand; it did not want to be stopped by a lack of the necessary constitutional powers. H. G. R. Mason, who became Attorney-General in the new government, had commented on the draft Statute of Westminster: 'I rejoice that the other Dominions have a better idea of their status, and I am sorry that in this country we should take pride in our insufficiency.'[46] The new government did not see why New Zealand should not exercise the same rights as other Dominions in the

43   Gustafson, *Cradle to Grave*, pp. 205-6.
44   *NZPD*, 248, p. 477 (29 Sept. 1937).
45   Quoted in Ross, 'Reluctant Dominion', p. 31. Statement is in *NZPD*, 199, pp. 33-34 (19 Feb. 1923).
46   Ross, 'Reluctant Dominion', p. 38.

external sphere. In 1939 it ended the practice whereby the Governor-General was both the representative of the British government and the representative of the Crown in New Zealand.

Certainly there was nationalism in the air. Both Labour and the scholars had some enthusiasm for New Zealand nationalism: 'We have developed in New Zealand a culture essentially different from that of older countries in the world and we are fast developing a New Zealand point of view, both in domestic and international affairs.'[47] J. C. Beaglehole wrote, in plainly sympathetic vein, of one significant impact of the Depression,

> the paradoxical conviction of separate identity forced on the country; the identity of New Zealanders in New Zealand, a particular people in a particular country, suffering together because of the position of that country in the economic world-complex; asking themselves if they, New Zealand, needed in the future to be subject to repetitions of such suffering, or whether New Zealand could not make its own policy, its own defensive wall, its own life.[48]

But in external relations, the nationalism of both the Labour leadership and the scholars stopped short of the Lee/Barnard approach.[49] The Labour government, it should be remembered, was a *British* government and it was a party of British Labour, with strong links with the United Kingdom Labour movement—Nash and Savage met Labour as well as government leaders on their visits to England; Hugh Dalton, one of the rising stars of the British Labour Party, visited New Zealand in February 1938 and talked to most of the Labour people.[50] Labour papers in England like the *New Statesman*, the *Daily Herald* and *Reynolds News* were natural allies of the government in New Zealand. The *New Statesman* on one occasion praised New Zealand, 'which had the courage to criticise severely the British attitude to the League and the Spanish War. New Zealand, once Britain's white-headed boy, has now, under

---

47 *NZPD*, 253, pp. 448-9 (15 Sept. 1938), Parry in debate on the New Zealand Centennial Act quoted in P. T. Enright, 'The First Labour Government and the Rise of Cultural Nationalism 1936-1949'. University of Otago, Postgraduate Diploma, 1979, p. 25.
48 'The Development of New Zealand Nationality', VUW History Dept, c. 1955, p. 7; Milner, *NZ and the Far East*, p. 84, makes similar observations.
49 In culture perhaps not quite so much—'the increased activity in literature and the arts since the great depression is not unconnected with the disillusionment of finding that the imperial connection carried no watertight guarantee of prosperity and security. The realisation ... that in spite of its small population New Zealand should attempt to achieve a greater sense of nationhood has coloured the outlook of younger writers just as it has persuaded the government to encourage industrial expansion.' A. R. D. Fairburn, 'Literature and the Arts' in Belshaw, *New Zealand*, p. 251. See also Rachel Barrowman, *A Popular Vision: The Arts and the Left in New Zealand, 1930-1950*. Wellington, 1991, pp. 2-3, 49, for comment on the 'internationalist' quality of cultural nationalism.
50 Diary, v. 56, Dalton Papers, London School of Economics and Political Science. Dalton met the local intelligentsia in Wellington: 'I was not very much impressed, their minds seem to skid on the roadway of reality. I suspect that the Left Book Club has something to do with making the surface greasy .... [most] are like not very clever undergraduates ....'

a Labour Government taken Australia's place as the most intractable member of the family.'[51] Nash and Jordan were English-born: 'Jordan, a truly English figure, who might have stepped straight from the ranks of Cromwell's new model army, not infrequently embarrassed the Council [of the League] by a tendency to quote the Bible.'[52] Perhaps it was no accident that it was Savage, Australian-Irish-born, who was least attached to some aspects of the British connection. But generally Labour New Zealand was as far removed as right-wing New Zealand from the isolationist and secessionist nationalism found in Ireland, South Africa and Canada and had little even of the left isolationist nationalism found in Australia.[53] As Nash put it on one occasion, 'the Commonwealth and the United Kingdom are loved by the people of New Zealand, and loved none the less because a different form of Government is in charge of its destinies.'[54] The commentary at this gathering made it clear that Labour's policies and its commitment to the Empire were issues for conservative opinion. Nash was reassuring his audience that New Zealand Labour was not radical. And as one respondent said on that occasion, 'He had had many Socialist candidates standing against him since 1922, but if he had one as eloquent, as moderate and as valuable a citizen as Mr Nash, he wondered what would have happened.'[55]

For Nash and his colleagues, independence could scarcely be enjoyed other than in 'close co-operation with the mother country, for history has shaped New Zealanders into a people British in sentiment, tradition and economic interest.'[56] Their concern for independence was grounded in internationalism, not isolationism, in renovation of the Commonwealth and of British foreign policy, not in any rejection of the Commonwealth or of Britain: 'her history has equipped her to live a life of her own as a small but not subservient member of the British Commonwealth.'[57]

Independence, loyalty and internationalism

National's criticisms were partly directed at Labour's internationalism, which seemed to some as potentially or actually disloyal as outright rebellion. Certainly internationalism was important to Labour, and it was an important element in scholarly conceptions of New Zealand's independence and

[51]   Monteith, p. 23.
[52]   Quoted from a history of the League of Nations by J. V. Wilson in 'New Zealand and International Organisations', *NZER*, pp. 66–67.
[53]   But a minority sentiment there: 'loyalty to Britain prevented isolationism being popular': Andrews, *Isolationism and Appeasement*, p. 193.
[54]   Walter Nash, 'New Zealand and the Commonwealth', *United Empire*, 28/ns 1 (Jan. 1937), p. 31.
[55]   Nash, 'New Zealand and the Commonwealth,' p. 34. The comment was made by Sir John Wardlaw Milne, M.P.
[56]   Wood, *NZ in the World*, p. 133.
[57]   Wood, *NZ in the World*, p. 133.

progress. The academics and intellectuals of associations like the Round Table, the Institute of Pacific Relations and the New Zealand Institute of International Affairs were particularly preoccupied with the issue of dependence.[58] They had frequently taken exception to the lack of interest in foreign relations displayed by New Zealand politicians and the New Zealand public and welcomed the changes that Labour ushered in, the 'outspoken rebellion', as Wood described it, against British dominance, the repudiation of the 'mother complex'.[59] They were excited to see New Zealand adopt an independent status in the League. They saw no fundamental conflict between such assertion and New Zealand's loyalty to Britain and the Commonwealth. A voice, not an exit, was their alternative to unthinking loyalty.[60] The Labour leadership agreed. Fraser in July 1938 spoke in ringing terms about the importance of New Zealand making 'up its own mind on international problems as a sovereign country—because under the Statute of Westminster ours is a sovereign country.'[61]

The internationalism of New Zealand Labour in the late 1930s was the internationalism of British Labour at the same time. Moreover, with the deepening crisis in international relations from 1937 on, the congruence of New Zealand Labour's aims with those of the British Conservative government became clear. At the 1937 Imperial Conference, when McKenzie King of Canada supported appeasement and resisted involvement in war, Savage opposed appeasement and offered unqualified support to Britain in the event of war. When Savage returned from the Conference he explained that New Zealand was concerned 'not only with the defence of our own shores but also with the defence of the whole British Commonwealth'.[62] During the Munich crisis, the prospect of war involving Great Britain and through it, New Zealand, did temper the government's zeal for speaking out on issues of war and peace; the imminent election fostered caution too. But this did not mean that the government would not be on Britain's side in the event of war— quite the contrary: it was the *appeasement* of Hitler that caused them anxiety. And the government did not want loyalty to be an issue: 'I think it inadvisable for me to make any statement', Savage was reported saying on 5 September.

[58] For the Round Table see John Kendle, 'The Round Table Movement: Lionel Curtis and the Formation of the New Zealand Groups in 1910', *NZJH* 1/1 (April 1967), pp. 33-50; for the IPR see Sinclair, *Nash*, pp. 81-84; for the Institute of International Affairs see NZIIA, 'New Zealand Foreign Policy: Choices, Challenges and Opportunities', NZIIA 50th Anniversary Conference. Wellington, 1984, pp. 1-3. And also *Round Table, Pacific Affairs*, and publications of the New Zealand Institute of International Affairs.
[59] Wood, *NZ in the World*, p. 133.
[60] The reference is to Albert O. Hirschmann, *Exit, Voice and Loyalty*. Cambridge, Mass., 1970, an essay by the distinguished economist on the different ways in which companies, and individuals in them, handle dissent and change.
[61] *NZPD*, 251, p. 133 (1 July 1938).
[62] Quoted in *Round Table*, 109 (Dec. 1937), p. 200.

'Should Britain become involved in a war the policy of the New Zealand Government is wellknown to the authorities at Home.'[63]

The different threads of Labour's critique could be identified just before the onset of the war in an outburst against British policy towards Japan and China. Through June 1939 the British had been under pressure from the Japanese in China and in particular in the Tientsin concession—Tientsin was blockaded by the Japanese and indignities were 'heaped' on British subjects there, according to the cable reports. It was a long way from Palmerston's ringing commitment to protect the rights of British subjects everywhere in the world. The crisis in Tientsin was at the farthest reach of British power at a time when the situation in Europe was graver by the day. The British agreed to talk to the Japanese and in the Craigie-Arita agreement conceded most of what the Japanese had asked for. *The Times* argued that it was not a 'Far Eastern Munich' but a 'local attitude which is to be adopted in the region of hostilities' but in Parliament in Wellington Labour M.P.s attacked it as a betrayal of the principles of British foreign policy: to Nordmeyer China had been sacrificed like Czechoslovakia, and McKeen blamed the international financiers.[64] The critics were accused of disloyalty, but they were arguing for a different kind of British foreign policy, exactly as the British Labour Party had. Only Sir Apirana Ngata weighed in with a different approach, questioning the roots of British foreign policy in an unexpected fashion, emphasising by way of contrast the very 'British' character of New Zealand dissent: 'An Empire founded on blood and rapine! An Empire extended by iron ruthlessness, the treading down of primitive peoples! That is the Empire which is saying to its latest rivals, "You must not do it. You must accept the principle of Christianity." What fools!'[65]

Defence and anti-militarism

The outbreak of war did bring to the forefront an issue which had simmered in Labour policymaking ever since it had become the government—the attitude of the Labour movement towards militarism. The notion of an articulate, moral, anti-Fascist foreign policy forged in collaboration with Conservative Britain might be workable in peacetime, but war meant fighting, possibly conscription, and tapped therefore the long-standing suspicion of worker movements about the morality of wars in general, and of capitalist wars which used working people as factory and cannon fodder, in particular. In the 1930s Labour anti-militarism had overlapped with and reinforced pacifist sentiment

63 *Press*, 5 Sept. 1938, quoted in Monteith, 'Czechoslovak Crisis', p. 40. See also pp. 42, 46 for further instances of support for Britain.
64 *NZPD*, 254, p. 738 (25 July 1939); *EP*, 26 July 1939. See also Wood, *NZ in the World*, pp. 127–8; Milner, *NZ and the Far East*, p. 91. Concern for New Zealand's defence did play a part too: see below, p. 40.
65 *NZPD*, 254, p. 724 (25 July 1939).

in the population as a whole. At the same time the rise of the Fascist powers raised awkward questions about the need for defence which anti-militarism was ill-equipped to answer.

One turning point had come in 1935. George Lansbury, a pacifist, resigned the leadership of the British Labour Party because he was opposed to sanctions against Italy over the invasion of Ethiopia.[66] When on 16 September 1935 Nash addressed Labour's first big meeting of the 1935 election campaign, he recognised that if the League decided to resist aggression, New Zealand might have to 'fight in sorrow for the good of the future'.[67] *Would* a Labour government fight though? A Defence League was re-established in 1936 to lobby on defence matters precisely because of suspicion of Labour's anti-militarism. After Jordan had presented New Zealand's proposals for reform of the League in Geneva in September 1936, Forbes, the former Prime Minister, seized on the contradiction between Labour's protestations of support for the League and its denial of any intention of sending men overseas in the event of war.[68]

The Labour movement was particularly suspicious of the army, associating it with conscription, sending men overseas to fight against their will and political hostility to the working class. Pressure from territorial force officers for conscription met with stonewalling from the government: 'I say quite definitely that the Government is opposed to conscription in all its forms ... there will be no compulsion in New Zealand while we are in charge.'[69] The 'colonels' revolt' in May 1938 was graphic evidence of political differences over the future of the army: four territorial force colonels publicly challenged government policy, and were posted to the retired list shortly thereafter.[70]

Shortly after the colonels' revolt, Savage met a deputation from the Defence League. He agreed that New Zealand had to 'prepare for the worst'. And at the time of the Munich conference the government moved very quietly towards organising a force that could be sent overseas, without actually saying so.[71] But were the government and its critics any closer to agreement on what preparation was needed? The conservative press talked a lot about defence in the first months of 1939, interspersing invasion talk with calls for national service—one correspondent to the *Standard* wrote that the daily press was whipping up a false sense of anxiety and distrust in the government.[72] At the

[66] Ben Pimlott, *Labour and the Left*. Cambridge, 1971, p. 71.
[67] Sinclair, *Nash*, p. 198.
[68] *NZPD*, 247, pp. 876-7 (adjournment debate, 21 Oct. 1936).
[69] 20 Feb. 1937, quoted in W. David McIntyre, *New Zealand Prepares for War*. Christchurch, 1988, pp. 182-3.
[70] Account in McIntyre, *NZ Prepares for War*, pp. 184-5.
[71] McIntyre, *NZ Prepares for War*, p. 187.
[72] *Dominion*, 7 March 1939, 'National service'; *Standard*, 13 April 1939. This correspondent quoted British Air Marshal Sir E. Ellington who had stated that the greatest number of soldiers the Japanese could transport for an invasion of Australia, provided they used the whole of their merchant fleet, would be 60,000, and this could not be reinforced in under two months.

Labour Party conference in April 1939 Fraser's claim that compulsory military service was obsolete because war would break out so quickly was greeted enthusiastically: 'Every one of us would be put in the line of defence. And not only human beings but every atom of wealth as well. (Cheers.)'[73] So officially compulsion, especially for service overseas, was out.

Left-wing opinion was suspicious. The *Workers Weekly* of 5 May reported that the Auckland Trades Council proposed to form a company of 200 men of which all ranks were to be bona fide trade unionists. According to the *Borer*, 'a patriot's duty is to defend not an abstract "Mother Country" but those democratic institutions, that freedom we now enjoy, against the enemy at home as well as abroad': an approach which was rejected by both the government and the Wellington Trades Council.[74]

The government searched for volunteers. On 22 May, Savage made a broadcast appeal for an increase of the territorial force from 9000 to 16,000 and also the establishment of a national military reserve, to be drawn from a wider age range than the territorials. The territorial appeal was originally set at 50,000 but this was thought to be too optimistic.[75] Neither appeal was very successful and the demand for conscription was repeated. Savage renewed the appeal on 8 June—'I say we can get the men'. Two weeks later Savage claimed that many centres had exceeded their quota.[76] For their part the RSA and the Defence League continued to advocate compulsory military service and put pressure on the government, especially when it looked as if the territorial recruitment scheme was not producing results.[77]

Early in June Semple visited works camps to drum up enlistments. Semple explained that the force was for home defence—enlistees were not being recruited for an expeditionary force: 'It is not a question of taking part in wars the world over .... I only ask for a pledge that New Zealand will be defended, not that we shall fight for the interests of groups like the shipping companies and the wool kings, but that we shall defend our own liberty.'[78] Semple stressed that if New Zealand did have to mount an expeditionary force another appeal for volunteers would probably be made. Savage took shelter: 'It has ... been said that if war comes we shall immediately dispatch an

73   Witheford, 'Labour Party and War', ii, p. 100.
74   Witheford, 'Labour Party and War', ii, p. 13 (second pagination sequence); *EP*, 26 July 1939.
75   Gustafson, *Cradle to Grave*, p. 251; McIntyre, *NZ Prepares for War*, pp. 235–6: McIntyre says that the NMR would include all volunteers between 20 and 55: those between 20 and 25 with two years' military experience would become the territorial reserve on mobilisation.
76   Witheford, 'Labour Party and War', ii, pp. 27–31 (second pagination sequence); *EP*, 8 June, 23 June 1939.
77   *EP*, 8 June, 23 June 1939, also editorial, 9 June, pointing out that Britain had adopted compulsory training and there was no objection from the Labour Party there.
78   Semple quoted in the *EP*, 5 June 1939: Semple was on a recruiting drive in the public works camps: there were clearly many in them who had strong feelings on the issues of military service and fighting overseas.

expeditionary force overseas. That is impossible. None of the experts are prepared to say at this juncture it can be done, certainly on the scale of 1914, until our sea communications are secure, and our ships can move with reasonable immunity from attack.'[79]

At the beginning of July, Nash got the government into hot water when he made a statement in Dublin that sounded as if it had ruled out the idea of an expeditionary force altogether. Under questioning from the Opposition, who charged the government with giving the impression of being 'unwilling to help Britain in time of danger', the government denied this, but clearly it was a sensitive issue.[80]

The speed with which the government offered an expeditionary force after the outbreak of war revived concern about conscription. The notion that it was acceptable to send volunteers away seems to have been acknowledged but suspicion of the government's denial that it was contemplating conscription persisted.[81] As before the war, the government hoped that with a sufficient flow of volunteers, conscription would prove unnecessary. In a joint Labour Party/FOL statement in February the anti-conscription commitment of the previous July was unconditionally reaffirmed: there would be no conscription in New Zealand while Labour was in power.[82] But Labour was hostile to the Peace and Anti-Conscription Councils which were set up over the summer in many towns and cities. At Labour's annual conference in March 1940 the movement was condemned as a political anti-Labour organisation contrived by the Communists: several Labour Party branches subsequently expelled members who belonged to the Peace and Anti-Conscription Council.[83]

Conscription was announced only in May 1940, when the Allied armies were reeling from the German blitzkrieg against the Netherlands, Belgium and France—the political atmosphere changed and what had been unacceptable and unwelcome to many became acceptable if not welcome. The government closed down the Communist newspaper, the *People's Voice*. A year later, when Germany invaded Russia, the Communists and Labour were on the same side.

Anti-militarism and pacifism had deep roots in British life, in British nonconformity in particular. Certainly in the 1930s pacifism had been a mass movement and it had remained significant at least until after Munich.[84] After that time, however, it was more an issue within working-class politics in both Britain and New Zealand. Conscription and anti-militarism remained the

---

[79] *EP*, 23 June 1939.
[80] Nash's statement and the subsequent controversy in Parliament are reported in the *EP*, 4–7 July 1939; *NZPD*, 254, pp. 171–4 (6 July 1939).
[81] For Canada see Thomas J. Socknat, *Witness Against War: Pacifism in Canada 1900–1945*. Toronto, 1987.
[82] *Round Table*, 119 (June 1940), p. 718.
[83] Taylor, *Home Front*, pp. 84–88.
[84] See Ceadel, *Pacifism in Britain*, pp. 263–6.

trickiest area for the Labour government, the sphere in which Labour opinion remained most radical and least ready to qualify dissent with loyalty.

The onset of war: how much independence?

The issue of conscription aside, what impact did the war have on Labour's conception of independence in foreign policy? If New Zealand followed Britain into war, would it not be evident that its independence was a myth?

The Munich crisis was the occasion on which New Zealanders had become alert to the fact that the events in Europe might commit the country to war: news broadcasts from London were recorded and re-broadcast and the government published the correspondence between the European powers over the crisis simultaneously with its publication in London: 'there was unanimity in the obvious practical issue—that in war New Zealand would follow Britain whatever the occasion of the war might be.'[85]

In April 1939 Savage told the public, 'let no one imagine that if Britain were involved in a general war this country could or would stand aloof enjoying undisturbed neutrality.'[86] And this proved to the case. The government identified itself with the cause of the war in a fashion consistent with the direction of its foreign policy since 1935.

On Friday 1 September, the government proclaimed a state of emergency, having received the news of the German invasion of Poland that same day. The House listened in 'grim silence', the only interruption a thunderstorm, fitting prefiguration of the war to come, fitting coda to the sometimes cold and politically rough winter. Two days later at 11.00 in its morning, Britain declared war on Germany, with New Zealand's declaration almost simultaneously made in its last hour of the same day. Fraser, the Acting Prime Minister, made the declaration. On 5 September, Savage broadcast to the nation from his sickbed, to which he had been confined since early August:

The war on which we are entering may be a long one, demanding from us heavy and continuous sacrifice. It is essential that we realize from the beginning that our cause is worth the sacrifice. I believe in all sincerity that it is. None of us has any hatred of the German people. For the old culture of the Germans, their songs, their poetry and their music, we have nothing but admiration and affection. We believe that there are many millions of German people who want to live in peace and quietness as we do, threatening no one and seeking to dominate no one . . . . The fight on which we are now engaged is one whose issue concerns all the nations of the world, whether they as yet realize it or not. . . . Nazism is militant and insatiable paganism. In its short but terrible history it has caused incalculable suffering. If permitted to continue, it will spread misery and desolation throughout the world. It cannot be appeased or conciliated. To destroy it, but not the great nation which it has so cruelly cheated, is the task of those who have taken up arms against Nazism. May God prosper those

85   *Round Table*, 113 (Dec. 1938), pp. 54, 56.
86   Quoted in Ovendale, p. 272.

arms . . . . Both with gratitude for the past and with confidence in the future we range ourselves without fear beside Britain. Where she goes we go. Where she stands we stand. We are only a small and young nation, but we are one and all a band of brothers, and we march forward with a union of hearts and will towards a common destiny.[87]

Savage's statement underlined the notion of independence espoused by the Labour government and its continuity with past practice in the conduct of New Zealand's external relations. It was an independence rooted in a progessive view of British politics and the British cause, one not afraid to stand up for itself, also seen as a British thing to do. His address, while taking the country into the war alongside Britain, eschewed the language of patriotism and Germanophobia for focus on the universal values that were at stake, values that linked New Zealand and Britain.[88] Anti-Fascism as well as patriotism linked New Zealand Labour and British Conservatism. Hamilton's statement that 'New Zealand gives unqualified support to the Motherland in her decision to stand with France and Poland against German aggression' gave a detectably different emphasis. While for some Britain was a country of reaction and of class conflict, to others it was the home of justice and freedom: 'The British people dislike ostentation . . . . they have retained a poise of unhurry and a habit of understatement', the *Dominion* said, and it reported with approval the support that came from different parts of the Empire, including the non-self-governing parts, at the outbreak of the war—not just from colonial governors either but from assemblies and peoples. The *Dominion* was impressed with Savage too: he had 'struck the right note, and placed the issues before the nation with clarity and force.'[89]

Labour's position on the war was sharply distinguished from that of the Communists and pacifist groups to its left. Indeed the period 1939–41 was one of the bitterest in the troubled history of Labour–Communist relations in New Zealand. Despite the Nazi–Soviet Pact, the Communist Party of Great Britain had initially endorsed the British war effort, saying that it was 'in support of all necessary measures to secure the victory of democracy over Fascism . . . . the essence of the present situation is that the people have now to wage a struggle on two fronts. The first is to secure the military victory over Fascism; and, second, in order to achieve this, the political victory over Chamberlain and the enemies of democracy in this country.'[90]

And this need to fight on two fronts, both against Hitler and against

---

[87] Text of Savage's address broadcast from his sickbed, 5 Sept. 1939, *Dominion*, 6 Sept. 1939.
[88] See also H. Witheford, 'The Political Parties and the War', p. 1: 'the most striking feature of the statements made by the spokesmen for the Government and the Labour movement . . . is their exclusive emphasis on the ideological aspects of the conflict and their expressions of sympathy for the German people as distinct from the Nazis'. WAII21/45c, NA.
[89] *Dominion*, 2 Sept., 8 Sept., 7 Sept. 1939.
[90] Carter, 'NZ Communist Party', p. 51.

Chamberlain—was also stressed in the *People's Voice*, on both 16 and 22 September. On 17 September though, the Soviet armies had entered and proceeded to annex eastern Poland in keeping with the secret protocol to the Nazi–Soviet pact which provided for such steps if an independent Poland should cease to exist. At the end of September the Soviet leadership had said the Western allies' war against Germany was unnecessary and should end. This stance was accepted by the *People's Voice* in its editorial of 6 October: 'peace now would enable the peoples of the belligerent countries to get rid of those responsible for the war'.[91]

For Labour this stance was either reason, or opportunity, or both, to attack the Communists. In its foreign policy too, Labour took a stand against the Soviet Union, in particular voting to expel that country from the League because of its aggression against Finland. The Soviet Union's invasion of Finland at the end of November 1939, even more than its non-aggression pact with Germany, its movement into eastern Poland, and its establishment of a sphere of influence in the Baltic countries, created difficulties for the Soviet cause in New Zealand. It was rhetorical ammunition for Semple: 'It seemed incredible to him that there were people in New Zealand who could attempt to justify the Russian invasion of Finland—a tiny country which wanted to live in peace under its Government of Socialists and Farmers . . . . Do you think these people are fit to be called New Zealanders? No!'[92]

But there was some uncertainty in Labour's ranks about the aims of the war. Anglo-French enthusiasm for Finland's resistance to the Soviet Union bothered some. There were 'a good many Labour supporters who had been very uneasy about Chamberlain's pre-1939 course and who were troubled now that New Zealand's government had identified itself completely with the British government's purposes. Such people felt that the war was slipping into a likeness of the imperialism of 1914–18, that it might crumble into an ill-advised Chamberlain peace or somehow . . . be switched against Russia.'[93] What Taylor describes as a 'broad swell of discontent' in the party fixed in part on the steadily deteriorating relations between Lee and his more senior colleagues in the parliamentary wing. Lee himself was vigorously in favour of the war—he wanted to be Minister of Defence—but he was 'critical of New Zealand being hitched to Chamberlain's chariot without visible safeguards'.[94]

Wood quotes Lee's ally Barnard saying early in February 1940 that there were 'many thousands of New Zealanders of unimpeachable loyalty who are . . . not satisfied with the oft repeated declarations about liberty and freedom

91   Carter, 'NZ Communist Party', pp. 60–61.
92   *Standard*, 14 March 1940, quoted in Roman Gershenfeld, 'The Russo-Finnish War and the New Zealand Press'. VUW History Dept research paper, 1989, pp. 23–24. Note also Semple's comment on Chamberlain, as being, although conservative, better than Stalin (p. 11).
93   Taylor, *Home Front*, p. 70.
94   Taylor, *Home Front*, pp. 46–48; Olssen, *Lee*, p. 149.

and democracy (equality is not mentioned) which are offered as sufficient reasons for the present sacrifice'.[95] It is difficult to assess how serious or widespread such sentiment was. In December the West Coast Trades Council had condemned the war as imperialist. This motion was rescinded after furore from many of its affiliates but it led to the aforementioned joint Labour Party/ FOL statement on war policy:

> It was an interesting statement, floodlighting Labour's image of itself.... it condemned Nazi aggression, and stressed that New Zealand's high standard of living, won by democracy and trade unionism ... depended on [the] Commonwealth. The British government was at last standing for collective security, as New Zealand had repeatedly advised; it would now be 'politically irresponsible or worse' if New Zealand Labour did not give Britain fullest support.[96]

British Labour's support for the war effort of the Chamberlain government was important to the government in New Zealand. The British Labour Party had expelled Sir Stafford Cripps from its ranks in 1939 for refusing to abandon his project of a popular front with the Communists and others. The six peace aims of British Labour were endorsed: no revengeful peace, but restitution to victims; rights of all nations to self-determination; the outlawing of war; rights of minorities; an effective international authority; an end to colonial exploitation and trade monopoly. In addition the statement called for the industrial and political labour movements to be represented in the discussion of peace terms.[97] Even after this the government was still cautious: when at the end of March 1940 the French wanted to bomb Soviet oilfields, Fraser objected: anything, he said, that might appear as British aggression against Russia would be both undesirable in itself and likely to arouse strong opposition in New Zealand.[98]

Labour rejected separatism along with Communism. Not for it Ireland's neutrality, South Africa's hesitation, or even the hidden qualifications in Canada's participation. But nor did Labour reject what it meant by independence. Its stance was nicely shown at the very beginning of the war when the New Zealand government declared war on Germany, whereas the conservative administration in Australia claimed to be bound by the British declaration[99]—independence was thus asserted for the purpose of proclaiming solidarity.

Some observers feared at first that war might slow down New Zealand's

95 Wood, *Political and External Affairs*, p. 111.
96 Taylor, *Home Front*, p. 85.
97 *Round Table*, 119 (June 1940), p. 718.
98 Wood, *Political and External Affairs*, p. 359.
99 David Day, *The Great Betrayal—Britain, Australia and the Onset of the Pacific War*. North Ryde, NSW, 1988, pp. 18-19. Of course the fact that it had to assert that this was the case was a contradiction in terms which had not arisen in 1914 and followed naturally from the assumption of the power to take the final decision on matters of peace and war by all the other Dominions.

constitutional emancipation, but even this proved not to be the case. Participation in war, even in the Middle East in association with Britain, became an expression of Dominion status: 'It involved constant consultation with the United Kingdom not only on the content of the war but also on the proper basis of the peace. It involved also decisions of great national moment concerning the uses of New Zealand forces in the course of which the habit of independent judgement was strengthened.'[100]

The experience of a Labour government in office and the advent of the Second World War had underlined the continuity of New Zealand's foreign relations. The idea of an independent foreign policy was a version of New Zealand's status as a self-governing colony, a loyal Dominion. The independence proclaimed was an independence compatible with loyalty, both ideologically and emotionally. It was the independence of loyal opposition (and of unavoidable circumstance). It was defined as much by what it was not, by its rejection of radical nationalism or socialism, as by what it was. Even in 1936–37 its internationalism, its most distinctive feature, was not profoundly at odds with British foreign policy, certainly no more so than was that of the British Labour Party. And after Hitler marched into Prague in March 1939, the concordance of means and ends, New Zealand Labour and British Conservatism, independently minded Dominion and imperial great power, was complete.

---

[100] R. R. Cunninghame, 'The Development of New Zealand's Foreign Policy and Political Alignments', in *NZER*, p. 21. The point is developed at greater length in Wood, *Political and External Affairs*, esp. pp. 100–103 on the status of the Expeditionary Force. 'The disappearance of these men into the general mass of British troops would be an offence to New Zealand's sense of nationhood' (p. 102): Freyberg, said Wood (p. 103), 'was truly typical of his country in his determination to combine independence with loyalty.'

3. Secure in the South Pacific?

In the preceding chapter we analysed the meaning of independence in foreign policy for the first Labour government and how that meaning conformed to characteristic notions of New Zealand's place in the British Empire, and in particular the idea of 'loyal opposition'. We did not consider the other accepted form of independence identified in the introduction, the idea of an independence grounded in the pursuit of interest. In the 1930s and 1940s interest mostly reinforced New Zealand's position within the Empire/Commonwealth. Sometimes it went beyond it.

While New Zealand was connected to England, and through England to the preoccupations of the world as a whole, it was also deeply insular, able, partly because of its remoteness, to assume the stance of onlooker rather than participant, a country which asked nothing more of the world than to be allowed to carry on with its own preoccupations undisturbed.

The return of good times after the depression of the early 1930s emphasised the gulf between New Zealand and most of the rest of the world. There was still massive unemployment in the United States, while in Asia and Europe to the economic woes were added political ones. Dictatorships succeeded democracies in many European countries, most notably Germany. War broke out in Spain, then in China. But in New Zealand, unemployment figures fell, real incomes rose, there were houses built, cars manufactured and public works under way at a rate far beyond that of the depression years. Labour politicians rejoiced in the prosperity: when Savage returned home from the Imperial Conference and Coronation in 1937, he told the New Zealand people that they 'lived in a veritable paradise'.[1] Business commentators and conservative politicians, in questioning how deep-seated the prosperity was, demonstrated a recognition that conditions had improved since the early 1930s. On the eve of world war, when the balance of payments was in deficit and the government had raised taxes, 'to all outward appearances ... the country was still in a prosperous condition'.[2]

Far away not just from Asia and Europe but even from Australia, most New Zealanders saw world history as 'a drama to be observed from a distance

---

[1]   *AIBR*, 21 Sept. 1937, p. 817.
[2]   *Round Table*, 117 (Dec. 1939), p. 219.

without any notion of audience participation.'³ In Nelle Scanlan's *Kelly Pencarrow* (1939), Scanlan has Genevieve, just returned from England, tell her brother that ' "The trouble out here, Kelly, is that you are all so engrossed in local politics that you don't notice what is going on in the outside world .... you all look pretty prosperous to me." '⁴ In his study on New Zealand and Asia, Milner commented on the lack of direct connection, be it commercial or any other kind, between New Zealand and Asia: 'At least until early 1939 most of the comment [on the war in Asia] is from the viewpoint of the detached spectator. On the same editorial page can be found one article stressing the need for further defence measures in New Zealand and another in which, for instance, a Japanese attack on Canton is discussed quite without reference to its implications for Australia and New Zealand security in the Pacific.'⁵ The sense of distance was also marked in the early stages of the 1938 Munich crisis: 'the [election] campaign went on virtually unaffected while the fate of civilisation visibly trembled in the balance'.⁶

The notion that New Zealand did not need to concern itself with the affairs of the world translated particularly into a caution in the expenditure of New Zealand resources, be they of men or money, on overseas endeavours. This was a very pronounced and, as we shall see, persisting interest, which in this study is sometimes referred to as insularity and sometimes, particularly when spending is the subject, as parsimony. It spilled over into a more general belief that New Zealand did not need a foreign policy at all—it was a Labour Party indulgence.

One particular interest did take New Zealand in unaccustomedly independent directions: the preoccupation with the country's security. This manifested itself in two ways in the late 1930s. Some feared that New Zealand would be cut off by an enemy power from its allies and indeed from the rest of the world, and would have to fend for itself. Self-sufficiency became an important consideration. This concern overlapped with the nationalist thinking of people like Lee and Barnard. The second and more persistent new direction was the need to have another guarantor, namely the United States. It was in this fashion that an internationalist independence became acceptable to the National Party, as Labour's pre-war activities had not been. Not only was it an interest that had to be pursued, it did not have any disloyal overtones, since the United States was Britain's principal ally.

Self-sufficiency

While New Zealand relied on British naval supremacy to keep it secure, there

3   Wood, *Political and External Affairs*, p. 24.
4   Nelle Scanlan, *Kelly Pencarrow*. London, 1939, p. 308.
5   Milner, *New Zealand and the Far East*, pp. 111-12.
6   *Round Table*, 113 (Dec. 1938), p. 53.

was always scope for anxiety, the anxiety of the defended about the capacity of the defender to do what might be necessary—against the French in the 1840s, the Russians in the 1880s, the Germans in the early 1900s; or against Asia—the Chinese in the nineteenth century, the Japanese after their victory over the Russians in 1904, the migrant Indians ('Hindus') and Chinese after the First World War. In the 1920s and 1930s New Zealand governments had supported British plans to establish a naval base at Singapore to facilitate the protection of British power in Asia. The construction of the base was dogged by party political changes of direction but it was completed in 1939. A new twist was given to the old anxieties about mass migration to New Zealand by the ideas of *Lebensraum*, of have and have-not nations, that circulated in Italy, Germany and Japan in particular and seemed to be an actual or likely influence on their foreign policies. These ideas overlapped with other German ideas about the return of the colonies it had lost after the First World War, including New Guinea, the phosphate island of Nauru and Western Samoa, this latter administered by New Zealand under a League of Nations mandate.[7]

In New Zealand, as in a number of similarly situated countries, the birth rate was falling, a fact which seemed to add to the apprehension that the heyday of the Caucasians might be passing, as had that of the Polynesians before them. A study often consulted and admired, Guthrie-Smith's *Tutira*, ended with a plea that 'compared with race admixture, the hundred necessary acts of economy and self-denial that must go towards true reform will be viewed as dust in the balance .... Black be the day that would surrender full British ownership of the farthest-flung Anglo-Saxon outpost.'[8] Barnard's 'New Zealand Five Million Club' was formed partly to combat popular hostility to increased immigration, with representation from labour as well as business and farming interest groups.[9] Savage talked on one occasion of the need for New Zealanders to develop their own economy, not just to guard against the possibility of isolation in the event of war but also because 'unless the country were used, we had no moral or economic right to it'.[10]

Concern about the intentions of Asian powers, coupled with awareness of Britain's concentration on Europe, and of the transformation wrought by the aeroplane, intensified preoccupation with the country's defence to an unprecedented degree, and one rarely matched in any subsequent period.

[7]   See Wight, 'The Balance of Power'; Ceadel, p. 188. Milner, *New Zealand and the Far East*, pp. 101–2, discusses in terms of Samoa.
[8]   H. Guthrie-Smith, *Tutira: The Story of a New Zealand Sheep Station*. 4th ed. Wellington, 1969, p. 421. A monumental study of the ecology of a Hawke's Bay sheep station by its owner.
[9]   *Round Table*, 106 (March 1937), p. 464; see also 'The Birth Rate in the Empire', *ibid.*, pp. 308–38; for an enlightened view of the problem, address by A. E. Butcher to the WEA, *EP*, 10 Oct. 1937; in June 1938 the *EP* wrote favourably on a report of the Five Million Club.
[10] *NZH*, 23 March 1939, quoted in Witheford, 'Labour Party and War', ii, p. 95; see also Donald Cowie, 'The Empire Through New Zealand Eyes', *Political Quarterly* (Oct. 1938), p. 583: 'More than any other single factor, [the invasion of the Asiatic mainland by Japan] has awakened New Zealand in recent years.'

David McIntyre has shown that the new government maintained and built on the defence programme initiated by its predecessor, albeit with a particular bias in favour of the Air Force. Air Force bases were established at Ohakea (midway between Whenuapai and Wigram) and at Woodbourne at considerable expense: more than £100,000 was spent on Woodbourne. The navy expenditure initiated by the previous government was maintained as well.[11]

Singapore was not discounted. But Savage told the public in June 1938 that despite the best intentions of the British, New Zealand might have to look after itself, to prepare for the worst. The country might be cut off in the event of a European war, the British unable to reinforce the Singapore base for a period, New Zealand vulnerable to the Japanese. In that same month Japan objected to proposals to fortify the Phoenix and Ellice Islands.[12] The government's determination to establish an iron industry was partly influenced by defence and self-sufficiency considerations, as was its embargo on scrap metal exports.[13]

The *Round Table* noted that in the second quarter of 1939 there was a stiffening of opinon on defence, not least because of this awareness that New Zealand might be isolated if trouble arose in the Pacific as well as in Europe.[14] In April the New Zealanders held a long-planned conference with the British (and also with the more modestly represented Australians) to discuss the issues. It did not reach any new conclusions nor were the British delegates able to offer cast-iron reassurances about Britain's capacity to reinforce Singapore, although the assumption held that New Zealand need only fear raids until the fleet reached Singapore.[15] The Defence League was active in canvassing alternatives and positing scenarios, in particular war with Japan, for instance at a meeting in Wellington in mid April attended by around 1700 people.[16]

For the Defence League, the danger of invasion and isolation was further ammunition in its campaign to commit what it saw as a socialist government with pacifist leanings to increased defence spending and improved defence preparedness. Coates, who was made a member of the War Cabinet in 1940, voiced similar views, but with a more marked emphasis on the need for national rather than Empire defence.[17] Such views were expressed by Labour

---

11 McIntyre, *New Zealand Prepares for War*, pp. 170–2, 181.
12 McIntyre, *New Zealand Prepares for War*, p. 191; *EP*, 3 June 1938. Phoenix and Ellice Islands (latter now Tuvalu) were British territories close to the Equator and to the Japanese League of Nations mandate, formerly German, islands of Micronesia.
13 *AIBR*, March 1938, p. 224.
14 *Round Table*, 116 (Sept. 1939), p. 878, and earlier. For instance, *Dominion* editorial, 27 Jan. 1939, stressing New Zealand's maritime lifeline to the Empire, and mulling over the lack of a British presence in the Pacific. *Dominion*, 23 March 1939, reports Fraser's comment that New Zealand might be cut off 'for years'.
15 McIntyre, *New Zealand Prepares for War*, pp. 189, 209–10.
16 *Dominion*, 20 April 1939: see also *Press* letters to the editor on the Japanese threat, 26 April 1939.
17 Wood, *Political and External Affairs*, pp. 164–5.

ministers too. But it was Lee and Barnard who linked self-sufficiency to an explicit nationalism. For some in the Labour movement, and for Lee and Barnard in particular, the prospect of the country's being isolated by war reinforced the case for a national defence and complemented their political and economic nationalism and emphasis on self-sufficiency. Indeed such commentators went beyond immediate concerns to question whether New Zealand needed a protector to quite the extent it was habitually assumed it did:

> New Zealand's strategic position in relation to trade is a comparatively simple one. She is 1200 miles from the nearest mainland in one direction of trade, 5000 in the other and 5000 miles from the nearest likely enemy.[18] Her commerce becomes oceanic the moment it leaves New Zealand ports, and on the main route across the Pacific passes only one focal point—the Panama Canal or Cape Horn, on the journey to Europe. It is thus easy to disperse the shipping on various routes across the ocean and so materially lessen interference. Her trade is very little canalized by geographical features. To this extent her isolation in the midst of the ocean is an advantage which is not vitiated by the fact that an overwhelming proportion of her trade is transpacific. Admittedly the trade does pass through one focal point en route to Europe and at the end merges into the densest shipping stream in the world, but by that time, it has passed out of New Zealand's strategic orbit and must be regarded as a problem for the Empire as a whole and for Great Britain in particular.[19]

One editorial in the Labour Party paper, the *Standard*, argued that as New Zealand had negligible strategic value and no important raw material resources, it was more in danger from its membership of the Commonwealth than from isolation: 'a probable objective of a raiding party would be to prevent or dissuade New Zealand from despatching any forces overseas to the assistance of any other part of the Commonwealth. New Zealand's Commonwealth membership renders her in this respect more likely to be attacked than if she stood alone.'[20]

It will be recognised that this species of opinion overlapped with the anti-militarist arguments against conscription and the dispatch of New Zealand forces overseas. But it had a greater resemblance to Lee–Barnard nationalism. Interest therefore could foster such nationalism. In the climate and circumstances of the late 1930s it was not a powerful or decisive impulse. Lee's expulsion from the Labour Party—and Barnard left with him—in March 1940 was one reason for this. So also was a change in Japan's foreign policy. The Japanese felt betrayed by the Germans when the latter concluded a pact with the Soviet Union in August 1939—Japan's armies on the Asian

---

[18] The nearest Japanese territory at that time, the Caroline and Marshall Islands, was around 5000 miles away.

[19] Quoted in Milner, *New Zealand and the Far East*, p. 94, no source given.

[20] Quoted in Milner, *New Zealand and the Far East*, p. 95. This overlooked the fact that even if it were outside the Commonwealth New Zealand might well be the victim of economic warfare as a supplier of food and raw material to a belligerent, namely Britain.

mainland had had repeated border clashes with Soviet forces through 1939 and the most recent clash at Nomonhan had been in the Soviet favour.[21] The Hiranuma government was replaced by one led by Noboyuki Abe, which was less hostile towards Britain and the United States. In talks after the war started, over sending a New Zealand expeditionary force to Europe, the British assured Fraser that the kind of breakthrough on the western front which might bring Japan into the war was remote and that Japan would therefore continue neutral.[22] But most important, opinion in New Zealand increasingly focused on the United States as a likely guarantor of the country's security, particularly when the event which the British had assured Fraser was 'remote' took place.

A guarantee of protection?

In the middle of 1940 Germany went from victory to victory in Europe—its western 'front' became the Atlantic Ocean and the North Sea. Japan responded opportunistically in Asia, where both the Netherlands, itself now occupied by Germany, and France, partly occupied and suing for peace, had territories. In August, Japan signed a tripartite pact with Germany and Italy, and moved its forces into the northern part of French Indochina. The British government told the New Zealand government in confidence that it might not be able to send a fleet to Singapore in the event of Japan's entering the war, although two months later another cable said that if Japan did attack Australia and New Zealand, Britain would 'cut its losses' in the Mediterranean and come to their aid.[23]

It was shattering news, and understandably the government's thoughts turned to the United States. Even in 1939 many comments from all parts of the political spectrum had been made about the value of the United States to New Zealand. 'Scarcely a day passes', wrote one overseas commentator, 'but a politician or newpaper appeals for closer identification of policy with the United States.' The United States was more popular with the left than was Chamberlain's government, being seen as more hostile to Fascism.[24] The mood was similar, but even more focused, in 1940. But would the United States respond?

21 Japan had occupied Manchuria—Northeast China—in 1931. The clashes took place at points on the Manchuria/Soviet frontier.
22 *Documents Relating to New Zealand's Participation in the Second World War* (hereafter *Second World War Documents*), v. 1. Wellington, 1949, pp. 335-6 (Appendix ii, Notes of a meeting held at the War Office, 6 Nov. 1939).
23 Wood, *Political and External Affairs*, pp. 194-6.
24 Cowie, pp. 584-5; see also Broadfoot and McKeen, *NZPD*, 248, pp. 497, 510 (30 Sept. 1937); Savage's praise of Roosevelt at the opening of the 1939 defence conference in Witheford, 'Labour Party and War', ii, pp. 1-2; Fraser in M. P. Lissington, *New Zealand and the United States 1840-1944*. Wellington, 1972, pp. 18-19; Lyon, *EP*, 17 Aug. 1939; Nash, *Dominion*, 2 Sept. 1939. For opinion on the left: see above, p. 23, n40.

Fraser, Prime Minister since Savage's death in March 1940, informed the British that, given the circumstances they had outlined, the New Zealand government wanted to establish diplomatic contact with the United States. He pointed out, with a degree of understatement, that 'the undertaking to despatch an adequate fleet to Singapore, if required, formed the basis of the whole of this Dominion's defence preparations', and went on to ask for British agreement to the dispatch of a New Zealand cabinet minister to Washington on a special mission, 'in the hope of strengthening the security of the Pacific and of reinforcing the representations already made to President Roosevelt on behalf of the Allies'.[25] Aware of British caution about such initiatives, Fraser, in a later message, stressed that the government had to satisfy public opinion and also that it wished to assist 'discreetly in establishing as far as possible the principle that the United States cannot be disinterested in the isolated British communities in this area and to lead as delicately as possible to the active co-operation of the United States in assisting to preserve the political integrity and economic well-being of these communities.'[26] The need to ensure the support of the United States influenced the government's opposition to Britain's closure of the Burma Road, in response to Japanese pressure, for three months beginning from July to October 1940.[27] For all that, political manoeuverings in Wellington meant that the decision to send a minister to Washington—Walter Nash, the Deputy Prime Minister—was not taken until November 1941, although in the interim a supply trade and diplomatic mission led by Coates and Frank Langstone, a Labour M.P. unpopular with his ministerial colleagues, did go to the United States.[28]

In the meantime, at the end of November 1940 the *Rangitane* was attacked and sunk with the loss of five lives some 650 kilometres off the east coast. The only aircraft available to track the attack craft were two flying boats, one of which was en route from Sydney and the other on the slipway. Neither could have attacked the raider anyway. Fraser reminded the British that at the outbreak of the war New Zealand had agreed to hand over to them the Wellington bomber aircrafts it had ordered, then on the point of delivery. Now the Air Force possessed 'not one single aircraft suitable either for reconnaissance or for attack against a raider at any substantial distance from the shores of New Zealand'. Understandably, said Fraser, 'The public are becoming restive at the repeated evidence that raiders can visit our shores with impunity....'[29] Churchill in response provided a small number of aircraft, a large dose of flattery and a reiteration of the 'main theatre'

---

25 GGNZ to SSDA, 15 June 1940, cited in Wood, *Political and External Affairs*, pp. 194-5.
26 Wood, p. 195, quoting GGNZ to SSDA, 9 July 1940.
27 Wood, *Political and External Affairs*, p. 198.
28 James Kember, 'The Establishment of the New Zealand Mission in Washington'. VUW History Dept research paper, 1971.
29 *Second World War Documents*, v. 3. Wellington, 1963, p. 215. (Fraser to Churchill, 4 Dec. 1940); McGibbon, *Blue-Water*, p. 347.

argument, that is, that the war would be won by defeating the enemy at the point its power was concentrated, in Europe.[30]

The Americans—or the possibility of them—became all the more important. Growing American support for the British war effort through 1941, most notably the inception of Lend-Lease economic and military assistance, was welcomed in New Zealand. The government was also aware of British and American discussions about likely responses to a Japanese attack in the Pacific. When New Zealand forces were involved in the difficult campaigns in Greece and Crete in April to June 1941, Lee and Barnard were alone in Parliament in setting the losses in dead, wounded and prisoners against the need for New Zealand to concentrate on its own defence.[31]

The attack when it came demolished American and British military and naval power in Asia and the Pacific far more completely than had been expected. The virtual destruction of the United States Pacific Fleet at Pearl Harbor, Hawaii, and the fall of Singapore and the British base there, raised real fears that New Zealand could be isolated and abandoned. How could the defensive shield of American and British power have been ripped away as roughly and completely as it was during the last three weeks of 1941 and the first six of 1942? The idea of a war in support of the British in Asia was ruled out with the sinking of the *Prince of Wales* and the *Repulse* on 10 December and the fall of Singapore on 15 February. By the end of February the British had no positions in Southeast and North Asia. And the Americans were not much better off, it seemed. Did New Zealand now lie open to attack?

Neither the British nor the Americans thought so. There is an element of hurt pride in Fraser's anger that the Joint Planning Committee in London believed that the only attack likely on New Zealand was 'sporadic raids by enemy cruisers and aircraft carriers' if Fiji and New Caledonia were held and 'one brigade group with naval and air support' if New Caledonia and Fiji were lost. 'It is impossible', said Churchill on 4 March, 'to say that the Japanese will not attack New Zealand in force, but there are other far more tempting objectives for them and their resources are not unlimited.'[32] Of course British military planners did not have a great deal of credibility in March 1942 and Fraser was only doing what was proper in looking after the interests of his own country. But there is a plausibility about the British observations in this instance. New Zealand was not a centre of Allied power. New Zealand was as fruit on a tree which the Japanese could harvest at leisure, once conditions were favourable.

---

[30] '. . . all hangs together and I hope that you will have good confidence in us.' *Second World War Documents*, v. 3, p. 216 (Churchill to Fraser, 14 Dec. 1940).
[31] Taylor, *Home Front*, pp. 293–4, 298; Olssen, p. 174.
[32] *Second World War Documents*, v. 3, p. 233 (Churchill to Fraser, 4 March 1942).

Fighting in the Pacific

Despite British scepticism, New Zealand did receive protection. It was well placed to act as a rear area for an American assault on Japanese positions in the Solomon Islands and New Guinea. American protection, or perhaps more accurately, a coincidence of American and New Zealand strategic interests, had come about.

The Pacific War therefore remained at a distance from New Zealand. But even in the first few months of 1942 the New Zealanders do not seem to have been as exercised about the Pacific theatre as were, for instance, the Australians. The fall of Singapore, which unleashed a wave of criticism of Churchill in Australia (a great many Australians were captured), did not elicit as strong a response. There was no clamour to bring back forces from the Middle East, except from Lee and Barnard. The *Listener* conducted an enquiry. Had the blow been accepted 'too calmly', it asked. One Member of Parliament, Bodkin, went so far as to say in March that he was 'just a little concerned at the attitude that appears to be taken up because America . . . has promised us great help. That seems to be made an excuse for complacency and almost a smug satisfaction.'[33] Another, Gordon, noted that he had 'even heard people say, "What does it matter if Japan wins?" They have also said, "Japan will probably buy our produce from us" . . . . The people should realise that they would be better dead than captured by the Japanese.'[34]

In the Legislative Council, one Councillor, Bloodworth, quoted a friend who was complaining about the complacency: 'what we needed here was one or two bombs.'[35] Some weeks later, in commenting on the news of the submarine raids on Sydney and similar activities by the Japanese, the *Auckland Star* thought that most New Zealanders were mentally prepared for some form of attack, but also that, with more than two years' experience of war, they regarded the shelling of Sydney and Newcastle as curious rather than important. Taylor argues that while there were 'preparations, practical curtailments, adjustments to thinking. . . . there was no sense of doom, no widespread break in values or ways of living.'[36] An academic commentator wrote that 'In 1943 New Zealand had returned to something like her pre Pearl Harbor status: she was a base behind the lines; a source of supplies and trained fighting men, not a potential firing post.'[37]

New Zealand's notion of security remained intimately bound up with the need to maintain British and American—particularly American—power in the Pacific. But there was not the same edge to this objective as in Australia

33 Barbara Angus, 'Public Opinion in New Zealand Towards Japan 1939–1945', p. 54: *NZPD*, 261, pp. 104–6 (19 March 1942), WAII-21/19a, NA.
34 Angus, p. 56: *NZPD*, 261, p. 145 (20 March 1942).
35 Angus, p. 52.
36 Taylor, *Home Front*, pp. 328–9; *Auckland Star*, 9 June 1942, is quoted by Taylor, p. 358.
37 Wood, *This New Zealand*, p. 169.

because New Zealand did not face the direct threat to its national security confronting Australia in 1942. The difference is paralleled by the responses on a number of occasions subsequently, for instance, in the negotiations over the ANZUS Pact in 1951 and over sending troops to Vietnam in 1965. But it was also demonstrated by New Zealand opinion about fighting in the Pacific theatre in the Second World War itself.

The possibility of an increased military involvement in the Pacific first became an issue in March 1942, when the Australians moved two of their divisions from the Middle East. Fraser accepted the promise of two American divisions to make up for the absence of the New Zealand Division and these duly arrived in New Zealand in June. At the end of 1942, when the issue arose again, Fraser was keen to see New Zealand play a role in the Pacific. Churchill demurred, a demurral reinforced by the Anglo-American Combined Chiefs of Staff, and in a secret session on 3 December the House of Representatives unanimously decided that the 2nd Division should stay in the Middle East for the time being. In part mitigation of the decision Fraser drew attention to the fact that New Zealand forces had now taken up forward positions in the Pacific as had always been intended (there were by this time forces on Norfolk Island and in Tonga and New Caledonia). Moreover, the decision was taken to build up the 3rd Division, as the forces in the Pacific were commonly labelled, to the status of a full combat division, on the assumption that in due course it would be reinforced from the Middle East.[38]

British pressure needs to be understood in relationship to New Zealand perceptions of the country's situation. By this time any direct military threat to New Zealand had passed. It is quite plain that public opinion in New Zealand was now overwhelmingly in favour of participating in the Mediterranean rather than the Pacific theatre. The nexus of loyalties and interests that made a major military commitment in the Mediterranean acceptable did not apply in the Pacific. New Zealanders recognised that the United States was helping protect New Zealand in the Pacific, but public opinion did not draw from that the same conclusions as it did in respect of the Mediterranean war. A meeting in Auckland in December 1942 of the local Chambers of Commerce, the Trades Council and the employers' and the manufacturers' associations concluded (with the subsequent assent of the Farmers' Union) that the development of United States power in the Pacific had removed the immediate menace to the country and that New Zealand should now move from maximum military defence to maximum utilisation of manpower in production for American demands: they had 'grave misgivings' about maintaining a large active force in the Pacific. Several newpapers commented on the conference, the *New Zealand Herald* remarking that the unanimity amongst such bodies was as rare as it should be influential.[39] One letter to the

38   Wood, *Political and External Affairs*, pp. 246–53.
39   Taylor, pp. 712–13, 710. In its editorial of 8 Dec. 1942 the *Herald* charged the care of the Pacific to the Americans.

Herald, signed 'Mother of a twice wounded hero', wrote that the NZEF should be returned home for a well-earned rest and also to 'look after New Zealand shores, and return to their own land and people.'[40] The fact that the Anglo-American priority was to concentrate against Germany meant that a Pacific offensive would be long delayed and in the meantime it would be better to concentrate New Zealand's limited labour resources on production.

The National Party was a firm supporter of keeping the 2nd Division in the Mediterranean, although it was not prepared to reject outright the notion of having forces in the Pacific.[41] Sid Holland, the leader of the National Party since 1940, commented in February 1943 that the government should not consider bringing the 2nd Division home at the end of the African campaign: the war effort would be damaged. Moreover there was no home front in New Zealand: it was up in the Islands, in the 'disease-infested tropical area'. Opinion in New Zealand generally was much more inclined towards bringing the 2nd Division home than sending it off to the Pacific. And the troops themselves had views: one wrote that the men of the 2nd Division had no wish after home leave to tackle the Japanese by serving in the Solomons, so unhealthy compared to the Middle East. There was also a feeling that the Pacific War was America's war, and that the United States was so much larger and so much less mobilised than New Zealand.[42] It was a view that complemented that of the American service chiefs themselves, who did not particularly want to accommodate their strategy and tactics to the requirements of one small ally.[43]

A concern that New Zealand not be seen to be evading the more unattractive war percolated the official reports. There was, said Fraser, a 'keenly felt realisation that the Government and people of the Commonwealth [of Australia] would undoubtedly regard New Zealand's action as one of reluctance not only to assist to the fullest extent of our resources, in the Pacific battle, ... but also to take our share in the burden arising from tropical disease which takes so grim and heavy a toll among those serving in the forward areas.'[44] And again,

---

[40]   3 Dec. 1942.

[41]   Wood, *Political and External Affairs*, pp. 250-1.

[42]   Taylor, *Home Front*, pp. 713, 717. It is interesting that in the 1986 opinion poll on defence and security, whereas 54 per cent of those polled were prepared to use armed force if requested in the event of an attack on Britain or British territory, only 36 per cent were prepared to act in the same way for an independent South Pacific country and only 42 per cent in the event of an attack on Cook Islands, Tokelau and Niue. Defence Committee of Enquiry, *Defence And Security: What New Zealanders Want*. Wellington, 1986, Annex, p. 20. See also below, pp. 261-2, 272-5.

[43]   Wood, *Political and External Affairs*, pp. 317-18.

[44]   Robin Kay, ed., *Documents in New Zealand's External Relations*, v. 1: *The Australia-New Zealand Agreement 1944* (hereafter *Agreement*). Wellington, 1972, p. 30: Fraser to SSD, 21 May 1943.

We are most anxious that there should be no feeling on the part of the Australians or Americans that we are in any way shirking, or leaving them to service in the tropics. Our men in New Caledonia and our airmen and naval units in Guadalcanal and Espiritu Santo, and no doubt in the areas which may later be captured, will necessarily be subject to all those tropical conditions which are causing so intense a strain and toll on men's endurance.[45]

No final decision was taken about the fate of the dual commitment. Fraser himself in May 1943 swung round to keeping the Division in the Mediterranean, a position which put him in agreement with Churchill and the Combined Chiefs of Staff, although not with the Australians.[46] In March 1944 the decision was taken to start withdrawing the remaining 3rd Division forces from the Pacific. The major New Zealand force in the Pacific conflict became the RNZAF: some 3000 RNZAF personnel in May 1943 had become 7500 by October 1944. In September 1944 the final decision was taken to keep the 2nd Division in Europe until the end of the war there. Meantime it had become evident that the United States was reluctant to share the war with New Zealand or Australia. Both were kept out of the ground fighting as it moved north across the equator in 1944, although their naval forces continued to be used as part of the British Commonwealth Pacific Fleet.[47]

The patterns that have already been identified in New Zealand attitudes to the war against Japan in 1942–44 can also be detected in the last year of the war. Public thinking was not in sympathy with contributing to a Commonwealth force against Japan in 1945, so opening up for the first time since the beginning of the war explicit debate on the role of New Zealand's forces and implicit reflection on the role New Zealand expected to play in the war. Wood himself comments that it was doubtful that the government's reasoning 'in essence that New Zealand was a Pacific country and should act accordingly, if necessary under American leadership—had made much impact on the Labour Party outside its responsible leadership. It is still more doubtful whether it could command much sympathy in the National Party—more particularly in the farming community.'[48]

The distance of Japanese forces now from New Zealand, the long-standing distaste for jungle fighting, the distaste too for the Japanese as adversaries, the feeling that it was America's war—all these factors identifiable in the 1942–44

---

45   Kay, *Agreement*, p. 32; Fraser to Berendsen, p. 31; Fraser was astonished to learn that 2NZEF men did not want to go to the Solomons: 'what exactly is in their minds if they don't want to go into the Pacific after they return? .... Has it been made quite clear to them that Americans are not here as garrison troops for the defence of New Zealand, but that they are using this country only as base ....? ': Fraser to Jones (Minister of Defence), 7 May 1943, *Second World War Documents*, v. 2. Wellington, 1951, p. 197.
46   Wood, *Political and External Affairs*, p. 256.
47   Taylor, *Home Front*, p. 720; Wood, *Political and External Affairs*, pp. 279–81, 318. And see below, pp. 50–51.
48   Wood, *Political and External Affairs*, pp. 296–7.

period were present and more openly so than before. The result, said Wood, 'was a fullblooded political discussion during which some of the deeper currents in New Zealand's politics and thinking, normally hidden, were brought spectacularly to the surface.'[49] By this Wood means—judging from the context of the comment—the range of attitudes about fighting in the jungle rather than the desert, about the Americans, even the idea that the Germans and Italians were preferable enemies to the Japanese. The Navy and the Air Force were both involved in the Pacific War—why should it be necessary to commit land forces as well? Neither the National Party nor Lee, who on this occasion was more in the mainstream of thinking, found the suggestion credible. In the campaigning for a by-election in Hamilton (26 May) National Party politicians stressed that New Zealand's population was overcommitted and it should concentrate on food production.[50] The assertion of the American commander in the South Pacific on 4 June that 'the most important thing that New Zealand could do now to help in the Pacific was to assist in the feeding of the American troops' did not help the government. Press opinion was mostly negative too: the *Hawera Star* said on 7 June, 'if our name hasn't been made good by sacrifices to date, nothing that we do from now on will achieve that end.'[51] Churchill's bitter attack on Britain's Labour Party at the opening of an election campaign in that country meant that an appeal from him was unlikely to have much effect on Labour voters in New Zealand.[52]

The government was nevertheless determined to do something. New Zealand could not desert her allies now, said Nash. After another by-election on 21 July it proved possible to reach agreement on committing a two-brigade division, with a complement of 16,000 men, to the war against Japan. Here was an echo of what the war might have been before the fall of Singapore: the New Zealanders were to be included in a British Commonwealth force to take part in the invasion of Japan, and one paper reported that after the war the forces would play a garrisoning role in British possessions in the Far East. The plan was finally put to Parliament for debate at the beginning of August: it was therefore overtaken very quickly by events.[53]

Wood's comment about 'deeper currents' implies that advocates of a more independent New Zealand foreign policy found the lack of enthusiasm for the Pacific War disconcerting, or perhaps frustrating. They wanted New Zealand to become more outward-looking, more aware of the world outside the Empire, more internationalist. It seemed to them that the Pacific War forced

---

49 Wood, *Political and External Affairs*, p. 297.
50 Holland, *NZPD*, 268, p. 143 (5 July 1945); see also Wood, *Political and External Affairs*, pp. 297–8.
51 N1724/0375, NA; see also other editorial comment on N1724/0320–0360, NA.
52 Wood, *Political and External Affairs*, pp. 299–300.
53 N1724/0347: *Mataura Ensign*, 4 Aug. 1945; Wood, *Political and External Affairs*, pp. 300–1. The Americans dropped atom bombs on two Japanese cities, Hiroshima and Nagasaki, on 6 August and 9 August respectively. Japan surrendered on 15 August.

such changes on New Zealand, required New Zealanders to adapt to new circumstances. But most New Zealanders did not see that necessity. Once the immediate threat from Japan had passed, the Pacific receded from popular consciousness, few argued that the national interest required New Zealand to have a bigger presence in the Pacific theatre than it did, and many argued for that presence to be limited.

Security after the war

During the war, New Zealand's need to act on its own behalf in the Pacific became for observers compelling evidence of the country's independent foreign policy. In the immediate aftermath of the war, the equivalent issue was the need to pursue its own diplomacy *vis à vis* Japan. It was of course really the same issue transposed from war to peace.

In January 1944 the Australian and New Zealand prime ministers met in Canberra. The Australians had been angered that Roosevelt and Churchill had met the Chinese leader, Chiang Kai-shek, at Cairo to discuss the progress of the war against Japan and the future shape of the postwar order in Asia. There was a particular concern lest the United States translate its temporary presence south of the equator into something more permanent: another echo, this time of the manoeuvering over air landing rights before the war.[54] Fraser's preparedness to meet the Australian Prime Minister, John Curtin and his Minister of External Affairs, H. V. Evatt, was partly grounded in his wish to mollify the government whose wishes he had disregarded in respect of the return of New Zealand forces from the Mediterranean.[55] The issues that the Australians raised which preoccupied him most were the need to ensure that New Zealand and Australia both had a voice in important wartime and postwar decisions—a classic formulation of independence and participation. The concern for the welfare of the colonial people of the South Pacific was a characteristic expression of Labour anti-colonialism.[56]

New Zealand accepted—although it probably would not have suggested— the Agreement, which asserted the right of Australia and New Zealand to participate in all decisions which concerned the South-west and South Pacific:[57] although Fraser discussed the agreement fully before signing, he

[54]   The advent of intercontinental air travel in the late 1930s—the first commercial flight from North America to New Zealand was in 1939—produced an Anglo-American contest for ownership of atolls in the Central Pacific of potential importance for landing rights. See McIntyre, *NZ Prepares for War*, pp. 195–200.
[55]   McIntyre, 'Peter Fraser's Commonwealth', p. 44.
[56]   For further discussion see below, pp. 65–67.
[57]   Kay, *Agreement*, p. xxviii. According to Kay all that was first envisaged by the New Zealanders was a series of talks in order to ascertain each other's viewpoint on various matters in which Australia and New Zealand had a common interest. Not until some time after the proceedings had commenced was it known that the Australians wanted a formal agreement.

was discussing an already prepared Australian draft.[58] The Agreement did implicitly treat the United States as an intruder in the South Pacific, as Germany, France, Russia had all been regarded in the past and Japan was emphatically regarded in the present. It included clauses which stressed that military bases constructed by one power in the territory of another could not provide the basis of territorial claims, and that there should be no sovereignty changes in the Pacific without their prior agreement.

There was a potential clash between these aspirations and New Zealand's expectation that its security would continue to rest in part on the United States. The War Cabinet secretariat, in January 1944, and the Chiefs of Staff, in October 1944, concurred in this expectation, and a War Cabinet paper spelt out how it might be accomplished:

> The occupation of [the] Japanese fortified islands [in Micronesia] by the United States would ensure the creation of a continuous defence line from the mainland of the United States through Hawaii and these islands to the Philippines. In addition, it would create a substantial United States interest in the Pacific and deny the force of the traditional body of isolationist opinion in that country .... We should at the same time, in consideration of the importance of strong imperial defence and our inability to provide sufficient forces for our own defence, ensure that substantial [British] forces in the Pacific be maintained. This will to some extent be ensured by [Britain's] continuing administration of Fiji [*et al.*].[59]

According to A. D. McIntosh, Secretary of External Affairs, the New Zealand authorities never had any doubt as to the desirability of permanent American bases in the central Pacific or at Pago Pago in American Samoa.[60] So American disquiet at the tenor of those parts of the Agreement which bore on its Pacific interests bothered the New Zealanders. During the talks Fraser himself had reassured Wellington that 'every care had been taken in drafting' to eliminate any reference which could have been construed as an intention to drive the United States out of the area. An apologetic reply was sent to the State Department and when Fraser visited Washington later in the year he made the appropriate *mea culpa*.[61]

[58] The full story of the pact is told in Kay, *Agreement*. See also Trevor Reese, 'The Australia-New Zealand Agreement, 1944, and the United States', *JCPS*, 4/1 (March 1966), pp. 3–15; see also below, p. 65.

[59] Kay, *Agreement*, pp. 60–61: War Cabinet secretariat, PM's Dept, paper on postwar security, Jan. 1944. New Zealand made the final point very firmly to Australia (Evatt had ideas about taking over British Pacific territories): Kay, *Agreement*, p. 104, notes by New Zealand representatives on draft agenda for Canberra talks, Jan. 1944; Chiefs of Staff paper, Oct. 1944 in Kay, *Agreement*, pp. 216–22, referred, to the assumption that the Japanese mandated islands would be under the control of or defended by the United States 'or some other power which will always remain friendly'.

[60] Kay, *Agreement*, p. 139: Fraser to Acting Minister of External Affairs, 22 Jan. 1944; McIntosh, 'Origins of the Department', p. 23. Substitute nuclear ships for bases and the issues raised in 1944 mirror the New Zealand-American conflict over port visits in 1984–86. McIntosh was Secretary of the Department from its inception in 1943 until his retirement in 1966.

[61] Reese, 'Australia-New Zealand Agreement', p. 12.

The pattern—concern about American intrusion coupled with hopes for American protection—recurred after the war. In November 1945 the United States first approached New Zealand, Australia and Britain, seeking negotiation over American bases which it wished either to retain access to or establish jurisdiction over. There was concern in New Zealand at the import of the American request—did it aim to annex New Zealand or other British territory? On the other hand, Nash and Fraser could both see the merit of committing the United States to New Zealand's security.[62] The latter, positive view proved dominant, but in the event a peacetime mood returned to the United States, and military spending, particularly on bases so distant from the United States, fell out of favour.

New Zealand was 'protected' by the American presence further away from its shores: the United States acquired a 'strategic trusteeship' over the formerly Japanese Micronesian islands. This was widely accepted by the international community, despite the fact that it involved a change in the provisions for trust territory administration.[63] Further, it was United States policy which New Zealand sought to influence in respect of Japan. Through the postwar years, New Zealand diplomats and politicians sought to ensure that Japan did not return to a position where it could make war in the Pacific.[64]

At the time of the Commonwealth conference on Japan in September 1947 (in Canberra) the press was generally sceptical about MacArthur's claims of reform, progress and 'spiritual revolution' in Japan.[65] While the *Press* was still concerned to include Russia in any peace settlement, the *New Zealand Herald* cautioned against Japanese-Russian rapprochement, suggesting the spectre of a red Japan, allied to a red China and Russia—the merging of the red and yellow perils.[66] In November 1947 the External Affairs Committee of the House of Representatives, in its comment on a Department of External Affairs paper, noted that it shared the view of the New Zealand delegation to the conference that the political and economic roots of Japanese militarism be eradicated and that the United Nations be secured against renewed aggression. It also warned that 'no single power, or two powers, should have a veto at this conference, but it should be a matter for further consideration whether those countries willing to accept simple or two-thirds majority voting should proceed alone with the conference.'[67] This was clearly a reference to the

---

62 847H. 20/9–1346, RG59, USNA; N2288/0085, Fraser to Nash, 29 April 1945: 'on the broad issue of American participation in Pacific defence there is no real difference of opinion' (in Wellington), EA 153/23/1, NA.
63 For more on trusteeship after the Second World War, see below, pp. 65–68.
64 Ann Trotter, *New Zealand and Japan 1945–1952: The Occupation and the Peace Treaty.* London, 1990, *passim.*
65 847H. 00/9–1947, RG59, USNA.
66 Some talked of the amalgamation of the yellow peril and the red menace into a sinister 'orange penace'.
67 Robin Kay, ed., *Documents in New Zealand's External Relations,* v. 3: *The ANZUS Pact and the Treaty of Peace with Japan* (hereafter *ANZUS Pact*), Wellington, 1986, pp. 195–7 (Report by the House of Representatives External Affairs Committee, 20 Nov. 1947).

American interest in proceeding to a peace treaty without Soviet participation.

In terms of New Zealand's security interest, the predominant fear was not of there being too much American power and influence but too little. At the Commonwealth Prime Ministers' meeting in October 1948 Bevin noted that America's new Cold War attitude to Japan might mean MacArthur was put into a purely supervisory role with the Japanese government in Japanese hands. Fraser did not at all like the idea that the occupation administration might be 'pushed over' and replaced by chaos.[68] While New Zealand was made anxious by some American initiatives, American withdrawal was an equally disturbing prospect; this pattern was to recur through the succeeding decades and is of course endemic in any unequal alliance relationship.

The key goal therefore was to keep the Americans in Asia and this inevitably entailed a certain encouragement and acceptance of the American presence. Foss Shanahan, Deputy Secretary of External Affairs, 1943–55, wrote to McIntosh about a conversation with Butterworth, Assistant Secretary of State, on 18 November 1949. He explained that he and Laking, the counsellor at the embassy, had 'stressed the fact that the government had been concerned for some time about developments in Japan and in other parts of the Far East, but had deliberately refrained from voicing publicly the misgivings they felt out of a desire not to embarrass the United States, whose difficulties and responsibilities they fully appreciated'; and that he had pointed out that his government was 'very sensible of the importance of close association between the United States, New Zealand and other countries of the British Commonwealth' in respect of Japan.[69]

There was another aspect to New Zealand's role in the peace settlement with Japan that echoes New Zealand attitudes to fighting in the Pacific. Ann Trotter notes that New Zealand was independent-minded in pursuit of its interests in Japan but also observes that those interests were fairly limited. New Zealand had not wanted to participate in the British Commonwealth Occupation Force (BCOF) and the Jayforce, as it was known, was always unpopular in New Zealand. In New Zealand (as indeed in many other Allied countries) the findings of the International Military Tribunal for the Far East, on which New Zealand was represented, 'were largely ignored'. Even with respect to security itself, Trotter emphasises that New Zealand reiterated 'at all times its specifically South Pacific view of Japan as a potential threat to security'.[70] Nor did South Pacific necessarily mean Australasian: Fraser told Field Marshal Montgomery when he visited New Zealand early in 1947 that Australian proposals for regional defence cooperation were a 'form of "Australian Imperialism"'.[71]

---

[68] For a full discussion, see Trotter, *NZ and Japan 1945–52*, pp. 106–7.

[69] Kay, *ANZUS Pact*, pp. 292, 293. Shanahan was Deputy Secretary of the Department of External Affairs until 1955 and held other senior official posts until his premature death in 1964.

[70] Trotter, *NZ and Japan 1945–52*, pp. 29–30, 183.

[71] Ian McGibbon, 'The Australian–New Zealand Defence Relationship Since 1901', *Revue Internationale d'Histoire Militaire*, 72 (1990), p. 140.

Conclusion

We have identified three interests animating New Zealand foreign policy in the 1930s and 1940s that can be described as 'independent', or which had or could have had independent consequences: the reluctance to relinquish the deep-seated insularity of New Zealand's circumstances and New Zealand life; the need for self-sufficiency and survival; and the quest for a new ally, namely the United States.

Of the three it was the latter which was, if not the most significant, then certainly the most discussed: 'It was the experience of World War II', McIntosh wrote in 1961, 'that led the New Zealand Government to recognise finally the risks of exclusive dependence on the United Kingdom and to establish diplomatic posts in four other countries (two of them not in the Commonwealth); to insist increasingly on recognition of its national interests, and to create new machinery for the formulation, administration and expression of an independent foreign policy.'[72] Wood similarly argued that the desire to encourage American participation in the defence of the Pacific produced 'a degree of regard to the reaction of a country outside the Commonwealth which was a new development in New Zealand foreign policy. Though less advertised at the time than the independence displayed at Geneva ... it was really both more novel and more solidly based ....'[73] In respect of matters of war and peace in the Pacific, New Zealand 'was and felt herself to be, a principal, a small power, no doubt, but one with direct and urgent interests ....'[74] New Zealanders 'over the years learnt', Wood said, 'to include an increasing element of Pacific-consciousness into their lives, and the strength of that element has been claimed as the best index to New Zealand's national maturity.'[75] Of the new diplomatic missions, the establishment of two—Washington and Canberra—was directly influenced by the imperatives of the Pacific War, as was the establishment in 1943 of the Department of External Affairs itself.[76]

For the scholars and diplomats of the 1940s, therefore, interest as well as dissent was a vehicle for the internationalising of New Zealand's independence. They had only good to say about the vigorous politicians, Grey,

72   A. D. McIntosh, 'Administration of an Independent Foreign Policy', in *NZER*, p. 33.
73   Wood, *Political and External Affairs*, p. 192.
74   Wood, *Political and External Affairs*, p. 206; see also McIntyre, 'Peter Fraser's Commonwealth', p. 41: 'Thus from 1943 onwards New Zealand took steps to assert itself as a nation. It began to shed the remaining trammels of "Dominion Status". Signing the Canberra Pact, attempting to revise the United Nations Charter in favour of small states, making its voice heard in the Far East Commission .... were all examples of the new assertiveness.'
75   Wood, *Political and External Affairs*, p. 191. Bernard K. Gordon, *New Zealand Becomes A Pacific Power*. Chicago, 1960, presents a similar perspective.
76   These had previously been the responsibility of the Prime Minister's Department and indeed the administration of the two departments was not separated until 1975. The existing External Affairs Department, which looked after the Western Samoa mandate, Cook Islands, Niue and Tokelau, was renamed the Department of Island Territories.

Vogel and Seddon, of the later nineteenth century, but were unanimous in seeing the early twentieth century, particularly the period since the First World War, as a period of 'decline' in independence. J. B. Condliffe talked of New Zealand's 'mother complex', which he described as 'more unreasoning and uncritical' than in any other Dominion and he cited well-known episodes such as Ward's offer of a battle cruiser to the British Navy in 1909, and Massey and Salmond's rejection of the post-First World War doctrine of 'equality of status'.[77] In Wood's *New Zealand in the World*, a chapter entitled 'Decline of Independence' looked particularly at the early twentieth century and at the urgings towards Empire unity of successive New Zealand premiers at a time when other Dominion leaders were seeking greater autonomy. The following chapter was called 'The Silken Bonds of Empire' and here Wood argued that the 'mother complex' developed strongly in New Zealand between 1919 and 1935, a 'thoughtful minority' of the population excepted.[78] In a later paper Beaglehole noted that 'In the period when the old fabric of the world began to break up, sentiment changed: New Zealand tended to ask Britain for advice rather than, like Seddon and Vogel, to proffer it.'[79]

For the scholars and diplomats of this generation there was something exhilarating about seeing New Zealand take charge—even if from necessity rather than choice—of its own external relations. Wood argued that Fraser's cable to Churchill on 15 June 1940, in response to the revoking of the Singapore commitment, had claims to be considered 'the most important single document in the formation of New Zealand foreign policy'.[80] It was in the Canberra Pact, J. C. Beaglehole thought, that New Zealand 'most clearly announced its independence of mind, its intention of pursuing a policy in the Pacific, intelligible in terms not of subordination to British hesitations and abstraction, but of the strategic needs, enlightened self-interest, and duty to Polynesian peoples of a quite independent power ....'[81] The diplomats and scholars welcomed the war because it provided a forcing house for their goal of seeing New Zealand exercise to the full the rights of Dominion status, with all that meant in terms of an ability and willingness to participate in the international as well as the Commonwealth community of nations.

The independence sought was one which drew New Zealand towards, rather than away from, the international community in general, but not, paradoxically, away from the Commonwealth and Britain—a crucial consideration. New Zealand was reaching out to the United States, but the United States was Britain's, and the Commonwealth's, most important ally in the war against Germany, Italy and Japan.

77 J. B. Condliffe, *New Zealand in the Making*. London, 1930, pp. 424–31.
78 Wood, *NZ in the World*, chs. 5, 6, esp. p. 106.
79 Beaglehole, 'NZ Nationality', p. 6.
80 Wood, *Political and External Affairs*, p. 194.
81 Beaglehole, 'NZ Nationality', p. 8.

The habitual insularity of New Zealand life before the war was, for the scholars and diplomats of the 1940s, limited and unappealing. But insofar as they grounded their argument for independence in changing interests they were on uncertain ground. They deplored the 'mother complex', but on occasion conceded that it was grounded in the same inclination to formulate policy in terms of interest that had produced the more vocal initiatives of the late nineteenth century. Beaglehole noted that while New Zealand leaders turned away 'with an appropriate shudder' from the Statute of Westminster, which formalised Dominion independence, 'the country had already negotiated a trade treaty direct with Japan, and ... was determined [to] have absolute control over its own immigration.'[82] Similarly, Wood observed that while to some Dominions 'security was not bound up with the British connection', to New Zealand 'security meant the British navy; and there was little reason why the navy should fight in the Pacific except to honour an imperial obligation.'[83]

Scholars did not quite know how to deal with what were in spirit plainly 'independent' actions—such as not wanting to fight in the Pacific—that were insular rather than internationalist in flavour but could not be explained simply by reference to 'mother complexes' or 'silken bonds'. In contrast, Trotter, a generation later, questioned the depth of 'Pacific mindedness' at the beginning of the 1950s as at the end of the war.[84] Independence of interest could translate into insularity as well as internationalism, into parsimony as well as participation.

---

[82] Beaglehole, 'NZ Nationality', p. 6.
[83] Wood, *NZ in the World*, p. 107.
[84] For 'Pacific-mindedness', see Trotter, p. 12, where she quotes Harry Batterbee, British High Commissioner, on the lack of interest in the Pacific in 1945, and pp. 181–2, where she quotes MacArthur to the same effect in 1951.

4. Independence and the postwar world order

The period 1944–46 is sometimes set alongside 1935–38 as a period of radicalism in New Zealand foreign policy. At the United Nations in particular, and also on colonial issues, New Zealand took stands, occasionally in conflict with British positions, which echoed pre-war initiatives. Close scrutiny reveals that, like the independence of the pre-war era, this independence did not present a radical challenge to New Zealand's place in the Commonwealth or the 'United Nations', as the alliance of wartime allies was known. Nor was New Zealand's stance in 1945–46 so different from its stance in the Cold War era that followed. Through both periods New Zealand foreign policy was aligned with that of Britain, which indeed now had a Labour government led by Clement Attlee, elected in July 1945 in the first British election in ten years. The difference lay in the orientation. Immediately after the war, dealing with the defeated enemy powers was a major preoccupation and therefore anti-Fascism was the focus—from 1947, relations with the Soviet Union were the major preoccupation and therefore anti-Communism came to the fore. But, as we have seen, Labour in power had a record of hostility to both Fascism and Communism.

Independence at war's end: the United Nations

The argument for Labour radicalism in 1945–46 revolves particularly around Fraser's activities in the United Nations. In the discussion and debate over the shape of the planned United Nations organisation, Peter Fraser played an active role. He wanted a strong United Nations, much as the Labour government had sought a strong League in 1936. When the draft for a postwar organisation, which had been drawn up by the great powers, was disseminated in August 1944, Fraser was critical because small states did not have enough influence. Berendsen told the British that the biggest failing of the draft was that the great powers had made 'no pledges, no guarantees and no undertakings'.[1] Fraser argued his positions with the British both at the

[1] McIntyre, 'Peter Fraser's Commonwealth', p. 49.

Australia-New Zealand conference in November 1944 and at a Commonwealth meeting in April 1945, and subsequently in the wider forum at San Francisco when the wartime United Nations alliance was finally transformed into a peacetime organisation. Fraser reiterated New Zealand's commitment to all members pledging themselves to cooperate in carrying out, by force if need be, any decisions taken by the competent bodies of the organisation for the preservation of peace. Additionally he stressed the need for the Assembly, on which all members were to be represented, to have final responsibility for all the organisation's activities.[2] His concern that the organisation take a strong stand against aggression led him to oppose the great power veto—this was consistent with pre-war Labour Party thinking about the League.

One writer has observed that 'the small group of officials which comprised the new foreign service had tasted the heady brew of independent foreign policy making, and under Peter Fraser's leadership engaged in it to considerable effect in the 1946 Peace Conference and from that "bully pulpit", the United Nations General Assembly, in its first sessions'.[3] Similarly, A. D. McIntosh wrote in the 1970s that

> during the later years of the Fraser administration the pivot around which New Zealand external policy turned was the United Nations Charter, with the General Assembly and the specialised agencies as the forum, and always with the continued advocacy of the principle of collective security—New Zealand had become an active member of the middle and smaller powers arraigned against the great, while staunchly advocating the United Nations as the best means of securing universal peace and justice and placing the fullest insistence on its organs for the solutions of international problems.[4]

But how radical was this stance? Britain had elected a Labour government at the end of the war—its first majority Labour government. Australia had had a Labour government since 1941. The New Zealand government therefore faced a more congenial situation than it had in the late 1930s. There were difficulties but they were incidental, not fundamental.

New Zealand's leaders *were* a little taken aback at the extent to which Ernest Bevin, the British Foreign Secretary, had taken up conservative Foreign Office positions on international issues. The most significant instance came at the Prime Ministers' meetings in April-May 1946. Nash, representing New Zealand, along with the Labour leaders Chifley and Evatt from Australia, was rather surprised at how far the official British line seemed to be dominated by anti-Russian sentiment and scepticism about the United Nations. Nash stressed that the Commonwealth countries had to 'work on the

2   Kay, *Agreement*, pp. 236-7.
3   Malcolm Templeton, *Top Hats Are Not Being Taken*. Wellington, 1989, p. 3.
4   McIntosh, 'Origins', p. 26. See also McIntyre, 'Labour Experience', p. 17: 'New Zealand's anti-imperialist, internationalist ideals surfaced again as post-war planning came under review'.

assumption that the United Nations has the fullest authority, and that everything must be done to secure this and make it effective'. The ideological currents were sharply expressed in a despatch from one junior officer at the 1946 meetings:

> [Bevin] hates Communism (because the Commies have double-crossed him and because they are his most bitter enemies at home in his own movement; Attlee hates them too because he loves individual liberty) and he's come to identify Communism with Russia; as Foreign Secretary of Britain he hates Russia because Russia is a power on the make, and she must make at the expense of [Britain], he doesn't get on with Molotov and he says he's not prepared to compromise with him any longer— though he probably would be if Molotov would be 'reasonable'. As a socialist and a man he doesn't like the United States, the home of big business ... but he has decided to play in with the States to stop Russia and to get the loan ....

And later on the same letter noted that 'Bevin doesn't like taking situations to UNO because Russia causes trouble in it, and because he is getting the Foreign Office way of looking at things. And it has been clear throughout the discussions that the top layer of the Foreign Office has the same contempt for UNO as it had for the League of Nations.'[5]

But whatever the Foreign Office may have thought, Britain was in the organisation. And so was New Zealand. Participation in the United Nations, although of course the international norm, did emphasise that New Zealand Labour's approach to foreign relations, while it might occasionally rub the British up the wrong way, was fundamentally in tune with theirs.

National Party and conservative press attitudes to the United Nations also help put Labour policy in perspective. National was somewhat suspicious of the United Nations as it had been of the League. In 1942 F. W. Doidge had warned of the risks to the Empire of collective defence (would the British Navy be handed over?) and of the cost to Britain of its adherence 'alone' to the post First World War Treaty of Versailles.[6] And conservative opinion in New Zealand was sceptical of Fraser's stand on the great-power veto in the Security Council. The *Otago Daily Times* thought that Fraser's vigour at San Francisco was a 'diversionary tactic to put New Zealand on the map ... and their ardent championing of lost causes at San Francisco is perhaps a cheap way of doing it.' It was also critical because of the implications for Anglo-New Zealand relations.[7] But this was tantamount to an endorsement, not a rejection, of participation in the United Nations. In its 1946 election mani-

---

5   Letter to McIntosh and Wilson, 27 May 1946. The officer is not identified but is almost certainly F. H. Corner. EA153/23/1, NA.
6   *NZPD*, 262, pp. 651–2 (9 June 1943).
7   See, for instance, *EP*, 28 April 1945; *NZH*, 26, 28 April, 7 June 1945; *ODT*, 21 April, 12, 19, 26 June 1945. For instance, in the 19 June editorial the *ODT* refers to the 'unprintable' attacks on Toryism by Evatt and Fraser at San Francisco: 'colonies' said the *ODT*, in apparent reference to New Zealand, 'do not cease to be colonies because they are independent'.

festo, the National Party did not have a foreign policy plank; its defence plank referred simply to the fact that 'New Zealand's future defence policy depends upon the nature of the arrangements made by the United Nations Organisation. These arrangements, and also the policy of the British Empire, are subject to negotiations already under discussion [*sic*] of which the National Party is unaware.' The manifesto also referred to the United Nations Organisation 'as the only means of ensuring world peace'.[8]

In fact by the middle of 1946, only a year from the organisation's inception, it was plain that the United Nations already faced serious difficulties in acting in such a fashion. The Soviet Union on the one hand and the United States and Great Britain on the other had opposing views on most aspects of the postwar settlement, be it over economic issues, or over the political character of the occupied countries, or over atomic energy. The Soviet Union frequently used the veto in the Security Council: the four other members—the United States, Britain, France and China—frequently took identical positions on issues.

Fraser's concern about the veto, which had had a more generalised significance in terms of small power–big power relations in 1945, was turned around to stress the destructive role of one big power, the Soviet Union, in the organisation. The United Nations could not be seen therefore as a forum in which Soviet and Western interests were of equal significance: it became one in which the West had the inside running, politically and morally, and the Soviet Union was on the outer. The New Zealand government had supported the alliance of the four major wartime allies—the United States, Britain, the Soviet Union and China—as essential to the postwar order. But Fraser was closer to the Americans and the British than the Russians. Near the time of the San Francisco conference, for instance, the government vigorously criticised Anglo-American acceptance of a new Soviet-Polish frontier, one generous to the former, and a new Polish government dominated by Soviet political allies.[9] In his report on the first session of the UN General Assembly, Fraser seemed to imply that the critical change had to come from that one unnamed power— the Soviet Union of course: 'I do not think that any nation can stand up against the overwhelming weight of public opinion all the time, and I look forward to the elimination of the veto, perhaps not within the next few years but ultimately . . . . and that, I believe, will be for the better, because it is very bad if one nation can hold up the advancement of mankind . . . .'[10]

Labour's dissent, its independence, was therefore of a very particular

8   Ms Papers 1624. 111/3, ATL.
9   Wood, *Political and External Affairs*, pp. 361–2; McIntyre, 'Peter Fraser's Commonwealth', pp. 49–50, 53–55.
10   *NZPD*, 273, pp. 535–42 (22 July 1946), reprinted in *New Zealand Foreign Policy: Statements and Documents*. Wellington, 1972, p. 108. Echoing in this respect Fraser's 1945 concern about Yugoslav activities around Trieste, see Roberto Rabel, 'Between War and Peace: The New Zealand Experience in Trieste, May-June 1945', paper presented to the New Zealand Historical Association Conference, Feb. 1987.

character, in both respects echoing the position it had staked out for itself in the late 1930s, in which independence within the Commonwealth and within the wider community of nations reinforced each other. In describing New Zealand's participation at the San Francisco conference, Wood referred to it as 'something like a climax in the development of her international status. She was fortified by prior consultation with sister British nations in London, and by their friendly presence in San Francisco. But "without impairment of the essential unity and solidarity of the British Commonwealth" she freely and candidly advocated her own individual policy ....' For Wood it was an emancipation from British tutelage but also the full realisation of the promise of British constitutional development, the fruitful relationship of 'small determined far-distant kindred communities' to powerful countries: 'behind [Fraser, Berendsen, Wilson and McIntosh] stood ... Seddon, Vogel and Grey; Hughes and Deakin and Parkes; Laurier and Macdonald; Smuts and Hertzog; and indeed Washington and Adams, Franklin and Burke'.[11]

Wood located Fraser and Nash within a Commonwealth tradition of independence; he could also have located them within a Labour tradition. Both bound them to England but in a fashion that allowed for independent action further afield: independence and loyalty, it seemed, could be combined. Another writer made the same point another way, noting in respect of Fraser's chairmanship of the Trusteeship Committee that Fraser had a 'complete ignorance of any language but his own, in a committee in which the Latin Americans took a great interest and seldom spoke in English and in which the French delegate always spoke in French'.[12]

It was also revealing that while New Zealand's constitutional independence could hardly be in question when the country had become a charter member of the United Nations, as of 1945 it was in fact still unresolved. During the war, Labour had thought about adopting the Statute of Westminster but had delayed in case the action was misconstrued by the Germans.[13] At the Prime Ministers' meetings in 1946, ideological uncertainties did not prevent Nash from seeking arrangements for the joint formulation of foreign and defence policy, not least because—in sharp contrast to the Canadian view—'almost any United Kingdom decision might affect the interests of the whole Commonwealth and might involve us in war.'[14]

The passage of the statute was finally accomplished in 1947, followed a year

[11] Wood, *Political and External Affairs*, p. 383. Hughes, Deakin and Parkes were architects of Australian Federation, Laurier and MacDonald of the united Dominion of Canada, Smuts and Hertzog of the Union of South Africa; Washington, Adams and Franklin were American leaders during the War of Independence and Burke the British thinker and defender of the Americans' right to secede.

[12] Eugene P. Chase, 'Peter Fraser at San Francisco', *Political Science* 11/1 (March 1959), p. 22.

[13] Wood, *Political and External Affairs*, p. 303, says that the Statute was not passed during the war 'for reasons never satisfactorily explained'.

[14] N2288/0063, NA.

later by a new nationality act. National was more cautious about adopting the statute than the government, convinced the action could be seen as weakening the Empire, a version of the concern that had delayed adoption in 1944.[15] The passing of the bills was partly achieved by parliamentary sleight of hand. Yet although Doidge spoke against them, while admitting the case on technical grounds, they were not opposed by National.[16]

Even with Labour, there was little sense of actively seeking these changes: they were rather precipitated by developments outside New Zealand—in the case of the nationality legislation, by the Canadians.[17] The independence which Labour advocated and practised was an independence moderated by a fundamental commitment to the Commonwealth, in which New Zealand participated, a commitment which put it in quite a different camp from isolationist Dominions like South Africa, Canada and Ireland, or fundamental ideological challenges like that from the Soviet Union. There was 'a tension between New Zealand the loyalist Dominion in a united Commonwealth and New Zealand the Labour-ruled small state determined to secure its own voice in a universal collective security system'[18] but it was one that remained under control, because of the congruence of the Commonwealth with the wider United Nations system.

The Commonwealth and decolonisation

Colonial issues had preoccupied the Commonwealth in the 1920s but in the 1930s Fascism had overshadowed colonial concerns—and made it seem that maybe colonial rule was not so bad after all. The defeat of Fascism, the advent of a Labour government in Britain, and Britain's alignment with two—albeit in very different ways—'anti-colonial' powers, the United States and the Soviet Union, all contributed to draw attention to colonial issues in the postwar world. In August 1941 Roosevelt and Churchill proclaimed an Atlantic Charter, which called, amongst other things, for self-determination for all nations. The discrediting or temporary usurpation of European colonial authority in both Asia and the Middle East, the mobilisation of colonial populations for war, and the development of revolutionary movements in some areas during the war, also played a part.

Accordingly, after the war, the Commonwealth faced a wave of decolonising pressure comparable with the assertiveness of the old Dominions after the First World War. It posed the old questions anew. Did secession threaten to blow apart the whole Commonwealth? Did Communism threaten the solidarity of the Commonwealth?

---

15 Shanahan to McIntosh, 3 Oct. 1946, PM 159/1/5, quoted in McIntyre, 'Peter Fraser's Commonwealth', p. 65.
16 McIntyre, 'Peter Fraser's Commonwealth', pp. 66–68.
17 McIntyre, 'Peter Fraser's Commonwealth', pp. 60–68 (Statute of Westminster), 68–71 (nationality).
18 McIntyre, 'Peter Fraser's Commonwealth', p. 47.

Where did the New Zealand government stand on such issues? In New Zealand and elsewhere labour movements had devoted attention to colonial issues in the 1920s, but rather less in the 1930s, as the international situation in Europe deteriorated. In wartime Fraser's government had unequivocally rejected the pursuit of nationalism at the expense of Commonwealth solidarity. The list of books banned in 1942 showed a sensitivity to colonial issues. Lenin's *Imperialism* was frequently seized by Customs until taken off the banned list in November 1942 but *Wartime Profits* by the British Labour Research Department, *The Empire and War* by the Communist Party of Great Britain, *India's Demand for Freedom* and *Why Must India Fight?* were still banned. Admittedly 1942 was an exceptional year: it saw the Quit India campaign and many Indian nationalists imprisoned by the British authorities.[19]

This was not a domestic issue. In the First World War, white New Zealand was reminded of its own colonialism. Waikato, Taranaki and Tuhoe Maori, who had suffered defeat and confiscation of lands one and two generations earlier, did not regard England's quarrels as their own. The introduction of conscription brought the issue to the surface: 'the attempted conscription of the most conspicuous of these disaffected tribes, which produced not one soldier at the front, obviously provides [an] example of the practical limitations of conscription'.[20] Maori were not conscripted in the Second World War. Good relations between Peter Fraser and the Waikato leader Te Puea ensured Waikato support for the war effort. Indeed the government-sponsored Maori War Effort Organisation became a model of Maori self-determination in cooperation with the Crown, one that has not been successfully emulated since.[21]

The major concern expressed in the 1946 New Zealand Institute of International Affairs publication, *Security in the Pacific*, was that nationalist and anti-imperialist movements might make Asia a centre of unrest and could embarrass New Zealand ('through its connection with one of the main imperialist powers') in the United Nations, if they opened up a division between the anti-colonialists and Britain or if they translated into conflicts on the ground. Though China was in the formal control of a Nationalist government and India became independent only in August 1947, New Zealand commentators believed they both had the potential to quarrel with Britain and the United States; but they did not believe that conflict would necessarily have an impact on New Zealand.[22]

[19] Taylor, *Home Front*, pp. 1005–8. Censorship was administered by a Controller of Censorship who answered to the Prime Minister. Books were handled in the first instance by a committee chaired by Nash.
[20] Baker, *King and Country Call*, p. 221.
[21] Michael King, *Te Puea*. Auckland, 1977, pp. 206–11; John McLeod, *Myth and Reality*. Auckland, 1986, pp. 24–25; Claudia Orange, 'An Exercise in Maori Autonomy: The Rise and Demise of the Maori War Effort Organisation', *NZJH*, 20/2 (April 1987), pp. 156–72.
[22] NZIIA, *Security in the Pacific*. Wellington, 1946, pp. 5–11.

In his first address to the House of Commons as Foreign Secretary, Ernest Bevin had spoken in terms of continuity with wartime policy, a stance that was taken to mean not just cooperation with the United States and the Soviet Union, which was axiomatic, but also the maintenance of British influence and interest in the broad arc of territory that stretched from western Europe, through the Mediterranean, the Middle East and Africa, to Asia and the Pacific. Everywhere in these regions there were Britons in place as colonial rulers, or as occupying or liberating armies, or as the dominant exporters, importers and investors.[23] British policy in these areas would be principled and enlightened, as one would expect of a Labour government—but it would be British policy, there would be no scuttle and British interests would be maintained by British power.

National politicians and conservative editorial writers like Leslie Munro, editor of the *New Zealand Herald*, who described the Indonesian nationalist Sukarno as a Quisling because he had cooperated with the Japanese, were relieved, at least for a while.[24] But the Attlee government's decision in 1946 to pull out from the Suez Canal base shocked Doidge and Holland and seemed to confirm that British Labour politicians were not as reliable as Conservatives: 'Our troubles', wrote Doidge, 'began—disarmament, appeasement and pacifism—when Ramsay Macdonald became Prime Minister. Now comes Attlee!'[25] Doidge deplored the plan to leave India and the withdrawal from Egypt and called for a policy of close cooperation among Empire countries to preserve the lifelines and territories of the Empire.[26]

Counterposing these opinions, the left was critical of British imperialism in the immediate postwar years. *Transport Worker*, the journal of a number of distribution unions, was critical of evidence of British support for colonial and Fascist regimes—Franco's Spain, Greece and the Dutch in Indonesia were favoured targets in 1945 and 1946. The watersiders were particularly active, as they had been against Japan in 1937: they banned Dutch vessels because of the situation in Indonesia through 1946 and 1947 and also considered a boycott of Spain—but the most effective action, blacking wool exports, was stymied by the fact that the wool belonged to the British government and the action would therefore force the New Zealand government to break a contract.[27] These positions were identical to those adopted on the left of the British Labour Party, a group frustrated by the new Labour government's evenhandedness between the Soviet Union and the United States and its maintenance of traditional British policies in the Middle East and Asia.

[23] Britain had the first postwar economic miracle, dramatically expanding manufacturing exports, for instance automobiles, over 1930s levels.
[24] *Weekly News*, 2 Oct. 1945. Quisling led the regime in wartime Norway that collaborated with the German occupation.
[25] Doidge to Holland, 13 May 1946. Ms Papers 1624. 55/3, ATL.
[26] 847H. 20/9-1346, RG59, USNA (Doidge in *NZPD*). Britain did not finally evacuate the Suez base until 1956.
[27] Moriarty, pp. 8-10.

What was the position of the New Zealand Labour government? Nash and Fraser had some reservations about the British government's outlook, even though it was a government formed by a fraternal Labour party. 'It is natural, therefore', wrote Nash at the time of the 1946 Prime Ministers' meetings, assessing the assumption that the United Kingdom had to take every practical step to secure the strategic position of the British Commonwealth,

> that Britain looks always at any development in international affairs to see what effect it will have upon the strategic position of the Commonwealth. Because they adopt this attitude there must certainly be times, and the question of disposal of the Italian colonies is a possible example of this, conclusions are reached which are not entirely based on the merits of the problem, but are taken in order to secure an immediate or long-range advantage.[28]

But Labour's approach did conceive of dependent territories becoming independent in cooperation with Britain, not in opposition to it. New Zealand grappled more directly with such issues in its own part of the world. Both the Australia-New Zealand Canberra conference, and the Wellington talks in late 1944, considered the future of the colonial territories of the South Pacific. Fraser and other like-minded individuals drew on their familiarity with British Labour Party and Fabian thinking about the colonial Empire. Articles 28–31 of the Canberra Agreement dealt with 'welfare and advancement of Native peoples in the Pacific' and argued that the doctrine of trusteeship was applicable not just to mandated territories but 'in broad principle to all colonial territories in the Pacific and elsewhere, and that the main purpose of the trust is the welfare of native peoples and their social economic and political development.'[29] The agreement proposed the establishment of a 'South Seas Regional Commission' but at the second meeting in November 1944 the two governments went further in advocating the establishment of an international body analogous to the Permanent Mandates Commmission, to which colonial powers should undertake to make reports on the administration of colonial territories.[30] This elicited a sharp rebuke from the British, not least because they had hoped to hold a Commonwealth line on the issue with the Americans and the two Dominions had made the announcement without 'any prior consultation'.[31] It might have looked as if Australia and New Zealand were lining up with the American anti-colonialists; but they were really taking sides in a British debate, with Labour and the Foreign Office on one side and

---

[28] N2288/0069, p. 10. Italy was to give up its pre-war African colonies — Eritrea, Libya and Somalia. Britain was interested in their fate. Note also one official comment at this time: the 'positive ideas of Bevin are taking second place. For one thing, most Foreign Office people have no feeling for them . . . . But Russia is the real stumbling block to his plans . . . .' 27 May 1946, p. 7. EA153/23/1, NA.

[29] Kay, *Agreement*, p. 144.

[30] Kay, *Agreement*, p. 237.

[31] Kay, *Agreement*, pp. 240–1.

Churchill and the Colonial Office on the other.[32] Peter Fraser, as has been noted, chaired the Trusteeship Committee at the United Nations San Francisco conference: its 'proceedings ... were indispensable in getting ... compromises accepted'.[33]

At the end of 1944 Fraser had visited Samoa, New Zealand's mandate under the League of Nations. The Samoans had heard of the Atlantic Charter: Tupua Tamasese Mea'ole, speaking on behalf of the Fautua, the three royal heads of lineage, told Fraser that self-government was 'the main point that you had in the charter in the conference that took place on the sea between the Prime Minister of England ... and the President of the United States .... that the big nations, as well as the small nations, would have the right to manage their own affairs. We have learnt about this and it has been confirmed by you, Sir, in the Parliament of New Zealand.'[34]

The visit had a big influence on Fraser and on New Zealand policy after the war. New Zealand placed Samoa under trusteeship and drew up a trusteeship agreement in consultation with the states directly concerned. It also determined to consult with the UN on its administration of the Cook Islands, Niue and Tokelau as non-self-governing territories, as defined in the UN Charter, and regularly transmit information about them to the Secretary-General, even though their formal status as New Zealand territory did not change.[35]

With respect to Samoa the changes were particularly dramatic. When the Samoan leaders were presented with the draft trusteeship agreement, they petitioned the United Nations for immediate self-government. Fraser wanted Samoans to control their own progress to self-government. This meant a 'radical departure' from British precedent. Samoa was to advance 'in one big step instead of several small steps from the non-representative stage of crown colony government to representative government'.[36] Differing Samoan and New Zealand conceptions of leadership and government were accommodated by the establishment of a Council of State of the New Zealand representative —to be known as the High Commissioner—and the three Fautua: 'It was to be consulted by the High Commissioner on all proposals for legislation which he intended to place before the legislature, [and] on "all matters closely

---

[32]   Mary Boyd, *Planning Decolonisation: New Zealand and the Practice of Trusteeship.* Wellington, 1987, p. 14.

[33]   Boyd, *Decolonisation*, pp. 16–17: the main differences were between Britain and the United States, not between the colonial and anti-colonial powers.

[34]   Witheford, 'Samoa, the War and Trusteeship', p. 40, WAII-21/22a, NA.

[35]   Boyd, *Decolonisation*, p. 17.

[36]   Boyd, *Decolonisation*, p. 18; J. W. Davidson, *Samoa mo Samoa.* Melbourne, 1967, pp. 163–87. Davidson writes as participant as well as historian and has a fine touch. See, for instance, his comments on the New Zealand public servants who ran Samoa before the changes: 'many had lived in Samoa for years without learning anything of importance about the country or the people ... and looking forward to the time when they would return to the New Zealand suburbs ... they looked on as home' (p. 168).

relating to Samoan custom" '.[37] The new policy was endorsed by the United Nations, New Zealand having deliberately followed a policy of enlisting the UN mission's help in persuading Samoans to accept the new direction.

The government's new Samoan policy was a sharp move forward, but it was suggestive of the general direction the government wished colonial policy to move in the Commonwealth as a whole. Not surprisingly the South Pacific Commission, foreshadowed in the Australia-New Zealand meetings in 1944, did not come up to expectation. The metropolitan powers, France, Britain and the United States, did not want a political organisation, nor one that directly involved the indigenous populations of the island countries. So the Commission, which came into existence in 1947, was not as extensive in its competence as the Australian and New Zealand governments had hoped for.[38] But New Zealand, like Australia, participated in it nonetheless; they did not challenge the metropolitan powers head on, or contemplate forming an alliance with the indigenous peoples.

A different dilemma was played out on the other side of the world. Palestine, a British League of Nations mandate, now a United Nations trusteeship, where Jews and Arabs had contended for power for a generation, had a peculiarly intractable politics and the 'Palestine question' reverberated in complex ways in New Zealand, as in British, foreign policy. Fraser was an enthusiastic supporter of the Jewish cause, the nationalist movement less favoured by the British. British motives were strategic—they wanted to retain influence in the Arab world, and that meant keeping the Arabs on side over Palestine; moreover, they were suspicious of some of the Jewish nationalist international connections, particularly with the Soviet Union. Did this make Fraser anti-British? Not necessarily. For one thing, the Jewish nationalists in Palestine had strong connections with the international labour movement as a whole. Many in the British Labour Party were unhappy with Foreign Secretary Ernest Bevin's handling of the Palestine issue. So was Fraser. At the same time, the issue was a running sore in Anglo-American relations—the United States actively sponsored the Jewish cause, called for increased Jewish immigration to Palestine while the British were in control, and immediately recognised Israel's declaration of independence, on 15 May 1948.

National was not as enamoured as Labour of the Jewish cause, not least because that position could put New Zealand at variance with Britain. The United Nations proposal to partition Palestine had provided for international

---

[37] Davidson, pp. 181–5, quote from p. 185. Davidson's account captures the personalities involved — Voelckler, the disillusioned administrator, Davidson himself, the imaginative and perceptive young scholar, Cruz-Coke, the most forceful member of the UN mission, a member of the Chilean Senate and a professor in the Santiago Medical School, and Tupua Tamasese, the most able of the three Fautūa. And in Wellington, Fraser and Nash, both committed to change.
[38] T. R. Smith, *South Pacific Commission*. Wellington, 1972, pp. 29–48. Equally, some of the tension between Australia and Britain over the issue was rooted in Colonial Office suspicion of settler (a.k.a. Australian and New Zealand) interests in the Pacific Islands.

enforcement of the partition, but could Britain and the United States, and New Zealand with them, afford to stand by and see Soviet troops in Palestine, even if under UN auspices? Comment in the New Zealand press suggested that the general public were largely in sympathy with Britain and its decision to leave; some editorial comment agreed with partition, although in the case of the *Press*, this was because it saw it as a check on the Jews. Letters to the editor tended to be highly critical of Jewish terrorist activities, especially those against British soldiers: the hanging of two British sergeants by the Jews in August 1947 was often referred to.

When the issue came before the General Assembly in November 1947, New Zealand voted, along with Canada, Australia and South Africa, for partition, but Britain abstained. To the British, trying to maintain influence with Arab governments and aware that the Soviet Union also welcomed Israel's independence and was probably feeding agents and sympathisers into the country, the outcome of the vote was a bitter blow. After independence the British told the Dominion governments that 'recognition of the Jewish state at this stage would in our view amount to a declaration of hostility to the Arab world. The effect could impair our relations with the Arab world for many years to come.'[39] Fraser was forced to accede to Cabinet pressure not to recognise ahead of the British: it was a rare occasion when Cabinet overruled him on a foreign policy matter. Holland commented with regret about Anglo-American antagonism.[40]

Tension continued through the remainder of 1948. The conservative press remained unsympathetic to Israel—but also to the Arab governments: an *Evening Post* editorial was critical of the United Nations failure to stop fighting between Arab governments and Israel, but believed that 'no great amount of sympathy' needed to be wasted on the Egyptians.[41] In January 1949 Britain came close to war: when Israel had ignored a call for a truce, Britain sent troops to Aqaba in Jordan, the Egyptians called on the British to honour the 1936 Anglo-Egyptian treaty, and the Israelis shot down five British planes. But at home, disquiet was building over British policy. Britain recognised Israel in that same month, after the government had faced a major rebellion in the House of Commons over the issue (its majority dropped from 160 to 90 on one vote), and New Zealand acted simultaneously. Some of the tension in the region abated.[42] Fraser's position was that of many in the British Labour

---

39   Quoted in M. Noelle Galvin, 'New Zealand and the U.N. Partition of Palestine, 1947–49'. Univ. of Canterbury, M. A. thesis, 1982, pp. 85–86.
40   847H. 00/6-1648, RG59, USNA. In November 1948 the British told Dominion leaders that 'the tone of the Jewish Press is becoming increasingly bellicose. If the Jews defeat the Legion with the aid of the aircraft and the arms they have bought from Czechoslovakia and elsewhere, the result might well be the extinction of our influence in the Middle East'. PM 277/5/2, quoted in Galvin, p. 99.
41   J. Mellor, 'New Zealand and the Formation of Israel 1947–49'. VUW History Dept. research paper, 1976, p. 21.
42   Galvin, pp. 99–103.

Party. He did not want to see the Soviet Union in the Middle East, nor for that matter the United States, other than as a backup for Britain. He believed that British policy could expect to keep both Israel and the Arabs as friends.

On the central issue for the Empire/Commonwealth, the future of India, the Labour government in Britain was committed to independence. Fraser indeed found himself in agreement with the British and out of sympathy with the Indians over the latter's wish to have the status of a republic within the Commonwealth, an arrangement never before considered, or thought practicable. India's objective was challenged by Fraser on the grounds both of its implications for the Commonwealth as a whole, and for New Zealand's relations to the Crown in particular: 'if we watered down the Commonwealth relationship so completely it would become as nebulous as an Atlantic Pact and our people would feel there was nothing in it.'[43]

In September 1948 Ireland had decided to end the role of the Crown in its affairs and it was not invited to the 1948 Commonwealth conference in consequence. Ireland was a sensitive issue with loyalists and Holland, pleading a prior engagement, avoided meeting De Valera when he came to New Zealand in May.[44] Did this mean that if India became a republic, it too would be unwelcome in the Commonwealth?

Even a left-wing Labour M.P. like Martyn Finlay saw disadvantages as well as advantages in the the Commonwealth decision to accept India as a 'special case', a republic within the Commonwealth. While Burma and Ireland might be drawn back into the Commonwealth, and the Benelux and Scandinavian countries brought into it, South Africa and Canada might move in the other direction.[45] Fraser himself was emotional about the Crown but he was also a realist who believed that republican status threatened the political unity of the Commonwealth—'If Nehru were to state that he would be in the Commonwealth in peace and war, the position would be vastly different.'[46] But this of course was just what Nehru would not do. Fraser was right, as the course of Indian foreign policy demonstrated, but so also were the British, who were determined to keep India in whatever the cost. The choice was not between Fraser's version of the Commonwealth and Nehru's but between Nehru's and an India outside the association altogether.

Labour, the left and the Cold War in the 1940s

We saw in Chapter 2 that anti-Communism was as important a part of the framework of Labour's foreign policy in the 1930s as support for the League of Nations, collective security or opposition to Fascism. What happened after

---

43 McIntyre, 'Peter Fraser's Commonwealth', pp. 80–81.
44 Holland to K. O'Shea, Irish National Council, 24 May 1948. Ms Papers 1624. 55/6, ATL.
45 *NZPD*, 285, pp. 326–7 (12 July 1949).
46 McIntyre, 'Peter Fraser's Commonwealth, p. 81.

1941, when Hitler invaded Russia and the Communists and the Labour movement, as well as the Commonwealth and the Soviet Union, became allies?

Even in these years Labour took great care to exclude the Communists from influence and rejected suggestions for common action. A joint declaration of the national executives of the FOL and the Labour Party in October 1941 stressed that approval of Russia's 'fighting valour' did not extend to local Communists and concluded that no useful purpose could be served by collaboration or association in any way with the Communist Party or its subsidiary organisations.[47] When the Westfield freezing workers struck in January 1942, the Minister of Labour, Paddy Webb, could extol Russia's war effort and fight against Hitler—but in contrast 'the half-baked Communists who were denouncing the government were just "wreckers and ratbags" who would not last twenty-four hours in Russia and whose real work for the Labour movement could be written on a tram ticket.'[48] For its part, however, the Communist Party advocated a united labour movement and worked for a Labour victory in the 1943 election.[49]

Even if Labour set itself so firmly against domestic Communists, it could not help but be influenced by the progressive atmosphere in international relations engendered by the alliance with the Soviet Union. Labour exchanged ministerial representatives with the Soviet Union in 1944, a move that the Opposition would probably not have initiated, although all the other British Dominions had done so, and which it criticised particularly on the grounds of expense.[50] Labour was also influenced by the general conviction that the populations of most countries had been radicalised by the war and that there would be a reluctance to see a return to the kind of policies that had produced depression in the 1930s. It was as if the rest of the world was catching up with New Zealand.

In the first eighteen months after the war, therefore, as during 1941–45, Labour's stance on Communism did not have foreign policy implications. Even Holland, the Leader of the Opposition, was prepared on occasion to say nice things about Russia: 'I don't believe there will be any peace in the world unless we can find a means of running along harmoniously with [Russia]. Some of the things Russia has been doing are difficult to understand but we in this country have a responsibility, as we have in every other part of the British Empire, of understanding the point of view of the other fellow. There can be no peace in the world if we are going to be at loggerheads with a great power such as Russia.'[51]

---

47   Taylor, *Home Front*, pp. 587–9.
48   Taylor, *Home Front*, p. 579.
49   Taylor, *Home Front*, p. 589.
50   Taylor, *Home Front*, p. 619.
51   On his return to New Zealand from an overseas trip in the middle of 1945. *EP*, 15 June 1945, EA 59/2/23, NA.

Only from 1947 did circumstances change and the issues and tensions of the 1930s, and in particular of the early war years 1939–41, return. Between 1947 and 1949 the breakdown of the hopes for a unified international order, the One World dream of individuals like Henry Wallace and Ernest Bevin and of public opinion in Europe, Russia and North America, forced the left to choose between the Soviet Union and international Communism and a labour movement aligned with the new centre of international capitalism, the United States, against a portion of the organised working class.[52] Anti-Fascism no longer provided a solvent of differences: anti-Communism made for different emphases.

This was as true in New Zealand as elsewhere. The issue reverberated through institutions both at home and overseas—the public service, the Public Service Association, the FOL, the Labour Party, the Society for Closer Relations with the USSR. Overseas it affected the World Federation of Trade Unions, the International Student Association, and a host of other bodies, all set up on a universalist basis at the end of the war and all now racked by bitter ideological division. And the pre-eminent victim of course was the United Nations itself, whose very name, once invoking the most powerful alliance the world had even seen, became a by-word for impotence.

National made political play of the claim that the Labour government was 'soft' on Communism. A memorandum to Holland from the National Party organisation in the aftermath of the 1947 Westland by-election pointed out that 'it is simply beating the air to denounce the Communists alone .... But, when these two groups (Communists and Socialists) were linked together, ... it is beyond question that our vote increased because of this.'[53] Webb wrote to Holland in May 1948 that in a series of addresses in the Waikato 'at each place I spoke on Foreign Affairs and linked the European set up with the spread of communism ... I am satisfied it is a good line for you to take.'[54] In 1948 National published the pamphlet, 'Tarred with the Same Brush', which explicitly linked Communism to the Labour government and party, to the detriment of the latter. National spokespeople made hay with statements drawn from Labour's past, in particular some of those of the two most vigorously anti-Communist members of the government, Semple and Fraser.[55] Martin Nestor, Holland's main speechwriter, stressed the need for

---

[52] Henry Wallace was Roosevelt's Vice-President, 1940–44, but was dropped in favour of Truman as a running mate for Roosevelt's third term. He was the leading figure on the left of the Democratic Party, resigning from Truman's Cabinet in September 1946 over the administration's increasingly hard-line policy towards the Soviet Union, and making an unsuccessful bid for the Presidency in 1948.

[53] Memo to Holland, 16 Dec. 1947. Ms Papers 1624. 50/4, ATL.

[54] Webb to Holland, 14 May 1948. Ms Papers 1624. 55/6, ATL.

[55] For instance: 'Any political party not based on perpetual enmity of the working class to the exploiting class was harmful and misleading .... the workers had to capture the State. The Labour Party was based on the class struggle'; quoted in David Bolitho, 'The Development of Anti-Communism in New Zealand Politics', VUW History Dept research paper, 1976, p. 8.

National to establish links between the Labour Party and the Communists.[56] One of Holland's correspondents, eager to see National win the 1949 election, wrote to him that

> the Slave Camps, the Canadian Espionage Scandal, the Iron Curtain, the bloodthirsty methods and irreligious and oppressive methods of Communist Russia could with advantage and safety be vigorously condemned with sufficient emphasis on past utterances of N. Z. Labour when Russia was so extolled—to stress the link between our extravagant socialism and the detestable Communism of Russia. The adroit manoeuvre of the Labour Party in attacking Communism in advance to defend themselves against this very attack would have to be exposed.[57]

Ronald Algie wrote to Holland at the beginning of 1949 that he had not found 'that there is much spontaneous interest in country districts on the subject of Communism: but when you talk about it you soon find out that the real menace is understood . . . we should . . . set to work to draw up our plans for dealing quickly and firmly with any outbreak of industrial trouble that may occur on our accession to power and we should also be ready to tackle any trouble that looks as if it was due to communistic influence'.[58]

But the Labour Party was not soft on Communism—and it never had been. After the war, as before and during, Labour had not relented in its determination to forbid any association with the Communist Party in New Zealand, even while friendship with the Soviet Union was still official policy. Communists' attempts to seek affiliation with the Labour Party were rejected. Undaunted, up until the 1946 election Communists persisted in support for the Labour Party.[59] But after the 1946 election, relations between the leadership of the Labour Party and the FOL on the one hand and the Communists and the left of the Labour Party on the other became much more contentious, a struggle over economic policy and foreign policy, a struggle for power. There were a number of leading figures in both the government and the FOL who were implacably opposed to Communists and to Communist influence in the labour movement: Fraser, the Minister of Works, Bob Semple, and Angus McLagan, the Minister of Labour and a former President of the FOL. In the Federation, F. P. Walsh, the single most influential labour leader, the architect on the labour side of the management of the economic stabilisation regulations during the war, and Ken Baxter, the Secretary of the

---

56   Nestor to Holland, 6 May 1949. Ms Papers 1624. 50, ATL.
57   W. R. Lascelles (Chch) to Holland, 28 Jan. 1949. It is not clear whether any specific attention was paid to this letter—Holland called it up on 11 June 1949, to check on a proposal Lascelles had made about compulsory military training. Ms Papers 1624. 113/1, ATL.
58   Algie to Holland, notes to letter of 30 Jan. 1949. In a subsequent letter Algie noted in passing that he was learning Maori. Ms Papers 1624. 24/2, ATL.
59   One candidate referred to it as being vital that the voice of the Labour Party be heard both in respect of social legislation and 'to introduce the voice of progress and reasons into our foreign policy'. 847H.00/8–846, RG59, USNA.

Federation, were also opposed to the Communists.[60] These men were neither temperamentally nor politically likely to accommodate the Communist-supported demands of varying unions. At the FOL conference in May 1947, Walsh and a number of his allies—though not Baxter—lost their places on the FOL executive to more left-wing individuals: they were determined to reverse those results in 1948. At the same time a number of steps which the government took or fostered showed its determination to limit and if possible extinguish Communist influence in New Zealand, in the New Zealand labour movement and in the island territories.[61]

The move from cooperation—albeit qualified—to conflict was rooted mostly in domestic circumstances. Inflation, even if suppressed by controls, was bothersome for many workers and bred discontent with the government. And a contest for power was always incipient in Communist-Labour relations—cooperation was the exception not the norm. The Labour leadership cannot have been unaware both that sympathy for the Communists was to be found within the Labour movement and that the Communist Party could enhance its position in the event of a favourable conjunction of circumstances. Armisted Lee of the American Legation noted early in 1948 that in all of the issues in which Communists had recently been involved—the overtime ban on the Auckland waterfront, the carpenters' go-slow and the strike at Mangakino against the transfer of the local union secretary—'[they] were able to appeal to a wide and sympathetic audience because of the legitimate grievances (from a strictly unionist point of view) of the particular workers concerned'.[62]

The issue of Communists in government was raised by Holland and Doidge as it had been by Menzies in Australia.[63] Their case was strengthened when the British government announced it would no longer employ anyone known to be a member of the Communist Party in work 'vital to the security of the state'.[64] Holland kept notes on a number of people linked to the left, for instance Jack Lewin, and there was discussion among the party leadership about whether the government should legislate against Communism. Algie, a former professor of constitutional law, was cautious about trying, for instance, to purge the civil service under the present regime. He also believed that 'our feeling that some independent workers are actually linked up with

---

60   Both were also ex-Communists.
61   For the Fraser/Walsh attack on the Cook Islands Producers Association, an organisation led by Albert Henry seeking better conditions for Cook Islands workers and producers, with links with Auckland trade unions, see Dick Scott, *Years of the Pooh-bah: A Cook Islands History*. Auckland, 1991, pp. 231–66.
62   847H.00B/3-3148, encl. RG59, USNA.
63   For Doidge, see *Bay of Plenty Times*, 4 March 1948. Ms Papers 1624. 55/6, ATL. Doidge argued that Parliament should be called into session to deal with the Communist threat. In a letter to Holland on 4 March he said that Fraser had 'thrown down the gauntlet' in a statement made after Doidge's address.
64   Editorial comment in *EP*, 16 March 1948. Ms Papers, 1624. 50/4, ATL.

Russian policy makers rests very largely on emotion and more upon guesswork than upon cogent evidence.' However, even he agreed that it was time to change the law, and that, although it might be difficult in peacetime, 'there must be a limit.'[65] Fraser suggested that the government would not allow Communists to occupy positions of trust and confidence in the public service. He did not indicate any retreat from his previously stated position of rejecting special legislation or a thoroughgoing purge of the public service, but approved of the British government's more limited steps.[66] National established a special committee to look into the question of the Opposition introducing a bill if the existing law were found to be deficient.[67]

At the 1948 Labour Party conference both Fraser and Semple devoted major portions of their addresses to denouncing Communism. As Fraser was reported saying, 'Labour's humanitarian policy of social reconstruction under Parliamentary democracy is the very antithesis of the Communist policy of revolution based on hatred, inhumanity and intolerance . . .'. In the past year the efforts of the Communists to disrupt the Labour Party had become more evident.[68] And Fraser went on to draw parallels between the activities of New Zealand Communists and Communists in Eastern Europe. The conference passed a resolution granting the party's national executive and its district committees the power to expel any member publicly critical of party policy. The emphasis of the conference was on controlling the economy rather than socialising it to any greater extent: there was considerable concern about inflation but it was channelled into resolutions seeking stricter price controls and endorsement of the Economic Stabilisation Act, which gave legislative force to the regulatory policy that the government had initiated during the war.[69] The political complexion of the FOL executive changed after the 1948 conference. The right wing sought successfully to amend the FOL constitution to provide for representation on the National Council by industry rather than by regions: according to the waterfront unionist, Toby Hill, they had taken up this cause after losing control of the National Council at the 1947 conference. Walsh recovered the office of Vice-President he had lost in 1947, while a number of Communist or left-wing members of the 1947–48 executive lost their positions. The full conference of the Federation reversed a number of the decisions taken by the outgoing executive, including its recommendation for the repeal of the economic stabilisation regulations.[70]

The FOL followed British leads. The British Trades Union Congress recommended that the World Federation of Trade Unions (WFTU), which

65   Algie to Holland, n. d. but probably March 1948. Ms Papers 1624, 50/4, ATL.
66   847H.00/5–1748, RG59, USNA.
67   Ms Papers 1624.50/4, ATL.
68   847H.00/5–1748, RG59, USNA.
69   847H.00/5–1848, RG59, USNA.
70   847H.5043/4–2748; 847H.00/ 5–1748, RG59, USNA.

had strong international Communist representation, be 'recessed' but in the upshot the British, along with the Dutch and the Americans, pulled out of the organisation at the Brussels conference in December 1948; the FOL followed suit at its 1949 conference. Another 'victim' of the Cold War in 1949 was the Society for Closer Relations with the USSR, which was identified by Semple in 'Why I Fight Communism' as having become a Communist-front organisation. After Labour's 1949 conference two of its M.P.s resigned from the society, membership having been declared incompatible with membership of the party.[71]

Anti-Communism shaped defence and foreign policy. Although Nash and Fraser had jibbed at some of Britain's expectations in the sphere of Commonwealth defence in 1946, they did not hesitate to proffer their support in the more tense international climate of 1948-49. The fact that a Labour government was in office in Britain limited the likelihood of the kind of tensions that had occurred between the New Zealand and British governments in 1936-37.

When in 1948 Britain and five other European powers signed the Brussels Pact, a forerunner to NATO, Holland stated that 'it would be a grand gesture to the mother-country and to the Western nations if we applied for what I might call, for want of a better term, associate membership of the Western nations ... There is no reference to a link-up with the Western nations or to any inter-Empire scheme of defence.'[72] If this was a jibe at the government, it had little substance. In May 1948, when Fraser left to attend the 1948 Prime Ministers' Conference, the Opposition emphasised the importance of bipartisanship in foreign policy—war was in the air in Europe, with a coup in Prague and tension in Germany, culminating in June in a Soviet blockade of the Western zones of Berlin. The Brussels Pact had emphasised the defence element in Western European solidarity. American bombers returned to England; New Zealand lent three RNZAF Dakota crews for the Berlin airlift. If Britain were defeated in war, Fraser said, it would only be question of time 'before New Zealand fell too'.[73] This was exactly like the thinking of the Second World War.

At further Commonwealth meetings later in 1948 and in 1949 defence was discussed but this time the focus was more on the Middle East than Europe. The Soviet Union was held capable of mounting a powerful offensive which might, unhindered, reach the Suez Canal in four months. New Zealand agreed to deploy forces in the region in the event of war comparable with those it had provided in the Second World War—an infantry division augmented with

---

[71] 644. 61/11-250, RG59, USNA.
[72] *NZPD*, 280, p. 327 (6 July 1948), quoted in Keith Sewell, 'N.Z. Perceptions of European Affairs, 1945-49: An Examination of Parliamentary Opinion'. VUW History Dept research paper, 1976, p. 25.
[73] Quoted in McIntyre, 'Peter Fraser's Commonwealth', p. 79.

additional formations plus contributions from the Air Force and Navy.[74] New Zealand also supported Britain in its efforts to retain control over former Italian territories in Africa, a course later criticised by a foreign service officer as being quite contrary to New Zealand's approach to foreign policy at that time.[75] New Zealand defence commitments to Fiji were revived and it made a contribution to British efforts in both Hong Kong and Malaya.[76] At the same time interest in Europe did not abate and the North Atlantic Treaty was warmly welcomed with the sole reservation concerning the relationship of Australia, New Zealand and their commitments to it—maybe a Pacific Pact could be established as well, it was suggested.[77]

For the Labour Party there was only one major stumbling block to domestic support for the Cold War. Political, diplomatic support was not contentious; conscription, to support mobilisation, would be. It was the same issue as in 1938-40. Conscription, like economic issues, touched people's lives directly and was not just a matter of votes in the United Nations or speaking up at a Commonwealth conference. Anti-militarism, like anti-capitalism, could thrive alongside anti-Communism. Conscription had too many overtones of standing armies, troops used against the interests of the working class in general and strikers in particular, to be widely accepted within the Labour movement. Fraser believed that it was crucial that New Zealand be able to prepare an expeditionary force more speedily than in 1939-40 but to some this seemed barely necessary when the Commonwealth was not at war—the fact that Australia had not introduced conscription nor was contemplating doing so reinforced the point.[78] The opposition to conscription had 'far deeper roots [than Communist agitation]', wrote an observer at the American Legation: 'it has been reliably reported that the only member of the present National Council of the Federation (of Labour) who would favour conscription is F. P. Walsh and he would have difficulty carrying his own Seamen's Union with him on this issue'.[79]

Fraser could not get his party conference to support compulsory military training outright; he had to resort to a referendum on 3 August, even though originally both Cabinet and caucus had rejected the idea.[80] National, after some hesitation in case it was walking into a government trap, supported the referendum, which was held in August. At the Dominion Council of the party Holland was recorded as saying that the 'government's decision to hold a

---

[74] Ian McGibbon, 'Defence 1945-1957' in *NZWA 1945-57*, pp. 154-5.
[75] Hugh Templeton, 'New Zealand and Africa', *EAR*, January 1967, p. 5.
[76] McGibbon, 'Defence 1945-1957', p. 157.
[77] *NZPD*, 285, p. 185 (6 July 1949).
[78] It was also true that in Australia the anti-conscription movement was far stronger.
[79] 847H.20/11-1748, RG59, USNA.
[80] 847H.00/7-2849, memo of conversation, Martyn Finlay, M.P., Wm Wilson (editor, *Standard*) and Robt Parker, VUW Professor of Political Science, with Armisted Lee, US Legation, is informative about Fraser's success in securing caucus support for a referendum.

referendum ... had caused a great deal of thought. ... it was decided that the [National Party] Organisation should throw its full weight in support of the proposal'.[81] Only publicity in favour of conscription could be broadcast, but there was a large vote against it and an even larger number of abstentions, which probably came from disillusioned Labour voters, who were, however, unwilling to oppose a measure sponsored by a Labour government.[82]

New Zealand, Britain and the United States in the 1940s[83]

We noted in Chapter 1 that while independence in New Zealand was not defined in nationalist terms, 'British' nationalism—loyalism—was an element in New Zealand thinking about international relations. That nationalism was mostly the province of the right. The right did not have a monopoly on loyalty and patriotism but it was better at them and particularly good at challenging the left's loyalist credentials. Liberals and the left fought back. They were hostile to flag-waving patriotism, to 'John Bullism', and to the use of either as a subsitute for intelligent thinking on foreign relations. But they were 'loyal', they claimed, to many aspects of British life, to British democratic traditions, rule of law, respect for individuals and minorities.

It was not an easy argument to win, and often they did not try. But in the 1940s a more congenial situation arose. In 1924, when a Labour government ruled at Westminster, Massey found loyalism provided little guidance for his conduct of New Zealand's external relations. So in the late 1940s, the Labour government in London tilted the loyalist balance some way towards the left. Doidge argued on one occasion to Holland that 'whilst realising that foreign policy must of necessity be determined in Whitehall, post war conditions require that Dominion Parliaments should be in agreement before imperial Parliament takes decisions affecting Empire defence.'[84] One of Holland's aides suggested that there be bipartisan representation at what he still called 'Imperial' conferences: 'I do not think the Empire creates the right impression with Americans when at the Conference three members of the Empire are Socialist—UK, Australia and New Zealand. Will an Imperial Conference consisting of three Socialist Governments, one capitalist (Canada) and one with a difficult racial problem (South Africa) reach decisions which are for the best for all the peoples in the UK and the Dominions? I think not.'[85] This was Massey's suspicion of socialists taking over the Empire, a quarter century on.

---

81 Minutes of Dominion Council, 18–19 Aug. 1949. Ms Papers 1624. 113/1, ATL.
82 533,000 in favour, 152, 000 against, a 60 per cent turn out (compared with 556,000 votes for National, 506,000 for Labour and a 94 per cent turn out at the 1949 election). Sinclair, *Nash*, p. 274; Stephen Levine, *The New Zealand Political System*. Sydney, 1979, p. 194.
83 Mike Ashby, 'Under Southern Skies: Sources of New Zealand Foreign Policy, 1943–1957'. VUW, Ph. D. thesis, 1989, was helpful in developing my thoughts for this discussion and the parallel one in Chapter 6.
84 Doidge to Holland, 13 May 1946. Ms Papers 1624.55/3, ATL.
85 Memo, 19 May 1948. Ms Papers 1624.55/6, ATL.

This tilt was encouraged by the growing significance of the United States in the affairs of the British Commonwealth. If conservatives felt close to the United States, the leading capitalist power, did this make them disloyal to Britain? In the event, the British and the Americans reinvigorated their wartime alliance, but there was always some potential for the issue to revive. Who was loyal? Who was not? Nationalism, it seemed, could be voiced by the left as well as the right.

The possibility of ideological conflict between the United States and Great Britain was canvassed in the immediate aftermath of the war. Truman appeared to many to represent a move to the right in American politics, while the election of the Labour government in England was as plainly a move in the opposite direction. One foreign service officer thought that if 'in 15 years there were war between U.S. and Russia ... it would only be [too] easy to see where New Zealand would then stand if we could envisage a Nationalist Government with the ideas that party had between 1920 and 1930—a postulate which the progress of events and ideas in New Zealand has probably ruled out.'[86]

The officer went on to argue that such a contest could conceivably see Britain and New Zealand on opposite sides, if Britain had become more socialist in the intervening period, as seemed likely. A commoner view was that Empire sentiment would encourage the alignment of New Zealand with Britain. In *Security in the Pacific* one group of opinion concluded that 'the country most likely to threaten New Zealand interests, directly or indirectly, is America .... There is an unawareness of the contradictions that are sharpening within American economic life and of the fact that the means that may be adopted to allay them, such as export of capital, may appear threatening to other peoples.'[87]

But this did not transpire. The United States and Britain became, and remained, allies. America's (eventual—Congress took six months to make up its mind) decision in July 1946 to lend $3.75 billion to Britain allayed many apprehensions in New Zealand and Britain. The Marshall Plan, announced in June 1947 and seen in New Zealand as the American parallel to New Zealand's own 'Aid to Britain' campaign, was welcomed by the right:

> ... woolly thinking socialists and communists, control-minded bureaucrats and intellectuals chatter about 'planning' and hold up Russia as a model of the art. America is criticised as a land of 'anarchic free enterprise'. This Marshall Plan is the most beneficent plan the world has yet seen .... American planning may not look as tidy as the theoretically minded people may like—it produces far more of the goods

86 Letter to McIntosh and Wilson, 27 May 1946, EA153/23/1, NA.
87 *Security in the Pacific*, p. 7. Theorists of imperialism at the turn of the century such as Hobson and Lenin had argued that, unable to make substantial profits in their home markets, predatory capitalists would compete in the colonial world, fostering thereby inter-imperial conflict and ultimately war.

and services of life and it does not take away people's freedom and self-respect in doing so. There is a wholesomeness and vigour and breadth of vision, decency and generosity in the Americans' actions that is in marked contrast to the petty, destructive, and nasty vapourings of the communists, intellectuals, Moohans and McLagans of the rest of the world.[88]

But some in the Labour government also welcomed the Plan. The very word 'plan' was helpful, with its overtones of the progressive strand in American history, Roosevelt's New Deal, economic rather than military solutions: the Plan was much preferred to the Truman Doctrine announced in March 1947, with its contention, voiced publicly for the first time by the President, that a state of virtual war obtained between the United States and its allies and international Communism. The Marshall Plan seemed to emphasise America's generous and forward-looking side, to be an echo of Roosevelt, not of Harding or Coolidge, those parsimonious 1920s Presidents seemingly more conscious of the size of Britain's debt to the United States than of its sacrifices in the First World War and the responsibilities for world peace it had shouldered since.

There was caution further to the left about the price that the United States appeared to be demanding. It was after the Marshall Plan was announced, and the Soviet Union had withdrawn from discussions on aid to Europe, that the Communists and the left concentrated their fire on the United States and characterised Britain as a country being unwillingly subordinated to America's quest for global domination. Marshall Plan aid was a 'good investment by the United States to protect the status quo against socialism'. Aid to Britain itself, said Toby Hill, was another government instrument to pressure and intimidate the militants in the union movement. The Communists went so far as to defend imperial preference against 'Wall Street lackeys' at the Geneva and Havana trade conferences, and argued that through the Marshall Plan the Americans would force a devaluation of sterling and the dismantling of the sterling area.[89]

Others of less radical temper did not necessarily disagree. Late in 1947, a time when the phrase 'Cold War' first came into general use, McIntosh questioned Berendsen's conclusion that it was 'quite unrealistic to base any policy upon, or to expect (in any circumstances other than complete submission to Soviet views) any agreement with Soviet Russia'. In a reply he drafted for Fraser, but which was never sent to Berendsen, he wrote, 'I cannot bring myself to conclude that the die is now cast; that the world has divided into two opposing camps and, for better or for worse, we must accept the leadership of America ....' And after discussion with Fraser, McIntosh drafted a paragraph in which he stated that 'the outlook and policy of the

---

88 MDW to Holland, 22 Dec. 1947, Ms Papers 1624.55/4, ATL.
89 847H.00B/3–3148 encl., RG59, USNA. See also below, p. 94.

present American Government and that of any possible alternative Government are very different from those of the Roosevelt regime and, moreover, they would appear to be completely opposed to the way of life of the United Kingdom and New Zealand'.[90]

But if Britain and the United States were in harmony, New Zealand would not stand aside. Although the same draft cable referred to the importance of New Zealand in the United Nations 'judging each case on its merits and not identifying itself necessarily with the American viewpoint', this would have been a lonely and thankless task indeed without the United Kingdom. In the second half of 1947 the British Labour government still had a residue of belief in the possibility of Britain's forging a middle way between America and Russia. But by the end of the year this had vanished: the Cold War alignment with the United States had hardened in Britain. It affected attitudes to the United Nations too, bringing to the surface assumptions implicit in the attack on the veto in 1945: 'by 1948 and especially after the Berlin blockade it became clear that great power unanimity in a world security organisation was a mirage and that the attitude of the New Zealand government would have to be modified.'[91]

Thereafter it was the left, not the Labour Party leadership nor the Department of External Affairs, that hoped for a middle way and saw British alignment with the United States as testimony to the power of American imperialism and a subversion of Britain's independence. Many on the left in New Zealand, as a way of adding greater force to their position, made a point of distinguishing between Russian Communism and British socialism: 'The British tradition of socialism comes from Robert Owen, William Morris, and others who inspired the Socialist movement in the British countries. Our British socialism is different from the Russian approach and we have no desire to go the Russian way.'[92]

Warren Freer, a young politician who had entered Parliament after a by-election at the end of 1947, caused an uproar by saying in March 1948 that the 'powers that be' in America wanted war. Other politicians, often from middle-class intellectual rather than trade-union backgrounds, such as Ormond Wilson and Martyn Finlay, had similar views. Later in 1948 the Fabian Society, a left-wing discussion group, an offshoot of the well-known British society, published a pamphlet, 'Martial Plan?', which concluded that Western Europe had to decide against both Russia and America and that any organisation set up in the continent had to be independent of both. George Fraser, the author of this pamphlet, was later transferred from his job in the Prime Minister's Department.[93] The annual conference of the FOL in April

90   McIntosh papers, MERT.
91   McIntosh, 'Origins of the Department', p. 27.
92   Ormond Wilson, *NZPD*, 280, p. 532, (13 July 1948), quoted in Sewell, p. 34.
93   744.00/3-750, RG59, USNA.

1948 urged 'the British Government to continue to base its domestic and foreign policy on the interests and aspirations of the mass of the people and consider that no effort should be spared to develop closer relations with those countries who are desirous of laying the basis of international peace and good will'. The American Legation noted that the significance of this 'wholly innocuous statement' could only be appreciated if it was recognised as the emasculated vestige of a strongly worded remit submitted by the Carpenters' Union, bitterly denouncing Bevin's foreign policy for alleged subservience to the United States and demanding an entente between Britain and the USSR.[94]

The government, said one trades council resolution in 1949, should 'resist any further alignment with the Western power politics group. Further we call on the government to press for a neutral bloc of British Commonwealth countries, and failing that, we call on the workers for united action to eliminate the possibility of another war.'[95]

Fraser paid no attention. In the election in November 1949, which ended Labour's term of office, foreign policy was not an issue. Labour was still in power in Britain. Both Labour and National in New Zealand stood for alignment with Britain on the great issues of the day.

There was more to link the 'independent' years of 1945–46 to the Cold War years of 1947–49 than there was to divide them. The differences had more to do with the international environment than with fundamental change in New Zealand foreign relations. It was inevitable that there should be greater scope for initiatives in the more benign postwar years than in the harsher Cold War environment. It was fairly likely that in the event of a deterioration in Anglo-Soviet relations, a Labour government in New Zealand would side with a Labour government in Britain. New Zealand's Cold War alignment was in the first instance an alignment with Britain, secondarily one with the United States.

94   847H.5043/11–1548;11–1748, RG59, USNA.
95   847H.20/11–1748, RG59, USNA.

5. New Zealand in the Commonwealth economy, 1935–65

Discussions about foreign policy frequently leave economic relations to one side. This is particularly true of much of the writing on Labour foreign policy. It may be an accurate reflection of the interests of the writers but it is not an accurate reflection of the world in which Labour governments operated.[1] Economic issues were more central than war and peace issues to the survival of governments in New Zealand and neither the first Labour government nor its successors could afford to ignore the external aspects of such issues even if they had wanted to. On the whole they did not. Through the 1930s, 1940s and 1950s there was vigorous debate about New Zealand's external economic relations. This debate provides us with a story which complements our discussion of independence in foreign policy generally.

The Depression had radicalised thinking about economic relations, both domestic and international.[2] In New Zealand this took the form of a greater readiness to contemplate industrialisation and protectionism as solutions to the country's unemployment problem. The Labour Party for its part also looked to balanced trade agreements and state trading to ensure the full employment of New Zealand's resources, particularly its human ones.

It was natural at a time of intense economic dislocation and uncertainty that ideas about limiting the connections between the New Zealand and the

---

[1]   It is not so much that writers leave out what should be covered, as that scholarly attention has focused on the political rather than the economic aspects of Labour's time in office. The two major biographies, Gustafson, *Cradle to Grave* and Sinclair, *Nash*, do address external economic issues, especially the latter. It is not possible to comment on the relative weightings in respect of National governments because no monographs have been written: Gustafson's biography of Muldoon, when published, will make a big difference.

[2]   And set the tone for a generation, until the 1960s: 'Since the onset of economic depression at the end of the 1920s, there had been in the Western world a progressively greater acceptance of the aims of the welfare state. Governments had intervened much more extensively in economic affairs when the ideal of a largely self-regulating economic system no longer seemed adequate. Scarcity and maldistribution of the material means of life led governments to act to ensure justice and more even distribution.' Smith, *South Pacific Commission*, p. 11. The crisis in the welfare state in the 1970s had the opposite effect.

international economies should gain some acceptance—such ideas were indeed common currency through most parts of the world. And in the economic as well as the political sphere such thinking could acquire separatist as well as radical overtones. Notions of breaking the hold of the bankers on the economy and of providing credit to those who needed it were widespread in the 1930s. There were echoes here of the debt bondage of the 1880s,[3] of the populist financial movements of agricultural regions like the Canadian Prairies and the American Midwest and of the repudiation of debts by revolutionary regimes, most recently and dramatically the Communist regime in Russia. Closer to home, there was the dramatic career of the New South Wales Premier, Jack Lang, whose government proposed suspending overseas debt servicing in 1931.

Would Labour act in such ways in office? In the economic sphere we find a rough equivalence to the idea of Dominion status, of independence in foreign policy. Labour accepted the framework of the Commonwealth as appropriate for economic relations but did seek to place those relations on a more equitable and balanced basis: this was very like the idea of loyal dissent. The exchange crisis in 1939 was, as we shall explain, a moment of truth.

Labour also pursued another form of independence—the vigorous pursuit of interest, which had characterised all colonial and Dominion governments in their commercial and financial dealings with the City of London and the British government. This is not to imply that New Zealand was not a dependent economy of course, because it was, but only to stress that the pursuit of interest was little hampered by filial sentiment. The pursuit of interest could have led New Zealand into a protectionist policy, as had already happened in Australia and Canada. But even though the need for some industrial development became widely accepted in the 1930s, protectionism as such gained less of a hold, in part because the Labour government itself had some hesitation about it.

If in these respects we can identify parallels between external economic relations and foreign policy, there are also points of difference to be addressed. One is that the international dimension was much less significant, or significant in quite different ways, than in the political sphere. New Zealand's economic eggs were so completely in the British basket that economic arrangements beyond the Commonwealth framework were a shadowy matter. In the 1940s the United States became of crucial economic importance to Britain and indirectly therefore to New Zealand. But because its significance was indirect, suspicion and caution were as evident as enthusiasm in New Zealand's position on Commonwealth-United States economic issues. Internationalism was therefore a weak reed in the economic

[3] 'Is the colony to govern itself, or to be at the mercy of a number of financial rings in London?', Premier John Ballance quoted in *NZH*, 19 Nov. 1891.

sphere. And this was true, to varying degrees, of other Commonwealth countries too. Accordingly, economic relations between the Commonwealth and the United States were more contentious than political ones.

In the 1950s the difficulties between England and America abated. International capitalism, which had to varying degrees been in crisis since 1914, recovered, with its focus now in New York, not London. The American economy was central, the British economy was a part of its system, as were Japan and Western Europe: the Commonwealth economic system was internationalised. Further, the prosperity and Keynesian welfare policies that characterised the recovery also helped mute the class conflict and ideological debate that had been characteristic of the 1920s, 1930s and 1940s. So it was that by the beginning of the 1960s 'economic independence' had acquired rather different emphases, and operated within different structures, from those of the 1930s.

Before the war: Labour and the City

How radical was Labour in external economic relations? It wanted to see economic relations internationally put on a more equitable and secure footing. Nash's proposal in 1936–37 for a balancing agreement between Britain and New Zealand was characteristic, a way by which the uncertainty could be taken out of international trade. Industrial development policies represented in part a commitment to a more stable economy and stable incomes for those in it; the same could be said of government purchases of butter, cheese and other dairy produce from the farmer, in exchange for a guaranteed income.[4] As far as business was concerned the government was 'interfering with private enterprise at a number of points'—the establishment of a Bureau of Industry, the Industrial Efficiency Act, the public works scheme.[5] In March 1938 the government presented the convention of the International Labour Organisation to Parliament for ratification; it had never been ratified before, and plainly many Opposition members were still reluctant.[6]

The government resisted pressure from some in the caucus and in the Labour movement generally to take more radical steps, such as exchange control, nationalisation of industry and revision of New Zealand's debt obligations. But the balance of payments crisis of 1938–39 forced the government's hand: it imposed import and exchange controls rather than taking the deflationary measures that had been the standard way of dealing with an import surplus before Labour took office.[7] But although import and

---

4   There are numerous studies of the Labour government's economic changes, including W. B. Sutch, *Recent Economic Changes in New Zealand*. Auckland, 1936. Sinclair, *Nash*, pp. 133–52, discusses Nash's London negotiations in 1936–37. See further below, p. 96.
5   Annual report of the Bank of New South Wales, *AIBR*, 21 Dec. 1937, p. 1071.
6   *NZPD*, 250, pp. 18 ff. (2 March 1938). See also Wood, *NZ in the World*, pp. 119-20.
7   The Coalition government had devalued the New Zealand pound in January 1933—the move was opposed by Labour on the grounds that it raised the cost of living. But it did not reverse it when elected.

exchange controls were emergency measures they did reflect an ideological predisposition and were certainly judged that way both by financial interests in London and conservative interests in New Zealand: one annual report for 1939 referred to the 'stigma of exchange control'.[8]

Having had an election success in 1938 outstripping its first in 1935, the government had a rugged few months as it grappled with implementing import control in the face of business opposition. In April Nash announced the import quota for the second half of the year—a dramatic reduction over the first half year's quota and an even greater shock therefore to business. But even this was not sufficient remedy for the financial situation: loans were falling due and it became plain that Nash would have to go to London to negotiate new terms.

In March 1939 Sir Harry Batterbee, the first British High Commissioner accredited to the New Zealand government, arrived in Wellington. Conservatives were resigned to this new evidence of loosening Empire ties;[9] it was all the more ironic that an event which was supposed to symbolise a new equality between Britain and New Zealand in fact took on neo-colonial qualities. Was Batterbee coming to tell the New Zealanders how to run their affairs? After all, Newfoundland had been 'put into commission' because of the extent of financial mismanagement there earlier in the decade. Batterbee himself referred on one occasion to the fact that 'flippant citizens delighted in repeating the rumour that his appointment had a more sinister significance'.[10] An acquaintance of Nash wrote to him en route to London about a 'piece of town gossip—to wit, that Sir Harry Batterbee had despatched an emissary to London to forestall you in London. If it's true, I don't suppose it will alarm you in the least for I take it all he can do is reiterate the viewpoint of the U.K. Manufacturers' Association.'[11]

The Opposition was in full cry after the government. This was not a national crisis—it was one which divided the country on ideological lines. The Opposition throughout took the line that it was the government's folly that had precipitated it and that it was quite natural that British financial interests and Whitehall should be rigorous in their demands and conditions. Adam Hamilton even attacked Nash for talking of turning to foreign countries for assistance: 'Perhaps Mr Nash finds it a bitter pill to swallow today to admit that his policy has crumbled of its own unbalance, but it would show gross miscalculation of the sentiments of the people if [he] endeavours to bluster his way through the difficulties with threats to British interests that he might turn to foreign interests for support.'[12]

8   Annual report of the Bank of New South Wales, *AIBR*, 21 Jan. 1939, p. 971.
9   See, for instance, 'The British High Commissioner', *Dominion*, 14 March 1939.
10   Quoted in *Round Table*, 115 (June 1939), p. 662.
11   John Malton Murray to Nash, 15 May 1939, N349/0229, NA.
12   *Auckland Star*, 29 April 1939.

The trading banks in New Zealand contributed their two cents worth: Nash arrived in London at the beginning of June to learn that they were refusing to provide funds to buy imports licensed for the second half year and would continue to do so until adequate funds were secured in London. The matter was sorted out but it was another pressure.[13] The Bureau of Importers in Auckland also made life complicated for Nash.[14]

Nash also found hostility in London, although British opinion was far from unified in its attitude. British exporters opposed New Zealand's import controls, indeed any protectionism, and were backed up in this by the Board of Trade. But Nash faced more serious problems in dealing with the Bank of England and the Treasury. They wanted to impose austerity on New Zealand, to teach the profligate, and as they saw it, rather self-righteous Labour politicians a lesson. They recognised that there had been over-importing but *their* target was inflationary government spending and the socialist principles they saw underlying it—the over-zealous concern for the wage-worker, the big public programmes, the use of Reserve Bank credit and other such aspects of Labour policy.

The partisan character of the crisis was given added credence by reports in *Reynolds News*, a pro-Labour paper, first, that New Zealand was the object of a whispering campaign that had swollen into 'open hostility' directed primarily at the import controls and later, that New Zealand was being blackmailed by the London financiers. Another pro-Labour paper, the *Daily Herald*, said New Zealand should be given a guaranteed loan.[15] And the official record of Nash's talks makes it clear that suspicion and criticism of the Labour government was endemic in financial and government circles in London. It must have been difficult for Savage to tell the public that Nash had assured him that the *Reynolds News* statements were incorrect and that no conditions were being laid down by either government or City,[16] when Nash had written a week earlier that Montagu Norman, the Governor of the Bank of England, 'required an offer of proportion of funds from export sales after September 30th to be allocated for redemption of debt. I would not agree but promised to work out in detail what funds would be required for imports to maintain our production also other charges and amounts that would be available for redemption.'[17]

In New Zealand attitudes to the crisis remained entirely partisan, with Opposition and press comment continuing to find fault with the government rather than the British: the *Evening Post* criticised the British critics of the

---

13   N349/0015, NA.
14   *Dominion*, 2 Sept. 1939. Nash alluded to this once he was back home.
15   N86/0001, N86/0001, NA; *EP*, 19 June 1939.
16   *EP*, 21 June 1939.
17   Nash to Savage, 9 June 1939, N342/0001, NA.

British government and argued that conditions in the City of London were generally unfavourable to long-term borrowing.[18]

But in London itself the mood changed. The lesson had been taught. Moreover, war was approaching and there was no point in hampering New Zealand's preparations. Chamberlain directed that New Zealand be given export credit guarantees to allow it to make defence-related purchases.[19] At the end of June non-Labour press opinion in London weighed in on New Zealand's side. The *Times* editorial on 29 June stressed New Zealand's defence significance and argued that 'misgivings over internal policy or financial management would be even more out of place in discussing the terms of a defence loan in New Zealand' than they would in respect of the Eastern Europeans. In its issue of 24 June the *Economist* contested the Federation of British Industries' notion of a trade boycott of New Zealand until the government changed its import regime, pointing out that New Zealand's import regulations had been drafted in such a way that the British proportion of New Zealand's imports could not decline and could possibly increase. In a letter to *The Times*, published on 7 July, J. M. Keynes, the Liberal economist, linked Britain's need to build up reserves of vital imports to a solution to New Zealand's difficulties: Britain should tell Nash that it would purchase whatever quantity of goods New Zealand could ship—an accurate foreshadowing of what would transpire once war broke out. And the *Financial Times* argued that although New Zealand had imposed exchange control, it was 'eminently reassuring' that bondholders could demand payment in cash.[20]

Nash was almost out of the woods. He signed an agreement with the Board of Trade in effect reiterating the Ottawa commitment to preserve reasonable opportunities for British exporters under the import licensing regime—it was a humiliating document and also in some ways a ridiculous one, given the preference New Zealand was giving to Britain compared to other overseas suppliers.[21]

The difficulties over trade could have occurred, and been resolved, with a conservative but protectionist government in Wellington. The financial settlement smacked more of an ideological judgment of Labour's monetary and social policies, although the tight loan market was a factor in the tough time Nash had too.[22] The Bank of England forwent the idea of tagging export

[18] *NZPD*, 254, p. 139 (5 July 1939); *EP*, 10 July 1939.
[19] Sinclair, *Nash*, p. 179.
[20] All on N86, NA, except *Financial Times*, reprinted in *EP*, 24 June 1939.
[21] Sinclair, *Nash*, pp. 180-1, 183-4. Commonwealth countries signed a series of mutual economic agreements at the conclusion of a Commonwealth economic conference in Ottawa in 1932. The most important agreements were those between Britain and the various Dominions, which all, to varying degrees, offered British manufactured exports some advantages in their markets in exchange for advantages for their farm exports in the 'Home', that is, British, market.
[22] Sinclair, *Nash*, p. 187.

receipts to cover the repayments, but the New Zealand government did have to issue an Order in Council promising repayment. New Zealand would be lent £16 million to cover the loan falling due in January 1940 but the sum was to be repaid in five annual instalments with no assurance that more generous terms could be arranged later.[23] Norman was in fact instrumental in ensuring that the loan was taken up: over three-quarters of it was left with the banks.[24] But Savage, a sick man, was angry at the settlement and at the budget measures which the New Zealand government had to take—increases in income tax and on petrol and beer—to help ensure that the loan could be repaid as agreed: £1 million of the principal of the loan on the due date, another £2 million in 1940, and £3.5 million in the four successive years.[25] It was the coldest winter spell in memory with snow on the hills around Wellington and also much further north: the financial and meteorological climates seemed in sympathy. 'A grim budget', the *New Zealand Herald* called it; 'Big increases in direct taxation' headlined the *Evening Post*.

Two days after the budget the news of the outcome of Nash's financial negotiations in London reached New Zealand. The *Round Table* correspondent, reporting on the events of the winter, observed that there was a 'widespread ... belief that the government may have reached a point where the road forks', the choice being one between financial orthodoxy and social policy.[26] But many in the Labour Party were profoundly unhappy. Left-wing Labour M.P.s, including Nordmeyer, Anderton, Macmillan, Boswell and John A. Lee, criticised British financial pressure on New Zealand and implicitly therefore Nash for negotiating the agreement and Savage for assenting to it. Nordmeyer said that if British financiers attempted to embarrass the government, New Zealand would be quite justified in mobilising overseas funds in the same way as Great Britain had done during the Great War, any attempt by London to dictate terms should be resisted and the reply should be given that 'we are capable of minding our own affairs'.[27] More dramatic interventions were to follow, however. Rejecting the charge that he was calling for debt repudiation, Lee nonetheless invoked it in all but name: 'the bondholder must have his "pound of flesh"', say our opponents, even if the nation rots ... the Labour Government can carry this country against "Shylock" any time it says it is prepared to trust the people first and "Shylock" second.' But, Lee continued, 'one of these days some political Vulcan will arise who will set fire to these paper chains and liberate New Zealand'.[28]

23 Sinclair, *Nash*, pp. 180-2, 185-6.
24 Sinclair, *Nash*, p. 186.
25 *EP*, 28 July 1939.
26 *Round Table*, 116 (Sept. 1939), p. 875.
27 Reported in *EP*, 27 July 1939.
28 *NZPD*, 255, pp. 131, 132, 137 (9 Aug. 1939).

Armstrong, the Minister of Housing, had ventured the defence that New Zealand had to accept 'the terms dictated by the financiers of Britain, who are the people who rule and will rule Britain till Britain has a Government strong enough to take charge of the finances of the country'.[29] But after Lee's attack, Fraser, the Acting Prime Minister, with Savage in hospital, responded swiftly: the Dominion would honour its obligations, repudiation was a 'wholly reprehensible and dishonest course of action', even the conception, let alone the contemplation of repudiation would be disastrous and ruinous to New Zealand.[30] The Opposition for its part had a field day, Endean claiming that Lee wanted to emulate Russia and Grigg attacking Labour M.P.s for their anti-British statements on both foreign policy and finance.[31] Further politicking on the issue within the Labour Party was expected when Nash returned at the beginning of September[32] but the outbreak of war put an end to it and to much other ideological manoeuvring.

In the exchange crisis of 1939 are the shadowy images of the fears and hopes with which capitalists and socialists invested Labour governments during the 1930s. It was the closest that New Zealand ever came to a rupture with international capital. And it was not very close. Savage, Fraser and Nash were firmly in control of the government and they were not economic radicals. They had no doubt that they were in office to reform capitalism, not to overthrow it. The City and the Bank of England and the Treasury could have been accused of ineptitude not malice if they had turned these political leaders into revolutionaries.

Sterling and the dollar in the 1940s

During and after the war the notion of economic independence for New Zealand was overshadowed by concern about the future direction of Anglo-American economic relations. American proposals for a new international economic order were greeted with a great deal of suspicion by conservatives because aspects of them seemed to portend an American takeover of the British Empire. Doidge warned of American designs on the British Empire in March 1942.[33] Anti-Americanism was a staple of conservative thinking, in New Zealand as in the United Kingdom. Hardly a systematic ideology, it nonetheless had some identifiable patterns. To British conservatives the United States alternated between being an ally and stout supporter of British interests and Britain itself, and being a predatory rival power whose industrialists wanted to steal British markets, buy up British industry,

29 *EP*, 9 Aug. 1939.
30 *NZPD*, 255, pp. 194–7 (11 Aug. 1939).
31 *NZPD*, 255, p. 165 (10 Aug. 1939); *EP*, 17 Aug. 1939. The foreign policy reference is to the Tientsin crisis, see above, p. 28.
32 *Round Table*, 117 (Dec. 1939), p. 227.
33 Taylor, *Home Front*, p. 636.

demolish British financial power and let Britain exhaust itself in a war for the common good while the United States stood ready to inherit what was left and to displace Britain at the centre of world politics. It was an ideological position, but one rooted in national rather than class orientation. The memory of the 'downside' of Anglo-American peacetime economic relations was fresh—the great corporate battles in the 1920s, the scheming and manoeuvering in South America, the Middle East and Asia.[34] It had echoes in attitudes to other countries as well, in particular France: the devaluation of sterling in 1931 was widely believed to have resulted partly from France's hoarding of gold. But in wartime it became particularly significant because the United States became so important to the British Commonwealth. Lend-Lease, primarily regarded as evidence of American generosity and commitment to the war effort, might have some liabilities. In debate about Lend-Lease in Parliament in 1944 both Doidge and Holyoake thought it possible that the United States might take a hard line on debt after the war, as it had with Britain after the First World War.[35]

At the same time it has to be stressed that those who were suspicious of American designs on the Empire were also enthusiasts for Empire-United States collaboration on acceptable terms: 'Will New Zealand', asked Doidge on one occasion, 'fit in under a system of Anglo-American partnership, where there will be control of the world's raw materials, where there will be an English-speaking bloc that will be the mightiest, the wealthiest, and the most irresistible combination of powers that the world has ever seen?'[36]

While conservatives worried about the impact of American economic power on the British Empire, Labour worried about its impact on the economic experiment in New Zealand. Many in the Labour movement were suspicious of Wall Street finance, and that suspicion had been well entrenched during the 1930s when there had been so much preoccupation with monetary issues. Labour's major concern in international economic relations was not so much the maintenance of British predominance as such, as the maintenance of a British commitment to a broadly collectivist solution to the management of the international economy—one that would take account particularly of the objectives of full employment, control over movements of capital and commodity price stabilisation—in other words, the agenda of pre-war Labour. The war saw a marked shift in British political thinking in a collectivist direction—would it survive the end of the war or fall victim to recession as similar attitudes had after the end of the First World War?

[34] See, for instance, J. A. Whelpley, *British-American Relations*. London, 1923; E. H. Davenport and S. R. Cooke, *Oil Trusts and US-UK Relations*. London, 1923; Parker Thomas Moon, *Imperialism and World Politics*. New York, 1926; Ludwell Denny, *American Conquers Britain: A Reward of Economic War*. London, 1930.
[35] *NZPD*, 266, pp. 786, 794 (10 Oct. 1944).
[36] *NZPD*, 360, p. 336 (27 Aug. 1941). Note that this was just after the Roosevelt-Churchill Agreement on the Atlantic Charter.

Suspicion of money power came from the Social Credit movement too. On 30 January 1942, under a headline 'Prepare for an American invasion', its newspaper, *Social Credit News*, stated that within three months American troops would be in New Zealand and behind them would be Wall Street, and the looming Frankenstein of financial interests. If the whole situation had been planned to eliminate hostility to the absorption of the British Commonwealth by American financial interests, it could not have been bettered.[37] Later in the year the activities of *Social Credit News*, later *Democracy*, and its editor John Hogan, generated a major censorship case. In replying to parliamentary criticism of the government's decision to suppress *Democracy*, Fraser replied that there was a need for the utmost goodwill to be engendered towards the 'gallant visitors', that is, the American forces in New Zealand. When 'a newspaper started to scare people by saying this was an attempt on the part of Wall Street to financially capture the country, drastic action had to be taken'.[38]

But what about after the war? The phraseology of Article 7 of the Mutual Aid (Lend-Lease) Act, passed by Congress in March 1942, was disturbing. The undertakings in Article 7 were inserted as a device to reassure the American Congress that the Administration was requiring some benefit from Lend-Lease beyond the defence of the United States: it stated that the terms and conditions of Lend-Lease

shall include provision for agreed action by the United States of America and the United Kingdom, open to participation by all countries of like mind, directed to the expansion, by appropriate international and domestic measures of production, employment and the exchange and consumption of goods . . . . to the elimination of all forms of discriminatory treatment in international commerce, and to the reduction of tariff and other tariff barriers.[39]

Would the British succumb to American pressure? Would they put pressure on the New Zealand government themselves, as they had in 1939? And not just in trade either. The Americans were contemplating a conservative international monetary regime with strict rules for managing balance of payments deficits and domestic economic policies which were anathema to Labour. British official opinion, however, hardened against American-style multilateralism in 1944 and New Zealand officials and politicians slept a little easier. At the end of the Bretton Woods conference in June 1944, at which agreement was reached on setting up an international monetary fund and bank for reconstruction and development, A. G. B. Fisher, one of New Zealand's delegates, reported that 'nothing in the

[37] *NZPD*, 261, pp. 397–8 (24 June 1942), quoted by Taylor, *Home Front*, p. 930.
[38] Taylor, *Home Front*, pp. 930–2.
[39] Richard N. Gardner, *Sterling Dollar Diplomacy in Current Perspective*. New York, 1980, pp. 58–59.

Agreement obliges any country to determine its currency or credit policy on account of any deficiency in gold supply'.[40]

Nash and Fraser accordingly recommended in principle that New Zealand join the two institutions, but in the postwar era they were to find their caucus still hostile. But even Fraser was firm with the Americans. He told the State Department, on his way home from the Commonwealth Prime Ministers' meeting in May 1944, that the doctrines of Adam Smith could no longer be accepted in their entirety even as an ideal. New Zealand had to develop greater diversity of production, and this involved industrialisation and therefore government regulation of imports.[41] It was not a Marxist comment but it did indicate an ideological gulf not only between New Zealand and the State Department and other agencies of the American government, but also between Government and Opposition in New Zealand: as in 1939, National did not endorse protectionism, certainly not against Britain. Labour ideology was also reflected in New Zealand's support at San Francisco for the elevation of the Economic and Social Council to be one of the principal organs of the United Nations. A New Zealand amendment to include the promotion of 'full employment' among the aims of the Council was passed and survived a subsequent American attempt to amend it.[42]

There were new anxieties about Lend-Lease, which had become a bilateral American-New Zealand arrangement after Pearl Harbor. The chief of the United States Lend-Lease mission in New Zealand wrote in January 1944 that

> the contribution of Lend-Lease to New Zealand is, in my opinion, producing more ill-will than goodwill at the present time. This is based upon hundreds of conferences in every community in New Zealand. The basis for the feeling comes down primarily to two things. In the first place, New Zealand does not consider Lend-Lease to be a gift, and is worried about the vague overhanging obligation that is mounting up to such large figures. No one can assure them as to the nature of the final adjustment, because the Act and the agreements do not contemplate anything definite until the war is over. The second difficulty lies in the fact that Lend-Lease accounting puts down figures for the obligation of New Zealand on the basis of current war-time prices. New Zealand considers her reverse Lend-Leases contribution as an offset to this obligation, and therefore feels extremely worried by the fact that the credit received for reverse Lend-Lease is in pre-war terms.[43]

The government stayed silent on the issue, possibly because it did not want to embarrass the Americans. In the event the continued accrual of credits on

---

40   Fisher notes on Bretton Woods, 14 Aug. 1944, p. 7, T52/880/2, NA.
41   Memo of conversation, 6 July 1944, 847H.50/7-644, RG59, USNA. It was a comment which owed more to List than to Marx: Friedrich List was a nineteenth-century German political economist who argued that countries would only be able to industrialise if their manufacturers enjoyed a protected home market. This thinking was very influential in the dominant Republican Party in the post Civil War United States, and also in the new German Empire established in 1871.
42   Wood, *Political and External Affairs*, pp. 354–5.
43   Blackwell Smith to John E. Orchard, 11 Jan. 1944, Box 2679, RG169, NRC.

the reverse Lend-Lease 'account' made it feasible at war's end for New Zealand to suggest that the final balance be 'washed out'.[44]

Even with a Lend-Lease settlement in the wind, conservatives were anxious about the United States. Not all the postwar portents looked good. Lend-Lease was ended abruptly on VJ Day and the British then had the humiliating experience of negotiating a loan with their erstwhile allies. The negotiations took three months—in Washington of course. While Britain then went ahead and joined the International Monetary Fund and the World Bank, as the United States wished, the United States Congress took weeks, then months, to decide on the loan. Churchill, now Leader of the Opposition, attacked the terms and in New Zealand Holland wrote to Clifton Webb that he was concerned

> over the prospect of control over international finance falling into American hands who will have more voting power than Britain and Russia together ... The experience of the Wall Street crazy boom and crash, the failure of so many private banks when Roosevelt took office, suggest that America doesn't know enough about the question to be invested with such terrific powers. London has for many years been the financial centre of the world. All she has done to lose her pride of place is to become poor.

Clifton Webb was sceptical: 'I hope we shall be able to convince you and Caucus that Bretton Woods should be supported ... Bill (Polson) feels we cannot afford to trust the Yanks. And Ron (Algie) and I feel that we can't afford not to ...'[45]

Most senior civil servants agreed. The British loan was approved by Congress in July 1946 and thereafter some of the tension eased. The more serious concern was the prospect of 'socialisation', a loose term National politicians, the press, business and farming interests used to describe Labour's import and price controls, nationalisations and management of trade, such as the export trade with Great Britain. Would the Labour government in Britain give further impetus to such policies? One paper, keen to warn New Zealand Labour politicians away from assuming that they would receive ideological sustenance from British Labour, warned that the government in New Zealand 'should not follow industrial policies that might render British workers idle, wherein an ideologically inclined UK Labour government might discriminate against New Zealand trade in return'.[46]

It was reported that Bevin had stressed the need for import boards and a continuation of the wartime bulk purchasing.[47] Paradoxically, therefore,

44 Memo, Under Secretary of State Acheson to President Truman, 12 Dec. 1945, Official Files, Harry S. Truman Papers, HST.
45 Holland quoted in Malcolm McKinnon, 'The New World of the Dollar', in Malcolm McKinnon, ed., *The American Connection*. Wellington, 1988, p. 116.
46 *NZH*, 1 Aug. 1945.
47 *Dominion*, 28 July 1945.

conservatives, while bothered in some respects by American policies, could welcome American pressure on England and New Zealand, for instance in the international trade talks, if they thought it might lead to the dismantling of import licensing: a paper by Kenneth Cumberland argued that the Atlantic Charter was not a prescription for economic isolationism,[48] while *Security in the Pacific* made the same point about Article 7 of the Mutual Aid (Lend-Lease) Agreement.[49] In 1947 many editorial writers were ready to lay the responsibility for Britain's acute balance of payments crisis at the foot of the Labour government in that country.[50]

New Zealand's preferences in England were not much more than a decade old, and in the postwar era of government-to-government contracts they were not even operative; moreover, they were flat rate duties, not ad valorem (percentage) preferences, and had therefore been eroded by wartime inflation. *Security in the Pacific* questioned imperial preference. 'It may be suggested', it said, 'that Imperial Preference has more sentimental than economic significance as far as New Zealand is concerned. Economically it is far less significant than the high tariffs of the USA and certain European countries.'[51] Nonetheless most producers, National politicians and editorial writers—although not all—remained profoundly hostile to any hint of a threat to imperial preference, which had acquired what one writer described as a 'talismanic' hold on the New Zealand imagination. And they had a knee-jerk reaction therefore to any American comment or proposal to dispense with it.[52]

If the Marshall Plan became a device to promote European unity at the expense of Commonwealth economic ties, that too was cause for concern: 'Where would we stand in New Zealand? ... If Britain goes in without us, what then?'[53] Doidge's characteristic anxieties in this instance echoed those of many others a decade and more later. And while National and Labour may have been in agreement over defending imperial preference, National remained unrelenting in its attacks on Nash's import and other economic controls and recorded evidence of the attached discomfiture: 'I gather Nash very embarrassing to UK at Havana re import control'.[54]

48   'New Zealand and the Post-War World', *Agenda*, 3 (1944), p. 36.
49   *Security in the Pacific*, p. 33.
50   Wellington to Secretary of State, 10 Oct. 1947. 847H.00/10–1047, USNA. See also summary reports, 5 and 18 Sept. 1947.
51   *Security in the Pacific*, p. 33.
52   There was a large measure of agreement in government too, certainly at difficult times in Anglo-American relations such as the 1947 sterling crisis: 'At the present time the United Kingdom is being subjected to considerable aggression in the economic field by the United States, particularly from such representatives as Clayton, Douglas (the American Ambassador in London) and Hawkins. They have adopted an extremely high-handed attitude over Imperial Preference and appear to me to be taking a most unfair and unworthy attitude ... at the time of Britain's greatest economic weakness.' Draft cable embodying sense of conversation with Fraser, McIntosh papers, MERT.
53   *NZPD*, 282, p. 2127 (8 Sept. 1948), quoted in Sewell, p. 30.
54   MDW to Holland, 22 April 1948, Ms Papers 1624. 55/6, ATL.

But while there were always individuals and lobbies ready enough to agitate for more imports from the United States (especially when supplies of British goods were inferior) or more investment, they were matched by British importers with their strong and habitual ties and by a certain reserve about allowing American capital untrammelled opportunities to operate in New Zealand: 'New Zealand conservatives interpret [their belief in the virtue of private enterprise] as freedom to operate their own parochial enterprises, not to sink themselves in America's mammoth business arrangements.'[55]

National Party caution was most evident in the continued reluctance of the parliamentary caucus to support New Zealand's entry into the International Monetary Fund, 'one of the hottest of domestic "hot potatoes" ',[56] and a great deal of reserve about the General Agreement on Tariffs and Trade (GATT), which was only reinforced when the United States secured its waiver allowing it to restrict imports of dairy produce. In respect of trade problems with the United States, official protests, according to the American mission in New Zealand, were, 'as usual', strongly echoed in the press: 'Picturing the United States as first shutting out the produce of her friends, next threatening their prospects on the world market by dumping, and finally protesting their trade with the Soviet Union and the satellites as unfriendly when the very restrictive policies of the United States force this trade upon them.'[57]

Senior civil servants were committed to taking New Zealand into the IMF. Holland adopted the cause in 1952 but had to abandon it in the face of caucus opposition. The possibilities of dollar investment were welcomed, not least because the British saw it as one way of improving the sterling area's balance of payments, but the approach was fairly leisurely. An interdepartmental committee came up with some proposals and the government finally acted on them in mid 1955. The government also explored borrowing commercially on Wall Street, having been helped by Vice-President Richard Nixon to gain a $16 million loan from the US import-export bank: 'One can never tell but we may need American money some day', Holland wrote to his Minister of Finance.[58] Ironically it was Labour, facing a balance of payments crisis in 1958, that was the first New Zealand government to borrow on the commercial market in the United States.

The protection of the British market

The other kind of economic independence, the pursuit of interest, on the whole linked New Zealand firmly to England in the 1930s, 1940s and 1950s. It

---

55   W. F. Monk, 'New Zealand and the United States' (Paper A), p. 7, 30 April 1953. EA58/9/1, MERT. I am indebted to Roberto Rabel for this reference.
56   611.444/2-2553, encl. memo of conversation, 28 Jan. 1953, RG59, USNA.
57   844.00/7-555, RG59, USNA.
58   Memo to PM, Feb. 1954, Ms Papers 1624, 98/3, ATL; NAC Minutes, 14 Sept. 1953, RG43, USNA; T61/1/8, NA.

was hard for anyone in the New Zealand community in the 1930s to imagine it as an entity completely separate from Britain, so close were the economic and defence ties. Could New Zealand survive without Britain? It seemed unlikely and unwelcome:

> New Zealanders are extremely loyal to British traditions and the imperial Crown, but they are also hard-headed farmers and business men who would be unnatural if they did not think of their own skins and livelihood first. So long as they depend upon Britain for defence and a ready market for their surplus produce, so long will they willingly subscribe to the doctrine of imperial unity. A future projected beyond those conditions is both unhappy and imponderable.[59]

Nonetheless at times, in the 1930s at least, that future had seemed uncomfortably close. Economic security had vanished in the depression of the early 1930s and the need, once prosperity returned, to anchor it in stable overseas trading arrangements as well as in more industrial development in New Zealand—a 'balanced economy'—was accepted by most political and business interests.

Like the Coalition government before it, Labour pursued the mirage of diversification—opening up new markets for New Zealand exporters. The Coalition had had talks with the Americans and signed a trade agreement with Belgium. Neither had produced much. Nash travelled to Berlin and Moscow in 1937, in between two rounds of negotiations in London. He came away with a trade agreement with Germany, but not with the Soviet Union. But the German one amounted to very little. Interestingly there was no political objection to it.[60]

Britain remained crucial. Walter Nash, like Coates, looked to Britain to provide a secure and stable market for New Zealand meat, butter and cheese. In 1935 the British abandoned the proposal to manage Dominion imports by a system of levy-subsidies i.e. a form of protection, in the face of Dominion opposition. Nash went on to the offensive. In a lengthy sojourn in England in late 1936 and into 1937 he tried to negotiate a balancing agreement where in return for Britain's guaranteed purchase of New Zealand's exportable surplus of meat and dairy produce at agreed prices, New Zealand would take in its import trade all that Britain could supply. The British did not agree. Unlike New Zealand, Britain was a global trader and did not want to place any of its trade on such a restrictive bilateral basis. Nash got only limited agreements from the British. Nonetheless when he returned home, he was given a dinner by the Wellington Chamber of Commerce, not usually a stronghold of Labour sympathy, and received a 'very friendly' welcome.[61]

---

[59] Cowie, p. 585.
[60] For discussion of one particularly unsatisfactory bilateral relationship see Keith Sinclair, 'Fruit Fly, Fireblight and Powdery Scab: Australia-New Zealand Trade Relations 1919-1939', *JICH*, 1/1 (Oct. 1972), pp. 27-48.
[61] *Round Table*, 111 (June 1938), p. 634. The quotas for 1937 for mutton and lamb Nash had negotiated were the highest secured since quotas were introduced in 1934.

The government did, however, also move slowly in a more protectionist direction in sympathy with a general belief that it was important to develop industry in an economy overly dependent on agriculture and therefore on price fluctuations beyond its control. In January 1938 tariffs on footwear from Australia, Canada and foreign countries (but not Britain) were increased.[62] The *Round Table* commented that in the 1938 election campaign, the Leader of the Opposition was talking in almost the same terms as the government about the virtues of developing industry as a way of increasing the national income.[63] Even a country-oriented paper like the *Dominion* ran an annual manufacturing supplement in which it lauded the value of the country's industries, although it saw the key to development in controlling costs rather than in promoting demand.[64] The fact that there were cheap imports from Japan made protectionism more acceptable than if the competition had been solely from British exporters (although the fact that Japanese buying brought buoyancy to the wool market in 1936–37 had the opposite effect). Holland told farmers that they must tolerate secondary industry: holding up a pair of trousers in Parliament, he said they were made in Christchurch from staple fibre, a wool substitute, which was less than half the price of wool. Farmers should have protection against that, he said, but manufacturers should have equal protection against cheaply produced goods from overseas.[65] But protection did not become a nationalist issue in New Zealand, uniting New Zealanders against overseas interests. For its part, the government, while keen on industrial development in theory, was rather cautious about imposing higher tariffs with consequences for the cost of living, despite pressure from manufacturers.[66] On the other hand, the Opposition attacked the government when protection came in by the back door with the 1938–39 exchange crisis, accusing it of mistreating British interests.

In international economic relations, the government welcomed both the US-UK-France monetary agreement of 1936 and the Anglo-American trade agreement of 1938. The British at the 1937 Imperial Conference either bludgeoned or cajoled the Dominions into agreeing to the negotiation of an Anglo-American agreement.[67] Savage was sceptical but stressed that New Zealand was in favour of an agreement—and in the event it did not, as had been anticipated, significantly affect New Zealand's trade in Britain—but nor did it open up trade prospects in the United States.[68]

62 *Round Table*, 111 (June 1938), p. 636.
63 *Round Table*, 113 (Dec. 1938), p. 194.
64 See, for instance, *Dominion*, special supplement to issue of 13 July 1937; and see also editorial, 14 July 1937.
65 *EP*, 27 July 1939.
66 *Round Table*, 110 (March 1938), pp. 421–2.
67 Ovendale, p. 17, 'moving appeal'; R. F. Holland, *Britain and the Commonwealth Alliance*. London, 1981, p. 150, 'bludgeoned'.
68 *Dominion*, 29 July 1937; *AIBR*, 21 Oct. 1938, p. 895.

New Zealand's interest in wartime was to ensure that the war did not precipitate any severe dislocation either through some interruption of supplies or exports or by a postwar slump. Britain agreed to buy all New Zealand's wool clip for the duration of the war and one year after at prices considerably above pre-war averages; this allowed New Zealand to envisage a major boost to its export receipts throughout the war. Britain also negotiated the purchase of large quantities of frozen meat, butter and cheese. These arrangements were rather more contentious though. In the first year of the war, the British market was oversupplied and there was a real danger of the butter price in particular collapsing. In 1940–41 there was a new threat—a shipping shortage, which raised the possibility of most of New Zealand's produce sitting in cool stores in New Zealand waiting for ships that might never come and for money which might not either. There was a lot of anguish and anger among meat producers when the British took supplies from closer Argentina in preference. The cry was to find other markets, a call which influenced the government to send a supply mission to the United States:

> The Labour government is being constantly criticised by the Opposition party as well as by local Chambers of Commerce and the press . . . for failing to take steps to cushion New Zealand against the impact of the war . . . . It is fair to assume that the Labour government is preparing the way to indicate to the electorate that by sending a trade mission to the United States, the only potentially important market apart from the British Empire, it has done what it could to extend New Zealand markets.[69]

Behind this mission lay a certain anxiety that the Americans would be allocated the British market instead and after the war New Zealand would find it hard to get back in. What, asked the President of the Chamber of Commerce in 1941, was New Zealand to make of

> the potential power of the United States in the new order and its effects on the New Zealand economy? The 'Lease and Lend' legislation, necessary as it may have been in Britain's interest, has at one blow given the United States almost a stranglehold on the trade of half the world, and after the war must she not command a much greater share of world trade if for no other reason than her possession of most of the shipping? . . . Does it not seem . . . possible there will be large blocks of nations for international trading purposes with the English-speaking world as one block operating through a clearing house at New York? . . . Not long ago Mr George Duncan returned from Britain and issued a statement encouraging hope in a market for New Zealand products in the Western Hemisphere. Against this the United States Secretary of Agriculture . . . only six weeks ago started the greatest food production programme ever conceived, and it is strongly backed by President Roosevelt.[70]

69 US Legation, Wellington, to Secretary of State, 16 May 1941. 611.47H31/117, RG59, USNA.
70 Associated Chambers of Commerce, *Annual Report*, 1941, President's Address to the Conference, November 1941.

But the apprehension proved to be unwarranted. By 1943, while the American market had not opened up to New Zealand, the British market had not faded. American production did not meet British expectations and the shipping situation improved. So Britain from 1943 committed itself to taking exportable surpluses of New Zealand meat and dairy produce. War's uncertainty, a by-product essentially of the Battle of the Atlantic, was followed by war's certainty, a by-product of Allied victory in that battle— Britain's near inexhaustible demand for all that New Zealand could produce.[71] In 1944 four-year contracts were signed for meat and dairy produce, and generous price rises were agreed to too. Moreover in 1942, primarily in response to Australian pressure, Britain had agreed to a 15 per cent increase in the price of wool. While Britain moved from creditor to debtor status during the war, New Zealand moved in the opposite direction. Britain had lent New Zealand the money to cover the sterling costs of its expeditionary force. By 1945 New Zealand was in a position to pay back most of what it had borrowed.

After the war Britain remained, despite fears about the United States, both principal market for New Zealand exports, and also principal source of imports. Both in 1946 and in 1947–48 campaigns were launched for economic assistance to Britain. These involved an extensive network of volunteer committees which replicated similar endeavours through the war, as publicity material for the Aid to Britain campaign implied: 'help Britain win the peace'. In March 1947 the government wrote off £10 million of its sterling balances as a 'gift' to Britain, a gesture that was universally welcomed. The welcome was grounded in realism as well as in loyalty: speeches and addresses in the postwar years are replete with references to the importance of Britain's recovery to New Zealand's own economic future. Similarly, although National on occasion criticised Labour for not accepting British tenders for certain postwar projects, the government did in fact provide around a 10 per cent margin to give British tenderers an advantage.[72]

The most public expression of solidarity with Britain in the economic sphere was in respect of the dollar shortage. New Zealand, like other Commonwealth countries, collaborated with Britain to curtail dollar expenditure as a way of building up the gold and dollar reserves of the sterling area. At the same time, New Zealand had to accept restraints on the supply of goods from Britain, as they were diverted from sterling markets to earn precious 'hard' currency.[73] But on balance New Zealand was a net consumer

[71]   Malcolm McKinnon, 'Equality of Sacrifice: Anglo-New Zealand Relations and the War Economy, 1939–1945', *JICH*, 12/3 (May 1984), pp. 66–67.
[72]   Malcolm McKinnon, 'The Impact of War: Anglo-New Zealand Economic Diplomacy 1939–1954'. Ph. D. thesis, VUW, 1981, pp. 216–17, 226–9.
[73]   A hard currency is one for which demand is greater than supply at a fixed rate; a soft currency the reverse. The United States dollar was the pre-eminent hard currency in the 1940s.

of dollars, at least until 1950 when wool prices soared, so it had a vested interest in maintaining the system. It was always possible to argue that New Zealand could have earned hard currency for its exports if it had not had bulk contract agreements with the British; but in the nature of things difficult to prove. Britain was by far the biggest purchaser—would it have paid hard currency to New Zealand, as it was forced to do to Argentina at one point? If it had, New Zealand could have waved goodbye to any long-term security of access to the British market. On the whole interest as well as sentiment counselled adherence to the sterling area.

In international trade negotiations New Zealand delegations, usually led by Nash, had to battle both the British and the Americans over New Zealand's wish to maintain import control, so dear to Nash's heart and to Labour's full employment ideology. Both—the United States for mostly ideological reasons, Britain for a combination of ideological and practical concerns as the world's largest exporter—wanted to ban import control. New Zealand argued that this was not protectionism in disguise, but a planned policy of maintaining a full-employment economy, a goal which required import control if the major alternative, deflation and unemployment in the event of over-importing, was to be avoided: 'the methods to obtain the objectives for highly industrialised countries may have an adverse effect for New Zealand and other countries similarly placed.'[74] At the critical tariff negotiations at Geneva in 1947 it was only after Nash returned home that the New Zealand delegation agreed to accept that New Zealand's case could be covered under Article 26 of the draft international trade charter, which made provision for import control in the event of balance of payments difficulties.

When Britain asked New Zealand to cut back on sterling imports, Nash agreed with alacrity, only to find the British suspicious that he was just using this request to cut back on all imports to advance the government's protectionist goals; Harold Wilson, who was at the Board of Trade at the time, had an early introduction to New Zealand negotiating styles and objectives. Meanwhile Holland launched a vigorous attack on the GATT treaty, which Nash had signed at Havana and which awaited ratification by Parliament, both on the grounds that it provided too much of an escape for Labour from the obligation to limit import control and also because of the possible threat from import control. In fact in 1948 and 1949 producers were becoming restless. They needed supplies which could be provided only from the dollar zone. The possibilities of liberalisation, of more trade with and capital from the dollar zone, in the air in 1948-49, were to grow in significance in the 1950s. In the final months of the Labour government ideas of dollar investment as a way of facilitating dollar imports were being canvassed, to the dismay of some of the left-wing intellectual Members of Parliament.[75]

74 *EP*, 8 Dec. 1945.
75 McKinnon, 'Impact of War', pp. 225-6.

The change of government at the end of 1949 did not make a big difference to the conduct of New Zealand's economic relations with Britain, except perhaps in an increased readiness to speak up on behalf of producer interests, who had close political connections with the National Party. Until 1954 the meat and dairy trade still operated under contract to the British Ministry of Food. There were occasional spats, particularly about prices: producers were particularly bitter at British stonewalling in the negotiations on dairy prices in the middle of 1950 and the government echoed their concerns in its talks with the Minister, Patrick Gordon Walker. Global prices were far above the contract prices and quite naturally the British wished to take full advantage of the terms of the contract. Farmers were joined by newspapers, which 'broke well established habits to print some angry denunciations of the British [government which] used language oddly reminiscent of that hurled at an unsympathetic Colonial Office eighty years earlier for it alluded cryptically to conduct which if persisted in might break up the Empire . . . .'[76] There were similar exchanges about meat early in 1952: on this occasion Holland's pleading 'not to squeeze the last drop of blood from Britain' was compared unfavourably with Holyoake's insistence on demanding increases.[77]

Holland himself was nonetheless quite capable of lambasting British business. One American observer caught the National leader well when he noted that he seemed 'temperamentally closer to the average American Rotarian than an average upper class Briton'.[78] He told exporters in London early in 1951 that while New Zealand gave preference to British suppliers wherever possible, there was a danger of British traders putting their heads together and offering one price for New Zealand tenders: 'you may think we can give you the business at any price but there may be a time when we cannot do that'. And New Zealand politicians also complained frequently about the quality of British imports, particularly of household goods.[79]

The British market though was far more important to New Zealand than the New Zealand market was to Britain. New Zealand was anxious about Japan, not just because it threatened New Zealand industry but because it threatened British markets in New Zealand—and elsewhere—too.[80] British government contracts for the exportable surpluses of meat, butter and cheese were not renewed after the 1953–54 season. There was apprehension among producers—what would a free market really be like? Diversification re-entered the lexicon of New Zealand's external economic relations. In 1955 Keith Holyoake, the Minister of Agriculture, visited Moscow on his way home

76 F. L. W. Wood, *This New Zealand.* Hamilton, 1952, p. 172.
77 And see also McKinnon, 'Impact of War', pp. 330–2.
78 744. 13/1-3151, RG59, USNA.
79 McKinnon, 'Impact of War', p. 302.
80 W. F. Monk, 'New Zealand Faces North', *Pacific Affairs*, 26/3 (Sept. 1953), pp. 223–4, 228; *Round Table*, 185 (Dec. 1956), pp. 76–77.

from an FAO conference in Rome. The visit was praised by the conservative press and producer interests, as well as Labour and Communist opinion, on the grounds that it was an opportunity to open up a new market. In fact the Soviet Union wanted bilateral, not just one-way trade, with hard currency settlement, and so the initiative languished. The United States looked more promising. When New Zealand exporters were still tied to British contracts in the early 1950s, they used to look longingly at the American market, the higher prices, the dollar earnings. Reality was less wonderful. In particular the Americans stopped imports of virtually all dairy produce in the early 1950s, despite this being in breach of GATT. The United States used its Defence Production Act to keep out butter and then secured the waiver from GATT legitimising the restriction.[81]

New Zealand had a run-in with the Australians when the latter abruptly tightened their import licensing policy in October 1955. Menzies and McEwen, the Australian Ministers involved, proved responsive to New Zealand concerns, but only after Holland had made an official visit to put New Zealand's case.[82] But it was the British market which remained crucial. After two good seasons of open market trading, in 1956–57 producers faced falling prices. In March the New Zealand government increased the car import allocation from Britain by £2 million as a way of helping the depressed British car industry.[83] In April Holyoake led a delegation to London to negotiate a return to a more protected market, but the British were resistant— there was nothing in it for them and indeed there was an unfamiliar element of bloody-mindedness about their unwillingness to make special concessions to New Zealand, as Holyoake, the chief negotiator subsequently explained: 'Sir David Eccles told us emphatically and unequivocally that the United Kingdom was not prepared to impose quantitative regulations under existing circumstances'.[84]

Holyoake achieved a certain notoriety on this occasion. Did he tell the British to 'stand and deliver'? On a BBC radio programme, when asked whether, if New Zealand had to look for other markets, 'our [British] privileges in the New Zealand market would be reduced', Holyoake answered, 'I'm afraid if you cannot use our produce at reasonable prices, prices that will cover costs, then of course it does mean that we must sell to other countries, we must then buy from other countries. We would regret it, but it would be an economic factor that we would just simply have to face.'[85] The prospect of New Zealand's reducing British preferences elicited a longer-

81   *AJHR*, 1956, H. 44, p. 39.
82   Ms Papers 1624, 78/5, 79/1–5, ATL.
83   Malcolm McKinnon, 'Trading in Difficulties', in *New Zealand in World Affairs*, v. 2, *1957– 1972*. Wellington, 1991, p. 156.
84   *NZPD*, 311, p. 89 (14 June 1957).
85   *NZPD*, 311, p. 127 (14 June 1957).

term commitment of duty-free entry for dairy produce than the British had originally offered and an agreement to consult. This was more acceptable than abandoning preferences.

When New Zealand approached the British in 1958, seeking the right to revise downward British preferences incorporated in the 1933 New Zealand tariff, the negotiations were arduous: at one point a letter was drafted for Nash unilaterally denouncing Ottawa; later on the British were insistent on their long-standing demand that New Zealand import controls or any bilateral trade agreements it might negotiate should not discriminate against British exports—echoes of the 1930s.[86] Agreement was finally reached in early September.

Phil Holloway, Labour Minister of Industries and Commerce in 1957–60, deplored what he described as delays in the hearing of an anti-dumping application by New Zealand in respect of butter: did Britain mean to turn its back on New Zealand? His statement was uniformly applauded by all interests, including the Opposition.[87] The issue was resolved only by a major improvement in market conditions in Britain in 1959, mainly because of the hot dry conditions of the European summer that year.

Much more substantial issues arose in the following years. After a great deal of debate and discussion through 1960 and into 1961 the British government announced a decision to apply for membership in the European Economic Community established by France, West Germany, Italy, the Netherlands, Belgium and Luxembourg in 1958. The visit by Macmillan's Commonwealth Secretary Duncan Sandys to meet the Cabinet of the recently elected National government at the end of June 1961 was a key moment. Macmillan said Britain would consult with the Commonwealth before proceeding with an application to join the Community. Would—or could—New Zealand or any other Commonwealth member veto the application? What would they want in exchange? Sandys said that it would be almost impossible for New Zealand to retain unrestricted duty-free entry: New Zealand would have to explore all other means of protecting its export trade. But this only confirmed what had already been suspected. Paragraph 4 of the communiqué recorded that Sandys had stated that if the British government did decide to negotiate, it 'would seek to secure special arrangements to protect the vital interests of New Zealand and other Commonwealth countries, and that Britain would not feel able to join the European Economic Community unless such arrangements were secured.'[88] In paragraph 5 New Zealand stressed that it could not see any other effective way of protecting New Zealand's vital

---

[86] The definitive discussion of these negotiations is in Sinclair, *Nash*, pp. 314–17. See also 844.00/8–2958, RG59, USNA, especially for comment on bilateral trade agreements.

[87] 844.00/4–1158, RG59, USNA. The anti-dumping issue seems to have attracted more interest than Ottawa revision.

[88] *EAR*, July 1961, p. 12.

interests than by the maintenance of unrestricted and duty-free entry. The closest it came to accepting the possibility of a fallback position at this time was in agreeing that it would be willing to examine any alternative methods for protecting New Zealand interests which might emerge in the course of the negotiations. But 'until specific proposals had been put forward, [it] would necessarily have to reserve [its] position'.[89]

The subsequent negotiations tested Anglo-New Zealand relations to the limit. Britain and the European Six started to talk about agriculture in February 1962. The British told the Six that they were prepared to participate in the Common Agricultural Policy. The British wanted to commit the Six to providing 'comparable outlets' for Commonwealth temperate foodstuffs that might be excluded from the enlarged Community.[90] The trip to Europe in May and June 1962 by the Deputy Prime Minister and Minister of Overseas Trade, J. R. Marshall, was not easy. There seemed to be a wide gap between what Britain and New Zealand understood by vital interests in respect of New Zealand's major products. Marshall and the British Ministers were unable to agree on a summary record or a series of conclusions for their discussions.[91]

A letter to the Prime Minister from Sandys towards the end of July 1962 made it look as if Britain had abandoned any attempt even to secure comparable outlets and that they would be unable to live up to the assurances given in the Sandys communiqué: they seemed to be in a rush to conclude the negotiations.[92]

Perhaps New Zealand might do better out of the Six themselves. Both Jean Monnet, the 'father' of European unity, and Sicco Mansholt, the Commissioner for Agriculture, had told Marshall in June that New Zealand should look to securing a special arrangement from the Europeans to be negotiated after Britain had reached agreement with them. When Anglo-European negotiations were adjourned in early August the Six told the British they recognised that New Zealand was in a special situation and were prepared to consider additional solutions. New Zealand officials were intrigued by the possibility although they recognised both the risks—that it might let Britain 'off the hook'—and the impediments, in particular both New Zealand's assurances to Canada and Australia that it would not try to cut a special deal and Britain's reluctance to favour New Zealand.[93]

A Commonwealth conference on Britain's quest to join the Community was

89 *EAR*, July 1961, p. 12.
90 The CAP had been settled amongst the Six only in January. Cabinet Committee on Economic and Financial Questions (CCEFQ), 13 Feb. 1962, Ms Papers 1403, 348/3, ATL; *AJHR*, 1962 A.17, 'New Zealand and the European Community 1962'.
91 CCEFQ, 26 June 1962. Ms Papers 1403, 348/4, ATL.
92 CCEFQ, 25 July 1962, Ms Papers 1403, 348/4, ATL.
93 *AJHR*, 1962, A. 17, p. 12; CCEFQ, 26 June, 7, 19 and 22 Aug. 1962. Ms Papers 1403, 348/ 4, ATL. For New Zealand and Australia, see Rita Ricketts, 'Old Friends, New Friends: Cooperation or Competition', *NZWA 1957–72*, pp. 183–8.

held in September 1962, but the timing was not good for New Zealand. The Anglo-European negotiations through the rest of the year made little progress: 'It was difficult to make progress, as far as urging any particular arrangement for New Zealand was concerned, until the dairy regulations and beef and veal regulations emerged. This was not expected before April.'[94]

As it transpired, French President de Gaulle's January 1963 veto ended this first round of Britain's attempt to seek admission to the Community. The prospect of special treatment did foreshadow the way New Zealand's case would be dealt with when Britain did successfully negotiate admission to the Community in 1970–71. In the meantime, the officials, politicians and producer interests involved in the negotiations with the British had had underlined for them the fact that British and New Zealand interests were not necessarily interdependent. The realisation that the British had a quite different agenda, that New Zealand was a nuisance rather than a long-standing associate, would not readily be forgotten.[95]

Moreover, the end of the Anglo-European negotiations did not mean that New Zealand could find security on the British market. The pressure to regulate that market had stemmed from factors unrelated to Britain's interest in joining the Community and these were still operative in the 1960s. In 1962 Britain introduced a managed market for butter and in 1964 for meat, thus ending the promise of unrestricted entry granted in 1952 for meat and in 1957 for butter.[96] It was hardly surprising that in considering New Zealand's direction after the veto, officials should conclude that while the British market would continue to be essential for butter, it was imperative to seek new markets and products.[97]

Britain was not of course alone in choosing its own ways of managing its markets and advancing its economic interests. New Zealand did so too. When Labour was in office in 1957–60 it gave some extra impetus to the use of protection to foster industrial development. The Department of Industries and Commerce in particular, under the energetic leadership of W. B. Sutch and J. P. Lewin and with the support of its Minister, Phil Holloway, embarked on a very active programme of promoting industrialisation. During 1959, decisions were taken to build an oil refinery and an aluminium-fabricating plant, to expand carpet production, to establish a steel industry and to set up a foreign exchange fund for industrial development. In 1960 the government took what was to prove the most controversial decision of its time in office—to

---

94   CCEFQ, 29 Nov. 1962, Ms Papers 1403, 348/4, ATL.
95   But not easily learnt either. One observer noted some years later, a 'sense of confusion, perhaps shock, at the blow which had been administered to the country with which our own traditions were most closely linked. The judgement that Britain was not yet prepared for a place in the grand design of Europe seemed in some way a reflection on New Zealand itself.' *NZFAR*, Nov. 1970, p. 45.
96   The changes are noted in *EAR* through 1961–64.
97   CCEFQ, 20 Feb. 1963, Ms Papers 1403, 351/2, ATL.

establish a cotton industry the future of which would be secured partly by offering the company involved a protected share of the domestic market. 'Manufacturing in New Zealand', said one business journal, 'is, indeed, at present enjoying an enlarged market which official policy appears determined to encourage, whatever the merits or otherwise of individual cases.'[98]

An open or a closed economy? National was not averse to the idea of industrialisation or for that matter to the government's playing a role in promoting it: it was a natural part of the developmental approach of the 1950s, with the government active in, for instance, the exploitation of timber and water resources. The cancellation of the Nelson cotton mill in 1962 looked like a blow for free trade,[99] but National did not abandon import licensing, and its approach to free trade with Australia was cautious. The News Media Ownership Act 1965 was overtly protective of local newspaper capital against overseas bids.

Economic independence—the waning of ideology, 1957-63[100]

While independence was as readily defined as the pursuit of interest at the beginning of the 1960s as in the 1930s, the ideological and nationalist beliefs in independence were waning. We can see this in two episodes, New Zealand's admission to the International Monetary Fund and the debate over Britain's bid to join the European Economic Community. The Labour Party was no longer as committed as it had been to the idea of keeping the New Zealand economy at arm's length from the international economy; this change of outlook was also influenced by global developments, however. By the end of the 1950s the boundary lines between the sterling area and the dollar zone had become blurred; there seemed little future in a separate Commonwealth economic bloc. As most plans for keeping New Zealand at one remove from the American-dominated international economy rested on keeping Britain at one remove too, Britain's actions were of crucial importance. This is what the debate over British entry to the Community demonstrated. Opinion in the National Party moved decisively away from preoccupation with Empire economic unity: Labour opinion, in which patriotic sentiment was reinforced by ideology, was more cautious.

The Labour Party had a traditional dislike of overseas borrowing[101] but

---

98 *NZE&T*, 16 May 1960.
99 For discussion of the cotton mill episode, see Sinclair, *Nash*, pp. 344-6, including his reference to D. J. Mitchell, 'Nelson Cotton Mill', Univ. of Canterbury, M.A. thesis, 1967; Austin Mitchell, *Politics and People in New Zealand*. Christchurch, 1969; Tony Simpson, *A Vision Betrayed*. Auckland, 1984. R. D. Muldoon, *The Rise and Fall of a Young Turk*. Wellington, 1974, pp. 56-58, notes backbencher opposition, partly because of complaints from manufacturers in various electorates.
100 This section appears in slightly altered form in Malcolm McKinnon, 'Trading in Difficulties', *NZWA 1957-72*, pp. 158-62.
101 744.00/12-957, 844.10/8-2258, RG59, USNA; see also Sinclair, *Nash*, pp. 306-8.

circumstances forced its hand in government in 1958. In the face of a severe payments crisis the government re-imposed full licensing for imports, an echo of 1938; but borrowing was also felt to be necessary to ensure that raw materials essential for the operation of domestic industry and therefore for the level of economic activity were admitted. The government raised £20 million in London but it was at a high interest rate (6 per cent) and an additional £7.5 million ($US48.9 million) was borrowed in New York.[102]

The borrowing, and particularly the dollar borrowing, the first ever undertaken on the New York capital market by the New Zealand government, could not help but change thinking about the desirability of New Zealand's joining the IMF and the World Bank. For one reason, if New Zealand was going to resort to emergency borrowing anyway, it was penalising itself by not having access to the IMF's short-term facilities. Secondly, it was evident that the general mood about participation in international financial institutions was changing. Labour did end the discriminatory treatment of imports from the dollar zone, a reminder of the acute dollar shortages of the 1940s and early 1950s but also a symptom of acceptance of the principle of liberalisation in New Zealand's economic relations.[103] But membership of the Fund was still too sensitive an issue for Labour and Nash had to defer again to this sentiment, as he had in 1946.[104]

Mainstream conservative opinion, however, had now moved decisively towards an international rather than an Empire framework for capitalism and finance. 'Unfortunately', said one new Member of Parliament, 'we cannot obtain enough from that [British] source. The writing was on the wall in 1958 when the Labour Government had to go to America, give a full report on the country's economy . . . and pledge our gold in America as additional security for the loan.'[105]

Labour fought National's bill to take New Zealand into the International Monetary Fund and the World Bank through an all-night sitting in 1961, with

[102] J. P. Morgan, the bankers, wanted New Zealand to make gold available as collateral. The government was agreeable, but resisted Morgan's insistence that the gold be transferred to Australia. The American Embassy in New Zealand was also unhappy about the gold transfer: 'anything that can be done to mitigate the impact of moving the gold would make the public reception of the loan more favourable'. Memorandum of conversation State Department, 25 June 1958, 844.00/6–2558, RG59, USNA; see also 844.10/8–2258. Eventually Bank of England gold was used as collateral, with New Zealand making an offsetting shipment to London (844. 00/9–2658).
[103] See, for instance, Nash's welcome to British liberalisation of dollar imports following on sterling convertibility, 1 Jan. 1959—it was, he said, consistent with the progressive removal of barriers to international trade supported by New Zealand. 844.00/6–559, RG59, USNA.
[104] The Secretary to the Treasury, E. L. Greensmith, told the State Department, 'New Zealand was following all the rules of members of the club, without getting any of the benefits'. But he explained that Nordmeyer, the Minister of Finance, was convinced that for political reasons, neither party would feel able to sanction membership: opposition to membership was in the Labour Party's election manifesto. RG59, 844.00/6–2558, USNA.
[105] *NZPD*, 327, p. 1109 (3 Aug. 1961).

Labour putting up every speaker and National none. Labour debated the issue essentially on ideological grounds and largely unhampered by its own overseas borrowing activities in 1958. Membership of the IMF would lead to unemployment, said Arthur Faulkner, invoking an argument put by one of the most best-known critics of membership, Wolfgang Rosenberg: 'Every country in the world belonging to the International Monetary Fund has a large percentage of unemployment on New Zealand standards, yet the Government ... proposes to pledge and shackle this country to an international organisation.'[106] Norman Kirk, then a new Member of Parliament, looked back to 1945 and American's cancellation of Lend-Lease at the end of the war:

> Many of the members sitting in this House will remember the concern there was at that time. There followed the extreme difficulty that had to be faced as a result of that arbitrary decision. It was reported at the time that the then Secretary to the Treasury in the United States, reporting to Congress on the actions of the President ... announced that that was the end of the sterling area; and the Congress cheered the statement ...

Kirk went on to quote evidence from the Congressional debate earlier in 1945 to prove that the United States wanted to, and believed that it did, dominate the International Monetary Fund.[107]

Ideological lines were also drawn over the prospect of Macmillan's Conservative government seeking to take Britain into the European Economic Community. Labour liked Macmillan's political attitude to the Commonwealth but found his enthusiasm for European economic unity all the more puzzling. After the Commonwealth Conference in September 1960, Nordmeyer said that if New Zealand's attitude had changed at all, it was in the direction of being against the Common Market rather than in favour of it, and on his return to New Zealand he commented that although he recognised that the division of Europe entailed political and economic costs, there were economic and political consequences to the Commonwealth if Britain entered the Community which should be taken into account as well. Moreover he also questioned whether the political stability or economic strength of Europe was dependent on Britain's joining the Community.[108]

Labour found an unexpected ally in John Ormond, chairman of the Meat Producers' Board, who still believed in the Empire, particularly one with a mother country which would take all the meat New Zealand could send it.[109] For Nash, emotional and practical attachment to the whole framework of

---

106 *NZPD*, 326, p. 752 (21 July 1961).
107 *NZPD*, 327, pp. 1132, 1134 (3 Aug. 1961).
108 Rob McLuskie, *The Great Debate: New Zealand, Britain and the EEC, the Shaping of Attitudes.* Wellington, 1986, pp. 28–30: Edward Heath, Macmillan's Minister of European Affairs, had made an unsettling statement.
109 For discussion of Ormond and of the Ormond/Nordmeyer/Nash connection, see McLuskie, pp. 21, 34.

Commonwealth trade played a part: this after all had been his world for a quarter century since his first official trip to England in 1936. Whatever his views about the need for more openness, he knew the value of the Commonwealth relationship (or at least the Anglo-New Zealand part of it: the 1960 Montreal Commonwealth economic conference did not suggest there was much hope for the Commonwealth as a whole as an economic unit, now that the days of sterling area collaboration were over) in providing a buffer between New Zealand and the wider world of international capitalism. National, in comparison, gave political support to European unity: 'New Zealand has, in principle, welcomed European economic integration as a means of increasing the political strength and the economic stability of the free world ... the successful accomplishment of a settlement between [the two economic blocs in Western Europe] could only lead to great advantage for the Western alliance in which New Zealand, at least indirectly, must share.'[110] Economically, it would be acceptable, provided it was accompanied by a liberalisation of world trade, in particular agricultural trade. This was an aspect of European unity in which the New Zealanders hoped the Americans would be especially helpful, given that New Zealand was not going to oppose British entry, on which the Americans were particularly keen. The communiqué of talks between Marshall and President Kennedy expressed agreement

> upon the desirability of European unity as well as the importance of liberalising world trade. The President described the trade legislation now pending before the United States Congress, explaining that with the passage of this legislation he expected an expansion of trade amongst the nations of the free world. The special problems of New Zealand were recognised with understanding. The President and Mr Marshall agreed that regular consultations between their two countries should continue.[111]

In November 1962 the United States Secretary of Commerce, Luther Hodges, visited New Zealand to discuss the new Trade Expansion Act: he stressed how much flexibility and authority the Act gave the President.[112] When de Gaulle vetoed British entry in January 1963, Holyoake expressed concern that 'the break in negotiations does not lead to any fracture in the Western alliance or an undermining of the economic growth and prosperity of the peoples of the free world'.[113]

Holyoake and Marshall faced commercial critics at home like Ormond and

110   'Britain and the European Economic Community: Implications for New Zealand 1961', *EAR*, July 1961, p. 9. A *Dominion* editorial, 10 March 1961, recognised that the new government was more positive about Britain's interest in joining the Community than its predecessor and attributed this to its recognition of the 'economic and political' imperative of a united Europe.
111   *EAR*, June 1962, pp. 46–47.
112   CCEFQ, 23 Nov. 1962. Ms Papers 1403, 348/4, ATL.
113   *EAR*, Jan. 1963, p. 21.

the Manufacturers' Federation, whose President, A. R. Dellow, asked whether it was 'unreasonable to suggest that we might now take another look at strengthening the Commonwealth as a trading bloc in the same way that was done in the Ottawa Conference of 1932'.[114] But Macmillan, backed up by Holyoake, was blunt about Commonwealth economic unity: 'Now I know that there are some people who talk as if there was an alternative system to the Common Market. The Commonwealth, they say, might form itself into a close economic unit .... I don't think that this idea has been a practical proposition for the Commonwealth in recent years ....'[115]

Commonwealth governments, said F. P. Walsh, had to talk over the heads of the British government to the British people. He had thought at one time that the dismembering of the Commonwealth would be accomplished with typical British finesse and diplomacy: 'I see now it is going to be brutal and with little or no consideration for the interests of the British Commonwealth. Mr Macmillan's masters, the United States Government and the big industrialists in both countries, have now evidently decreed that the gloves are off.'[116]

Similarly P. G. Connolly argued that the British industrialists and the United States were playing a major part in British entry.[117] Nash was more concerned, as were many other Labour politicians, with the idea that the British were abandoning their responsibilities to their colonial and ex-colonial possessions—to the third world—to join a rich men's club. In London he attended a meeting of Commonwealth Labour parties at the time of the 1962 Commonwealth Conference. A joint meeting of the FOL and Labour Party executives before Nash's departure had concluded that Britain should stay with the Commonwealth. Nash was influential in hardening the attitude of Gaitskell and the British Labour Party against British entry.[118]

For Labour the Commonwealth represented a different political and economic idea from that of Europe and the Atlantic alliance, one which accorded better with Labour concerns about colonialism and with the need to provide breakwaters against the power of international, particularly American, capital. So Labour speakers found themselves arguing that whether or not New Zealand itself got a good deal was not the only issue: 'we need to look at this question from three angles. Is it good for Britain herself to join? Is it good for the Commonwealth as a whole that she should join? Is it good for New Zealand in particular that she should join?'[119] British Labour opposition to entry provided a point of reference for Labour in New Zealand.

114   *New Zealand Manufacturer*, 2 Oct. 1961.
115   *EAR*, Sept. 1962, p. 42. For Holyoake, see *NZPD*, 332, p. 2049 (11 Oct. 1962).
116   Quoted McLuskie, p. 142.
117   *NZPD*, 330, p. 434 (26 June 1962).
118   J. D. B. Miller, *Survey of Commonwealth Affairs, 1952–1969*. London, 1974, p. 328; Sinclair, *Nash*, pp. 353–4.
119   *NZPD*, 332 p. 2037 (11 Oct. 1962).

'I am satisfied', said Nash, 'that the Labour Party at Home is a party to whom we can make representations ... it has said that if the Community does not comply with the Labour Party's conditions it will not support the Conservative Government proposals but will fight them.'[120] Nash and Nordmeyer both supported British Labour's concern that the Community was a rich men's club that would ignore the concerns of the third world, of which the Commonwealth was so predominantly composed. Labour spokespeople were more sceptical about the United States pressure to push Britain into the Community and saw it in ideological terms.

Conclusion

Through the 1930s, 1940s and 1950s the idea of independence was an important part of Labour thinking about New Zealand's place in the Commonwealth economy: it focused on New Zealand as a haven of full employment and high living standards in a fallible world. But Labour was more reconciled to that world in 1960 than in 1935.

For conservative opinion, independence was, unsurprisingly, expressed in the pursuit of interest, an interest usually, although not exclusively, identified with the maintenance of the closest possible economic relationship between New Zealand and Britain.

New Zealanders also attached importance to the survival of the British Commonwealth as an economic association. The internationalisation of Commonwealth economic relations, the weakening of distinctively Commonwealth links, meant that this objective would not be as significant in the future as it had been in the past.

---

[120] *NZPD*, 332, p. 2033 (11 Oct. 1962).

6. The 1950s consensus

Throughout the fourteen years of the Labour government, National had been ready to charge it with disloyalty if ever its 'independent' policies looked to be creating complications for Britain. National won the 1949 election. Would loyalty now become the watchword of its foreign policy? Would there be a sharp turning away from the course of Labour foreign policy? 'Loyalty' certainly dominated National's rhetoric. And National did give an ideological emphasis to foreign policy issues which was different from Labour's. But in practice the differences were minimal. Labour had after all argued in word, and shown in deed, that independence and loyalty were compatible. The two parties had taken similar, albeit not identical, ideological positions over the struggles against Fascism and Communism. Both placed relations with Britain and the Commonwealth at the centre of foreign relations and saw those relations as a model for international relations generally.

While a consensus prevailed, the Department of External Affairs nonetheless found the new government difficult. Fraser and Nash had been passionately interested in international affairs; Holland and most of his colleagues were not. Necessity sometimes dictated that the government reach out beyond the familar world of the Commonwealth, which many in the National Party still called the Empire. But not always. Parsimony remained a more powerful imperative than participation. Further, there were times when loyalty jibbed at the pressures of the wider world on New Zealand, on Britain, and on the relationship between the two.

Loyalty and parsimony

For the new government, solidarity with Britain was deeply rooted in the political culture. Many of the important links with Britain were with the more conservative parts of that country's political, social and economic structure — the armed forces, the Crown and the City, for instance. The Navy in the 1950s still had as its head a British admiral. The establishment of the Security Intelligence Service (SIS) was done in consultation with the British, and in particular with MI5, the counter-espionage service (combatting enemy activities), and many of its early personnel were recruited from MI5, which found it had surplus staff as colonies became independent.[1] Freyberg was the one exception before the 1960s to the recruitment of Governors-General from the ranks of the British aristocracy (Freyberg's New Zealand origins and wartime command of the New Zealand forces in the Second World War were important—but it should also be remembered that he had made his pre-war career in the British, not the New Zealand, army and that he returned to England—and a peerage—at the end of his vice-regal term). And as we have seen in Chapter 5, the business classes still looked primarily towards England as a source of imports, finance, professional knowledge and services of all kinds.[2]

It was to Britain that New Zealand returned for defence equipment, once wartime American supplies were exhausted. At least one of the three New Zealand chiefs of staff at any one time was a British officer on secondment, a pattern which continued through the 1950s. It was with Britain—and Australia—that peacetime defence cooperation and planning was developed. The British were seen as clearly the dominant military and naval power after the Americans, and the dominant power in the Indian Ocean and adjacent regions.[3] It was with the British that there were discussions about atomic energy in the 1940s, not the Americans—it was a Commonwealth concern.[4]

On numerous occasions, Holland took up Savage's phrase, 'where Britain goes we go', to the extent that it completely lost its original context and became a partisan motto for the foreign policy of his government.[5] Holland proffered full support to Britain's Middle Eastern policy and expressed disappointment at Egypt's failure to do likewise.[6] He agreed to support the British in the Middle East with an expeditionary force in the event of war, and deployed an RNZAF squadron in the region in 1952. In his thesis, 'New Zealand's Palestine Policy 1949-1976', C. D. Ritchie has demonstrated how overwhelmingly the daily press interpreted events in the Middle East in a pro-British fashion; indeed most papers were critical of the New Zealand government if it was felt to be less than complete in its support for British

---

[1]   The SIS was constituted only in 1956, when Holland secured a New Zealand officer who had done intelligence work in Melbourne and London, H. E. Gilbert, to head the new service. According to Michael Parker, *The SIS*. Palmerston North, 1979, p. 20, Holland backed off establishing a security service in 1951 because he did not want it run by the British—the ASIO (Australian Security Intelligence) representative at a December 1951 meeting on a possible SIS was British, as were many ASIO personnel. According to Parker, p. 21, the Petrov case (see below, p. 128) changed Holland's mind. For the establishment of the SIS in 1955-56, see Sir John Marshall, *Memoirs*, v. 1. Wellington, 1983, pp. 242-4.

[2]   See above, p. 95.

[3]   See McGibbon, 'Defence 1945-1957', pp. 147-8, for further comment.

[4]   EA2111/18/3. NA.

[5]   See, for instance, *EAR*, Nov. 1951, p. 10 (in connection with the Middle East); also *NZPD*, 305, p. 21 (24 March 1955), in respect of a military commitment in British Malaya; *Round Table*, 185 (Dec. 1956), p. 7, in respect of Suez.

[6]   *EAR*, Dec. 1951, pp. 2-3.

foreign policy.[7] New Zealand committed itself to help the British in Malaya in 1955 and to support their nuclear testing programme in the Pacific in 1957. Holland was ready to identify instances of the importance of Britain in international affairs and the recovery of its prestige after the difficult postwar years, for example at the Commonwealth Prime Ministers' Conference in January 1955 and at the time of the Bulganin-Krushchev visit to London in 1956.

Despite fourteen years of Labour 'independence', such rhetoric did not cost National politically. Loyalty to Britain was still a central element in the political culture. The visit of the Queen and Duke of Edinburgh in 1953-54 was one occasion on which the strength of the emotional tie with Britain was affirmed, and dissent was noticeable only by its absence.[8] There were many other more ordinary occasions; as one British visitor noted in 1952, 'They will ask you "How are things at Home?" and, when you tell them, will nod their heads knowingly, as though Manchester and Liverpool were places they visited every day.'[9]

National was not just patriotic, it was insular. National leaders had frequently been critical of Labour's 'independent foreign policy', not just because of its supposed disloyalty and radicalism, but also because it was wasteful. Holland had almost no interest in foreign affairs. Revealingly he took the Finance rather than the External Affairs portfolio in addition to the prime ministership. When he did intervene in the field he frequently made gaffes. In 1951 he claimed he would be quite happy if Japan was rearmed. He once offered all of New Zealand's meat to Britain for free. In 1953 he promised the then very large sum of £250,000 to help the Dutch with flood relief, and in that same year in Parliament he revealed the existence of ANZAM—even the term was top secret.[10] In 1957, when admittedly his powers were clearly failing, he claimed to have been surprised when the British detonated their bomb on Christmas Island—'Explosion a bombshell for Holland', said an uncharacteristically witty *New Zealand Herald* headline on 17 May, reporting Holland as saying that he was preparing to talk on the issue when to his great surprise the explosion occurred. The Commonwealth Relations Office said that Holland had been told over three months before that the explosion would be

7   See C. D. Ritchie, 'New Zealand's Palestine Policy', Univ. of Auckland, M. A. thesis, 1986, pp. 128-58.
8   Peter Attwell, ' "The Cheering Never Stopped": The Royal Tour of New Zealand 1953-1954'. VUW History Dept research paper, 1989.
9   Henry Deschampsneufs, 'Role of the Southern Dominions in South-East Asia', *New Commonwealth*, June 1952, p. 557.
10   744.00/5-1853, RG59, USNA; NZPD, 299, p. 308 (28 April 1953); ANZAM — Australia/New Zealand/Malayan region — a contingency planning organisation for the Eastern Indian Ocean, Southeast Asia and the Southwest Pacific established in 1949, largely as a result of an Australian initiative. It was based on Australian defence machinery with the British and New Zealand defence forces involved through their liaison officers in Australia. See Ian McGibbon, *New Zealand and the Korean War*, v. 1 (forthcoming, Auckland, 1993), ch. 3.

as soon as possible after 10 May, and that even Macmillan had been told of the event itself only after it had taken place.[11]

Doidge, Webb and Macdonald, Holland's Ministers of External Affairs, were more interested. Doidge retired from politics at the 1951 election and became High Commissioner in London, ending Bill Jordan's long tenure of the office. His passion, as befitted a one-time journalist and leader writer for the pro-Empire Beaverbrook press in London, was Empire unity. To this he added a preoccupation with Anglo-American solidarity, by which he usually meant American support for the Empire. Clifton Webb retired from politics at the 1954 election and followed Doidge as High Commissioner. Webb was more liberal, possibly more internationalist by inclination. Certainly he brought the attitudes of his legal profession to his portfolio. He believed New Zealand should recognise the Communist government in Peking because it was appropriate that de jure and de facto recognition coincide. This got him into hot water with the Americans. He did not trust the cable system and penned longhand reports which were mailed even during international crises, like Suez. Macdonald was probably the most predictable and easiest to work with of the three. The Americans preferred him.[12]

National caution could be identified even in the area where it might have been least expected, given the rhetoric—Empire defence. Approaches from the British government were almost invariably met with excuses, prevarication, anything rather than willingness to do what was suggested in the way of spending money or providing armed forces. At an early Cabinet meeting of the new government in March 1950, plans to deploy to the Middle East ran into the government's economising policies. Holland was irritated at Major-General Stewart's insistence on pressing the issue of the commitment. When the Chief of the Imperial General Staff, Field Marshall Sir William Slim, visited in June, the British had still not been notified that the Middle East commitment would be fulfilled. Slim's advocacy achieved what the New Zealand defence chiefs could not.[13]

Nor was the government keen on ANZAM. According to McGibbon, this in part derived from a fear of domination by Australia, even dislike of Australians, which was found in official circles in Wellington. McIntosh noted early in 1950 his belief that it was 'never in our interests to work in double harness with the Australians' and that New Zealand would be better to stick to its own line, even though in the long term New Zealand and Australia had to keep in line on defence issues. Behind the intra-Dominion prejudice one can sense here a different security evaluation. New Zealand did not, said

[11] N12/0816 (NZH); N12/0812 (EP, 18 May 1957), NA.
[12] Macdonald had to wait until National's return to office in 1961 to get the High Commissionership. He was in London until 1967.
[13] McGibbon, *Korean War*, v. 1, ch. 3.

Shanahan, 'regard the ANZAM region as a theatre vital to the successful outcome of a future war'.[14] It was 1943 all over again.

It was not just in the defence sphere that parsimony ruled. Although the government agreed to provide some assistance in kind in the first year of the Colombo Plan, 1950–51, it refused to contribute financially on the grounds of lack of resources—a stance with which the press for the most part agreed.[15] Holland, the great loyalist, even squabbled at length with the British as to who should pay for the expenses of the *Gothic*, the Royal Navy ship the Queen used on her visit to New Zealand. Holland's parsimony won an easy victory on this occasion.

Mark Pearson provides ample evidence of the parsimonious way the government handled its participation in SEATO. The establishment of a secretariat was opposed on cost grounds and then accepted only provided it was kept as modest as possible. And similarly, 'the expenditure implications of economic aid made political measures, such as publicity and rhetoric, the most attractive options'.[16]

Most of the government's supporters, indeed most New Zealanders, were probably quite comfortable with its lack of interest in external relations: 'New Zealand has been so preoccupied with internal development that she has not felt the need to develop a tradition of public interest in external affairs. And it is a just criticism of both the Labour and the National Governments that they have made little effort to guide the community by giving it effective leadership ....'[17] Did New Zealand need a spendthrift government, extravagant on behalf of the lazy at the expense of the hardworking and thrifty? If New Zealand did not need foreign relations, why should it spend money on them? If New Zealand interests were not directly engaged, why waste resources? The cost of foreign missions, of the contribution to the United Nations, of aid to other countries, were all bugbears at different times. Even more caution attached to the notion of involvement in anything military, particularly where it came close to a fighting war.

Yet the discontinuity and the sense of regression should not be exaggerated. The new government did not undo the specific changes made by Labour—the establishment of the Department, the passing of the Statute of Westminster, the representation at the United Nations and at various other international organisations. And it did find that interest impelled it, however reluctantly, to one major diplomatic initiative: the negotiation of what would become known as ANZUS.

14   McIntosh and Shanahan both quoted in McGibbon, *Korean War*, v. 1, ch. 3.
15   The government changed its mind in 1951: *EAR*, April 1951, pp. 2–3.
16   Mark Pearson, *Paper Tiger*. Wellington, 1988, pp. 45, 54 (quote).
17   W. F. Monk, 'New Zealand and the United States', p. 2.

Anzac dilemmas:[18] the Korean War and ANZUS, 1950–53

The belief that New Zealand needed protection was as powerful in the 1950s as in the 1930s and 1940s. As in the 1930s concern about security was linked to debate about immigration, over the 'threat' from Asia. Would the Chinese prove to be like the Japanese? Or was it the Indian 'takeover' in Fiji that was a portent of things to come? Letters to the editor in 1950 produced a flurry of comments defending the native New Zealand small business against Indian and Chinese fruiterers.[19] Much political and intellectual opinion was also preoccupied with Asian 'expansionism'. In discussions about an alliance with America, politicians recognised that 'as the long-term objective was an American guarantee against Asian expansionism from any quarter, [Australia and New Zealand] should seek to avoid close military and political association with Asian countries.'[20]

And the academic commentator, Winston Monk, noted in a paper in 1953,

> the danger of invasion, whether by direct assault or by infiltration, of people of different culture who cannot or will not be assimilated to the existing developing New Zealand way of life. The most obvious danger in this respect at present seems to result from the presence in the Near North of comparatively dense, fertile Asian populations, whose immediate prospects are poor but whose aspirations are mounting .... The direct threat from any does not seem immediate; if it came it would probably be as a result of a new resolution of major world forces. But such might result, for example, from the alignment, even for a short time, of any or all of these countries with Soviet Russia.[21]

The country that could be expected at best to stave off such an outcome, at least to protect New Zealand, was the United States. The 'richest prize', Doidge described it, would be a security guarantee from the United States. National was as committed, if not more committed, to this goal as its Labour predecessor. It was more successful in obtaining it. But it was not a straightforward matter. It is impossible to separate our discussion of the quest for security from two connected considerations—National's interest in avoiding undue military involvement in Asia, and its vulnerablity to charges of disloyalty when drawing closer to the United States and away from Britain. That was an ironic charge for a party for which loyalty was second nature. It provides us with an important insight into the meanings of independence in foreign policy in the 1950s.

[18] The term is drawn from an article of the same name by F. L. W. Wood in *International Affairs*, 29/ 2 (April 1953), pp. 184–92.
[19] And again in 1952: 744.00/7-252, RG59, USNA.
[20] A. D. McIntosh, 'Notes on Discussions held in the Department of External Affairs, 19 March 1951', Kay, *ANZUS Pact*, p. 663. The discussions were held with Alan Watt, the Australian Secretary of External Affairs: in response to the quoted comment, he said that a guarantee against Asian expansionism generally, which he agreed was the strongest reason for having the guarantee, 'could not be made public'.
[21] Monk, 'New Zealand and the United States', p. 3.

As an anti-Communist party, the more anti-Communist of the two main parties, National could not escape a certain warmth (present in a much more muted form in the Labour Party) towards the United States as the leader of the anti-Communist alliance. The elections in both Australia and New Zealand in 1949 followed by only a few weeks the Communist victory in China. Anti-Communism had been such a dominant theme in the election in New Zealand, albeit a domestic one, that it was almost inconceivable that the new government could turn around and straight away recognise the new regime— moreover Fraser advised against it. Also, although the two issues were not strictly comparable, National had made great play of its intention to close down the New Zealand mission in Moscow. The Attlee government was, however, keen to recognise the People's Republic of China. Part of this was realpolitik—Britain had major investments in China; it also had its position in Hong Kong to consider. But part of it was ideological. The British put pressure on the New Zealanders and the other Commonwealth governments to agree on recognition so that it could be announced collectively at the upcoming Commonwealth Foreign Ministers' conference at Colombo: in the event both Britain and India announced recognition before the conference on the grounds that agreement would not be reached there. New Zealand's refusal to recognise at this time linked it to the newly elected conservative government in Australia, to the United States and to anti-Communist regimes in Asia.[22]

Did the refusal amount to much more than party politicking? The outbreak of war in Korea at the end of June 1950 created more immediate pressures and opportunities. On the one hand the government saw that the war, and in particular the American commitment to Asia it was likely to elicit, might resolve its concerns about security. On the other hand, it put pressure on New Zealand to contribute and also raised fears of a larger, more destructive war.

The government took a decision to make a naval deployment into Korean waters very quickly. It was primarily the British approach that led New Zealand to decide fast on this and subsequently on a land-force contribution:[23] New Zealand was 'unprepared to undertake a military, and through it a political commitment which required it to act independently of a familiar and secure British-led Commonwealth'.[24] The land-force contribution was the harder—partly because it was seen as a diversion from more important strategic obligations, but also for less elevated reasons. Holland changed his mind several times and eagerly received news of United Nations victories in the hope that the force would not have to be sent.[25] When the *Washington Post*

22   See McGibbon, *Korean War*, v.1, ch. 3.
23   Ian McGibbon, 'New Zealand's Intervention in the Korean War, June-July 1950', *International History Review*, 11/1 (May 1989), pp. 278, 283–5.
24   Rob Eaddy, 'New Zealand and the Korean War: the First Year'. Univ. of Otago, M.A. thesis, 1983, p. 75.
25   McGibbon, *Korean War*, v.1, ch. 15.

in 1951 criticised New Zealand and other countries as 'laggards' in contributing to the struggle in Korea, both Doidge and Holland came to the rescue of New Zealand's reputation.[26]

During the early stages of the Korean War there was concern that the war for South Korea might re-ignite the Chinese civil war—with American connivance. Nations which were united on the issue in Korea would be divided.[27] The government was apprehensive about America's insulation of Taiwan in case a clash with China resulted, leading to the intervention of the Soviet Union through invocation of the 1950 Sino-Soviet Treaty.[28] Through the Korean winter of 1950–51 the United Nations forces suffered major reverses. In the United States, criticism of the Truman Administration's foreign policy reached new crescendos, with isolationist voices a part of the chorus. At the same time there was talk of using the atomic bomb against the Chinese armies that had intervened in the war on the side of the North Koreans—maybe even bombing China itself. Attlee flew to Washington to discourage the Americans from this latter course, with the support of all New Zealand editorial and official opinion. Similarly in the new year, there was a great deal of scepticism in New Zealand about America's determination to have China branded in the United Nations as an aggressor and the fear that this would lead to a wider war. Holland, while believing the Americans had to be supported in their call to have China declared an aggressor, was apprehensive: 'I cannot estimate what will be the course of events which this resolution will set in train, [but] I think we will have to face up to the fact that this action may very well precipitate a major war.'[29]

In Wellington an urgent meeting of Cabinet was called to consider the American resolution. Cabinet supported Holland but felt the same degree of apprehension, Britain's initial reluctance to support it adding to their discomfort. At the United Nations the British succeeded in modifying the resolution so that members would not be obliged to impose sanctions if the resolution was passed. New Zealand's remaining reserve was met and it voted for the resolution in full.[30] Voluminous comment in the editorial and letters columns of the papers suggested that on balance opinion was overwhelmingly opposed to sanctions against China, that a blockade and bombardment would do more harm than good.[31] American criticism of Britain for giving priority to

---

[26] McGibbon, *Korean War*, v.1, ch. 20. The editor of the *New Zealand Herald*, Leslie Munro, later appointed Ambassador to the United Nations, had visited the *Washington Post* a few days before the editorial appeared.

[27] McGibbon, *Korean War*, v.1, ch. 10.

[28] Ibid.

[29] Holland to Doidge, 18 Jan. 1951, EA153/3/4, NA.

[30] McGibbon, *Korean War*, v.1, ch. 16.

[31] Although the National government clearly had reservations about following the Americans' China policy, they did not feel they could do much about it. Labour believed it could, it was much more critical of American policy, and sensing an issue to which the public was not unreceptive, committed itself to recognition in the post Korean War era. See, for instance, 744.00/2-251, 2-1651, 2-2051, RG59, USNA.

its relationship with India and its economic ties with Malaya and Hong Kong, i.e. what the Americans saw as a British preparedness to appease China, also influenced New Zealanders against the United States. The issue surfaced during the Brooklyn by-election campaign: 'the very fact that [the issue of New Zealand relations with the United States] should be introduced into [an] election campaign is symptomatic, for as recently as 1949 there seemed to be no foreign policy issues.'[32] Carl Berendsen, however, New Zealand's representative at the United Nations and a strong supporter of the Americans, nonetheless made a speech in which he much more vigorously praised the United States and condemned the Chinese than did any other Commonwealth representative save the Australian.[33]

The sanctions issue between Britain and the United States was resolved, much to New Zealand's relief. But the turmoil in American foreign policy in the northern winter of 1950–51 was double-edged. American belligerence was intimidating. But an American retreat into isolationism was unwelcome too. Fear of this seems to have been at the bottom of Holland's pro-American statements on his overseas trip at the beginning of 1951 and explains his vigorous defence of the United States both in public and private when he was in London for the Commonwealth Prime Ministers' Conference. The tendency, he wrote to Doidge, on the part of the UK, 'to criticise and oppose the United States especially publicly was, in the situation we are all now facing, unwise and for the Conference to adopt a similar line would be equally so and untimely'.[34] Holland was reported in London as saying that the Commonwealth should stand behind the United States, through thick or thin, right or wrong. Labour and the left had a field day, claiming National was pro-American and anti-British: 'For quite a while now the National Party has shown a tendency to be touchy about America, regarding criticism of the United States as almost an act of disloyalty. No doubt this derived in the first place from the feeling that the capitalists of the world must hold together; and while Britain was going socialist, in America at least private enterprise was firmly entrenched.'[35]

After the release of the text of the tripartite security treaty (ANZUS) in July 1951 there was so much comment in the press about the implications for New Zealand's obligations to Britain that Holland issued a statement denying that New Zealand was moving away from Britain. He agreed that New Zealand was 'moving towards closer solidarity with the the United States but argued that this was not incompatible with devotion to the mother country'.[36] He and

---

[32]   744.00/2-1651, RG59, USNA. The by-election was to fill the seat vacant because of Fraser's death.
[33]   Berendsen memoir, v.3, Berendsen Papers, VUW.
[34]   McGibbon, *Korean War*, v.1, ch. 16.
[35]   Ormond Wilson, 'ANZUS and Us', *Here and Now*, Dec. 1952, p. 16.
[36]   744.00/7-2051, RG59, USNA.

Doidge rejected the argument presented by Willis Airey, Associate Professor of History at Auckland University, that both peace treaty and security pact 'further lessen the chances of Great Britain playing an independent and healthy role in the world, that the Commonwealth is being disrupted through disregard of the Asiatic dominions and that New Zealand is being irrevocably committed to a watertight division of the world into two hostile camps.'[37]

In fact the negotiations with the Americans over the security treaty demonstrated the precisely delimited interest that a conservative New Zealand government had in an alliance with the United States, Berendsen's lobbying notwithstanding. In the face of the difficulties in Korea late in 1950, the American military accepted the State Department view that the United States urgently needed both a peace treaty with Japan and a pact with Pacific countries, provided in the latter case that the United States was not committed to the defence of British territories in Asia, in particular Hong Kong.[38] Doidge told Dulles, the American negotiator, that a presidential declaration, preferably with Congressional approval, would have been ideal for New Zealand. It was unlikely that the Americans would have worn this—it had too much the feel of something for nothing. But the Australians were not keen either—it was for them not enough of a commitment from the United States. Doidge and Holland seem to have recognised that New Zealand might become committed with a conventional alliance to 'join in the defence of other parties should they be attacked'.[39] In the face of British pressure the Americans accepted the exclusion of both Japan and the Philippines from the alliance. With American bases in both countries the practical significance of this was small: in answer to a question in April, Dulles explained in a cable to Doidge that he had been 'asked whether the pact would come into play if US troops in Japan were attacked. I replied extemporaneously "It would mean that if there were an attack upon the US forces that were stationed in Japan, Okinawa or the Philippines that that would be deemed to be an attack on the US in the Pacific for purposes of that pact, assuming that is made clear in the final drafting." '[40] Nonetheless the exclusion of the Asians was important in emphasising to New Zealand opinion that the arrangement was a backup to Commonwealth defence, not a new association.

For Doidge and Holland and others in the Cabinet, the value of the security treaty was not so New Zealand could fight in a Pacific war, but precisely because it might not. The Second World War pattern was envisaged—New Zealand would be denuded, its forces fighting with the British in the Middle

---

37 Quoted in 744.00/8-351, RG59, USNA; see also Airey in *Here and Now*, May 1951, pp. 15-17.
38 *Foreign Relations of the United States*, 1950, v.6, *East Asia and the Pacific*. Washington, 1976, pp. 1359-60, 1363-7; 1951, v.6, *East Asia and the Pacific*. Washington, 1977, pp. 132-7.
39 Kay, *ANZUS Pact*, p. 574, Holland (in Washington) to Doidge, 7 Feb. 1951.
40 Kay, *ANZUS Pact*, p. 718.

East, and the Americans, as in 1942, would make up the difference. Nor was this an abstract issue: British difficulties in 1951 with Egypt and Iran, particularly the latter, took the Commonwealth to the brink of war. And it was always assumed that behind any such difficulties lay the Soviet Union.[41]

The British Labour government accepted its exclusion from the new alliance in public while being disappointed in private, but Churchill, in Opposition, and as soon as he became Prime Minister, in October 1951, raised it with Truman, and also both Holland and Menzies.[42] Holland and his government's situation was made the more invidious by the fact that the Labour Party was making hay with the issue. When Webb came back from the first meeting of the ANZUS Council, the communiqué of which declared that there would be no change in the membership of the alliance, there was an uproar in New Zealand.[43] Churchill raised the issue with Menzies and Holland in London at the end of the year: Holland told Cabinet that he had pointed out to Churchill that New Zealand had not complained when Canada and Britain had joined NATO and that in 1950 the British Chiefs of Staff had made it quite clear that in the event of war, Britain could not defend New Zealand.[44] It was a response which stripped some of the sugar coating from the relationship, while in public Holland could claim that the problem had been resolved.

The government supported the pact because of the security guarantee, but it was made most uncomfortable by any recurrence of friction between Britain and the United States over policy in Asia. When truce talks stalled in Korea early in 1952, there were renewed fears of American belligerence and American attacks on British trade with China continued to exercise the press.[45] In articles in *Landfall* in March and June 1952 James Bertram asked whether it had been wise to follow American rather than British policy in Asia. The new Republican administration's decision to withdraw American patrols from the Taiwan Straits early in 1953, 'the unleashing of Chiang', attracted little support. After the ceasefire in mid 1953 Clifton Webb, the Minister of External Affairs, argued for the early admission of China to the United Nations. Holland knocked Webb back but characteristically blundered badly in describing the Korean War in public as 'costly, futile and pointless'.[46] Yet it was probably a sentiment that many in New Zealand shared. The Holland

41   *FRUS*, 1951, v.6, p. 220 (Dulles, 25 June 1951).
42   And again after the ANZUS meeting in 1953. But did not do anything about it in government: when Nash was in London at the end of 1959 he was asked whether there had been any discussion of Britain joining ANZUS: Nash replied that it was not discussed, but that nothing could be done in ANZUS which the United Kingdom did not know about: *New Zealand News*, 17 Nov. 1959, N1733/0378, NA.
43   Press clippings EA111/3/1, NA; 744.00, RG59, USNA.
44   Meeting held 23 Dec. 1952, CM (53)38, NA.
45   744.00/2-1552; 744.00/2152, RG59, USNA.
46   *NZPD*, 299, p. 408 (12 Aug. 1953): reference made by Nash to Holland's comment.

government found itself in trouble again when Webb returned from the second ANZUS Council meeting with no decision on China. The left-wing M.P. Clyde Carr asked whether the 'changed attitude' of the Minister of External Affairs was dictated by the Prime Minister's declared policy of following America 'right or wrong'. Instead of a written answer, Holland intervened at once to deny that the United States had any control over New Zealand or that he had ever given such a pledge. The rapidity of Holland's reply reflected not Carr's political influence but a realisation of how disturbing New Zealand public opinion found the exclusion of Britain from ANZUS. Most of the daily press was critical of the failure of the ANZUS Council to address the issue, the *Dominion* said the country would accept the Prime Minister's assurance with relief, since 'many responsible people' were disturbed as to where some phases of American post-war foreign policy were leading.[47] Renewed American criticism of what the virulently anti-Communist Senator Joseph McCarthy called Britain's 'blood trade' with China also angered much New Zealand opinion.[48]

The ANZUS treaty, the first New Zealand signed with a foreign power, without the United Kingdom, has been seen by some commentators as a mark of New Zealand's independent status.[49] It was ironic but revealing that a government traditionally suspicious of 'independence' was responsible for taking New Zealand into the agreement. It was a demonstration of the power of interest, not of ideology: National's attachment to the United States, whatever its critics might have said, remained very circumscribed.

In one sense New Zealand was more independent, but in other ways less: 'In her nineteenth century colonial status, New Zealand enjoyed greater freedom than she possesses today as a free nation of the Commonwealth.... for contemporary power purposes the Commonwealth is not a great power .... Its members, not excluding Britain herself, are obliged to make terms individually with the Two-Power reality.'[50] Monk went on to say that 'American economic dictation' would be greatly felt,

a fact sufficiently demonstrated by our resentment at recent American trade restrictions which affect us, materially, only slightly. Our reaction to American political attitudes, as, for example, in the occupation of Japan, the war in Korea, the Japanese Peace Treaty, indicates how sensitive we are to our changed status, our dependence on America instead of Britain for the maintenance of our physical security. After a similar fashion we are inclined to resent American trade policy, financial power and social restraints (cf the McCarran legislation and negro persecution) to an extent we rarely felt occasion to resent British policies.[51]

47 744.00/9-3053, RG59, USNA.
48 744.00/8-553, RG59, USNA.
49 '... the ANZUS Treaty was at once an unmistakable expression of independence and a decisive act of commitment'. Bryce Harland, 'New Zealand, the United States and Asia: The Background to the ANZUS Treaty', in Peter Munz, ed., *The Feel of Truth*, Wellington, 1969, p. 194.
50 Monk, 'New Zealand Faces North', p. 224.
51 Monk, 'New Zealand and the United States', p. 4.

The United States did not fit neatly into New Zealand's world, or into the world in which New Zealand wished to find a place. The prospect of the United States becoming more important and Britain less so in New Zealand's affairs was not one that either public opinion or policymakers welcomed.

Anzac solutions: Indochina, SEATO and the thaw

The pattern of diplomacy over the Indochina crisis in 1954 and the organis-ation of an anti-Communist alliance in Southeast Asia was very similar to that over Korea. The government again found itself caught between the wish for security tempered by caution about involvement and the wish to gain an American commitment but not do so in a way that angered the British. But the outcomes were different. The United States did not become directly involved in the war in Indochina; Britain and the United States reached agreement on a Southeast Asian alliance; and as a backdrop to these developments, relations between the Soviet Union and the West improved markedly.

When the American Secretary of State, John Foster Dulles, first made his call (at the end of March 1954) for 'united action' in French Indochina, to avert the possibility of a French defeat and a Vietnamese Communist victory, the New Zealand response was cautious. Webb told American Ambassador Scotten on 2 April that New Zealanders would be reluctant to take part in a military enterprise, given their other commitments and the fact that they would have to rely on volunteers. It was classic diplomatic evasion. New Zealand was prepared to act if the British did, but the British too were fearful of what the Americans might do: Makins, the British Ambassador in Washington, told Munro that the US possession of the hydrogen bomb, recently tested, did not make matters easier. There were emergency ANZUS meetings at both the Geneva conference on Indochina and Korea and in Washington: the full implications of being an ally of the United States began to be apparent. Webb said on one occasion, after leaving talks with Dulles in Washington in the middle of May, that he 'could not conceive of a satisfactory alliance being made [in respect of Southeast Asia] that would not include Britain'. Some American press comment saw this as indicative of a divergence from Dulles. Webb was annoyed at the journalists but they had seized on an important difference in emphasis between the two governments. There was still more American pressure: at an informal ANZUS meeting with the two Ambassadors in Washington in early June, Dulles sought renewed commit-ments to participation in resisting 'overt unprovoked military action in the Western Pacific or South East Asia'. New Zealand was unhappy, and was perhaps fortunate that the Americans did not keep up this line.[52]

52   Ian Dowman, 'N.Z., the U.S. and "United Action": A Study of NZ–US Relations April-June 1954', VUW History Dept research paper, 1985, *passim*. Some editors commented privately to the American Embassy that the government was 'ahead' of public opinion on participation in Southeast Asia. It was probably ahead of itself: under the circumstances its relief must have been all the greater. 744.00(W)/7–254, RG59, USNA.

Shortly after this a settlement was reached at Geneva which ended French rule in North Vietnam, but which also allowed for a non-Communist regime to continue in the south. Direct intervention was now ruled out and it was possible for Britain and the United States to move forward jointly with the organisation of collective defence in the region. Politicians on the left continued to question National's loyalist credentials. The refusal of the Americans to countenance trade with China was instanced to their disadvantage. Labour M.P. John Mathison claimed National supported the American ban on British trade with China.[53]

In October 1954 Webb attended the Manila conference which saw the signing of the Manila Treaty binding Britain, France and the United States to a (qualified, particularly in the case of the United States) commitment to resist aggression in Southeast Asia (SEATO). New Zealand was unhappy about the pact's specifying 'communist aggression', wanting vaguer language which might leave the organisation freer to respond to other threats and at the conference itself Webb momentarily disrupted proceedings when he said that if Dulles's proposed reservation to the treaty were accepted, other parties would bear a heavier burden than the United States.[54] In the end all the countries present at Manila—the United States, Britain, France, New Zealand and Australia, Pakistan, Thailand and the Philippines—signed; the American caveat remained. But New Zealand was pleased that Britain and the United States were at last both within the same organisation. Charges of 'disloyalty' were heard less frequently from Labour after October 1954. Some commentators expected ANZUS to be superseded by SEATO, although ministers themselves, expressing their own perception of New Zealand interests, were opposed.

Asia was calmer after 1954. Nonetheless, early in 1955 New Zealand became particularly involved in a crisis over Chinese offshore islands because it was on the Security Council at the time.[55] The New Zealand representative sought to place the issue on the Security Council agenda including an invitation to a representative of mainland China—in effect acting as a proxy for the United States. New Zealand's Ambassador, Leslie Munro was, like his predecessor Carl Berendsen, an enthusiastic supporter of the United States. For the government, the advantage of the UN initiative was that it took the pressure off the possibility of the United States invoking the ANZUS alliance. The People's Republic declined the invitation, whilst Nationalist China declared the New Zealand delegate 'had tried to lead the Security Council out

---

53 Adjournment debate, *NZPD*, 311, pp. 11–85 (12–13 June 1957).
54 Roger Dingman, 'John Foster Dulles and the Creation of the Southeast Asia Treaty Organisation in 1954', *International History Review*, 11/3 (Aug. 1989), pp. 467–8, 472–3.
55 The islands, right against the Chinese mainland, were still held by the Nationalist forces, based in Taiwan.

of the hard, world of facts into the soft atmosphere of Alice in Wonderland'.[56]
The fighting abated without any further international initiative.

In the middle of 1955 Duncan Rae, a National backbencher, argued for establishing relations with China, and was supported by the *Dominion*. While Holland rejected the idea, he did not rule it out in the near future and he made it clear that there was only one principal reason holding up recognition and/or admission of China, 'which I think all Members are aware of'—that was, of course, American policy.[57] In 1956 attention was drawn to China when a group of academics and others visited the country. Their impressions and activities were extensively reported in the New Zealand press. *Here and Now* was certain that Holland advocated trade liberalisation with China at the 1956 Prime Ministers' Conference: the Americans did allow some relaxation later in 1957.[58]

A readiness to contemplate the normalisation of relations with Communist China was matched in 1955-56 by a responsiveness to the post-Stalin thaw in both Soviet domestic politics and in Soviet-Western relations. New Zealand opinion was inveterately optimistic about opportunities for détente. While anti-Communism had deep roots in domestic political life, it was a much more shallow plant in respect of international relations. This was partly because it was no longer Britain, but the United States, that was the leading antagonist of the Soviet Union. This meant that even conservative New Zealanders felt at some distance from the conflict. As early as the end of the Korean War Holland was looking approvingly on the prospects for an amelioration of international relations in the wake of Stalin's death.[59] Despite its anti-Communist rhetoric the government ruled out 'McCarthyism' in New Zealand: 'we have not yet reached the position in this country—and I hope we never will, when we say that Communists should be hounded out of office.' An anti-Communist diatribe by Berendsen, back in New Zealand from Washington on his retirement, was not particularly well received.[60] When Holyoake visited Moscow in 1955, the visit was approved of on political as well as commercial grounds.[61] The visit by the Soviet leaders Bulganin and Krushchev to London in April 1956 was also welcomed, not just because of the evidence of the thaw, but also because it seemed to emphasise a certain recovery in Britain's international standing after the postwar years of

---

[56]   Ms Papers 1624/132, ATL; 611. 44/5-2455, RG59, USNA; *EAR*, Jan-Feb. 1955, pp. 7-11, 27-34, 45-46.
[57]   *NZPD*, 305, p. 16 (24 March 1955); *Dominion*, 18 June 1955; 744.00/7555, RG59, USNA.
[58]   N1749/0004, NA.
[59]   *NZPD*, 299, p. 71 (15 April 1953), pp. 401-2, 405-6 (12 Aug. 1953).
[60]   Holland quoted on 744.00/9-1952, RG59, USNA; response to Berendsen noted in 9-3053, RG59, USNA; for general press attitudes to McCarthyism, see 744.00/10-1752, 8-1953, RG59, USNA.
[61]   See Roman Gershenfeld, 'The Holyoake and Nash Visits to the USSR', VUW History Dept Honours essay, 1989. See also Ms Papers 1814. 51/6, ATL.

economic travail and stringency and in its capacity therefore to introduce more balance into international relations.[62] In New Zealand, as in most European countries, there was not the boundless commitment to an ideological and geopolitical contest with Communism and the Soviet Union that animated political life and foreign policymaking in the United States. New Zealanders wished to extend the Commonwealth model of state-to-state relations with which they were familiar to international relations generally.

Labour and dissent

While National had to face *intermittent* charges of disloyalty, Labour had the more major task. The Cold War dominated the 1950s as it had the later 1940s. Labour in opposition did not abandon anti-Communism—quite the contrary. Electoral defeat seems to have deepened the shadow cast by the Cold War and increased the fear of being labelled 'soft on Communism'. However convincing Labour's anti-Communist credentials might be, they could always be outbid by National. Opposition, far from radicalising the party, seems almost to have had the opposite effect: 'despite the mild protests from the Labour Party, the fear of being dubbed pro-Russian or Communist seems to have prevented them from expressing the increasing sense of uneasiness which [the National party pro-American policy] is causing'.[63] Through 1950, its first year in opposition, Labour, a depleted minority in Parliament, was led by a sick and aged Peter Fraser. His anti-Communism and support for the Western alliance against the Soviet Union was so pronounced in 1948–49 that it was not at all surprising that he vigorously supported the United Nations intervention in Korea.

The bitter and long-drawn-out dispute between the Waterside Workers' Union and the government from February to July 1951 underlined the choice that Labour had made. The ports closed and the government brought the army in before establishing new port unions, from which members of the deregistered union were excluded. The government accused the watersiders of being part of a Communist conspiracy and, in its more rhetorical moments, of undermining the United Nations effort in Korea. The trade union movement itself was split—some unions supported the watersiders but the FOL, under the influence of F. P. Walsh, was opposed to them. Deep-seated and bitter hatreds were involved here between Walsh and the WWU leadership. Nash, the new leader of the Labour Party, was not as dogmatically anti-Communist as Fraser, nor was he close to Walsh—quite the contrary. But arbitration, to which the WWU was hostile, was dear to Nash and he had little affection for the WWU leadership either—nor they for him. So at its 1951 conference Labour passed a strong resolution against Communism. Nonethe-

---

62 Ms Papers 1624/133, ATL.
63 Ormond Wilson, *Here and Now*, March 1953, p. 7.

less, Nash did not completely endorse the government's methods of dealing with the watersiders, and in this he had the support of much of the Labour Party. It was all too easy therefore for National to use Communism as a weapon against Labour in the 1951 campaign, despite the latter's professed anti-Communism, and to charge Nash, using an unkind but accurate turn of phrase, with being 'neither for nor against'.[64] 'While the government was unable to reveal any direct link between the Kremlin and the militant unions', one American diplomat reported, 'it did manage to convince many people that the left-wing labour elements in the country were, consciously or unconsciously, serving the interests of Moscow. It was easily demonstrable that the tying up of the country by crippling strikes had crippled New Zealand's capacity to ship food to Britain and train troops for Korea and Commonwealth defence.'[65]

Nash and his senior colleagues did endorse the Japanese peace treaty and the ANZUS security treaty, although hardly as enthusiastically as National. In debate in Parliament when the two treaties were introduced for ratification, Nash said that there was no better policy than to support the treaties and argued that the Pacific security treaty did not have much bite—and presumably could not therefore be used by the Americans to force New Zealand into unwelcome conflicts. Others were more cautious, Nordmeyer saying a big risk was being taken with Japan, Mathison contending that the security treaty was a 'great mistake'.[66]

Tensions eased after the 1951 election. However, this did not mean that anti-Communism had faded: it remained deeply entrenched across the political spectrum, as the outcome of the waterfront dispute and the election result had both confirmed. While the government resisted the idea of purging Communists from the public service, it did continue, through the Public Service Commission, the policy of transferring known Communists and fellow travellers from sensitive departments such as External Affairs, Defence and the Department of Scientific and Industrial Research: but it was a policy initiated under Fraser.[67]

The drama of the Petrov spy affair in Australia in May 1954 underlined for much of public opinion the legitimacy of these measures and Nash made little comment on it.[68] The Labour Party conference, held that same month, did resolve by a 3:1 majority to abolish the Special Branch (the Security Intelligence Service not having been established), but Walsh reminded the delegates

---

[64] Nash himself had said, 'We are neither for the watersiders nor against them ....', Michael Bassett, *Confrontation '51*. Wellington, 1972, pp. 174–5, quoting *EP*, 14 May 1951.
[65] 744.00/9–551, RG59, USNA.
[66] 744.00/9–1351; 9–751, RG59, USNA.
[67] Alan Henderson, *The Quest for Efficiency: The Origins of the State Services Commission*. Wellington, 1990, p. 206; 744.00/9–1952, 7–2354, RG59, USNA.
[68] Petrov, a Soviet Embassy official in Canberra, successfully sought asylum in Australia at the end of his tour, defeating strenuous efforts by the Soviet authorities to repatriate him.

that Labour had established the Special Branch and subsequently the motion was rescinded.[69]

In the foreign affairs debate in July 1954 there was a great deal of criticism by Labour speakers of both the Americans and the French: of the former's stance on the admission of China to the United Nations; of Syngman Rhee, the Americans' South Korean client; of the continued exclusion of Britain from ANZUS. Nash praised Ho Chi Minh, the leader of the Vietnamese Communists, and castigated the French puppet Bao Dai.[70] But Labour agreed to SEATO. This approval was sharply criticised by left-wing observers: 'The Southeast Asia Collective Defence Treaty ... may well prove to be a bad bargain .... The appeal of the Manila Pact is clearly to those who believe that the present turmoil in the Far East is of Communist origin, and that all things Communist are evil: the Pact is seen as an attempt to prevent the further spread of Communist influence in Southeast Asia.'[71] Similarly when the pact was ratified, 'Scrutineer' in *Here and Now* commented that 'the fact is that neither the whole New Zealand Army, nor the Australian Army, nor the armed forces of all the signatory powers put together, can protect a people that does not wish protection. Neither can they defeat a continent almost unanimously hostile to such protection ....'[72] 'Scrutineer' also recorded the editorial opposition to SEATO in the press in both India and Indonesia. But for Nash the fact that SEATO involved the British, and might also lend itself to stabilising independent Asia and thereby avoiding Western intervention, were important considerations.

National took decisions to commit forces to Malaya in support of the British in 1955 and again in 1957. A decision to send troops, even volunteers, overseas in peacetime tapped traditions of opposition to conscription, the First World War, the debate in 1939–40, the 1949 referendum. The Malayan Labour Party opposed the sending of Australian and New Zealand troops on the grounds they might be used to help prolong colonial rule. Nash learnt that David Marshall, the leader of the Singapore Labour Party, was unhappy with the plan too.[73] The Australian Labor Party opposed the Australian commitment. Wood noted that 'the suggestion that New Zealand should help garrison Singapore or other Asian strongholds had been made repeatedly in the past and firmly rejected, partly on the general ground that troops stationed in Malaya, for instance, might be used for internal as well as external security and might in fact, be a police force as well as a strategic one.'[74]

But it was after all a Labour government which had agreed to some military

---

[69]   744.00/5–2754, RG59, USNA.
[70]   744.21/7–754, RG59, USNA.
[71]   *Here and Now*, Oct. 1954, p. 3.
[72]   *Here and Now*, Feb.-March 1955, pp. 9–10.
[73]   Michael Green, 'New Zealand and the Malayan Emergency', VUW History Dept research paper, 1969, p. 18.
[74]   F. L. W. Wood, 'NZ and Southeast Asia', *Far Eastern Survey*, Feb. 1956, p. 25.

involvement in Malaya in August 1949. Moreover, Nash thought Labour would lose votes if its sole policy was one of opposition.[75] Nash convinced the Labour Party conference in May 1955 that 'no objection [could] logically be raised against our assisting Britain to remove the communist terrorist activity which is the biggest stumbling block to Malaya's progress to self-government and development.' The qualification was that Malaya be given self-government as soon as possible and that the wealth of the area be used to improve the standard of living of its population. In the aftermath of decision and conference Nash drafted a statement which reconciled the decision with Labour principles: terrorism in Malaya, it stated, was not a legitimate expression of desire for self-determination. Predictably, that is, Labour chose to interpret the commitment in terms of a reformist approach to Western involvement in Asia rather than as an act of old-fashioned imperialism.[76]

Wood reckoned that it could be broadly postulated that the commitments entered into in Asia by 1956 were 'quietly accepted and endorsed' by the community: 'Such judgements are necessarily speculative, but it is notable that there has been no significant current of criticism directed against current trends comparable to that voiced by prominent Labour men in the 1930s.'[77]

The 'ban the bomb' movement voiced a more vigorous dissent. In the frozen ideological landscape of Cold War international relations, the anti-nuclear movement became one of the few areas of change, of questioning. In New Zealand this meant that it reinforced the characteristic pattern of independence in foreign policy rather than undermined it. It was not a revolutionary movement, it stressed it was not anti-Communist. It was a classic instance of loyal opposition and met with favourable response from some who could not in any way be described as of the left.

Concern about nuclear weapons was first evident during the Korean War. During the Brooklyn by-election, at the height of tension between the United States and China, canvassers for the international Stockholm petition seeking an end to all nuclear weapons collected signatures from as many as 90 per cent of the houses in some streets.[78]

The advent of the hydrogen bomb, so much more powerful than the atomic bomb, revived anxieties. American hydrogen bomb testing in 1954, when a Japanese fishing vessel was exposed to radiation, and in 1956 both aroused some concern in New Zealand, but public opinion was much more vocal in 1957 and thereafter. Late in 1956 the Holland government announced it

---

[75]   D. J. McCraw, 'Objectives and Priorities in New Zealand's Foreign Policy in Asia 1949-75: A Study of the Issue of the Recognition of the People's Republic of China and of Security Policies in South-East Asia', Univ. of Otago, Ph. D. thesis, 1978, pp. 351–2; Green, p. 18.

[76]   McCraw, 'NZ Foreign Policy in Asia', p. 355.

[77]   Wood, 'New Zealand and Southeast Asia', p. 26.

[78]   744.00/2-2051, RG59, USNA. For peace movement activity during the Korean War, see Glenn Swafford, 'The Opposition to New Zealand's Involvement in the Korean War', VUW Hist. Dept. research paper, 1982.

would support the British in monitoring tests they would conduct on Christmas Island in 1957 by deploying two New Zealand vessels, *Pukaki* and *Rotoiti*, in waters adjacent to the test site. The participation of the RNZN vessels meant that New Zealand itself was now taking part in the tests; such participation, said an Auckland University physicist, called for 'solemn reflection on the part of every thinking New Zealander'. Many other New Zealanders agreed, including well-known names from the world of letters such as James K. Baxter and Allen Curnow. One couple wrote to the Prime Minister to ask whether it had been made clear to the personnel of the New Zealand frigates that they would jeopardise the health and well-being of any future children by reason of their proximity to the test location.[79] In talking later in the year about the inception of the organised movement against nuclear weapons, Robert Chapman noted that when four student clubs called a meeting about the issue, 'although it was at short notice in an inconvenient room and was competing against other meetings, it drew one of the largest student attendances in years. The "apathetic" younger generation at least demonstrated strong feeling on this.' A short time later a meeting was held in Auckland to which Chapman claimed 1600 people came.[80]

Many people from different walks of life opposed testing. There was protest from the expected sources, such as the FOL and peace groups which had links with the Communist Party, but also from less predictable quarters. An organisation called the New Zealand Federation of Business and Women's Clubs sought an end to testing and the eventual prohibition of nuclear weapons. The International Relations Committee of the Presbyterian Church, convened by J. D. Salmond, sought a ten-year moratorium. The Helensville Borough Council wanted the tests to cease until assurances could be given that there would be no climatic changes. A long petition from Kaikohe, submitted in both English and Maori, called for the promotion of peaceful means for the settlement of all international disputes.[81]

The volume of protest did not fade away as the 1957 test date approached, nor was the government's position helped by Britain's failure to inform New Zealand of when exactly the first explosion was to take place. In his address, broadcast on 23 May, Holland alluded to the volume of correspondence, including what he described as numbers of letters from Communists and Communist-influenced organisations. He defended the holding of the tests essentially in Cold War terms: 'the course being followed by Britain is the right course, and we must continue to support her. Her aim is the security of the Commonwealth and the Free World and our safety lies in that security.' He contended that 'neither ship was affected in the slightest and they have received the thanks of the Task Force Commander for the part they played'.

79 EA121/5/3, NA.
80 *Here and Now*, 62 (Nov. 1957), p. 16.
81 EA121/5/3, NA.

Pukaki had been at about 80 kilometres from the test site, *Rotoiti* about 320 kilometres: *Pukaki* had a 'good view and was much impressed'.[82]

National's response was predictable: it remained to be seen how Labour would handle the issue.

Commonwealth, common ground

Willis Airey argued in 1954 that 'Under the conditions that have developed since the Second World War, in New Zealand there has been a drawing together of the formerly opposed strands of British imperialist superiority, continued in the National Party, and the rather naive humanitarian internationalism introduced by the Labour Party in 1935.'[83] The change of government in 1949, the first since 1935, raised in a very immediate way the issue of continuity in foreign policy. But Airey was right: the record of the 1950s underlined the commmon ground, rather than the divisions, between the two main parties and therefore the continuity in foreign policy from before 1949.

It was a shared, or at least overlapping, conception of the Commonwealth and beyond it, the United Nations, that was at the core of the consensus. For National, the Commonwealth meant the exercise of British influence, a barrier to Communism and radical nationalism in what had once been the Empire. To Labour it also meant the exercise of British influence, the influence of enlightened policies of independence, development and multi-racialism. Either way the Commonwealth was a 'good thing':

> Except in an emergency it would be hard to persuade [New Zealanders] that association with the United States offers a satisfactory moral alternative to the United Nations on which they so readily placed their hopes as an instrument of peaceful—and to them comfortable—change. There remains a stronger belief in the utopian virtue of the Commonwealth as an instrument of world peace, as a practising world-wide community of 'united nations' which might in time give a lead to the world.[84]

A British writer gave a related but revealingly different emphasis, in noting that he had found 'many New Zealanders believing that the Commonwealth could still provide an answer to most of their problems'.[85]

For that reason, if no other, Indian policy did cause some anguish during the Korean War. There was a great deal of criticism in the New Zealand press when it became clear that India would not ally itself with other Common-wealth countries. The *Evening Post*, for instance, saw Nehru as naive: 'The

82   *EAR*, May 1957, pp. 19–20.
83   In 'Siegfried after 50 years', *Political Science*, 6/2 (Sept. 1954), p. 49.
84   Monk, 'New Zealand and the United States', p. 8.
85   Don Taylor, 'A World of Their Own', *Listener* (UK), 5 April 1956, p. 337.

Kremlin, the Indian Government seems to believe, will reciprocate this goodwill and permit the quasi-socialist India under the Congress party majority to live in peace in a Communist-dominated Asia.'[86] And Nehru was criticised again a year later for keeping India away from the American-sponsored Japanese peace treaty.[87] In an article in *Landfall* in March 1951 Philip Matthews pointed to the difference between the New Zealand and Asian perspectives on the relationship between Communism and nationalism.[88]

But there were more expansive attitudes as well. The Commonwealth, by taking on as full members India, Pakistan and Ceylon, and later in the decade Malaya and Ghana (its first black African member), had also demonstrated its progressive and pluralist character, while remaining a reference point for more conservative attitudes:

> one of the reasons for our enthusiasm about the Commonwealth is the belief that by the time a course of policy has been evolved which is acceptable to the diverse members of the Commonwealth, this course is likely to be well-balanced and therefore likely to find wide acceptance outside the Commonwealth. The Commonwealth is of great assistance to New Zealand in reconciling a constant problem of its foreign policy, namely, to follow a policy towards Asia which will be broadly acceptable to those countries whose security is involved in Asia, including the United States, ... and to the people of Asia, whose well-being and security can, in the last resort, only be ensured if they approve the measures being taken and freely cooperate in them.[89]

On the colonial or ex-colonial, as on the Communist world, New Zealand opinion enjoyed a consensus that stretched from conservative to more liberal ends of the spectrum. South Africa was an example. On the one hand, conservatives associated apartheid with the anti-British attitudes of the Afrikaner Nationalist government of D. F. Malan. The *New Zealand Herald* made a characteristic comment in favourably comparing the advantages of 'full cooperation between Dutch and English and a very gradually liberalised treatment of the African majority' to Malan's dream of a 'Utopia in which a million or more British will accept Afrikaner doctrine in toto and the non-European will be kept permanently in his proper station'.[90] Opposition to apartheid was also linked to New Zealand's own race relations, regarded by most Pakeha as 'good':

[86] 11 July 1950, quoted in Sara Knox, 'Something is happening in Asia', VUW History Dept. honours essay, 1989. See also *EP*, 22 Aug. 1950, 'Can Nehru compromise with Communism?'
[87] 744.00/9-751, RG59, USNA.
[88] *Landfall*, 5/1 (March 1951), p. 63, 'Lucknow in Retrospect' (Report on the most recent conference of the Institute of Pacific Relations).
[89] 'New Zealand Foreign Policy', *EAR*, July 1955, p. 55.
[90] Quoted in 944.61/8-2252, see also 2-2952, RG59, USNA.

New Zealand has had a fortunate experience of race relations and it is this experience, extending over more than a century, which colours our thinking: it puts us out of sympathy with policies such as apartheid and, indeed makes such a policy almost incomprehensible to us, so far is it outside the range of our thought, our emotions and our history. In New Zealand Maori and 'Europeans' are both doing work of the highest quality . . . . we are one people and our various qualities overlap . . . . most of the time we do not think in terms of differences between Maori and other inhabitants of New Zealand, so much do we take each other's presence as inevitable. . . .[91]

Plans for further advances in Samoan self-government, drawn up by the High Commissioner, Sir Guy Powles, were 'after some doubts and hesitation' accepted by the Holland government. It would 'free New Zealand from a troublesome responsiblity. It was in line with the traditional goals of *Samoa mo Samoa*. It would win friends for New Zealand among the anti-colonialists in the United Nations and would ensure a close and special relationship with an island neighbour.'[92] Elsewhere in the world, where, if not New Zealand, then British interests were engaged, support for nationalist movements was more qualified. Thus while opposing apartheid, the New Zealand government rejected the notion that the United Nations could exercise jurisdiction in respect of the domestic affairs of member nations:

The Charter of the United Nations is built on many compromises, many delicate balances. Of these, the balance between the rights of man and the rights of states is one of the most important . . . . we wish both South Africa and this Organisation to develop on healthy lines . . . . there is time to move in orderly fashion . . . . we must oppose any resolution providing for the continuation of the Commission of Investigation on South Africa, or calling upon the Union Government to alter specific policies, or declaring the situation to be a threat to peace.[93]

It was the Commonwealth Foreign Ministers, meeting in an Asian capital for the first time, who in 1950 established the Colombo Plan, a British version of Point Four, itself a replica of the Marshall Plan, but directed at poorer countries.[94] The importance of the Colombo Plan in establishing barriers to Communism was never concealed. What was stressed though was that it was an enlightened way of establishing those barriers, not a backward-looking way relying on military intervention or colonial rule:

---

[91] *EAR*, Nov. 1955, p. 18: statement to the United Nations Ad Hoc Political Committee, 2 Nov. 1955.
[92] Boyd, *New Zealand and Decolonisation*, p. 20.
[93] *EAR*, Nov. 1955, p. 22: Statement by the NZ Rep. to the UN, F. H. Corner, to the Ad Hoc Political Committee, 2 Nov. 1955.
[94] Point Four was an American-sponsored aid and assistance programme initiated in 1949: it took its name from the fourth point of President Truman's January 1949 inaugural address.

New Zealand has been a pioneer in the field of social legislation and our modest prosperity . . . is spread among the whole of our population. There are no very rich people in New Zealand and no really poor; doubtless that is why Communism is no great problem inside our country. Because this is the bent of our thought, the Colombo Plan makes sense to us, and to it we have contributed sums which are quite large by our standards.[95]

Thus were conservative and liberal stances interwoven. The 1955 Bandung (Indonesia) conference of non-aligned nations elicited some not unfriendly reaction from the New Zealand press:

For us in Australia and New Zealand the most significant fact of the conference was the final appeal by Nehru to these countries to become more closely associated with Asia. Our destiny must be affected by events in that vast continent: accordingly our relations must become ever closer. There are so many problems to solve, so many ways in which we can help without being charged with seeking domination and our own self-interest.[96]

In private, however, the Secretary of External Affairs believed that attendance at Bandung could be a source of real embarrassment to New Zealand.[97] In the briefs for the September 1955 ANZUS Council meeting New Zealand's attitude to the non-aligned movement was canvassed. The arguments for becoming involved were grounded in the assumption not that Australia and New Zealand would be moving closer to the Asian countries but that they would be able to play a role in keeping the Asian countries closer to the West. Similarly a conservative Member of Parliament, speaking of his attendance at a Colombo Plan meeting at the end of 1956, noted the way in which ex-colonial attitudes to Britain had changed: 'They spoke in terms of high praise of English civil servants who had spent their lives fighting battles against the British Colonial Office. They spoke in high praise of the way in which they had been prepared for the time when they would assume the responsibility for self-government.'[98]

National accepted that Malaya should become independent, reassured as it was that the pro-British regime that took over would not threaten Commonwealth security interests, particularly the Singapore base.[99] But it was the Colombo Plan, not military involvement, that remained central to the

---

[95] 'New Zealand Foreign Policy', *EAR*, July 1955, p. 51. The article went on to say that during the first four years of the Plan New Zealand had contributed nearly £3.5 million of capital assitance with additional commitments for technical assistance. See also McIntosh, 'Origins', p. 32.
[96] *EP*, 26 April 1955.
[97] EA440/9/3, NA.
[98] Leon Gotz, *NZPD*, 311, p. 74 (13 June 1957).
[99] At the end of 1956 the government told the British that it supported Britain's approach of deciding to give Malaya independence as the best way of ensuring that the Singapore base remained in British hands.

New Zealand conception of its relationship with that continent.[100] In 1960 the *External Affairs Review* ran a series of three articles on the Colombo Plan and New Zealand's part in it. The first article stressed that the very nature of the problems of South and Southeast Asia 'makes a strong appeal to the humanitarian instincts of New Zealanders, themselves pioneers in the field of social legislation . . .'. The second article stated that 'New Zealand considers the Colombo Plan to be one of the most hopeful developments of recent years . . . the Prime Minister, Mr Nash, spoke of the pride of the Government and people of New Zealand in the part they have been able to play in helping to initiate and develop it.'[101]

The United Nations was not forgotten, although insofar as it was favoured this was because it resembled the Commonwealth, rather than the other way around. Fraser's sponsorship of the United Nations in 1945 was remembered favourably in the 1950s. His opposition to the veto, and the persistent use of the veto by the Soviet Union since then, had made that stance, and with it support for the United Nations, acceptable to conservative as well as more liberal opinion. As Doidge said, 'The world will not be safe from the risk of armed aggression, unless and until the collective resistance that is to come to the aid of the victim is both automatic and immediate.'[102] Similarly, Macdonald, defending the United Nations some seven years later, referred to the fact that 'New Zealand had built up a good record, a sound record, and a worthy record in the United Nations. Our influence there is much greater than our size would appear to warrant. Certain names spring to mind from the very early days of the formation of the United Nations. We remember the late Peter Fraser and Sir Carl Berendsen. Then there is our present representative, Sir Leslie Munro.'[103]

Suez

The Suez crisis of 1956 was a contest of wills between the leader of Egypt, Gamel Nasser, and the British and French governments, essentially over the extent of European influence in the Middle East. The crisis broke early in November, when Britain and France intervened militarily in Egypt, ostensibly to separate Egyptian and Israeli armies, but in fact in collusion with Israel. The intervention ended almost as quickly as it had begun when the United States refused to support Britain and France and their action was condemned by the United Nations. Anthony Eden, the British Prime Minister, retired a disgraced leader. The diplomacy of his successor, Harold

100   See Wood, 'New Zealand and Southeast Asia', p. 26, for further comment.
101   *EAR*, March 1960, p. 9; April 1960, pp. 11–12.
102   *NZ Foreign Policy: Statements and Documents*, p. 229 (speech by Doidge to the UN First Committee, 11 Oct. 1950).
103   Macdonald in the House of Representatives, 12 June 1957, quoted in *EAR*, June 1957, p. 21.

Macmillan, helped restore Anglo-American relations to their more normal harmonious state, but few would have predicted that this would be the last severe Anglo-American crisis.

The crisis demonstrated the power of loyalism, of patriotism to Britain, in both the National and Labour Parties and public opinion generally. It created a crisis for the progressive internationalist dimension of the new foreign policy—in this instance, not the Labour Party, but the officers of the Department of External Affairs.

Forced to choose between Britain and its Empire interests on the one hand, and the more recent formulations, the United Nations, the Colombo Plan, the Commonwealth, on the other, many National Party members did not hesitate. The traditional enemies, the socialists and the nationalists, were invoked: 'we know that members of the Socialist Party, both here and in England, have spoken of their desire to see the liquidation of the Empire. We know that had it not been for the Socialist Government in Britain we would probably still have Burma as part of our Commonwealth and it is doubtful whether India would today be a republic.'[104] Another National M.P. wanted to 'show the true strength of our Commonwealth in the interests of the welfare of mankind, despite our weakened state following the spate of secessions from the now historic British Empire.'[105]

New Zealand had one particular, and revealing, involvement in the crisis. The British had palmed off an unwanted battle cruiser, the *Royalist*, on New Zealand. Holland was in Britain for the Prime Ministers' conference some months before the crisis and at this time he agreed to a request from Eden that the *Royalist* stay on with the British Navy, with which it had been exercising in Mediterranean waters. This meant that when the crisis broke in the first days of November, the *Royalist* was actually off the Egyptian coast. The Admiralty, for rather different reasons from those of Eden himself, was keen to have the *Royalist*, with its anti-aircraft capability, to hand. Only at the eleventh hour was the vessel released to New Zealand, which thereby just avoided becoming a virtual belligerent in the conflict. This episode was part and parcel of a general breakdown in communication between the British government and the Dominions in the days immediately before the intervention. Even Holland was shocked by this lack of consultation, and it may have contributed to the relatively cautious official New Zealand response thereafter. But it did not seriously undermine the ties of loyalty.[106]

It was a measure of the strength of pro-British sentiment that within the two

104 Gotz, *NZPD*, 311, p. 77 (13 June 1957).
105 G. A. Walsh, *NZPD*, 311, p. 49 (13 June 1957).
106 This account relies heavily on Malcolm Templeton, 'Ties of Blood and Empire: New Zealand's Involvement in Middle East Defence and the Suez Crisis, 1947–1957', MERT, Wellington, 1988, Ch. 9. Quotations from McIntosh correspondence cited in the following paragraphs are also drawn from this manuscript.

political parties it was Labour rather than National that faced difficulties taking a stance over the crisis. Labour spokespeople were prepared to recognise that Egypt had a case in nationalising the Canal, Mathison indeed regarding it as a 'good thing'.[107] Regional councils of the FOL in Dunedin and Auckland both condemned the invasion and Holland's support for Britain. Nash received a lot of mail critical of Britain's actions.[108] Moohan and some others wanted to condemn the Eden government. But elsewhere in the party opposition was far more qualified—to the point where it was barely opposition at all. The FOL as a whole avoided making any official statement. The *Standard* avoided editorial comment.[109] Nash was pro-British: he was also mindful of the negative consequences of being seen to criticise Britain, and rejected condemnation: 'The Labour Party', wrote McIntosh, had 'a very shrewd sense of public reaction ... while they didn't approve generally of what the British were doing, they were delighted to think that the old lion still had a throaty roar and a sharp claw which, on occasions, he was still prepared to use.'[110] Nash also exemplified traditional Labour support for Israel, one of Egypt's other antagonists in the Suez conflict.[111] Walsh supported Nash: Nash issued a statement that would mollify Moohan and others of his persuasion, but too late to seriously embarrass the British.[112]

As in the 1940s, many on the left tended to refrain from criticism of British foreign policy, even with the Conservatives in power, in favour of criticism of the United States.[113] Britain was seen as a bulwark of values and attitudes which should be more acceptable to New Zealand and it was a much more problematic matter to criticise Britain to a New Zealand audience than to criticise the United States. Even the left-wing Clyde Carr blamed the Suez crisis on the Americans rather than the British, even though it was a British *Conservative* government that was involved. Nash himself, while more pro-American, favoured Britain and the Commonwealth: 'I believe that the British people—the people of the British Commonwealth, with its freely associated sovereign nations—can and will, render great service to the United Nations.'[114]

The Department of External Affairs might have felt differently about Labour if that party had been the government—as it was, the department's

---

107   *NZPD*, 309, p. 949 (8 Aug. 1956).
108   N2069/1632–1643, NA.
109   *Here and Now*, Nov. 1956, p. 7.
110   McIntosh to Herbert Norman (Canadian Ambassador to Egypt), 20 Dec. 1956. McIntosh Papers, MERT.
111   See, for instance, *NZPD*, 309, p. 895 (7 Aug. 1956): 'In the ten years since the close of World War II, these people have brought more wealth out fo the soil than was ever dreamed of. I have never known a body of men and women who have worked so hard for the benefit of all ....'
112   *Round Table*, 186 (Feb. 1957), p. 185, discusses Labour uneasiness; note also Moohan comment in *NZPD*, 311, p. 79 (14 June 1957). See also, 744.00/1–3157, RG59, USNA.
113   Adjournment debate, *NZPD*, 311, pp. 35–36 (12–13 June 1957).
114   *NZPD*, 311, p. 17 (12 June 1957).

New Italian representative arriving at Parliament, escorted by 'Black Shirts', 1930s.
Evening Post *Collection, Alexander Turnbull Library.*

'Out of the hole', cartoon by Gordon Minhinnick, *Evening Post*, 29 July 1939.

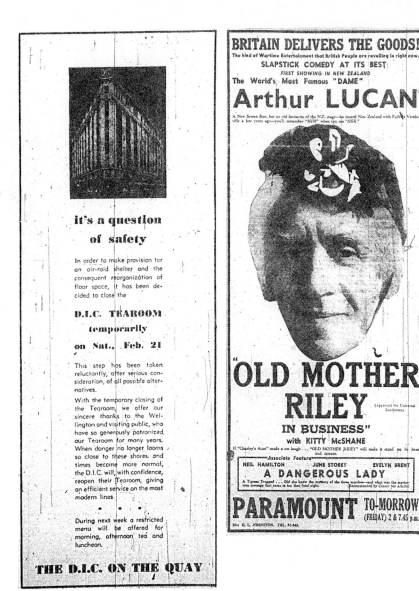

Wartime advertisements, *Evening Post*, 16 February, 19 February 1942.

VE Day, Perrets Corner, Wellington, 8 May 1945. *John Pascoe Collection, Alexander Turnbull Library.*

Aid for Britain campaign advertisement, 1947–8. *National Archives.*

Governor-General's tour, Mangaia, Cook Islands, July 1948. Lady Freyberg talks to Mrs Sally Taripo. *National Publicity Studios Collection, Alexander Turnbull Library.*

'Sorry — I've already invested', cartoon by Sid Scales, *Otago Daily Times*, 25 February 1955. *Sid Scales collection.*

The Mayor of Wellington,
Frank Kitts, Queen Sirikit of
Thailand and Keith
Holyoake, 20 August 1962.
Evening Post *collection,
Wellington Newspapers.*

'Break away', cartoon by Neville Lodge, *Evening Post*, 12 November 1965. *Neville
Lodge collection.*

Student anti-Vietnam War march, Wellington, 1 August 1967. The *Evening Post* reported 5000 at the demonstration in the grounds of Parliament on the occasion of the Clifford-Taylor visit. Evening Post *collection, Wellington Newspapers.*

Captain P. Loginov, of the Soviet research vessel *Gorets*, visits Karori Normal School, Wellington, 17 March 1976. Evening Post *collection, Wellington Newspapers.*

Japanese Minister of Agriculture and Forestry, Ichiro Nakagawa, and members of the Japanese delegation at Japan-New Zealand trade talks, Wellington, 29 June 1978. Evening Post *collection, Wellington Newspapers.*

'One false move', cartoon by Tom Scott, *Evening Post*, 2 March 1985. *Tom Scott collection,* Evening Post.

wrath was focused on the government itself. McIntosh spoke, in unusually strong language, of 'the criminal folly of Eden's policy. In my view he ought to be impeached.'[115] In respect of New Zealand, he wrote to one confidant that Holland's policy had 'kept the whole country united on the issue, except for the enlightened left-wingers and the fellow-travellers, and, I am afraid, I must include the Department in this group: it has been very sick about the line we have taken. Needless to say, our name stands fairly low in the U.N.'[116] An academic commentator observed in the aftermath of the crisis that 'there can be no doubt that in the eyes of the greater part of the world New Zealand is now numbered among those countries which support the U.N.O. when, in their judgement, it suits them to do so. Moreover, the New Zealand Government chose to do this not that it might support a genuine *United Kingdom* policy, but in support of a *rightwing Conservative* policy ....'[117] Another described New Zealand support for Britain's actions as equivalent to excusing 'one's mother, should she be caught shoplifting—and to describe her, perhaps, as a plain clothes policewoman.'[118]

This was not of course how it appeared to conservatives. In the aftermath of Suez there was a great deal of disillusionment with and criticism of the United Nations, a feeling among conservatives that in disciplining Britain and France but not the Soviet Union it had shown true or new colours: Macdonald took on the brief of defending the Organisation which he did in pro-British terms: 'I do not think we would be wise to [reduce or remove our support] .... Our friends, such as Britain, would be attacked again and again in the United Nations by the Communists and by the extreme anti-colonialists. We would be doing Britain no service whatever. Indeed we would be doing her a disservice ....' He confronted head on the debate about double standards:

> there has been much talk of a double standard having been applied by the United Nations in the case of the Suez Canal and in the case of Hungary. What are the facts? The General Assembly in both cases made the same recommendation .... for the withdrawal of forces .... Britain and France complied, not because they had been forced to comply, but because they were law abiding. It should be realised that the Assembly's recommendation was not binding in either case because its enforcement in either case against the will of the party concerned would have resulted in a major war.[119]

These were hard words for most New Zealanders to hear. The fact that they had to be said suggested what a fragile hold internationalism had in the

115 McIntosh to F. H. Corner, 12 Dec. 1956. McIntosh Papers, MERT.
116 McIntosh to Norman, 20 Dec. 1956. McIntosh Papers, MERT.
117 E. A. Olssen, 'Suez and New Zealand's Foreign Policy', *Landfall*, 11/1 (March 1957), p. 68 (italics in original).
118 Keith Sinclair, 'Independence and Morality', *Here and Now*, Oct. 1957, p. 13.
119 *EAR*, June 1957, pp. 2–3. On 4 November 1956 Soviet forces had intervened in Hungary to restore a pro-Soviet regime.

political culture. On the other hand, the crisis was over almost before it had begun. The power of loyalism, of British nationalism, would never again be played out in quite the fashion that it was over Suez. The interplay of independence, nationalism and internationalism would continue, but against a different background and in different contexts.

Labour in power, 1957–60

The foreign policy record of the second Labour government confirmed the continued commitment of Labour to a stance of 'loyal dissent'. We can see this in its positions on issues as diverse as China, Antarctica, and nuclear weapons. In 1957 this had implications for the United States as much as for Britain. Americans had been clear in their minds for some time that National was a better bet for them than Labour:

> There is an aversion to the United States in minority segments of both parties, but in the Labour Party it is proportionately larger and merges into some degree of hostility whereas in the National Party it seldom exceeds a certain coolness. Also, the former embraces a block of opinion which holds that closer ties with the United States automatically bring about a weakening of ties with the United Kingdom, while in the latter there appear to be few believers in this supposed antithesis. Or if there are a few, it does not seem to disturb them.[120]

As one New Zealand diplomat reported from Washington in 1957, after Labour's return to office, 'Since the relations between the United States administration and the New Zealand National Government had been cordial and had been promoted by happy personal relationships with members of the National Cabinet, some regret is expressed that these friends of the United States are now out of office.'[121]

Labour was widely believed by the Americans—and the British—to be 'soft' on China. What would happen in practice? American warmth for National, wrote the same official, 'isn't antagonistic to Labour, under Nash wellknown here and record of Labour Government in cooperation with United States in Asia is remembered. No doubt about where Labour stands on Communism—more certain in this respect than with [the Australian Labor Party].'[122] There was some truth in the Americans' view. Labour had long amalgamated anti-Communism and more progressive elements in its thinking. But the Americans also had hopes of the government's advisors:

> the attitude of Mr Nash and his Government towards [these issues] will undergo gradual change with the assumption of responsibility and through facing the logic of

---

120   744.00/9–551, RG59, NA.
121   G. D. L. White to SEA, 13 Dec. 1957. EA26/3/1, NA.
122   White to SEA, 13 Dec. 1957. EA26/3/1, NA. Syntax is correct.

basic international relationships. The competent professional staff of the Department of External Affairs is well prepared to review with the new ministers the factual background of present policies and their presentations will undoubtedly be persuasive on many points. Forces within the Government itself will be operating to check any hasty action and assure deliberation, thereby preserving opportunities for us to consult with the Government in good time without appearing to be impatient and without giving any new grounds for resentment of imagined pressure or lack of confidence in the new officials.[123]

An American diplomat noted that 'It has been official Labour Party policy for several years to urge recognition [of] Red China and its admission UN. While it is unlikely new government will extend recognition it is probable that where Holland and Macdonald in general supported US on this issue, Nash will tend support British policy.'[124]

It was ironically Macmillan who first put pressure on the new government not to move on the China issue: ironic because the Conservative government in Britain had maintained the diplomatic relations with China that had been established by its Labour predecessor in 1949. Macmillan visited New Zealand at the beginning of 1958, the first (and to date the only) visit by a British Prime Minister while in office. In talks with the new government at the end of January he counselled them to stall on the China issue: 'I don't want a major rift with the United States', the Secretary of External Affairs recorded him as saying.[125]

Shortly thereafter Nash attended the SEATO meeting in Manila in March. The American Ambassador wrote to the State Department subsequently: 'Since the Manila meeting Nash has spoken on numerous occasions both privately and publicly in praise of Secretary Dulles' efforts for peace ... and has said that while as a matter of principle recognition should be extended to Communist China, New Zealand will take no action without consulting its Allies and in any event it is likely to require a considerable period of time.'[126]

At the party conference in May resolutions supporting recognition were defeated.[127] Nonetheless the government, in choosing not to challenge American policy on China, did not feel obliged to accept the American position on the offshore islands issue, which erupted again in 1958. Although it deplored the use of force in the Taiwan Straits and the 'brutal methods employed' by the Chinese authorities against the people of Tibet', the 1958–

[123] 744.00/12–957, RG59, USNA.
[124] 744.00/12–557, RG59, USNA.
[125] Notes on talks, 23 Jan. 1958, EA59/3/4, NA. The American Ambassador got inserted in an Eisenhower-Macmillan letter thanks to Macmillan for his helpfulness to the Americans in New Zealand (611.42/2–1458, RG59, USNA) — one instance of how New Zealand preoccupations with conflicts of interest between their allegiance to Britain and their security link with the United States were ill-founded.
[126] 744.13/7–2858, RG59, USNA.
[127] 744.00/5–2058, RG59, USNA.

59 report of the Department of External Affairs also contended that 'the claims of the Communist Chinese to the offshore islands of Quemoy and Matsu are soundly based'.[128]

On the nuclear-testing issue the balance between principle and practice was very like that on recognition of China. Labour had not criticised National during the testing in 1957, but in the election campaign later in the year Nash did take a stronger stance. The Americans were alerted: 'The Labour platform called for the abolition of nuclear bomb testing, without stating any conditions which should be sought. Since the election, Nash has specifically stated that he favours an agreement for the cessation of tests which would not be conditional upon agreements in any other field of disarmament. In this matter, however, he will be confronted by British interest, which is identical with that of the United States.'[129]

The peace movement was to be disappointed. On 3 March 1958 the Acting Prime Minister, Jerry Skinner, explained that New Zealand was concerned to give help to the United Kingdom in ensuring that all necessary safety precautions were taken with any further tests which the British might conduct in the Pacific. Accordingly a frigate would be made available, as had been done the previous year.[130] Nash told Chapman that the government remained 'strongly in favour of ending tests'. But there was no international agreement to end them and 'in the meantime the United Kingdom tests are going on. Our part in the tests is merely that of assisting them with safety measures and is therefore not at all inconsistent with our desire to have an effective international agreement which would halt all further testing of nuclear weapons.'[131]

Protest continued through the winter of 1958 but some of the heat went out of the issue when in October 1958 the Soviet Union accepted the Anglo-American proposal to suspend all atmospheric testing.[132] But the peace movement itself was careful to stress that it was not a Communist or Communist front movement.[133] And the New Zealand movement lay well within the framework of an independent foreign policy, just as the British movement located itself firmly within the mainstream of reformist movements in British politics.

The years 1959–60 were the high point of the Easter marches in England,

128   *AJHR*, 1958, A. 1; see also, Nash, *NZPD*, 318, p. 1721 (11 Sept. 1958): 'the offshore islands belong to Communist China'.
129   744.00/12-957, RG59, USNA.
130   *Christchurch Star-Sun*, 3 March 1958, N12/0762, NA.
131   EA121/5/3, NA. Labour abolished compulsory military training. But although a move hard fought by National, the (Conservative) British government was also ending it, and the fiscal burden of keeping it was a major influence on the decision. Brief reference in Sinclair, *Nash*, pp. 318–9.
132   For details of protest see *Press*, 28 July 1958 (N12/0751, NA); *Evening Star*, 14 Aug. 1958 (EA121/5/3, NA); *NZH*, 13 Sept. 1958 (N12/0748, NA).
133   *Here and Now*, Nov. 1957, pp. 15–19, interview with Chapman.

organised by the Campaign for Nuclear Disarmament, from the nuclear weapons establishment at Aldermaston to London. The first relatively small march was held in 1958. The 1959 march attracted around 15,000 on its last day and 20–25,000 to the final rally in Trafalgar Square, the 1960 march some 60,000 to 100,000 (estimates varied) to the Trafalgar Square rally.[134] A first Easter march was held in New Zealand in 1959. It started from Featherston in the Wairarapa and ended at Parliament. The climb over the Rimutaka summit made it a more strenuous achievement than the English stroll down the Thames valley. One report from the American Embassy in the middle of 1959 alluded to the then current 'widespread feelings (resulting from the feeling that the United Kingdom believes compromise with the USSR is possible) that the United States is too stubborn and inflexible in its relations with the Communist countries'.[135]

Like the atmosphere, Antarctica was another unpopulated but contested zone. Nash was keen to see the continent internationalised, an objective less than welcome to the United States and Britain who feared it would enhance Soviet influence in the region. Nash deferred and an Antarctic Treaty was signed involving only those powers with a presence on the continent, a grouping in which the Soviet Union could not be so influential. At least one commentator identified interest as well as ideology in New Zealand's argument for internationalisation: 'it is arguable that an entirely hard-headed analysis of New Zealand's position, devoid of any idealism, would have reached the same conclusion.'[136] New Zealand had no significant interests in its Ross Dependency, was ill-placed to guard what interests it had and made a claim which neither of the superpowers recognised: internationalisation had something to commend it.

Nash visited the Soviet Union in 1960, twenty-three years after his first trip. He tried to have a dialogue with Krushchev and convince him that Western leaders wanted disarmament too.[137] He was accused, when he returned to New Zealand, of supporting the Russian rather than the Western disarmament proposals and National Party pressure caused him to tone down his comments.[138] Similarly in 1960 Ruth Bacon in the American Embassy noted that 'National Party leaders fortunately do not share Mr Nash's soft approach to the Soviet disarmament proposals'.[139]

[134] Taylor, *Against the Bomb*, pp. 49, 57.
[135] 844.10/6–959, RG59, USNA.
[136] C. Beeby, *The Antarctic Treaty*, Wellington, 1972, p. 10. See also Sinclair, *Nash*, p. 325.
[137] Sinclair, *Nash*, pp. 327–30.
[138] 'Since his visit to the USSR in March 1960, . . . Nash has spoken of Khrushchev, of general conditions in Russia, and of Soviet objectives in laudatory terms which have gradually become more restrained largely because of National Party denunciation of his statements, his fear lest Soviet action in Africa prove harmful to the United Nations and to UK interests, his concern over Khruschev's increasing stridency', 611.44/9–1060, RG59, USNA.
[139] 611.44/12–1660, RG59, USNA. Bacon's observations were prompted by a phone call from Nash asking her to continue, now that he was in Opposition, the Ambassador's practice of sending him information on American disarmament policies.

Conclusion

National in office did not undo what had changed in foreign policy since 1935. National and Labour were ideologically close, drawn together by anti-Communism, but also by a common belief in the Commonwealth and the United Nations. New Zealand's interests were pursued, its critique articulated, within this framework. The Commonwealth was at the centre of this scheme, the UN lay beyond it, the United States somewhat to one side. Suez demonstrated the power of patriotism to disrupt the pattern, the sequence of ever-wider circles. But the continuum was rapidly restored. At the end of the decade, the idea of independence in foreign policy first pursued in the 1930s acquired its definitive formulation.

An independent foreign policy, 1961

F. L. W. Wood wrote in 1956 that:

> For half a century or more the basic principle of [New Zealand] political life has been common-sense humanitarianism, guided by a short-term shrewdness and a preference for general decency in human behaviour, not by foresight or theoretical analysis. New Zealanders, from the Prime Minister downwards, hope implicitly that this same formula will continue to be an adequate guide in world politics.[1]

We can take this statement and build on it an analysis and summary of the idea of an independent foreign policy at the beginning of the 1960s. The publication *New Zealand's External Relations* gave an excellent perspective on the orthodoxies of New Zealand foreign policy at the beginning of the new decade. It was a collection of papers delivered early in 1961, mostly by members or former members of the Department of External Affairs. McIntosh, still Secretary of External Affairs, identified the beginnings of New Zealand foreign policy with the election of the 1935 government: 'The changes which the pre-war government brought .... were broadly—independence of outlook (stemming in part from the fact that it was the only Labour government in the British Commonwealth); a profound belief in collective security; an eagerness to make the League of Nations effective; and a conviction that international political dangers could be relieved by action against conditions of economic and social distress.'[2] We can elaborate on this by identifying the following seven central elements which provided the context for understanding what independence in foreign policy meant at this time:

- a belief in the Commonwealth as a framework for New Zealand's foreign relations and for the defence of the principle of multiracialism in the world as a whole: 'New Zealand must be especially interested in the contribution which the Commonwealth can make towards bringing about partnership between peoples of different race'.[3]

---

[1] Wood, 'New Zealand and Southeast Asia', p. 27.
[2] A. D. McIntosh, 'Administration of an Independent Foreign Policy', in *NZER*, p. 32.
[3] R. R. Cunninghame, 'Foreign Policy and Political Alignments', *NZER*, p. 29. The focus was on Africa. F. H. Corner's discussion of New Zealand and the South Pacific (pp. 130–52) is also pertinent here. It is discussed in Chapter 11.

- a belief in the United Nations: '. . . in the postwar period [New Zealand] has been especially alert against any possible repetition of the disaster which overtook [the League]. That the lessons of the past are still vivid was apparent as recently as the 1960 General Assembly session when confronted with the Congo crisis and Soviet attacks upon the Secretary-General, New Zealand was among those to concentrate with most evident concern on the dangers for the future of the United Nations itself. Support for the United Nations has thus been for New Zealand more than a pious expression; it has involved the expenditure of considerable efforts.'[4]

- a belief in a multilateral global economic order rather than closed economic blocs: interestingly this is implicit rather than explicit in *New Zealand's External Relations* and indeed it was a much more divisive area than political relations, as the debate over New Zealand's joining the International Monetary Fund demonstrated.

- a belief in economic and social rather than military solutions to international problems: 'It has been observed that to New Zealand, a pioneer in the field of social legislation and a country in which income is spread through all levels of the population, the Colombo Plan has a special significance . . . . some steps have recently been taken which indicate that New Zealand recognises a measure of responsibility in Africa also.'[5]

- a belief in the possibility of peaceful relations with adversary states, particularly the Soviet Union and China: here the more perceptive comment comes from an American observer: 'while Government leaders firmly oppose Communism, many New Zealanders have been shielded from any harsh contact with Communism and have been blessed with abundance necessities of life. They are tired Cold War and disposed toward trying turn-other-cheek philosophy as solvent world problems. Naive tendency in certain quarters public opinion equate Soviet objectives with Free World objectives and attraction towards neutralism constitute public relations problem for us of growing dimensions.'[6]

- a belief in the moral value of the Western alliance, i.e. anti-Communism, a belief which for some overlapped with belief in the United Nations. Thus J. V. Wilson compared New Zealand statements about the Chinese in Tibet in 1960 with the pre-war stand against appeasement in 1936-37: 'words as true as those with which New Zealand delegates had inveighed against the

---

4   Cunninghame, 'Foreign Policy and Political Alignments', p. 23. See also C. C. Aikman, *NZER*, p. 154 (report of conference discussion); J. V. Wilson, 'New Zealand's Participation in International Organisations', *NZER*, p. 69.
5   Cunninghame, 'Foreign Policy and Political Alignments', pp. 27-28.
6   Wellington to Secretary of State, 24 Dec. 1960. 611.41/12-2460, RG59, USNA. Syntax correct—text is a cable.

pre-war Fascist aggressions, and as ineffectual. The United Nations, itself more and more influenced by the initiatives and inspirations of the Communist states and certain neutralist auxiliaries, seems unlikely to take any continuing interest in the fate of people overborne by Communist pressure.'[7]

- loyalty to Britain and in particular a preparedness to fight alongside Britain in the event of a major war: 'the doctrine of "where Britain goes we go" is still firmly implanted in New Zealand hearts—no New Zealand Government could ever ignore an attitude so firmly entrenched in our tradition.'[8]

Alongside these seven principles can be placed another three fundamental objectives: 'interests' in the sense in which we discussed the term in the introduction:

- a reluctance to commit significant material or human resources to any of the above principles (save the last).

- a commitment to New Zealand's physical security, '... the ultimate goal of New Zealand's defence and foreign policies are essentially the same—to obtain as much external security as possible for New Zealand and to maintain as far as possible the character of New Zealand society in a form desired by the majority of New Zealanders.' This was to be attained through keeping major friendly powers active in the wider region, there being no direct threat to New Zealand: 'New Zealand has sought security in friendship and formal defensive arrangements with Australia and the United States.'[9]

- a commitment to New Zealand's economic security: 'If we are to maintain an adequate rate of economic growth in New Zealand it will be necessary to ensure not only that domestic resources are employed to the best advantage but also that overseas markets are open for the products of our export industries. This must be the major objective of New Zealand's external economic relations.'[10]

New Zealand looked to secure the first of these last objectives by not committing resources, or, where it felt the pressure from others to do so, by pleading poverty, a balance of payments constraint, competing commitments, or a combination of all three. It looked to secure the second goal

7   Wilson, 'NZ's Participation in International Organisations', p. 77.
8   McIntosh, 'Administration of an Independent Foreign Policy', p. 31.
9   McIntosh, 'Administration of an Independent Foreign Policy', pp. 37, 41.
10 N. V. Lough, 'New Zealand's External Economic Relations', *NZER*, p. 112.

through an American guarantee and the third through a British/European guarantee, possibly backed up by other countries.

We can identify in conclusion two familiar elements in the notion of independence that were as valid at the beginning of the 1960s as in the 1930s. Firstly, independence was about articulating certain principles, in external relations as in other spheres of political life. Secondly, it was about interest and its pursuit within an existing, accepted framework. Putting these two elements together, independence in New Zealand was not about fundamental conflicts of power. New Zealand did not, in 1960 any more than in 1935, conceive of itself as a nation alone in the world. Its independence had, after all, been granted rather than wrested. Diplomacy for New Zealand possessed more of the characteristics of parliamentary or bureaucratic politicking than it did of the world of Machiavelli or Metternich, of power politics, or of war and peace.

Independence and progress

We have above a snapshot picture of the idea of an independent foreign policy but to capture exactly the meaning of the term both in 1961 and over the preceding generation we have to take into account the dynamic, progressive element in the idea. For the advocates of independence in foreign policy believed, as we have seen in earlier chapters, there had been significant changes, and for them, it was these changes which were a key factor. Between 1935 and 1945 New Zealand had participated for the first time in a systematic and committed way in the community of nations, as well as in the community of the Empire. 'Internationalism', then, was a hallmark of this idea of independence. And the stages in the acquisition by New Zealand of an international personality—the independent line at the League, the Embassy in Washington, the establishment of the Department of External Affairs, the active role in the formation of the United Nations—were fondly and proudly recalled.

The National Party had an interest-based notion of foreign policy but it embraced 'interests' which did not always dovetail with the Department's commitment to internationalism and participation. One newspaper editor, sympathetic to National, questioned 'whether New Zealand had any future role at all in world affairs. The suggestion that it could disperse its sympathies, money and military resources around the world was the greatest nonsense he had heard. New Zealand could not act as though it were many times bigger than it was. He saw no point in proliferation of posts abroad . . . .'[11]

A National politician was more likely to link diplomacy to commerce than to ideology: 'the effectiveness of New Zealand's foreign policy would depend on the strength of its economy; [diplomatic] posts should therefore be

11   Comment by E. V. Dumbleton, editor, *Auckland Star*, *NZER*, p. 160.

established wherever they could assist New Zealand's trade'; and to contest the notion that New Zealanders should 'ask themselves whether they wished merely to sit in a little safe corner of the Pacific or whether they were part of the wider world. In fact they were part of the wider world and had to act accordingly.'[12]

Like Holland, Holyoake, Prime Minister from 1960, had no particular interest in foreign affairs and in this respect he was a characteristic conservative New Zealand Prime Minister: 'Holyoake is known as one who thinks that the country must stand on its own two feet and deal with Britain in a more independent manner, recognising that [Britain] is primarily concerned with its own self-interest.'[13] This made Holyoake seem different from Holland, but the real difference was in the perception that New Zealand interests had changed, from the need to protect the British market at all costs, to the need to find other commercial partners.

But the difference can too readily be exaggerated. The independent foreign policy was not under threat—National had accepted that New Zealand had, and had to have, an international personality. It did have a different view of what that personality should be, but that was natural given its ideology.

We can credit the Department of External Affairs for articulating so clearly the idea of an independent foreign policy at this time. If it had not done so the idea would still have been around but its clear expression by the Department makes the historian's task—and one suspects that of scholars at the time—easier. As has been noted, most of the contributors to *New Zealand's External Relations* were members of the Department, or enjoyed a close association with it. Writing about the origins of the postwar colonial policy, Mary Boyd noted that

> McIntosh was a friend and Corner a recent student of Professor F. L. W. Wood and Dr J. C. Beaglehole, scholars and teachers of Commonwealth history at Victoria University College, advocates of New Zealand's adoption of the Statute of Westminster .... R. O. McGechan, Professor of International Law at Victoria, lectured on the legal aspects of the evolution of Dominion status and among his students was C. C. Aikman, constitutional advisor to the New Zealand government when power was transferred to Western Samoa and the Cook Islands.[14]

Most had also been active in the New Zealand Institute of International Affairs, which, like the Institute of Pacific Relations, with which it merged in 1939, had been an élite group fostering a wider awareness of international

12 Aikman, *NZER*, p. 159.
13 744.00/11-1457, RG59, USNA.
14 Boyd, *Decolonisation*, p. 9. Mary Boyd was herself a student, later colleague, of Wood and Beaglehole. See also, Peter Munz, 'A Personal Memoir', in *Feel of Truth*, pp. 11-24. The subtitle of *Feel of Truth* was 'Essays in New Zealand and Pacific History presented to F. L. W. Wood and J. C. Beaglehole'. McGechan and Winston Monk were both killed in a plane crash in 1954.

issues for a generation. Branches of the Institute in the main centres met regularly to discuss international issues, and it also held conferences and published literature on international relations.[15]

Members of the Department were distinctive in the methodical way in which they expressed a philosophy of foreign policy. There were variations—Shanahan was more conservative, more preoccupied with defence and security, George Laking, who succeeded McIntosh as Secretary in 1966, had a greater familiarity with, and was more relaxed about, the role of the United States in New Zealand's affairs. But they were variations of degree, not kind. Other departments of state also had perspectives on external relations, but these by and large ran parallel to those of the Department of External Affairs. Treasury was committed to economic multilateralism; Customs participated conscientiously in GATT; for the armed forces, collaboration with Australian and British forces was almost a definition of their mission. The Department of Industries and Commerce under W. B. Sutch (1958–65) had a more distinctive position, but stripped of some of the rhetoric, its policies clearly belonged to the family of Dominion protectionism, something that had been around for a very long time in intra-Commonwealth relations, as we saw in Chapter 5. But it was External Affairs which was particularly identified with the idea of an independent foreign policy. New Zealand's overseas missions were in London, Paris, New York, Washington, Canberra, Ottawa, Tokyo and Singapore: the United Nations, the Commonwealth, the Western alliance, were New Zealand's diplomatic world. And the very fact of an independent diplomatic service provided the opportunity to combine independence and loyalty.

The Department was less than two decades old at the beginning of the new decade, a product of wartime exigency but marked also by the political outlook of the times in which it had been founded and at which it had recruited many of its (then) young staff. It could be described as to the left of National for the most part, but closer to Labour not in a party political sense but in terms of solidarity with Labour internationalism and participation in global tasks. Its officers recalled President Franklin D. Roosevelt, America's wartime leader, the promise of the Atlantic Charter and the Four Freedoms, of the United Nations and the Marshall Plan.

It believed that independence entailed the abandonment of an insular, provincial attitude to the world for an international, confident one. They hoped to take the new National government which took office at the end of 1960 with them. Fraser had been a hero, Holland was not. Nash's practices were disliked but his ideas were congenial; Holyoake did not seem to have ideas. So it was National rather than Labour who were the adversary.

[15]   A number of items of which have been cited in this study. See especially NZIIA, *New Zealand Foreign Policy: Choices, Challenges and Opportunities.* Wellington, 1984, pp. 1–3.

Looking forward

In 1961 commentators on foreign relations for the most part looked back, back on a generation of accomplishment. The idea and practice of independence in foreign policy had been achieved in the face of an orthodoxy about New Zealand's foreign relations that was loyalist and insular. The scholars, diplomats and occasional politician who sought change could welcome the fact that the National Party as well as Labour had come to accept that independence was not disloyal, and that New Zealand had an international as well as a Commonwealth personality. They were aware of the continuity with the past, with Dominion status, but did not place such stress on it.

Having arrived at a long-sought destination, there was, somewhat naturally, not a great deal of preoccupation about what was to come next— other than more of the same. With the benefit of hindsight, we can identify three elements in the history of New Zealand's foreign relations in the generation to come. Was there any inkling of them? And in what particular way might they affect the new orthodoxy, as we can call it, the independent foreign policy of 1961?

We have seen two components of independence in foreign policy—interest and dissent. In the 1930s–60s generation both had encouraged New Zealanders to look outward. What if that changed? Insularity and parochialism had supposedly been banished by the attainment of this particularly internationalist independence. But it did not require a great deal of effort to locate them still. Could an independent New Zealand exhibit some of the same inward-looking qualities as colonial New Zealand?

The late 1950s and early 1960s were an 'end of ideology' era, as we noted in Chapter 5. If this was true of society as a whole, why should it not remain true of its foreign relations? The seeds of what was called the New Left lay in the ban-the-bomb movement.[16] But few would have guessed that protest would escalate in the fashion that it did later in the 1960s and reinvigorate ideological divisions.

In 1961 New Zealand's internationalism grew from its close association with Britain, its membership in the Commonwealth, into the wider world. But what if the Commonwealth association, or elements of it, weakened or even vanished? What would then happen to New Zealand's idea of independence? Would it be exposed to the world of power more directly?

Of course we have seized on these three factors for a reason. All played a part in the history of New Zealand's foreign relations over the next generation and meant that 'independence', after another generation, although it had points in common with the accepted meaning of 1961, had also some different elements.

---

16 The British journal *New Left Review* started publication in 1960.

7. The Vietnam War and New Zealand

In the mid 1960s the framework of New Zealand's foreign policy was tested by involvement in the Vietnam War in alliance with the United States. That involvement provoked the first substantial debate there had ever been in New Zealand on foreign policy: Labour and National disagreed as they had not since the mid 1930s; the consensus on an independent foreign policy collapsed. From 1968 onwards the United States was as committed to disengagement from the conflict as it had been in 1965 to engagement in it. Some of the points of difference between the parties and within public opinion in New Zealand over the war abated. But the war, and events associated with or parallel to it, also gave new meanings to the notion of independence in New Zealand foreign policy. We will consider those new meanings in a section following this chapter.

We can identify the characteristic elements of the independent foreign policy in the way different segments of opinion responded to the issues raised by the Vietnam War. Conservative opinion stressed publicly that participation in the war was necessary to stop Communism; privately, the importance of securing New Zealand's security guarantee was emphasised. In this formulation independence was defined in terms of interest, and interest clearly required New Zealand to cooperate with the United States, Australia, and their Asian allies. Domestic considerations fostered the pursuit of another interest—keeping the commitment of New Zealand resources to the war to a minimum. Labour opinion drew on elements from the independent foreign policy consensus of the early 1960s that were particularly important in its ideological tradition: the importance of economic and social rather than military solutions and of the role that both the Commonwealth and the United Nations could and should play in the resolution of the conflict.

New Zealand in Southeast Asia before 1965

Before 1965 involvement in Southeast Asia was broadly acceptable to both political parties. There were differences of emphasis between them but not of fundamentals. New Zealand forces were deployed in the region, but their combat involvement was both limited and within a Commonwealth context. New Zealand's activities in the region were predominantly, and acceptably, socio-economic rather than military: the Colombo Plan, rather than SEATO, was the important and preferable agency in the minds of most New Zealanders who concerned themselves with Southeast Asia.

Labour resisted American pressure for greater involvement in the region under SEATO auspices when Labour was in government in 1957-60. SEATO's non-interference in trouble in Indonesia in 1958 was reassuring for Nash.[1] But towards the end of 1958 there was a flare-up in Laos: the 1954 Geneva settlement on Indochina had not brought stability. In September 1959 the Laotian government, which was pro-Western in sympathy, asked the United Nations for military aid to stop North Vietnamese aggression. At the meeting of the ANZUS Council in October Nash *was* extremely outspoken against American views and New Zealand also tried to ensure that SEATO military planning did not blur into planning for intervention.[2] But the pressure from the United States was not as intense as it would be two years later.

As Prime Minister, Nash retained his earlier enthusiasm for economic and social solutions to political and international problems and voiced his belief in such approaches during his visits to Colombo Plan projects, to the ECAFE conference in Kuala Lumpur in 1958, and to Indonesia late in 1959 for a Colombo Plan conference.[3] In government Labour associated New Zealand with the Anglo-Malayan Defence Agreement in 1959. There were close links with some of the Malaysian leaders, Lee Kuan Yew of Singapore for one, and Charles Bennett had got close to Malayan leaders when High Commissioner in Kuala Lumpur.

National, in office from the end of 1960, also faced pressure from the United States to become involved in Indochina. Over Laos in 1961 National maintained the Labour position that a neutral Laos was the goal and that military action by SEATO was not itself a cure for the Laotian problem.[4] In

---

[1]   Nash at the Labour Party conference in May 1958 defended SEATO as a purely defensive organisation: 'that is why there is no interference in Indonesia'. 744.00/5-2058, RG59, USNA.
[2]   In an interview for the Dulles Oral History Archive in 1968 Nash said there was more evidence of the Americans than of the North Vietnamese in Laos at the time, N2432/0389. For a discussion of Nash's reservations and wish to use the United Nations, see Pearson, *Paper Tiger*, pp. 81-84. See also Sinclair, *Nash*, pp. 323-4. Pearson's account details the activity at SEATO meetings about which Sinclair could only speculate: at one meeting in January 1960 New Zealand was the only delegation to object to a more restrictive definition of insurgency: 'not only was the Government in the highly unusual situation of openly disagreeing with all of its Western allies, it was also holding up the process of military planning critical to stopping a communist advance' (Pearson, p. 83). On the other hand Pearson notes that the Australians, the British and the French were privately supportive (p. 84).
[3]   Sinclair, *Nash*, pp. 322, 326-7.
[4]   *EAR*, April 1961, p. 33. Holyoake told Rusk in March that New Zealand would fulfil its SEATO obligations but had to draw a distinction between the obligations under the Treaty to come to the assistance of the victim of aggression and the more obscure situation arising out of subversion or indirect aggression. EA63/1/14/1, notes for Holyoake report to Cabinet, 7 April 1961.

March 1962 the Thanat-Rusk statement had made it clear that the United States would act to aid Thailand under SEATO, even if the other allies did not. SEATO unanimity was no longer a shelter for New Zealand.

We do not know how Labour would have handled this change if it had been the government. National fell into line, though reluctantly. An ANZUS Council meeting was held in Canberra in May, after which Secretary of State Dean Rusk visited Wellington. The Americans initiated the meeting, the first in two years: with its principal SEATO allies, Britain and France, unenthusiastic about the involvement in the region, ANZUS had become important. A few days later Kennedy announced the dispatch of American forces to Thailand and New Zealand followed suit: 'Mr Holyoake thought it most important that we should join with our allies in demonstrating solidarity with Thailand at a time when the military situation in Northern Laos has deteriorated and Communist forces had moved very near to the borders of Thailand.'[5]

Labour's support for SEATO and involvement in Indochina remained qualified in opposition, as befitted a party which had resisted military intervention in Laos so firmly when in government. Martyn Finlay told one gathering that he was unhappy about both SEATO and ANZUS but was prepared to adhere to them in the absence of any alternative: he would have preferred to see a United Nations force backed by a strong international police force and he noted the ability of the UN to despatch emergency forces to the Middle East and the Congo as a promising development.[6]

There was a marked contrast between the evaluations of Sukarno, the nationalist leader of Indonesia, and the praise which greeted independence in both Western Samoa (1962) and in Malaysia (1963).[7] In neither of these cases did independence entail any challenge to Western influence. In the case of Malaysia, independence was plainly a way of preserving it, an ideal way, said one Department of External Affairs comment, of forestalling Indonesian aspirations.[8] Nordmeyer, the new leader, supported the establishment of Malaysia and Nash hoped that New Zealand's defence obligations would continue to the new country.[9]

---

5   *EAR*, May 1962, p. 25, Sept. 1962, pp. 34–35. New Zealand sent SAS troops: they were withdrawn, the crisis having abated, in September. In August, the King and Queen of Thailand visited New Zealand, the first visit of an Asian head of state.
6   *NZER*, p. 156.
7   Malaysia, a union of the independent Commonwealth state Malaya and three British territories—Singapore, and Sarawak and Sabah on the island of Borneo—came into being in September 1963. Singapore seceded two years later.
8   DEA thoughts on Airmail Bulletin, 61/25, EA63/1/14/1, MERT. The Australians, for instance, told New Zealand they liked the Malaysia idea because it would keep Singapore and its base within the Western alliance. New Zealand High Commission Canberra to Wellington, AB61/26, MERT.
9   McCraw, 'NZ Foreign Policy in Asia', pp. 377–8, quoting parliamentary statements, 9 July 1963.

Over the next months/years the Holyoake government was more preoccupied with Malaysia than with Indochina. Malaysia's legitimacy had been and was questioned by President Sukarno, who saw it as neocolonialist device to maintain Western influence in Southeast Asia. Many in National Party circles were 'gung-ho' about Indonesia, seeing Sukarno as another Nasser, who should also be dealt with summarily. One journal reckoned early in 1964 that it was an open secret in Wellington that 'some influential people, particularly in defence circles, are increasingly irritated by what they regard as the timidity of the New Zealand attitude towards Dr Soekarno .... quite a lot of ordinarily sober opinion supports the view that, given displays of meekness, the Indonesian leader becomes more and more ferocious'.[10] But the government itself was more cautious and in this respect probably echoed public opinion. Holyoake visited Sukarno in April 1964 after attending a SEATO meeting in Manila: '... it does not seem sensible to be in the area and not make the gesture .... all I want to do is to tell him where we stand if there is actual fighting with Malaysia, and perhaps to add another voice of caution and restraint for what it is worth.'[11] Uncertainty about the intentions of the United States, which had acquiesced in the transfer of West New Guinea to Indonesia in 1962, may have contributed.[12]

The crisis between Indonesia on the one hand and Malaysia and Britain on the other—'confrontation', as it was known—escalated in August 1964, with Indonesian forays on to the Malayan peninsula; and at this time the government did accept the need for direct military involvement. Labour was more hesitant than National about New Zealand forces being committed on the Borneo frontier between Indonesia and Malaysia.[13] Ironically, the involvement was soon to be used by both the Cabinet (in private) and the Labour Party (in public) as an argument against the more controversial involvement in Vietnam.

What had been happening in Vietnam? The Laos crisis had passed, but that in Vietnam had intensified. The narrowly based Ngo Dinh Diem government was under increasing pressure in the countryside from an insurgent movement, the National Liberation Front or Viet Cong, which had close links with the North Vietnamese government, and it faced sectarian opposition as well. In 1963, following renewed urging from Washington, New Zealand agreed in principle to send a non-combatant unit to South Vietnam: a field engineer detachment of two officers and twenty other troops. The force was sent only in May 1964, being delayed because of disturbed conditions in

10 *NZE&T*, 1 Feb. 1964.
11 Holyoake to Marshall, 1 April 1964, Ms Papers 1403, 268/3, ATL.
12 For West New Guinea, see Gregory Pemberton, *All The Way: Australia's Road to Vietnam*. Sydney, 1987, pp. 83–106.
13 See *NZH*, 7 Sept. 1964.

Saigon after the overthrow of Diem. By the time it arrived, American pressure was intensifying again.

Labour had only reluctantly agreed with National's decision to send the engineers to South Vietnam and was unhappy when the force went. 'It is true we have not sent a detachment of men who are armed or are aggressive, but it is absurd to say . . . that an engineering unit in New Zealand uniform is a non-combatant force.'[14] The issue would not go away. Twelve months later, American involvement in Vietnam had escalated, and New Zealand had decided to make a combat commitment to the war.

The government and the war

The government's decision to make a combat commitment in Vietnam can be readily explained in terms of the principles of the independent foreign policy of the early 1960s. The government—and the Department of External Affairs—wished to keep the United States (and Britain) militarily and politically involved in Asia and the western Pacific.

The silent component of the independent foreign policy—reluctance—also played a part, a point made particularly by David McCraw in his appropriately named article.[15] After President Lyndon Johnson had written to Holyoake in December 1964, referring to the fact that he could not ask the American people to make sacrifices without support from America's 'closest allies in the area',[16] Cabinet decided that Malaysia would have first claim on New Zealand's armed forces as a matter of principle. It also took a decision that New Zealand would not contribute combat forces to Vietnam.[17] When Holyoake wrote to Johnson in February, still declining to make a commitment, he explained that it was, at that time, 'just not possible for us politically to step up our military aid while coup succeeds coup and the whole situation in Vietnam remains so chaotic'.[18]

---

[14]   *NZPD*, 338, p. 331 (25 June 1964); in 1963 Nordmeyer had agreed 'that non-combatant aid may well be justified under existing conditions . . . . whatever form of aid is decided on we agree that, provided it is non-combatant aid, under the special circumstances that aid is justified.' (*NZPD*, 335, p. 407, 9 July 1963)
[15]   See David McCraw, 'Reluctant Ally: New Zealand's Entry into the Vietnam War', *NZJH*, 15/1 (April 1981), pp. 49-60; Roberto Rabel, 'Vietnam and the Collapse of the Foreign Policy Consensus', *NZWA 1957-72*, pp. 40-63; W. S. McKinnon, 'New Zealand Military Involvement in Vietnam' (in author's possession).
[16]   Johnson to Holyoake, 12 Dec. 1964, EA 478/4/6, MERT. Such letters, on notepaper, signed by Johnson (or any other head of government), were not common.
[17]   Cabinet agreed that the defence of Malaysia was the first priority within New Zealand's defence commitments and obligations in Southeast Asia. CM (64) 49, 14 Dec. 1964. Ms Papers 1814, ATL.
[18]   Holyoake to Johnson, 24 Feb. 1965: DEA suggestions are on SEA to PM, 19 Feb. 1965. EA478/4/6, MERT. A similar attitude obtained to any overseas commitment: 'Holyoake . . . loathed overseas expenditure . . . . "most people in the Department assume that the government wants overseas posts or indeed that it really has much belief in an External Affairs service. Of course it does not." ': McIntosh, quoted in Malcolm Templeton, 'Moving on from Suez', in *NZWA 1957-72*, p. 7.

Only American pressure and Australia's decision to commit troops forced the government to change its mind. The latter was particularly crucial—if Australia had decided not to get involved, New Zealand would almost certainly not have done so either. But in contrast to 1942-43, a New Zealand government committed to the cause in principle could not stand aside once Australia had decided to go ahead. On 24 May Cabinet approved the dispatch of an artillery battery of approximately 120 men.[19]

The fact that pressure was applied does not mean that the idea of an independent foreign policy was in ruins, that power had replaced consent and cooperation. The response, though controversial, was materially very meagre. Moreover, the majority of the public were accepting and undoubtedly this was also because participation was linked with America's security guarantee, felt by most, including the government, to be as necessary in 1965 as in 1951:

> if the allies of the U.S. do not stand by it in Vietnam to the fullest extent of their capacity, the U.S. attitude to them will inevitably be affected. It is relevant for us in this respect that the ANZUS Treaty is not precise, that Congress is questioning whether the allies of the U.S. are bearing a reasonable share of the mounting burden on Vietnam; and that a significant segment of Congress and public opinion in this country is tending towards a 'neo-isolationist' attitude—questioning whether, in the light of modern weapons of war it is, in fact, vital to the security of the United States to protect such countries as Vietnam from the encroachments of Communism. Against this background, the visit of Cabot Lodge assumes considerable significance, the point at issue being not the immediate one of whether or not we can provide forces in Vietnam ... but what effect our decision will have on the U.S. attitude, in the long term towards problems of more immediate concern to our security.[20]

This was George Laking, New Zealand's Ambassador in Washington, speaking, but all the circumstantial evidence suggests that his view was shared by a majority of New Zealanders. At no stage did the American—or indeed the British—commitment to Asia look entirely secure to the Pearl Harbor/ Singapore generation. So New Zealand's involvement in Vietnam was consistent with one of its most traditional foreign policy goals—keeping a friendly great power on its side of the Pacific.

So powerful was this objective, and also the wish to keep New Zealand's own commitment of resources to the region to a minimum, that they made for continuity in New Zealand policy even when the military circumstances in Vietnam changed dramatically after the Tet offensive and the United States began to retrench. Indeed arguably the first consideration became *more*

---

[19] Rabel, 'Vietnam', p. 47.
[20] New Zealand Embassy, Washington, to DEA, Wellington, 15 April 1965. McIntosh made very similar arguments in a lengthy memorandum to Holyoake dated 1 May. EA478/4/6, MERT. President Johnson's envoy, Henry Cabot Lodge, visited Wellington in April.

important after 1968, when America's will was faltering, while the second was more important in the earlier years, when American pressure was insistent.

The decision to become involved was controversial. The government talked about anti-Communism, of the need for New Zealand to participate with other countries in the defence of one small country against aggression, rhetoric deliberately designed to make Labour uncomfortable. In 1964 Holyoake had thanked America for its 'efforts to maintain peace and to ensure that Communist aggression does not succeed in engulfing those countries who wish to preserve their independence and freedom'.[21] In a televised statement on 13 May, in which he foreshadowed the decision to send a force to Vietnam, Holyoake referred to 'the ruthless and undeclared war which Communist North Vietnam, aided and abetted by Communist China, is waging against South Vietnam'. The Communist aggression was now 'flagrant'. Holyoake stressed that the war was not a civil war, nor a popular uprising, that the South Vietnamese people themselves were fighting for their own freedom, and that if South Vietnam fell to the Communists, then it would be the turn of Thailand, Malaya, of 'every other smaller country in the region'. The *Dominion*, 14 May 1965, assessed that the Prime Minister

> spoke for the vast majority of New Zealanders when he said that South Vietnam must not be abandoned to the Communists. He need have little fear that, save among a fringe of well-meaning demonstrators, there is confusion in the public mind about the basic issues involved in the present fighting. A more forceful gesture of aid to back up the American position is due if it can be made without impairing our support to Malaysia, our primary commitment.

For the government and its supporters the public frame of reference for defending the conflict was the Cold War, not colonial or neocolonial rebellion:

> Have we already forgotten Czechoslovakia and Greece in Europe and all the Communist campaigns in Asia? New Zealand became involved in containing open Communist aggression in Korea in 1950 and Communist insurgency in Malaya in 1955. By virtue of the ANZAM relationship, and in accordance with the terms of the Manila (SEATO) Treaty, we have established regional defence arrangements which recognise that New Zealand security is directly connected with events in South-East Asia .... Indonesian 'confrontation' is ... an offshoot indeed of Communist tactics, and a result perhaps of their success elsewhere.[22]

Hostility to Communism merged with traditional New Zealand fear of attack from 'the north'. Behind North Vietnam lay China. Good relations with China had been a popular goal in the mid 1950s and early 1960s, but not a deep-seated one. It was not difficult to arouse anxieties about China, a country about which people knew little, certainly about its relations with Vietnam. If

21   *EAR*, Aug. 1964, p. 21.
22   *EAR*, May 1965, p. 6.

there was a war in Vietnam, then many people drew the conclusion that the Chinese were not the friendly people they thought. A canvassing of opinion by the *Waikato Times* demonstrated that conservative-minded people thought of the issue overwhelmingly in terms of Communism, and placed the participation in the war firmly within the context of support for the Americans and hostility to China. Another section of the poll suggested that such attitudes were linked to many socially conservative and anti-Communist attitudes in domestic politics.[23]

The argument was apparently, if not substantively, helped by the outbreak of the Cultural Revolution in China in 1966. Although in fact it meant that Chinese activity in foreign relations declined—and the anti-Communist coup in Indonesia at the end of September 1965 was significant in this respect too—it made China seem much more menacing. George Laking, now Secretary of External Affairs, argued in May 1967 that 'behind and adding a further dimension to [other Asian] problems, vast enough in themselves, had been the growing power of Communist China—a China whose leaders (whatever their internal differences) have shown themselves united in their determination to make dogma and conceptions of the historic role of a united China the moving force of the new Asia'.[24] Holyoake vigorously endorsed the ANZUS Council communiqué in April 1967 which stressed that 'the most dangerous threat to the security of the world continues to come from Peking's brand of militant Communism and from Communist armed aggression and subversion in South-East Asia. The focal point of this threat is the aggression by North Vietnam against the Republic of Vietnam.'[25]

Certainly after the initial heat generated by the decision abated, informed observers judged that most New Zealanders supported the war. One journal reckoned in August 1965 that 'the public had accepted commitment in Vietnam. Sniping may keep on ... but at the political centre things are, presumably, more or less orderly.'[26]

Opposition to the war

There *were* those on the left who from the inception of American involvement in Vietnam and New Zealand's association with it had criticised from a stance exactly the same as in the Korean War; but they were a minority of those opposing the war. For the Communist Party of New Zealand, North Vietnam

[23] From 'Vietnam June 1965–June 1966', ATL. A collection of press cuttings accumulated at the time, mostly, but not entirely, from the *Waikato Times*.
[24] *EAR*, May 1967, p. 16. See also Ian Templeton, *NZE&T*, 1 Aug., 1 Sept. 1967; Marshall in *NZPD*, 353, p. 3683 (26 Oct. 1967), 'the southward pressure of Communism'.
[25] *EAR*, April 1967, p. 30. Similarly Laking, *EAR*, March 1967, p. 17, who described the 'growing power of Communist China—a China which has shown itself determined to shape the future of Asia in accordance with the dictates of dogma ... has introduced new techniques of subversion and aggression to disturb an already fragile social and political fabric'.
[26] *Comment*, 24 (Aug. 1965), p. 1.

was entirely in the right and the issue was not whether or not it was involved in South Vietnam but whether it could provide enough assistance, with the support of China and the Soviet Union, to the National Liberation Front of South Vietnam to enable that organisation to achieve victory. As one May 1965 flyer put it, 'There is no threat to New Zealand in allowing the Vietnamese people the government of their choice. The Americans and Ngo Dinh Diem prevented elections in 1956 in South Vietnam because they would have lost them. What humbug to talk of the Vietnam people aggressing against themselves. The only foreign troops in Vietnam are the Americans and their satellites.' The polemic did go on to claim that 'there are virtually no North Vietnam people in South Vietnam', even though it would have been consistent with the earlier argument to regard this as an irrelevant matter.

Much of the opposition to the war came from other perspectives. A number of writers and scholars made public comments. W. H. Oliver stressed the legitimacy (and implicitly the loyalty) of dissent: 'I do not think we should pursue a separate policy outside the Western bloc .... I seek to see such a policy pursued *within* that bloc—as one of the many influences which the Americans must heed .... I want basically New Zealand to join the saner side of the debate within the west.'[27] C. K. Stead wrote in November 1966, 'Why did I sign a petition calling for withdrawal of New Zealand troops from Vietnam? Why, if President Johnson had visited Auckland, would I have embarrassed those who welcomed him by carrying a placard? These are questions asked of me by people who know I am not a Marxist, not a pacifist and that I have never joined or been committed to a political party.'[28] The university teacher and writer, Vincent O'Sullivan, preferred democratic to communist regimes, but did not think New Zealand should be in Vietnam and noted that in the eyes of most of Asia and Africa it should not be.[29]

Criticism of the war from anti-militarist and anti-colonialist perspectives was evident from the very beginning. One of the first demonstrations against the war, at Wellington Airport when Cabot Lodge arrived, was partly mounted by CND people, in Wellington for their Easter conference; thus there was an overlap between the anti-war, ban-the-bomb movement and opposition to the war in Vietnam.[30] Opposition to the war itself was a driving force behind church leaders' criticism of New Zealand's involvement. The graphic television coverage of the damage wrought by aerial bombardment gave an added intensity to opposition to the war as war.[31] Dissenting church leaders focused on the horrors of war, the bombing of North Vietnam, the use of napalm and the like. The ebb and flow of debate and controversy in the

27 W. H. Oliver, 'Moralism and Foreign Policy', *Landfall*, 19/4 (Dec. 1965), p. 381.
28 *Auckland Star*, 21 Nov. 1966.
29 Committee on Vietnam, *Intervention in Vietnam*. Wellington, 1965.
30 Barry Mitcalfe, *Salient*, 8 Aug. 1965.
31 Rabel, 'Vietnam', p. 57.

United States was mirrored in New Zealand, but New Zealand responses also tapped characteristic attitudes to war and conflict. At a meeting with a deputation from the churches, Holyoake was told by one church leader that he had 'never known such a weight of communication to a President of the Methodist Church as there had been on the Vietnam issue .... what would gain public approval [it seemed to him] was not the contribution of New Zealand troops but aid in any other way such as under the Colombo Plan'. The National Council of Churches, in a statement on Vietnam issued by the Commission of the Churches on International Affairs, rejected a military solution to the problem and counselled the virtue of recognising China. In his reply to the churches Holyoake pointed out that without the military campaign by the United States and its allies, the result would be a military victory by the North.[32] Throughout the course of the war, criticism surged whenever some particularly bloody aspect of the military operations, or some new military initiative by the Americans, hit the headlines. This was particularly true of the on-again, off-again aerial bombardment campaign. The resumption of bombing in June 1966, while the ANZUS and SEATO Councils were in session in Canberra, was a case in point. Labour M.P.s were particularly vigorous on this occasion—it was a more straightforward matter to oppose bombing than for a party hostile to Communism to formulate a stance on the war as a whole.[33] In February 1968 when a large anti-war delegation met the Prime Minister under the auspices of the Committee on Vietnam, the burden of criticism was largely the evils rather than the politics of the war.[34]

The colonialist aspects of the war also exercised many. This would have been even clearer if the French had been one of the protagonists; as it was, many drew parallels between the situation of the Americans in 1965 and that of the French in 1954 and earlier and saw South Vietnam as a colony in all but name. One publication, *Vietnam*, by Barry Mitcalfe and Conrad Bollinger, from the Wellington Committee on Vietnam, stressed the anti-imperialist argument: 'The West finds it difficult to admit that the revolts of the Asiatic and African people against Western domination could be prompted by noble sentiments of independence or patriotism. They seem to want to believe that only fanatics, terrorists or communists are prepared to take up arms against Western dominance.'[35]

Critics also charged the United States and its New Zealand ally of pursuing an essentially imperialist policy of wishing to deny China the right to an independent existence. In this instance criticism of the war and its foreign policy underpinnings drew on the long-standing New Zealand scepticism

32 Holyoake to National Council of Churches, 17 Sept. 1965. Ms Papers 1814, 278/2, ATL.
33 See exchanges on Ms Papers 1814, 369/5, ATL; *NZPD*, 346, p. 988 (30 June 1966).
34 Ms Papers 1814, 455/5, ATL.
35 Wellington Committee on Vietnam, *Vietnam*. Wellington, 1965, p. 18.

about America's cold war with China, and its refusal to either recognise the People's Republic or accept its admission to the United Nations.[36] Keith Buchanan, Professor of Geography at Victoria University and in 1965 one of the most prominent critics of the war, published *The Chinese People and the Chinese Earth*.[37] Jim Cairns, a young Australian Labor Party politician, published *Living With Asia* in 1965 and introduced it by noting that 'Asia, in spite of our growing awareness of it, remains foreign and not understood. Fear and suspicion of Asia are felt not only by many ordinary Australians, but by many of those who form public opinion and foreign policy.'[38] A publication such as *New Zealand and Southeast Asia* made similar points both in its content and by the very fact that it was produced.[39] It arose out of a lively, well-attended conference.

In these early years of the war too, most critics argued that the opposition to the government in South Vietnam was essentially indigenous, with little support and no control from North Vietnam—a response in part to the American and New Zealand governments' argument that the war was in essence an act of aggression by North Vietnam against South Vietnam. The South Vietnam National Liberation Front, it was argued, was just that, a mass movement, not one fostered by Hanoi: 'the leaders of the Front insist that the affairs of South Vietnam must be settled by the South Vietnamese themselves'.[40] Or as one New Zealand critic put it ironically:

> Reading tendentious rubbish such as: 'the NLF is a shadowy organization brought into being by the ... Vietnamese Communist Party for which it is indeed a "front" ', [my public would] nod their heads in agreement, cut the item out to show their friends, stick it up on the kitchen wall under the calendar of the (New Zealand) Chinese greengrocer; or use it as a marker in the current issue of *Hoofbeats*.[41]

Labour's position on the war—and the discomfort it felt about the issue—was entirely explicable if we remind ourselves of its perspective on the independent foreign policy consensus of the preceding decade. The belief in

36   See, for instance, G. J. C. McArthur, 'The China Image: Is China The Aggressor?', *Monthly Review*, Nov. 1965, pp. 13-20; C. P. Fitzgerald, 'China's Place in the World', *Listener*, 5 Nov. 1965, p. 5; 'China: A Threat in Southeast Asia?' in R. Alister Taylor, ed., *Peace, Power and Politics in Asia*. Wellington, 1969, pp. 64-77. Fitzgerald was Professor of Far Eastern [*sic!*] History at A.N.U. and later Australia's first Ambassador to the People's Republic of China in 1972.
37   London, 1966.
38   Jim Cairns, *Living With Asia*. Melbourne, 1965, p. 1.
39   See, for instance, Michael Bassett and Robert Nola, eds., *New Zealand and Southeast Asia*. Auckland, 1966.
40   Jean Lacouture, 'What is the NLF?' in *Peace, Power and Politics*, p. 97.
41   Sarah Campion, 'If only I had seen the light', *Monthly Review*, March 1966, pp. 12-13. Contrast this and the previous comment with the analysis of the NLF and the nature of the revolutionary movement in the South and its relationship with the North in Gabriel Kolko's leftist history of the war, *Vietnam: Anatomy of a War*. New York, 1985, pp. 102-8.

economic and social, not military solutions, anti-militarism and hatred for war, support for détente, the Commonwealth and the United Nations—all can be identified in Labour's attitude. So also can anti-Communism. Unfortunately for Labour, it was difficult to settle on a policy which accommodated all of these goals or values.

With the pressure from New Zealand's allies to do something, with the party unwilling to break with the foreign policy consensus in any other respect, it found itself in an unappealing situation. Nordmeyer made a statement on 28 April 1965. He stressed that the issue should be handed over to the United Nations, that it was not for one nation, no matter how powerful, to decide, and that ANZUS did not pledge New Zealand to a war.[42] This was definitely leaning to the side of opposition to the war without actually saying so. At the Labour Party's annual conference in May the party decided to oppose the sending of New Zealand troops to Vietnam. Nordmeyer called for a negotiated settlement that would end Communist aggression. Any action to resist aggression should be undertaken only through the United Nations or any other international authority. Nordmeyer also told the conference, when speaking in support of the resolution against the deployment, that New Zealand's integrity among the newly emergent nations depended on not sending troops to Vietnam.

The fact that Nordmeyer was talking in terms of Communist aggression gave an indication of the limits of Labour's challenge to the government. Not only was Labour, like National, an anti-Communist party, it was either unable or unwilling to define the war as other than a war against Communism. Labour's anti-Communism and its healthy respect for the public's anti-Communism qualified that criticism: the comment above about 'only fanatics, terrorists or communists' wanting to fight the West was a classic instance of the demarcation line which even the anti-war movement (as distinct from the Labour Party) drew between Communism and legitimate dissent.

Was Labour's position convincing though—opposition to the war and to New Zealand military involvement, but opposition also to Communism? Nordmeyer did argue that as the Americans had refused to send troops to Malaysia because they were too heavily committed in Vietnam, New Zealand should refuse to help in Vietnam because it was too heavily committed in Malaysia. But it was difficult to make that distinction, as the government itself had found. It served only to underline Labour's dilemma. The connected set of assumptions had come adrift: on the one hand, the belief in economic and social rather than military solutions, always particularly strong in the Labour Party; on the other, anti-Communism.

Friction within the party was inevitable. A minority, led by Timaru M.P. Basil Arthur, rebelled against the party's official policy; America should

[42] *Christchurch Star*, 28 April 1965.

receive support, he said, for what the government was doing in Vietnam—North Vietnam was the aggressor. The Associate Minister of Finance, R. D. Muldoon, forwarded a letter to Holyoake from the Palmerston North City Council employee members of the Wellington Drivers' Union, describing it as 'typical of a very large number of letters that have come in since the Vietnam television debate and which have been virtually 100 per cent favourable to the government'. The letter stated that the members 'fully endorse Government action on the troops to S. Vietnam proposal. We do this not only because we believe it is right, but because we fear that Communist members within the union and the F.O.L. are using this proposal and the union members who don't know better, to further their own and China's political views.'[43] Similarly in July 1965, for instance, the Chairman of the Auckland Labour Representation Committee said that the Labour Party 'strongly resented' attempts being made by certain people to implicate it in support of the Committee on Vietnam: he stated that since one public meeting had been held by the Auckland LRC and the Auckland Trades Council on Vietnam, it did not want to support another meeting being organised by the Committee because the Commonwealth Prime Ministers' initiative, which Labour strongly supported, was now under way, and it was now evident that the responsibility for peace rested with North Vietnam and China.[44]

Others disagreed. Martyn Finlay was one of the M.P.s who was most articulate and vocal in his criticism of American policy. But even he, though arguing that a Labour government would not have committed troops to Vietnam, refrained from committing Labour to withdrawal if it became the government:

> Once they [the troops] have gone there a somewhat different situation is created.... If you are asking me to make a positive assertion that we would certainly withdraw them I say that this cannot be done and that it would be a foolish gesture for anyone to embark on .... The suggestion that we might withdraw, that there are limits beyond which our patience will not go, could very well enable us to exercise a degree of importance much beyond the warrant that our population and military contribution gives us the right to exercise.[45]

This was not a party that believed in its policy or thought anyone else did. The cry that just because Labour opposed the government's policy it was not necessarily being duped by Communism, was also heard far too often for the Labour Party to look like a party on the attack. In the first opportunity to debate the issue in Parliament after Holyoake had announced the combat

---

43 Ms Papers 1814, 323/3, ATL.
44 *Auckland Star*, 23 July 1965, quoted in J. A. Elder, 'The New Zealand Labour Party and the Vietnam War: Traditions and Policy Until 1973', Univ. of Auckland, M. A. thesis, 1973, p. 143.
45 Martin Finlay, 'Labour Party View on South-East Asia', *New Zealand and Southeast Asia*, p. 52.

commitment, many Labour M.P.s absented themselves; there was a strong belief in the parliamentary party that there was no gain for Labour in the issue.[46]

At the end of 1965 Norman Kirk replaced Nordmeyer as leader. In some respects Kirk was seen as a leader with more links with the trade union movement, and the FOL had taken a stronger stand over Vietnam than had the Labour Party. But Kirk was not necessarily to the left of Nordmeyer on that issue. Initially Kirk restated Labour's commitment to withdrawing the New Zealand force but on one occasion, in February 1966, he suggested that the forces could stay but in a non-combatant role. Kirk clearly wanted to prevent Labour's being tied to an electorally unpopular policy, i.e. withdrawal. His task was complicated when the Joint Council of Labour (a body with representation from both the party and the FOL) reached agreement on a Vietnam policy. Kirk argued that the joint statement allowed for troops to continue to play a defensive role: 'if a noncombatant force of engineers does go to Vietnam to build a hospital it is not going to do much good if the hospital is burnt down the night after it is completed'. And in the External Affairs Committee of the Labour Party conference, the pre-election conference, a little later in the year, Kirk attempted to get the statement modified. But the amendments proposed by Tizard were withdrawn when it became clear that a majority of committee members were opposed to them. Similarly an attempt by Finlay to amend the motion in full conference to commit Labour to a noncombatant force also failed, 360 to 64.[47]

1966–68

An American commentator noted on the eve of President Johnson's brief visit to New Zealand in October 1966 that the 'National Party considers New Zealand involvement in Vietnam a plus in the coming campaign . . . . [there] is no systematic opinion polling in New Zealand, degree of popular support for American involvement not known, but generally believed to be majority . . . even Labour Party supports humanitarian efforts'.[48] Big welcoming crowds turned out to greet Johnson in Wellington. At the end of 1966, despite more controversy, in particular over renewed bombing of North Vietnam, some of this mood survived. Holyoake, according to one journalist,

> quite clearly had no doubts from the beginning of the campaign (whatever doubts he may have entertained earlier) that his Vietnam policy was a winning policy. His first meeting in Christchurch must have reinforced him in this view—if indeed the remarkably fervent welcome to President Johnson from professedly phlegmatic

---

46 Interview with Sir Wallace Rowling, 12 Sept. 1989.
47 Elder, pp. 156, 160, 162.
48 'Attachment A', United States Embassy, Wellington to State Department, 9 Oct. 1966. I am indebted to Owen Wilkes for this reference.

Wellingtonians had not already done so. At every occasion, from every platform, Mr Holyoake spoke about Vietnam. If there had been some doubt that it would be an issue at all, he removed that doubt, too.[49]

National's 1966 victory confirmed this analysis. So did another 'poll'. When Roger Horrocks surveyed 250 essays on Vietnam by teenagers he found that over 80 per cent of them supported New Zealand's Vietnam policy, instancing most often the argument, 'the Communists are coming to get us, so we've got to stop them'. Sixty per cent also argued that by participating in the war New Zealand ensured it would be protected if it were directly threatened.[50]

Some commentators questioned whether Vietnam was an issue in the election at all, but most thought it had played a role, and one beneficial to the government.[51] And the government had achieved this not by breaking with the independent foreign policy and taking the country into a major military commitment in Vietnam, but by working within the framework of the policy. It paid heed to New Zealanders' insularity as well as to their wish to be protected: 'Setting aside almost instinctive responses to appeals from Britain, we did not, I think, feel ourselves necessarily involved during this period in the affairs of the world at large. It is not always surprising that some vestiges of this attitude remain. Perhaps they explain in part the reactions of some people to the war in Vietnam.'[52]

A conservative American commentator, William F. Buckley, who visited New Zealand early in 1967, commented on the population as a whole:

During the [1966] election the Left tried very hard to encourage the voters to punish the Government for sending 150 soldiers to Vietnam but the people, churlishly, refused to do so. Not so much because they approved New Zealand's presence in Vietnam, as because they do not really care about foreign policy. Their exquisite islands are so far removed from strife that they cultivate their isolation. To the dismay of the Left, which is involved in mankind and very much wants the Americans out of Vietnam.[53]

But the strife came closer. Early 1967 saw major demonstrations in city streets against the visit of the South Vietnamese leader, Nguyen Cao Ky, a contrast to the relatively benign welcome accorded Johnson and a clue perhaps to the way New Zealanders saw the alliance with the United States.

---

[49]   *NZE&T*, 1 Dec. 1966. For a 'Vietnam not involved' comment: the 'electorate preferred genuine local issues . . . . Vietnam did not involve in the voter's mind the Grand Passions which the Returned Servicemen's Association and the Committee on Vietnam found in the topic.' Owen Gager, 'Nowhere Men: the 1966 Electioneers', *Dispute*, Jan.-Feb. 1967, p. 5.
[50]   Roger Horrocks, 'The Vietnam Mythology', *Dispute*, April 1967, pp. 7-8.
[51]   Muldoon thought Labour lost the Miramar seat because of Vietnam. Muldoon, *Young Turk*, p. 81.
[52]   George Laking, *EAR*, May 1967, p. 15.
[53]   *Marlborough Express*, 1 March 1967. I am indebted to Roberto Rabel for this reference.

Under pressure from the Americans and the Australians the government increased its deployment in Vietnam twice in 1967. The second announcement followed some weeks after a visit from two American envoys, Maxwell Taylor and Clark Clifford—again, there were major demonstrations, in contrast to Johnson's visit ten months earlier. In the United States too, 1967 was a turning point in the war, the year in which the foreign-policymaking elité split over the war, in which millions of ordinary Americans were drawn into protest actions of which the large-scale mobilisations were the most memorable. The view that the war was a betrayal, rather than a defence, of American values had found a home in the American political mainstream.

Labour's position on the war did not shift significantly in 1967. Kirk stressed in May that Labour was not anti-American; he also joined in the welcome to the American admiral, D. L. McDonald, visiting New Zealand for the twenty-fifth anniversary celebrations of the Battle of the Coral Sea.[54] At the same time he discussed the need to get beyond SEATO and ANZUS and explore new forms of relations with Asia. But this did not necessarily mean China—or North Vietnam. Labour committed itself very strongly to Malaysia and Singapore as a way both of emphasising the acceptable aspects of New Zealand involvement in Asia, and separating out Vietnam from other aspects of New Zealand foreign policy.[55] In a lecture to a National Party audience in 1967, F. L. W. Wood attempted to steer the government in a similar direction: he elegantly defended the old consensus and enjoined the government to speak up to its allies, accepting its argument about the importance of Asia whilst neatly turning the point:

> Looking at the world today, realistic New Zealand eyes see not *two* great powers, not even three, by the addition of Russia, but *four*. And this is not all, and what follows is perhaps the core of the problem and the nature of the opportunity for us. My New Zealand eyes see not only super powers today, but a host of lesser ones . . . becoming increasingly present and compelling in Asia . . . . For New Zealand the tragedy of Vietnam has at least compelled us to get just a little more definite knowledge of an Asian people and its problems.[56]

Change came, but from outside, rather than within, New Zealand. With 'confrontation' with Indonesia over in 1966, pressure mounted in the ranks of the British government, besieged by balance of payments difficulties, to pull back from its expensive overseas deployments. In March 1967 George Laking took comfort from the fact that the British government had 'given an undertaking that it will not withdraw from its commitments to help maintain

54 *NZPD*, 350, pp. 668-9 (18 May 1967).
55 See, for instance, *Auckland Star*, 21 Jan. 1968.
56 *New Zealand and the Big Powers: Can a Small Nation Have a Mind of Its Own?* NZ National Party, Sir Sidney Holland Memorial Lecture. Wellington, 1967, p. 8.

the security of South-East Asia'.[57] But in its defence white paper of July 1967 the British government announced it would withdraw its forces from Southeast Asia completely by the mid 1970s. In January 1968, in the aftermath of a long-fought but now lost battle against devaluation of sterling, this was brought forward to 1971.

There was resentment in New Zealand at the speed and likely consequences of the British decision. Neither Malaysia nor Singapore was 'ready' to go it alone, isolationist pressure in the United States would be increased.[58] At the same time no one in New Zealand expected that it or Australia or both could take Britain's place. 'The sooner', said one newspaper editorial, Malaysia and Singapore 'appreciate that Australia and New Zealand can never fill the gap left by Britain, the sooner will they be ready to examine alternatives . . . .'[59] In Australia in particular there was debate about whether that country should also withdraw from Southeast Asia to a 'Fortress Australia', particularly if American intentions were uncertain.[60]

And the war was taking an increasing political toll. The pressure in Vietnam, in the United States and on New Zealand foreign policy, was increasing. American forces were besieged at Khe Sanh, in the hill country in the north-west of South Vietnam. In the Tet offensive, NLF and North Vietnamese forces demonstrated that South Vietnam's cities were not secure.

At the end of March, two conferences assembled in Wellington. At one end of the city, the SEATO and ANZUS Councils and the seven countries contributing forces to South Vietnam met; at the other, gathered the 'Peace, Power and Politics in Asia' conference.[61] This latter brought to the city such luminaries as Jean-Paul Sartre, Krishna Menon, Jean Lacouture and Conor Cruise O'Brien. It was a moment when the war reached its turning point. On the third day of the alternative conference, delegates learnt of President Johnson's dramatic announcement that he would not run for re-election and had ordered a halt to the bombing of North Vietnamese cities: 'The SEATO conference which was meant to be a platform on which Mr Holyoake could be seen exercising his statesmanship, turned out be a trapdoor—through which Mr Johnson dropped Mr Holyoake and other Vietnam allies.'[62] A mixture of 'joy and cynicism' greeted Johnson's statements at the rival conference, said

57   *EAR*, March 1967, pp. 18–19.
58   *Press*, 8 Jan. 1968; *Dominion*, 10 Jan. 1968.
59   *NZH*, 17 Jan. 1968.
60   *Auckland Star*, 8 April 1968, quoting Australian Prime Minister, John Gorton, 'Australia would have to do everything possible to ensure that America remained interested and retained a presence in South-East Asia'; see also J. L. Richardson, 'Political and Strategic Relations: A View from Canberra', in Bruce Brown, ed., *Asia and the Pacific in the 1970s: The Roles of the United States, Australia and New Zealand*. Wellington, 1971, pp. 137–8.
61   *Peace, Power and Politics in Asia*, pp. 7–11.
62   Ian Templeton, *NZE&T*, 1 May 1968.

one commentator some months later, 'but events have proved that Johnson was indeed serious ....'[63]

Conrad Bollinger wrote, 'we have had sporadic, almost underground resistance to our participation in foreign wars from the Boer War onwards, but we have never had opposition on this scale before'.[64] And some of the biggest demonstrations against the war took place in subsequent years—the biggest in 1971, the year New Zealand militarily disengaged from Vietnam. But in fact at the precise moment when President Johnson made his announcement, the most significant threat made by the war to the existing pattern of New Zealand foreign policy had passed.

Retreat?

Holyoake may have 'fallen through the trapdoor' but he knew what to do next. After 31 March 1968, and in the face of British as well as American retrenchment, one of the enduring mainsprings of New Zealand policy—to foster a continued great power commitment in Asia and the western Pacific— took on of necessity a new lease of life. Other things being equal, it was a more manageable task than handling the pressure as American involvement in the war was increasing. It is difficult to judge whether New Zealand policymakers thought it likely that the United States would do a complete scuttle from Asia: they must have thought it highly unlikely it would leave the Philippines, Taiwan or Japan.

In the meantime there was the task of doing what could be done to maintain British and American interest in the region. Before a five-power (Britain, Australia, New Zealand, Malaysia and Singapore) meeting in June 1968, Cabinet agreed that New Zealand should secure the maximum possible continuing British interest and role in the defence of Malaysia and Singapore, and for New Zealand's own part, avoid any commitments of a long-term or specific nature and discourage any disposition on the part of Malaysia and Singapore to look to Australia and New Zealand to pull their chestnuts out of the fire.[65] Australia was even more cautious than New Zealand: Malaysian-Philippine tension over the Malaysian state of Sabah contributed to its unease. It was not until February 1969 that both governments declared their willingness to keep forces in the Malaysia-Singapore area after 1971.[66] The Malaysia-Singapore commitment was also bipartisan: at the Labour Party conference in 1968 Kirk said that 'The last thing we ought to do is ... close off assistance to our neighbours, especially to members of the British

63 Taylor, 'Introduction', *Peace, Power and Politics in Asia*, p. 7. Taylor himself referred to 'turning-point'.
64 *Monthly Review*, May 1968, p. 9.
65 Record of Cabinet meeting, 4 June 1968. Ms Papers 1814, 456/1, ATL.
66 Chin Kin Wah, *The Defence of Malaysia and Singapore: The Transformation of a Security System 1957-1971*. Cambridge, 1983, pp. 145-50, 153-65.

Commonwealth.'67 Limited commitments to Malaysia/Singapore were a viable part of the independent foreign policy consensus because of the Commonwealth context.

New Zealand's commitment was qualified: the decision to stay on was not a decision to take on Britain's former treaty obligations—'there was no legal obligation ... to maintain forces in Malaysia or to follow specific courses of action for its external defence'. This position was underlined by New Zealand's reiteration after the May 1969 post-election riots in Malaysia that under no circumstances were New Zealand's forces to be used to maintain internal order.68

The New Zealand decision was taken, not because New Zealand on its own could foster the stability of Southeast Asia, but to help encourage the United States to commit itself to the region as a whole:69 for similar reasons, in November 1968 Holyoake announced that the New Zealand deployment in Vietnam would be expanded by the addition of an SAS squadron.

To what exent *was* the United States committed to the defence of Malaysia and Singapore? According to the *New York Times*, 'American officials had worked in close consultation with Australia and New Zealand over future security arrangements'.70 Holyoake claimed in September 1969 that all three ANZUS powers recognised that Malaysia and Singapore were part of the ANZUS area, although 'the United States has never spelled out in detail, nor have we ever asked them to spell out in detail, any hypothetical case in which the provisions of ANZUS would be triggered off'.71

President Richard Nixon told Holyoake that if the United States was humiliated or allowed itself to be pushed out of Vietnam, 'it would cease to be an Asian power', and he stressed that he had no intention of letting this happen.72 But what would happen? On his first trip as President to Asia Nixon had spoken at Guam about the future direction of American policy on the continent, stressing that the United States had to be emphatic about 'two points: one, that we would keep our treaty commitments .... And, two, that as far as the problems of military defence, except for the threat of a major power involving nuclear weapons, that the United States was going to encourage and had a right to expect that this problem would be increasingly

67 *Auckland Star*, 9 May 1968.
68 *NZEAR*, June 1969, p. 61; *NZPD*, 360, pp. 561-2 (5 June 1969). See also discussion in Chin, pp. 164-5.
69 Hugh Templeton, *NZPD*, 369, p. 4158 (20 Oct. 1970), quoted in McCraw, 'NZ Foreign Policy in Asia', p. 494.
70 Keith Jackson, ' "Because It's There ...": A Consideration of the Decision to Commit NZ Troops to Malaysia beyond 1971', *JSEAS*, 2/1 (March 1971), pp. 29-30, citing *New York Times*, 25 Feb. 1969.
71 *NZEAR*, Sept. 1969, p. 17, quoted in McCraw, 'NZ Foreign Policy in Asia', p. 486. For Malaysian and Singaporean concern at Australian and New Zealand reservations, see McCraw, 'NZ Foreign Policy in Asia', pp. 496-8.
72 Ms Papers 1814, 513/6, ATL.

handled by, and responsibility for it taken by, the Asian countries themselves.'[73]

Nixon argued that New Zealand and Australian support was essential to the successful development of regional cooperation: their forward defence policies were 'heartwarming'.[74] Very heartwarming, it might be surmised. The Americans had by this time announced two reductions in their troop numbers. Holyoake told the Nixon administration that having hoisted the New Zealand flag in Vietnam, the government would ensure that it would stay flying, 'so long as his party is in office'.[75] Despite public pressure, he refused to fix any date for the withdrawal of the New Zealand contingent in Vietnam. The renewed prospect of American isolationism made it all the *more* important to shore up America's commitment, if not to Vietnam itself, then certainly to Asia and the western Pacific.

But both Holyoake and Marshall told the Americans that while they would not reduce the numbers of New Zealanders in Vietnam, they would not increase them either, in view both of New Zealand commitments in Malaysia and the mood of domestic opinion: the government had 'stretched about as far as it could go'.[76] In April 1970 Holyoake endorsed the American intervention in Cambodia but he did so cautiously, a week after the initial action and stressing that New Zealand forces were not involved.[77] Nevertheless, the crisis, and the consequential need to stress solidarity with the United States, delayed plans to reduce the New Zealand deployment. Both Australia and New Zealand announced a withdrawal on 20 August 1970.

The New Zealand commitment to Malaysia and Singapore took on a different character after a Conservative government was returned to office in Britain in May 1970. The new Heath government was much more strongly committed to collaborating with the United States in the third world, including Southeast Asia, than was the outgoing Wilson Labour government. The British did not return in force to the region, however. When the five-power (Australia, Britain, Malaysia, New Zealand, Singapore) defence arrangement came into force in November 1971—at about the time that New Zealand's last combat forces left Vietnam—Holyoake again stressed that commitment extended to consultation, 'no more than that, in the event of an attack externally organised or supported or the threat of such an attack against either or both Singapore or Malaysia'.[78]

The quest for security—at limited expense—drove government policy towards Vietnam and Asia. It did so as powerfully, if not more powerfully,

73 *New York Times*, reported in *NZEAR*, July 1969, p. 15. Reported speech in text.
74 Shepherd to Laking and Corner, 19 Sept. 1969. Ms Papers 1814, 513/6, ATL.
75 Ms Papers 1814, 513/6. ATL.
76 Shepherd to Laking and Corner, 19 Sept. 1969. Ms Papers 1814, 513/6, ATL.
77 *NZFAR*, May 1970, pp. 37–38.
78 *NZFAR*, Nov. 1971, p. 69.

when America was retreating from involvement in Asia, as when its involvement had been deepening. How far would the Americans retreat? If it was as far as Hawaii, then New Zealand's efforts would have been wasted. Time alone would tell.[79]

Apprehension and dissension changed in tandem. As one waxed, the other waned. Further withdrawals of New Zealand forces were announced in the first months of 1971 and the last combat forces left Vietnam at the end of the year.

The end of the war and Labour in power

During the 1969 election campaign, the Labour Party was as committed as in 1966 to ending New Zealand's military involvement in Vietnam. But despite the changed circumstances of the war, Kirk was still careful to avoid the charge of being soft on Communism: 'Labour Governments and the Labour Party in this country have always been significantly and substantially, indeed totally, opposed to any form of Communism. It has been completely opposed to aggression; it has been completely opposed to the use of violence and force ....'[80] But in 1969 Vietnam was not an issue that National could exploit as readily as it had in 1966 and Labour's dissenting tradition seemed more apposite: 'It is said that we should attempt a more "international" and independent role such as we played in the League of Nations in the late 1930s and in the formative period of the United Nations',[81] observed one diplomat, while the historian, David McIntyre, invoked F. L. W. Wood, who, he said, had suggested that in the 1930s 'New Zealand's views often carried far more weight than derived from her own power because her spokesman often summoned up important minority opinion in other parts of the Common-wealth.'[82] Richard Kennaway, writing in 1972, argued the case for qualified alignment, noting that there was nothing in the letter or spirit of either ANZUS or SEATO which precluded member countries from 'exercising considerable independence of judgement'.[83]

Changing circumstances were an even more powerful determinant, if not of

---

[79]   See the discussion in *Asia and the Pacific in the 1970s*, pp. 135-6.
[80]   *NZPD*, 360, p. 594 (5 June 1969).
[81]   Graham Ansell, 'New Zealand and Australia', paper given to the 1970 Otago Foreign Policy School. Dept of Univ. Extension, Univ. of Otago, p. 10.
[82]   David McIntyre, 'The Future of the New Zealand System of Alliances', *Landfall*, 21/4 (Dec. 1967), pp. 344-5. Wood himself in a paper presented in 1972 made comments that bore the traces of the thinking of the earlier generation—'in general however [New Zealand's] stance in international affairs has been one of independent-minded co-operativeness'—and he argued that for the 'apprehensive—some would say for the realist or the prudent'—there was 'no escape from the necessity for keeping the American umbrella over one's head; and after 20 years, the ANZUS Treaty still gives a firm basis for the hope that it will remain there indefinitely'. ('The Problem of National Security: Political and Strategic Background', paper given to the 1972 Otago Foreign Policy School. Dept of Univ. Extension, Univ. of Otago, p. 15.)
[83]   Richard Kennaway, *New Zealand Foreign Policy 1951-1971*. Wellington, 1972, p. 103.

Labour policy, then certainly of its acceptablity, through 1969 and thereafter. Not only did the United States pursue its disengagement from Vietnam, it also initiated a détente in relations with China and the Soviet Union. Kirk was able to argue in his 1971 address, *New Zealand and Its Neighbours*, that while China was not 'in any way prepared to throw overboard long-standing basic policies', it seemed likely that more conciliatory relations would develop between it and other countries. By the time Kirk's speech had been published, Nixon had made his dramatic announcement that he would accept an invitation to visit China in 1972. It was now National, committed to Taiwan and to its cautious and apprehensive Asian allies, that was on the back foot: only in January, Holyoake had stressed that China still had a revolutionary anti-American foreign policy and Nixon's announcement came unheralded, in the middle of an allies' meeting.[84] Revealingly Kirk opened his address with a discussion of the impact of recent British and American decisions. More than any change in New Zealand this let Labour off the horns of its dilemma about policy in Asia—the sponsors of the existing policy were changing course: 'Now some people will insist that SEATO is an important cornerstone of New Zealand's defence and of the collective security of the region. I think I have demonstrated clearly enough that the changes which have taken place involving the powers are such as to make it an unreliable vehicle on which to establish confident expectations of collective security.'[85] Similarly, Kirk argued the new defence arrangements with Malaysia and Singapore might not last much beyond a five-year period. In sum, he was able to reclaim New Zealand's Asia policy for Labour: 'for the most part all the other collective security arrangements in which New Zealand has participated and for which it has worked over the last twenty years have evaporated.'[86]

How pleasant too, to find a respected scholarly British commentator make the related point that 'very broadly speaking, New Zealand involved herself in Southeast Asia because Britain wanted it'. New Zealand's security depended not on what went on in Southeast Asia, but on 'the effective functioning of the great trading and financial system which links [Australia and New Zealand] with the United States, Western Europe and Japan'.[87] Kirk noted that ANZUS had 'quite specific functions and was established for particular reasons':[88] he was in the business of separating out the American guarantee from involvement in Asia.

Kirk's thinking in this particular respect was paralleled by scholars who questioned whether New Zealand's own strategic circumstances required it to

[84] *NZFAR*, Jan. 1971, p. 25. A reminder to many there, presumably, of Johnson's similar timing in March 1968.
[85] *New Zealand and its Neighbours*. Wellington, 1971, p. 5.
[86] *New Zealand and Its Neighbours*, p. 6.
[87] And which was not itself any too healthy at the time. Michael Howard, 'Lonely Antipodes', *Round Table*, 245 (Jan. 1972), pp. 77, 83.
[88] *New Zealand and Its Neighbours*, p. 6.

be involved in Asia. The earliest was Keith Sinclair, who in a 1966 paper challenged the idea that New Zealand was *in* Southeast Asia:

> There has never been a sense in which this was true .... Our thinking on relations with Asia, while recognising that we are nearer Asia than Europe, should not ignore how far we are away. Peking is closer to London than to Auckland; Hanoi is about as near to London as it is to Wellington. Though, in the 1940s, we have been threatened from Asia, we should avoid supposing it is under our doorstep. The Chinese are not under the bed.[89]

Sinclair questioned military involvement in Southeast Asia, being cautious even about Malaysia and certainly about anything more remote: 'our interests require as little involvement as possible in the shifting and slippery swamps of mainland Southeast Asian politics—and wars .... Involvement in Malaysia should make us uneasy. Over the Thai border our interests do not go; nor should our armed forces.'[90] This was a critical reformulation for the conception of New Zealand's interests. From the beginning of white settlement and right through the 1930s, 1940s and 1950s, the assumption that New Zealand was vulnerable to external attack, that it needed a protector, and that it should act in support of that protector, was axiomatic. The quest for this kind of security was a central New Zealand interest. We have seen how it informed policy during the era of British and American retreat as much as it had before.

The public may not have been ready to be convinced that 'all threats were off', but Sinclair's ideas were certainly popular with other scholars. W. David McIntyre, who lived in Canterbury, amended Sinclair's dictum: he pointed out that Hanoi was closer to London than to Christchurch: 'Is not the "logic" of New Zealand's geography that we are remote from anywhere except Polynesia, Australia and Antarctica and on the main road to nowhere—except perhaps the South Pole? How does the "logic" of geography make us any closer to Asia than the Europeans and the North Americans are?' This comment was sufficiently compelling to be quoted by two other writers on international affairs shortly afterwards,[91] while another, Bruce Brown, a New Zealand diplomat and Director of the New Zealand Institute of International Affairs, noted by way of variation that New Zealand was almost as far from Saigon as from San Francisco or Santiago and that there were 'reasonable limits to the risks and costs which New Zealand is likely to be politically able to incur to influence any situation in the region, which, while it may bear on our future, does not directly threaten that future.'[92]

[89] Keith Sinclair, 'New Zealand's Future Foreign Policy', *Political Science*, 18/2 (Sept. 1966), p. 71.
[90] Sinclair, 'New Zealand's Future Foreign Policy', pp. 72–73.
[91] McIntyre, 'New Zealand System of Alliances', p. 342; Alexander MacLeod, 'Foreign Commitments in Dispute', *Round Table*, 237 (Jan. 1970), p. 93; Keith Jackson, 'New Zealand and Southeast Asia', *JCPS* 9/1 (March 1971), p. 6.
[92] Bruce Brown, 'Political and Strategic Relations: A View from Wellington', in *Asia and the Pacific in the 1970s*, p. 123.

McIntyre himself followed Sinclair in questioning whether it was in New Zealand's interests to be militarily involved in Southeast Asia and indeed went further than Sinclair (or more accurately stayed closer) in identifying differences between Australia and New Zealand: 'Australia has a frontier in South-East Asia . . . and an Indian Ocean coastline. New Zealand has neither . . . there are potentially serious conflicts of interest and aspiration.'[93] McIntyre recognised that asking who was likely to attack New Zealand was 'an embarrassing, indeed improper question—one that the now rather woolly doctrine of collective security forbids'. Dissent and interest overlapped. Military alliances and intervention were unpopular in the Labour Party—but maybe they were not necessary either. On another occasion Kirk described ANZUS as 'solely an anti-Japanese fence. It has never involved a soldier . . . .'[94]

The interplay of dissent with interest did mean that, when it took office at the end of 1972, Labour was both eager, and felt able, to break completely with the previous government's military and political involvement with South Vietnam and with America's policy of containing China, both in respect of China and of Asia generally. While this policy had some similar effects to America's own détente with China, it had different roots and it was not entirely welcome to the United States or to its allies in the region. In the event, Labour modified its agenda.

The radical steps Labour took are well remembered, the subsequent modifications less so. The new government withdrew the New Zealand training teams that were still in Vietnam and Cambodia. Kirk also protested very sharply when the United States resumed bombing of North Vietnam over Christmas 1972.[95] At the same time diplomatic relations were established with the People's Republic and broken off with Taiwan. The government made provision for a substantial rehabilitation grant for Indochina in July 1973, lifted the trade embargo on North Vietnam and in September 1973 established diplomatic relations with Hanoi. Kirk endorsed the idea of the newly elected Labor Prime Minister of Australia, Gough Whitlam, for SEATO's replacement by 'an organisation genuinely representative of the region, without ideological overtones, conceived as an initiative to help free the region of the great power rivalries which have bedevilled progress for so long, and which would be designed to insulate the region against ideological interference from the great powers'.[96] New Zealand and Australia persisted with these plans despite American reserve. Moreover, Kirk refused to have the 1974 SEATO Council meeting in Wellington or to invite the Secretary-

93 McIntyre, 'New Zealand System of Alliances', p. 342.
94 Margaret Hayward, *Diary of the Kirk Years*. Wellington, 1981, p. 206 (2 Jan. 1974).
95 Hayward, p. 108.
96 *NZFAR*, Feb. 1973, p. 20.

General of the organisation to visit.[97] In respect of the Soviet Union, Labour re-established an embassy in Moscow, and later in 1974 recognised the incorporation of Latvia, Lithuania and Estonia into the Soviet Union.[98]

But Kirk did specifically allude to the 'force of circumstances' too: '... with the ending of American military involvement in Asia, tensions have been lowered and the danger of war breaking out in areas of direct concern to New Zealand has receded. The need has greatly lessened for New Zealand to consider its relationships with other countries, and particularly those of Asia and the Pacific, in terms of security.'[99]

How greatly? National had been cautious about China not just because of inertia but also because of the extent to which its diplomacy linked it to Taiwan, to Taiwan's Asian friends, and to the scepticism of most non-Communist Asian governments about China's intentions. Labour could not completely ignore this concern either.[100] Asians feared that the new government in New Zealand, like that in Australia, was being unduly friendly to China in ways that might harm their security, while Americans wanted the two countries to continue to play a role in the security of the region, as outlined in the Guam doctrine.[101] So Labour backtracked a little. Kirk acknowledged that Malaysia and Singapore valued the five-power defence arrangements. New Zealand committed itself to the deployment even though Australia was planning to withdraw its forces by 1975.[102] Kirk stressed that it was not really a military commitment but was 'mainly a political device to foster stability',[103] while Thailand also valued SEATO 'as a symbol of other countries' support for Thailand'. Kirk said New Zealand was not prepared to impose its views on a partner country.[104] This was exactly the view of the Opposition. Con-

---

97   Pearson, *Paper Tiger*, pp. 107–8. Australia's reform proposals, which were more moderate than New Zealand's, formed the basis of the final compromise.

98   *NZFAR*, Sept. 1974, pp. 25–26. See also David McCraw, 'New Zealand and the Baltic States: Principle versus Pragmatism in Foreign Policy', *Australian Outlook*, 35/2 (Aug. 1981), pp. 191–200.

99   *NZFAR*, June 1973, pp. 7, 8. And again, *NZPD*, 390, p. 987 (19 March 1974). New Zealand 'has not drawn away from Britain or the United States, it has not turned its back on its old friends .... Old policies were certainly abandoned, but they were not abandoned by New Zealand; they were abandoned by our allies and friends who turned to new policies, and we in the region are left to replace those policies with new ones.'

100   And did not necessarily want to: at home, at any rate, Kirk was an anti-Communist: 'there are things that I would really like to do. Deport the man who caused that union trouble at the Kawerau paper mills to Australia. Make it compulsory for all trade union secretaries to be born in New Zealand.' Hayward, *Diary*, p. 196; also p. 137, attack on *People's Voice*.

101   *Dominion*, 12 Oct. 1973; Leszek Buszynski, 'SEATO: Why It Survived Until 1977 and Why It Was Abolished', *JSEAS*, 12/2 (Sept. 1981), p. 290, records American Ambassador Marshall Green's warning to Australia that SEATO 'contains a fundamental commitment [and] is essential for the security of Thailand and for the confidence of people in the area', and talks between Secretary of State Rogers and the New Zealand and Australian Ambassadors in Washington on the future of the organisation.

102   *NZFAR*, Feb. 1973, p. 3; July 1973, p. 17.

103   *NZFAR*, June 1973, pp. 23–24.

104   *NZFAR*, June 1973, pp. 23–24.

versely, the Whitlam idea, supported by Kirk, of an Asia/Pacific regional organisation, including China, fell by the wayside. Like National too, Kirk saw Japan as a central country in Asia, one that was 'an important factor in the sustained growth and development of South-east Asian countries'.[105]

Nonetheless, the end of the Vietnam War, and the circumstances, the new patterns of international relations, which had been engendered by its end, meant that Labour could take its initiatives in an atmosphere relatively free from party political bitterness or conflict with the United States or other allies. While National objected, for instance, to the manner in which Labour ended diplomatic relations with Taiwan and established ties with Peking, there was no likelihood that it in its turn would reverse the decision. The Guam doctrine and the American military disengagement from Vietnam seemed irreversible; and so the scope existed for a reinvigorated consensus on foreign policy, with many points in common with the consensus of 1961. As we shall see, however, the war, and other developments in the 1960s, had given new meanings to the notion of 'independence' in foreign policy. And in the 1970s new areas of disagreement with the United States appeared. It was not easy to go back.

[105] *NZFAR*, Feb. 1973, p. 29.

Independence and power

The Vietnam War broke the foreign policy consensus of the early 1960s and even the end of the war did not fully restore it. But the war was important for other reasons central to the approach of this book. New Zealand's involvement in it was part of a wider series of developments that marked the end of the Commonwealth phase in the history of New Zealand's foreign policy. The linkage between the war and these developments is most concisely expressed by the fact that New Zealand fought the war alongside the United States, not Britain. Britain's retreat from global power was a central event for New Zealand in the 1960s and early 1970s. That in turn markedly weakened the role of an association that had been at the centre of the conception of an independent foreign policy. How would New Zealand deal with this new world, in which power might press much harder than before against the interests and values of this particular national community? Could New Zealand have an independent foreign policy, as that had been understood at the beginning of the 1960s? Would not it have to turn into something entirely different?

We can discern two ways in which the issue was approached in the later 1960s, ways which correspond to our categories of interest and dissent. The right was most preoccupied with the British and American retreat, the prospect of New Zealand isolated and powerless in a hostile world. The left was preoccupied with the unpalatable and unwelcome American pressure for New Zealand to support America's role as global policeman. In both cases, national, or nationalist, considerations played a part, and in both respects therefore the notion of independence in foreign policy took on new meaning. The formulation of thinking in these new ways was particularly evident in 1968-69, against the backdrop of rapidly moving events in Asia. We conclude this short section by considering the 'independent foreign policy' of the third Labour government.

Nationalism

Fifteen years before the Vietnam War, unease in New Zealand over too close an association with the United States in respect of the latter's policy towards

China had expressed itself in pro-British sentiment. Such sentiment was ruled out by the changed circumstances in 1965:

> military action . . . can make enemies and induce moral uneasiness. It is a novelty for New Zealand to find herself in this position without the kind of solution which active British participation would confer. New Zealand . . . does not have with the United States a bond of union similar to the emotional unity which has bound her to Britain and has made it seem right and proper for her to support British actions . . . . reliance on the United States instead of Britain tends to induce irritation . . . .[1]

Thus the Winston Monk argument, fifteen years on. The difference was that unease about New Zealand's involvement in the Vietnam War alongside the United States was now couched in nationalist terms. The radical left had argued in such a fashion since the beginning of the war[2]—it was after all a part of the left critique of New Zealand foreign policy that went back many decades. But it was only in 1967-68, when the war became more unpopular, that nationalist arguments were widely articulated on the left and in the Labour movement. In 1966, Labour Party conference remits on foreign policy were talking of the importance of the United Nations: in 1968, even the toned-down remit that came from the party's policy committee called for an 'independent policy' on foreign affairs: 'independence' had become a partisan term again.[3] Journalists covering the 1969 election campaign observed that any conversation with Kirk was 'heavily sprinkled with references for New Zealanders "to run their own affairs", to "accelerate our journey towards nationhood", to "retain initiatives in our own hands", to "resist dictation of our affairs by overseas organisations" '.[4] *Towards Nationhood*, consisting of extracts from Kirk's speeches, was published to coincide with the 1969 Labour Party conference.

The journey metaphor was misleading. This nationalism was a local version of left-wing British nationalism: 'in the wider sphere of international relations Kirk is in the strong Labour tradition of being closer to Britain than any other country . . . . And he reflects as well the suspicions of the militant unionists and intellectuals in his party about the United States.' There was a strong belief in the Labour Party, observers noted, that 'the United States should not have the trust New Zealand previously gave to Britain. Kirk has said "Our people should realise that Britain is the only country in the world New Zealand can

---

[1] NZIIA, *New Zealand Foreign Policy with Special Reference to South-East Asia* (Report of an NZIIA Study Group). Wellington, 1968, p. 23.
[2] 'This new Foreign Policy will no longer be able to lean on . . . the easy and lazy way of blindly following the Foreign Policy of a great power, whose values and ultimate interests, might not, at all times, and in all issues, correspond with ours.' Rabel, 'Vietnam', p. 52, quoting *A Source Book on Vietnam: Background to our War*. Wellington, 1965.
[3] New Zealand Labour Party, 50th Annual Conference, April 1966, *Report*, p. 34; 52nd Annual Conference, May 1968, *Report*, 1968, p. 21.
[4] Ian Templeton and Keith Eunson, *Election '69*. Wellington, 1969, p. 82.

expect automatically and certainly to come to our aid if we were in military difficulties".'[5]

A programmatic nationalism would have addressed New Zealand's relations with Britain rather than with the United States:

> English influence dominates at all levels of New Zealand society. A lot of people will query this assertion, not because it isn't true but because it is true. Accustomed from birth to an all [-pervasive] English influence New Zealanders accept it without question. English influence is unnoticed because it is dominant. Brash, self-assertive Americanism on the other hand is noticed. And not only is it noticed but it rouses hostility . . . because it is so obviously alien to the New Zealand way of life. American influence is resented in New Zealand because, rather than in spite of, its being only a minor factor in New Zealand life. People can challenge it and at the same time conform.[6]

Left-wing nationalism in the late 1960s was about power, about some New Zealanders resenting being corralled by the United States into a war they opposed. But although it was novel to identify such nationalism with New Zealand's independence, the nationalism itself was not new—like much else in New Zealand life it affirmed rather than rejected the country's British antecedents.

An American 'Commonwealth'?

In 1972 Ralph Mullins, a foreign service officer, referred to

> the inhibitions imposed by attitudes built up in New Zealand over the century of the colonial and Dominion periods. The residue of the 'Little-Britain-of-the-South-Seas' attitude has been sympathetic to continuing links with the United Kingdom and the South Pacific, and even to the transition from colony to member of the Commonwealth, but to little else; a diffuse internationalism has been acceptable but not a bilateral relationship with other countries of the Pacific area. Much New Zealand reaction to international affairs has instinctively reflected this attitude: anything to do with Britain, the South Pacific, the Commonwealth, the United Nations or aid has been regarded with favour, and anything to do with the United States, Australia, Japan, South-east Asia or defence with disfavour or at least reserve.[7]

Mullins's analysis, while emphasising the British origins of the New Zealand debate over the Vietnam War, also draws attention to another direction that was discussed and considered in the mid 1960s. Just as the Labour movement was developing a nationalist response to New Zealand's involvement with the United States in Vietnam, others were considering

5   *Election '69*, pp. 82, 83.
6   Bruce Jesson, 'Newsview', *Dispute*, April 1966, p. 3.
7   *NZFAR*, July 1972, pp. 7–8.

whether the United States could provide some kind of substitute for Britain, whether an American 'Commonwealth' was a possibility.

The relative novelty of the close defence ties developed between Australia and New Zealand, without the British alongside them, in Vietnam; the close involvement with the United States; the development of new relations with America's Asian allies—all played a part in this thinking. The relationship with Australia, a Commonwealth member itself of course, seemed to be acquiring a new closeness in the mid 1960s, with the joint involvement in Vietnam paralleled by the signing of the New Zealand-Australia Free Trade Agreement (NAFTA), partly as a response to British interest in entering the European Economic Community. In a discussion paper published in the middle of 1965 by the New Zealand Institute of Economic Research, the political scientist Alan Robinson argued for the gradual establishment of a defence as well as an economic union between Australia and New Zealand. He saw two factors acting as a spur: developments in Southeast Asia and the growth of economic and political regionalism in Europe. The Minister of Defence, Dean Eyre, in September 1966 also firmly supported closer ties to Australia, suggesting they might lead ultimately to political union.[8] In an address in Auckland on 6 June 1967, Paul Hasluck, the Australian Minister of External Affairs, said that 'facing the broader questions of our place in the world and our participation in world politics, I am unable to see any room for choice. It is unthinkable that we should not work together.'[9] It was perhaps no accident that the *External Affairs Review* in its February 1968 issue published a seventeen-page historical perspective on Australian-New Zealand relations concluding with a discussion of the New Zealand-Australia Free Trade Agreement of 1965 and the recent intensified political and defence cooperation.

We have traced the ways in which New Zealand was drawn into association with Asian countries in the 1950s and early 1960s—the Colombo Plan, SEATO, AMDA and so on. During the Vietnam War the engagement with Asia intensified. New Zealand was a founder member of the Asian Pacific Council—ASPAC—in 1966. Its members were Japan, South Korea, Taiwan, South Vietnam, Thailand, New Zealand, Australia, Malaysia, Singapore, and the Philippines and it was the first exclusively Asian organisation of which New Zealand had become a member: this was frequently reiterated by official spokespeople, despite the manifest fact that it was essentially an association of allies of the United States, including the American-protected halves of all the divided countries. For Laking, New Zealand's involvement in Asia was the most dramatic change he could identify after eight years away from New Zealand: it involved not just Vietnam but also North Asia—Japan, South Korea and Taiwan.[10]

---

[8] *NZE&T*, 1 June 1965, 1 Oct. 1966: on this latter occasion the journal itself added 'Mr Holyoake, instead of pooh-poohing the idea, might well encourage it'.
[9] *EAR*, June 1967, p. 29.
[10] *EAR*, March 1967, pp. 16–17, 21–22.

The enthusiasm with which New Zealanders greeted President Johnson on his brief visit in October 1966 seemed to suggest some popular receptivity to the idea of a 'transfer of allegiance' from Britain, the old mother country, to the United States. In February 1968, New Zealand's Ambassador in Washington, F. H. Corner, advocated a closer association between New Zealand and the United States on the lines of the old Commonwealth relationship with Britain. The British had helped New Zealand economically, they had learnt the art of managing an alliance; these bonds were what Corner called 'hoops of steel', which were to his mind part of what was necessary to 'transform New Zealanders and Americans from friends and allies into a band of brothers so that they may march forward with a union of hearts and wills towards what I have little doubt should be a common destiny.'[11]

New Zealand alone?

For other diplomats it was independence that was New Zealand's fate, albeit a harsher independence than the one they were used to. There was irony here for some diplomats, attacked now for not following an independent foreign policy, when the notion of such a policy was virtually an official ideology in the Department of External Affairs. Diplomats went on the offensive, attacking the critics of foreign policy who 'sometimes fulminated against the absence of a really "independent" foreign policy .... [but what they] want usually turns out to be a vociferous rejection of foreign entanglements, of alleged subservience to United States policy or some similar man of straw'.

For George Laking, 'our approach to issues of external policy is fully independent'. The great revolution of nationalism in Asia was concurrent with a 'smaller revolution in our own country ... our awakening to full nationhood', as some years earlier that had related to 'the diminution of British naval power in the Pacific'.[12] Holyoake presented the 1969 decision to maintain forces in Malaysia/Singapore as a national one, that of an independent nation, a decision consistent with long-established objectives and approaches in New Zealand foreign policy.[13] An *Auckland Star* editorial on Labour and nationalism in foreign policy generally took the National Party position that New Zealand was standing on its own two feet, instancing both economic diplomacy with the United States and the Malaysia/Singapore decision in February.[14] But the very determination to identify the decision as

[11]   *EAR*, Feb. 1968, p. 23, note the echo of Savage. See also Corner to Holyoake, 10 June 1968, for a less rhetorical elaboration of the same idea. Ms Papers 1403 86/3, ATL.
[12]   *EAR*, March 1968, pp. 31, 32.
[13]   Holyoake address to the NZIIA, March 1969, reproduced in *EAR*, March 1969, pp. 3–14: 'we cannot take the British role in South-east Asia. We can take a New Zealand role' (p. 13). See also *EAR*, Feb. 1969, pp. 30–37, for text of Holyoake's announcement and subsequent amplifications.
[14]   13 Nov. 1969; for economic diplomacy, see below, p. 210.

an 'independent' one marked a shift from not much more than a decade before, when 'independent' decisions had to be defended against charges of disloyalty.

Laking's 'nationalism' was different from that of the government's critics: it was rooted in the politics of interest, not of dissent. But those interests were demarcated more sharply from the interests of allies and friends than in the past. Laking, perhaps because he was through those years in such a pivotal position, had an acute feel for the change in New Zealand's situation: 'It seemed clear', he said in August 1969, just after Nixon had spoken in Guam, that 'in many areas of international endeavour where we enjoyed British and American company, we may feel a little chill wind of loneliness.'[15] New Zealand now needed 'to make a conscious effort to stand off and retain a certain independence of thought and action in our dealings with larger states, and especially the great commercial and political powers'.[16]

This 'national' response was exhibited most clearly in the economic sphere, and in that respect will be discussed further in Chapter 9. But the formulation was not confined to that sphere. Laking was taking the tradition of independence as interest and combining it with ideas drawn from the realist approach to international relations, which focused primarily on power relations amongst sovereign states, in which the contest of interest was paramount. New Zealand was of course not well equipped by size or resources to engage in such a contest, but Laking did not believe this disenfranchised it, even in relations with the United States:

Most of New Zealand's international experience involves dealing with countries that outweigh us in many respects. Dealing with the United States presents that problem in its most exacting form. We would be foolish to expect too much from the United States but I see no reason why we should expect too little . . . . we shall not be seeking a dependent relationship. There will always be areas of independence which we must insist upon preserving so that relations between us can be mature and confident.[17]

Laking was even prepared to venture a similar opinion in respect of New Zealand's relations with Australia: 'One can envisage circumstances in which a series of Australian decisions—each of which failed, if only marginally , to take account of New Zealand interests—could provoke a strong reaction here and encourage the pursuit of a deliberately independent line in foreign affairs and other areas.'[18]

At the beginning of 1970 the Department of External Affairs changed its

[15] *EAR*, Aug. 1969, p. 17.
[16] Holyoake to Corner, 10 July 1968. Ms Papers 1403 86/3, ATL.
[17] George Laking, 'International Problems Confronting New Zealand in the 1970s', in NZIIA, *Foreign Policy in the 1970s*. Wellington, 1970, p. 40.
[18] Laking, 'International Problems', p. 38.

name to the Ministry of Foreign Affairs. It is as good an event as any to symbolise the shift from a world of Commonwealth, 'external' relations (with High Commissioners), to a world of international, 'foreign' relations (with ambassadors).

The third Labour government and independence in foreign policy

In the eyes of many of its supporters, the third Labour government implemented an independent and a moral foreign policy. It was making a clean break with the compromises of the past; it was refusing to me-too the Americans. It was a government that was in the honourable tradition of the first Labour government, particularly its advocacy of the League of Nations in 1936-38 and of the United Nations in 1945. To a later generation it would be a forerunner of the fourth Labour government and its anti-nuclear policy. The image of Kirk, dead at fifty-one after only twenty months in office, reinforced the sense that this was a special period in which special things were done.[19] The sweeping nature of the 1972 election victory, the speed with which certain decisions were taken, the subsequent initiatives, in particular the active protest against French nuclear testing—all combined to foster a sense of possibility, of excitement and of change.[20]

Nationalism was certainly a part of the style of the new governing party. In debate at the end of the 1973 parliamentary session, Michael Bassett commented, 'In the 1920s it used to be said that every time Whitehall sneezed Wellington caught cold. In the last twenty years every time Foggy Bottom coughed, the National Party ran in with a hanky. This has been changed with the Labour Government.'[21] At the personal level, Kirk did not have the same fellow feeling for the American defence and foreign policy establishment that had characterised his predecessors. This may have had something, although not everything, to do with the incumbents during his prime ministership— Nixon, under siege over Watergate, and Kissinger, the 'Metternich man' in Washington. In different ways they both represented alien political traditions. Kirk did not visit the United States except to speak in New York at the United Nations.

[19] See, for instance, David McCraw, 'From Kirk to Muldoon: Change and Continuity in New Zealand's Foreign-Policy Priorities', *Pacific Affairs*, 55/4 (Winter 1982-83), p. 640; Michael Bassett, *The Third Labour Government*. Palmerston North, 1976, pp. 26-27, 45, 104; Alexander MacLeod, 'A New Foreign Policy', *Round Table*, 255 (July 1974), p. 296; Keith Sinclair, 'New Zealand's Metamorphosis', *International Journal*, 29/3 (Summer 1974), pp. 412-21. On the other hand some other writers emphasised continuity: Richard Kennaway, 'Foreign Policy', in Ray Goldstein & Roderic Alley, eds., *Labour in Power. Promise and Performance*, pp. 163-72; Nigel Roberts, 'Foreign Affairs: The Legend and Legacy of Norman Kirk', *Islands*, 3/4 (Summer 1974), pp. 421-9.
[20] Warren Page and Brian Lockstone, *Landslide '72*. Dunedin, 1973; Jim Eagles and Colin James, *The Making of a New Zealand Prime Minister*. Wellington, 1973. For the campaign against French testing, see below, p. 189.
[21] Bassett, *Third Labour Government*, p. 104: 'Foggy Bottom' was a Washington colloquialism for the State Department.

Interestingly, in view of the observations quoted earlier, there was also a certain coolness evident towards Britain. Both Labour and National were upset at the changes Britain made in its immigration laws in 1972, and for much the same reason—the access of some New Zealanders to Britain was curtailed.[22] But Kirk did not find the Conservative government of Edward Heath particularly congenial anyway. He was unhappy with the way they had handled the Commonwealth, in particular relations with white South Africa and the matter of entry into the EEC, which so directly affected New Zealand.[23] Kirk introduced the Royal Titles Bill which changed the Queen's status in New Zealand from Queen of the United Kingdom in the first instance to Queen of New Zealand.[24] Kirk met the Queen in New Zealand but never made the traditional visit to London almost obligatory for New Zealand prime ministers.

Coolness towards Britain, however, reflected as much a decline in, rather than untoward, British interest in New Zealand—it was fuel for Laking's realism rather than for nationalism. And Kirk did articulate a sense of New Zealand independence which drew on a perception of changes in New Zealand's circumstances as well as change in values and attitudes. In his most substantial explanation of his government's foreign policy, Kirk proclaimed that

> New Zealand for its part intends to follow a more independent foreign policy. It has emerged from the phase in its national development where it allowed its policies to be determined by the views and interests of its most influential ally: at one time Britain, more recently the United States. From now on, when we have to deal with a new situation, we shall not say, what do the British think about it, what would the Americans want us to do? Our starting point will be, what do we think about it?[25]

But circumstances militated against the adoption of a notion of independence in foreign policy that focused on New Zealand's separateness rather than its involvement with other countries. We have already examined the circumstances of Labour's Asia policy, and the limited impact its new departures had on the United States. More generally, détente had introduced an entirely new atmosphere into international relations in the early 1970s compared with the late 1960s, one with which the more traditional notion of independence in foreign policy fitted very well: recall the enthusiasm for détente in the 1950s, for better relations with China. Much of the sense that the new government was doing new things stemmed from foreshortened perspectives: Vietnam had been such a controversial war that the *status quo ante bellum* had been forgotten.

---

22 For National, see Muldoon, *Young Turk*, p. 192.
23 For more discussion see below, pp. 211-12 (EEC), 241 (South Africa).
24 *NZPD*, 389, pp. 1-3 (4 Feb. 1973).
25 *NZFAR*, June 1973, p. 7.

The one exception to this pattern perhaps arose in respect of attitudes to and dealings with France over the latter's nuclear-testing programme in the Pacific. But France had not been a central country in New Zealand's external relations and it was unlikely that the shape and character of New Zealand foreign policy would turn on that one relationship. Generally, we will see that ideas of independence in the 1970s can be as readily understood in relation to earlier ideas of an independent foreign policy as to the newer notions of state, nation, and the world of power. It was in the 1980s rather than the 1970s that these newer ideas were to be more frequently invoked.

8. The 1970s: a new kind of independence?

We have seen that independence acquired new meaning at the end of the 1960s: power became an element in thinking about independence. But in the 1970s the older ways of thinking also remained significant. The anti-nuclear movement, although interwoven with a radical critique of ANZUS, derived its strongest impetus from environmental concerns. National, in government again after 1975, with Muldoon as Prime Minister, talked of independence, as Holyoake had at the end of the 1960s, but we can see powerful echoes of the traditional preoccupations and assumptions of conservative parties about New Zealand's place in the world.[1] There were no defining moments in alliance relations comparable with those engendered by the Vietnam War and the British retreat from Asia.

The revival of the anti-nuclear movement

What had happened to the anti-nuclear movement since 1960? Ban-the-bomb activity had revived in 1961–62 when the moratorium on testing agreed to by the Soviet Union and the United States had collapsed. The two countries signed a partial test-ban treaty in 1963, but by then anti-nuclear sentiment had been given a strong 'local' dimension with France's announcement that it planned to move its testing programme from Algeria, which had become independent, to French Polynesia. There was an immediate hostile reaction in New Zealand. In September 1963 Parliament was presented with an 80,000-signature petition seeking a nuclear-free Southern Hemisphere. Students at their summer congress advocated that the government station ships in the test zone and CND supported similar action and also a trade boycott; this latter was supported by some trade unions too. A women's petition and an open letter was forwarded to de Gaulle by Holyoake, whilst some students established the Committee for Resolute Action Against the French Tests (CRAFT).[2]

[1]   Labour 'idealism' and National 'realism' in the 1970s are also discussed in John Henderson, *NZIR*, May-June 1977, p. 7; McCraw, 'Kirk to Muldoon', pp. 640–59.
[2]   Roderic Alley, ' "The Awesome Glow in the Sky": New Zealand and Disarmament', in *NZWA 1957-72*, pp. 84–86; *Salient*, 21 Sept. 1964.

CND activity waned in the mid and later 1960s when protest focused on the Vietnam War, but there were some significant developments. The Canterbury student newspaper, *Canta*, stirred up a hornets' nest by claiming in June 1968 that the government wanted to establish a 'spy station' in New Zealand under the guise of Omega, an American navigation system. *Canta*'s dramatic 'special Omega edition' provoked an immediate demonstration involving around 1500 students, with other demonstrations following both in Christchurch and in other university towns. Debate about Omega raged for the next months, with the Royal Society becoming involved along with the government and protest groups.[3] Neither side convinced the other—the critics continued to believe that if New Zealand had an Omega station, it would be exposed to greatly increased risk of attack in a nuclear conflict; defenders of the project argued that it was a low-level navigation system with no special security uses. In the event Omega was not proceeded with.[4] In the early 1970s installations with actual or claimed links with American defence activities were targeted by protesters—notably the United States Air Force installation at Woodbourne in Marlborough and the USAF satellite-tracking station at Mt John in South Canterbury. The University of Canterbury, from which the USAF sub-leased the land at Mount John, withdrew from the arrangement in 1972, which became one between the government and the USAF.[5] The Woodbourne operation closed in 1973. Holyoake cited United States budgetary considerations—Wilkes thought the protest played a role.[6]

The agitation against the various installations arose on the left and the radical student Progressive Youth Movement was particularly active in the protests. But it did seem that the concern about the installations tapped a more widespread apprehension. Owen Wilkes thought that 'the ultimate cause of the June 1968 events was . . . that this was the first time that New Zealanders were faced with a direct, immediate and unpleasant consequence of alliance with America'.[7] He noted that even the right-wing populist weekly paper *Truth* became involved in the campaign against Woodbourne—it thought that

---

3   Owen Wilkes, *Demonstrations Against the American Military Presence in New Zealand.* Wellington, 1973, pp. 7-16; Royal Society of New Zealand, *Report of the Ad Hoc Committee on the Omega Navigation System.* Wellington, 1968 (the report played down the significance of Omega); *EAR*, June 1968, p. 23, July 1968, p. 17, Aug. 1968, p. 45; *NZEAR*, Jan. 1969, pp. 44–45, April 1969, pp. 63-64, 65; Ms Papers 1403, 234/1, ATL.
4   Perusal of SEA to PM, 21 April 1969, would suggest that the government was caught between wanting to demonstrate that the station was under New Zealand control and wanting to avoid the costs that would be entailed in establishing and running it. It was also noted that if the station was sited in Australia, New Zealand would still get the benefits. Ms Papers 1403, 234/1, ATL.
5   Wilkes, *Demonstrations*, pp. 31-40; *NZFAR*, June 1972, p. 88; Ms Papers 1403, 104/1, ATL.
6   Wilkes, *Demonstrations*, p. 29; *EAR*, Jan. 1965, p. 19; *NZFAR*, Jan. 1971, pp. 69-70; Aug. 1972, p. 93.
7   Wilkes, *Demonstrations*, p. 16.

'Kiwis have a right to know' and that Holyoake could not go on saying that the base was not 'secret' but refusing to amplify.[8]

Most significant in 1972 was the escalation of protest against French nuclear-weapons testing in the Pacific, which had commenced in 1966. Direct action—ships voyaging into the test zone, trade boycotts—was pursued. In 1973 the Labour government gave a degree of official approval to such activities while taking its own steps, with the Australians, to protest French activities—taking France to the International Court of Justice and sending a frigate for observation and witness purposes into the test zone. In 1974 the French ended atmospheric testing and started testing underground—a limited victory for South Pacific protest.

Opposition to French actions had readily taken on a nationalist flavour. In Auckland the Mayor handed out medals to some of those embarking for the test zone during the 1973 protest. Daily newspapers normally sympathetic to National attacked the Opposition for its criticism of government policy: 'there are many New Zealanders', preached the *Daily News*, 'to whom the thought of adjusting the frequency of our moral protest to suit the amount of pecuniary fallout ... on our trade negotiations is particularly repugnant.'[9] The *Marlborough Express* noted on 19 July that 'New Zealanders have been showing immense interest in the saga of Mururoa. Support for the decision of the Government to send a frigate into the area has been widespread. It is the type of direct positive action which has appeal.'[10] In 1971 81.7 per cent in one poll supported New Zealand government opposition to French nuclear-testing plans for that year, and the following year a large minority—39.8 per cent—supported the FOL ban on the handling of French ships in New Zealand ports. In 1976 60.4 per cent supported the Peace Media protest movement sending vessels into the testing zone.[11]

Opposition to a French presence in the Pacific, of whatever species, had deep roots. Siegfried, writing of colonial sentiment in the middle of the last century, noted the protests that had been raised against the French annexation of New Caledonia: ' "What are these French Catholics doing", they murmured, "in a part of the world which providence has certainly reserved for Englishmen and Protestants? Why did the British Government allow these intruders to come into a region where, with a little foresight, British isolation might have for ever remained absolute and indisputable?" '[12]

The issue of a nuclear-weapons-free zone overlapped with the campaign against French testing and it was natural that renewed attention should be

---

8   *Truth* quoted in Wilkes, *Demonstrations*, p. 18.
9   13 July 1973. There was also favourable editorial comment in the *Auckland Star*, 10 July, and by the columnist John Halifax, in the Dunedin *Evening Star*. See EA121/5/2b, MERT.
10   Editorial on EA121/5/2b, MERT.
11   David Campbell, *The Social Base of Australian and New Zealand Security Policy*. Canberra, 1989, p. 100.
12   Siegfried, *Democracy in New Zealand*, p. 351.

given to the idea with Labour in power. In its 1972 manifesto Labour had committed itself to calling a conference of Pacific nations with a view to establishing a nuclear-weapons-and-test-free zone.[13] In his substantive August 1973 address (and the point was reiterated in an address to the General Assembly in September) Kirk said that 'New Zealand was studying the proposition of a nuclear-free zone in the South Pacific'. In 1974, with Kirk ailing, the momentum on the issue was not maintained, nor did it feature in either of the two South Pacific meetings held that year.

It was Rowling, Kirk's successor as Prime Minister, who picked up the issue and attempted to make headway with the cause. At the South Pacific Forum in July 1975, New Zealand raised the concept of a nuclear-weapons-free zone and the Forum agreed that 'it would be desirable for a wider endorsement of the idea to be sought through the adoption of a resolution by the General Assembly of the United Nations'.[14] Taking action on the Forum decision, New Zealand and Fiji sought inscription of an item, 'establishment of a nuclear weapons free zone in the South Pacific', on the agenda of the General Assembly.[15]

Port visits by nuclear-powered naval vessels or vessels carrying nuclear weapons also became an issue in 1974-75. In 1971 the National government had told the United States it would not accept visits by nuclear-powered vessels until the United States agreed to accept liability in the event of accident and/or widespread contamination.[16] Under new Congressional legislation passed in 1974 the United States government accepted such liability for incidents occurring outside the United States,[17] but the Labour government continued to take a definite line against visits. 'The American position has changed', said Acting Prime Minister Tizard at a press conference, 'but I can't imagine the political question would change—that if we are in the middle of an argument with someone about nuclear testing we are not going to have a side issue introduced by the visit of a nuclear-powered ship, even if there is a guarantee against damage.'[18]

[13] New Zealand Labour Party 1972, election manifesto, p. 30.
[14] *NZFAR*, July 1975, p. 61.
[15] *NZFAR*, Aug. 1975, p. 61. For background to the issue in the 1974 session and Non Proliferation Treaty meeting, for New Zealand statement on the Forum approach, Fiji/New Zealand explanatory memorandum and draft resolution, see *NZFAR*, Sept. 1975, pp. 41-42, 55-57.
[16] Kevin Clements, *Back From the Brink: The Creation of a Nuclear-Free New Zealand.* Wellington, 1988, p. 84.
[17] *NZFAR*, April 1975, p. 55. Note that in his comment in answer to the parliamentary question, 24 April, Rowling referred to 'the decision of the Government that no nuclear-powered vessels would be offered port facilities in New Zealand' (p. 56). In May, Tizard referred to the fact that Kirk had indicated some time back that New Zealand was going to look at each request for a nuclear-powered ship to come to New Zealand, and that at the time of French testing he had suggested it might not be appropriate for a British nuclear-powered warship to visit New Zealand: *NZFAR*, May 1975, p. 79.
[18] *NZFAR*, May 1975, p. 79.

As with the ban-the bomb movement in the 1950s and early 1960s, and as would be the case with the anti-nuclear weapons movement in the 1980s, the anti-nuclear movement in the 1970s arose out of a compound of overseas and local influences. Environmental preoccupations acquired salience throughout the Western world at the end of the 1960s and this naturally had an effect in New Zealand. The 'Save Manapouri' campaign in 1969–70 was the most significant environmental movement within the country, and there was a clear connection between the philosophy of that campaign and the opposition to French nuclear-weapons testing. And when port visits by American navy ships became an issue in 1974–75, popular concern was focused almost entirely on the possibility of a nuclear accident; the question of nuclear weapons was not so systematically addressed. As with the protests against US defence-related installations in the late 1960s and early 1970s, we can hypothesise that the environmental protest movement could reach out to a larger, not necessarily radically minded public because it tapped sentiments of unwelcome and unnecessary intrusion. It is also noteworthy that though ideologically it had quite different origins from the long-standing concerns about 'Asian hordes' or 'reds under the bed', the notion of intrusion was very similar.

The National government, elected at the end of 1975, did not continue to lobby in the United Nations for the South Pacific nuclear-weapons-free zone, and it announced it would invite nuclear-powered United States naval vessels to visit New Zealand. These were contentious decisions. A 1978 poll produced 70.9 per cent support for a South Pacific nuclear-weapons-free zone.[19] A survey of opinion conducted on the day of the election revealed a strong distrust of nuclear power as an energy resource and a fear that safety arrangements might never prove sufficiently adequate.[20] The result of the Nelson by-election in 1976 suggested that while the public wanted good relations with the United States, it was also suspicious of nuclear power and port visits.[21]

A 'Peace Squadron' was formed at the beginning of March 1976, organised in part by members of St John's Theological College in Auckland. It planned to blockade Auckland harbour if and when nuclear-powered ships attempted to enter. One of the organisers, the Rev. George Armstrong, stressed that the movement was entirely non-violent.[22] The flotillas of small craft that sailed out

---

[19] Campbell, *Social Base of Australian and NZ Security Policy*, p. 101. There does not appear to have been a question asked on this issue before 1978.

[20] Stephen Levine, 'Public Opinion and the ANZUS Treaty', *NZIR*, May-June 1976, p. 18.

[21] The new Labour candidate, Mel Courtney, held the seat, vacant because of the death of Stan Whitehead, with an increased majority, 'defying predictions' that the National candidate would win comfortably, just four months after National's massive victory in the general election. The Values vote also increased. Colin Moyle, for the Labour Party, thought the nuclear issue was an important factor in Labour's favour (*EP*, 1 March 1976). Levine noted that a survey conducted in Nelson immediately after the by-election suggested that either Labour's attacks on the port-visit issue or National's retreat from active support of the South Pacific nuclear-free-zone proposal had helped Labour, 'Public Opinion and the ANZUS Treaty', p. 18.

[22] *EP*, 1 March 1976.

into Wellington and particularly Auckland harbour on the occasions of visits by nuclear-powered ships did become one of the most visible symbols of the protest movement in the following years and the names of the ships became a protest litany—the vessels *Truxtun* and *Longbeach* (1976), the submarines *Pintado* (1978) and *Haddo* (1979).[23] Polls showed significant, although not majority, levels of support for opposition to visits by nuclear-powered ships of between 33 and 39 per cent over the period 1976–82.[24]

The future of ANZUS

Throughout the Vietnam War the idea that New Zealand should separate itself from all military alliances was a popular radical cause. But if there was a particular moment when the campaign for non-alignment became a political issue for the Labour Party, it was March 1968. Alister Taylor recorded in his account of the 'Peace, Power and Politics' conference that after the news of President Johnson's 31 March 1968 decisions had reached delegates, a 'spontaneous and deeply felt plea for a New Zealand policy of non-alignment had erupted at the conference . . . . all the 1400 conference delegates—and the thousands more who attended the public sessions—felt the need for an independent and positively peaceful New Zealand foreign policy'.[25] 'For the first time in New Zealand history', wrote Wolfgang Rosenberg, 'there is a substantial body of people who believe and think that the time has come for New Zealand's foreign policy to divorce itself from the powers.'[26]

At the 1968 Labour Party conference remits demanding withdrawal from all regional security alliances were rejected in favour of a restatement of the principles of the United Nations as the centre of Labour's foreign policy.[27] Nonetheless the conference did vote for New Zealand withdrawal from SEATO.[28] A former Secretary of Defence, J. K. Hunn, supported the idea in a *Listener* article in the middle of the year. 'It is suggested', said one diplomat in 1970, 'that we should become prominent in the group of smaller and relatively non-aligned nations, that we should ask ourselves whether or not the risks of our alliance are greater than those which would pertain if we opted out.'[29]

I do not want to explore the international law debate over whether if New

---

23   Philip Soljak, 'New Zealand Confuses Nuclear Ships Policy', *Monthly Review*, July 1979, p. 10. *Truxtun* visited Wellington, the rest, Auckland.

24   Campbell, *Social Basis of Australian and NZ Security Policy*, p. 94. Campbell's data is drawn from nationwide polls in New Zealand. The question asked in 1976 referred to allowing 'nuclear warships of ANZUS nations' rather than 'American nuclear-powered ships', the phrase used in the other years.

25   *Peace, Power and Politics in Asia*, p. 9.

26   *Peace, Power and Politics in Asia*, p. 220.

27   New Zealand Labour Party, 52nd Annual Conference, May 1968. *Report*, p. 21.

28   *Auckland Star*, 9 May 1968. The *Star* noted that the parliamentary party was not bound by the resolution.

29   Ansell, 'New Zealand and Australia', p. 10.

Zealand did not want to stay allied with the United States it should adopt a foreign policy of non-alignment *or* one of neutralism.[30] It suffices for our purposes to be aware that the cause of taking New Zealand out of alliances was now on the political agenda in a way it had not been before the later 1960s, and that it had become an issue with which the Labour Party leadership had to grapple, much as it had in the past grappled with the charge of being 'soft on Communism'.

The rise of the anti-nuclear movement in the 1970s increased the salience of the anti-ANZUS critique (SEATO now being moribund) in political life. The shift in the focus of anti-nuclear protest from a preoccupation with the French in the South Pacific, to a preoccupation with the presence of any nuclear weapons in the South Pacific, to a preoccupation with visits by nuclear-powered ships to New Zealand ports, brought the movement closer and closer to a point of difference with the United States and with New Zealand's membership of the ANZUS alliance.

The Americans were not happy with the notion of a nuclear-weapons-free zone in the South Pacific and they were not happy with the prospect of their nuclear-powered ships being banned from New Zealand ports. Their unhappiness in neither respect was rooted in central strategic concerns—the South Pacific was peripheral to American strategy. But there was no gain for the United States in encountering such restrictions in the ability of its Navy to manoeuvre freely in the Pacific and there was always the danger of precedent, of an idea not too inconvenient for the United States in the far South Pacific catching on in some more significant place, perhaps Japan or West Germany.

If support for a nuclear-weapons-free zone and opposition to visits by nuclear-powered ships caused problems for the United States, then it caused problems for New Zealanders. ANZUS was popular in the mid 1970s: 69.2 per cent of the electorate in 1976 opposed withdrawal, including 76.7 per cent of National voters, 65.8 per cent of Labour voters, 64.7 per cent of Social Credit voters and even 44.8 per cent of Values voters (compared with 37.9 per cent of Values voters supporting withdrawal).[31]

Labour's difficulties in reconciling its anti-nuclear stance with continued membership of ANZUS were exploited by the National Party. It was also able to exploit the debate within Labour over whether New Zealand should stay in ANZUS. While support for withdrawal may have been only a minority position among Labour voters it was popular with many of the delegates to party conferences.

---

[30] If interested, see Holyoake, 'A Defence and Foreign Policy for New Zealand', *EAR*, March 1969, p. 12; Kennaway, *NZ Foreign Policy*, pp. 93–104; and for a later discussion, Ramesh Thakur, *In Defence of New Zealand: Foreign Policy Choices in the Nuclear Age*. Boulder, Colo., 1986, pp. 109–48.

[31] Stephen Levine, 'Public Opinion and the ANZUS Treaty', p. 17. Values was a conservation-oriented party which was founded in 1972 and won 5% of the vote in the 1975 general election. It was an early manifestation of 'green' politics.

Muldoon and members of his new government stressed that if New Zealand wanted the alliance, it had to agree to port visits. The United States had accepted liability for accidents; New Zealand should now do its bit. How could New Zealand have a dependable and active relationship with the United States if it continued to insist that a large and growing part of its ally's most modern naval units should be banned from visiting ports and harbours? It was scarcely what could be called being a good ally: 'If we do refuse admission to nuclear-warhead-carrying ships, we have to say we're getting out of ANZUS', said the new Minister of Foreign Affairs, Brian Talboys.[32]

National's attitude to Labour's South Pacific Nuclear-Weapons-Free Zone resolution was linked to its perception of ANZUS. Muldoon stressed that the resolution was 'carefully tailored to be widely acceptable' and that National would continue to support any resolution to 'move towards' anything that was nuclear-free.[33] But the new government also assured both the United States and the newly elected conservative government in Australia that it considered the idea both impracticable and inconsistent with the objectives and provisions of ANZUS treaty.[34]

Muldoon claimed that Rowling and his deputy, Tizard, had been told by the Americans that there would be a problem for ANZUS if nuclear-powered vessels were excluded from the area covered by that treaty but that such opinions were not publicised at the time.[35] Muldoon quoted official submissions to the previous government in support of his view. One such document revealed that in October 1975 Ministry of Defence officials had told their Minister that their Australian and American counterparts had expressed considerable alarm over the development of the nuclear-weapons-free zone proposal.[36] When asked, the Americans would always say that port visits were necessary.

Muldoon played on Labour's traditional defensiveness in the face of 'soft on Communism' accusations: 'My Government will stand firmly against the protests, such as they are, of concerned New Zealanders who are genuinely apprehensive, but more importantly of New Zealanders who owe less allegiance to their country and their people than they do to an aggressive foreign power.'[37] On another occasion he observed that 'it would be fair to say that we have gone through in the last six months perhaps a period of some slight—and I emphasise slight—uneasiness as far as the United States was

32 *Listener*, 10 April 1976.
33 Henderson interview with Muldoon, *NZIR*, May/June 1977, p. 8.
34 Malcolm Templeton to J. K. McLay, 5 June 1986.
35 *NZFAR*, April-June 1976, p. 50; R. D. Muldoon, *My Way*. Auckland, 1981, pp. 77-78.
36 Grant Tweddle, 'The U. S. Military Presence in New Zealand'. University of Canterbury, M. A. thesis 1983, p. 116. The document was quoted by Muldoon in Parliament, 25 June 1976 (p. 61) and had been published in the *Bulletin*, 12 June 1976, in Australia—reported in the *Listener*, 4 Sept. 1976.
37 *NZFAR*, April-June 1976, p. 11.

concerned .... I think we are past that now, because publicly and officially we've made it clear to the Americans that we want ANZUS to continue in the fullest possible respect.'[38]

It was difficult for Labour to keep the anti-nuclear issue and ANZUS apart. In 1977 (although not in 1976 or 1978) the annual party conference passed a remit calling for a 'positive non-aligned foreign policy and withdrawal from all military alliances with nuclear weapons states'.[39] The party's leadership was not bound by such resolutions, which went to its policy committee for consideration. But the sentiment could not be ignored. Rowling and other senior party members directed their energies at reconciling anti-nuclearism with the American alliance rather than requiring the end of latter for the accomplishment of the former. Labour argued on slender evidence that a port ban would not be a problem for the Americans.[40] It believed that it could have reached a compromise, making New Zealand de facto non-nuclear while keeping the alliance. The visits were not necessary—'encouraging visits by these ships really means giving New Zealand a new-found strategic importance.'[41] Questioning of the US State Department in July 1976 elicited the response that 'the entry of warships into ports is an operational question not specifically addressed in the ANZUS treaty. Operational questions are left to less formal arrangements.'[42] And at times even Muldoon downplayed their significance: 'We will have visits from American warships, I promise you. They will not have a strategic context .... They will be here simply to further cement the goodwill between our peoples ....'[43]

What did the Americans think of Labour? Officials and political people in Washington who were involved in matters of Pacific defence and security undoubtedly found National a more congenial partner. That had been the pattern right through the 1950s and 1960s. And even if the inflexibility of the conservative parties in both New Zealand and Australia had become less than helpful,[44] in a general sense the pattern still held good. Within the Labour Party, although not so dominantly in the caucus, there was a discomfort with

---

38 *NZFAR*, March 1976, p. 20.
39 New Zealand Labour Party, 61st Annual Conference, May 1977, *Report*, p. 26.
40 Labour M. P. Fraser Coleman, for instance, quoted a response to a question put to Vice-President Rockefeller on his visit in 1976, in respect of American reactions to New Zealand moves to ban American vessels from its ports: 'I never cross bridges until I come to them and that is an iffy question totally unrelated to reality ....' See Stephen Levine, 'ANZUS: the American View', *NZIR*, May-June 1977, p. 15.
41 Rowling reported in *Auckland Star*, 28 April 1976, quoted in Juliet Lodge, 'New Zealand Foreign Policy in 1976', *Australian Outlook*, 31/1 (April 1977), p. 83.
42 Quoted by Stephen Levine in 'ANZUS: The American View', *NZIR*, May-June 1977, p. 18.
43 *NZFAR*, April-June 1976, p. 11.
44 Henry Albinski, 'American Perspectives on the ANZUS Alliance', *Australian Outlook*, 32/2 (Aug. 1978). p. 134: 'The reappearance of conservative governments ... in December 1975 brought to office Fraser and Muldoon, two strong-willed Prime Ministers. Both were committed to the American alliance, but neither was fully attuned to Ford and Carter Administration conceptions and priorities.'

the Americans, a critical evaluation of the United States role in the world in general and the relationship with New Zealand in particular. To some extent these feelings were reciprocated. American visitors from the politico-military establishment did not usually seek out Labour Party politicians and when they did, the results were not always fortunate.[45]

Questioned about the issue in 1978 Rowling commented that Labour had got to 'persevere so that present [United States] administration understands exactly what the situation is . . . . neither country should take an action which would upset even a significant minority group in the other country if that action can be avoided. I believe the nuclear ships visit is such an area.' He also stressed that New Zealand had 'a lot of affinity with the United States and I believe most New Zealanders would like to see a strong relationship sustained.'[46] Rowling's talk of perseverance and affinity was a 1970s version of loyal dissent. Ample amounts of both would be required when and if Labour took office again.

National security?

How did the formulation of interests, most particularly the question of security, intersect with anti-nuclear sentiment, the debate on ANZUS and the meaning of independence?

Labour tried to make the ideological critique of ANZUS more acceptable by stressing that there was no significant threat to New Zealand's security. Rowling in 1976 stressed the limited strategic significance of the South Pacific to the great powers.[47] National thinking was rooted in the notion that New Zealand still needed ANZUS for security reasons and that the public shared that belief. Were Muldoon's actions influenced by polling on ANZUS, by a well-honed political instinct for an issue which would work to his adversary's disadvantage? Maybe, but there was substance, as well as politicking, to his concerns about security; in particular he was anxious lest isolationist tendencies in the United States, already pronounced in the post-Vietnam era, would intensify: 'there is some pressure in the American Congress to abandon their strategic interest in this part of the world in the interests of economy. We'd be very cold if they did, and furthermore it would be very expensive for New Zealand if they did.'[48] This was a preoccupation which others of Muldoon's generation would respond to. For them, for National and for the Ministry of Foreign Affairs, it was axiomatic therefore that 'the United States should remain an active force for peace in our part of the Pacific'. National was firm about helping the United States (and Australia and Western interests

---

45   Interview with Sir Wallace Rowling, 12 Sept. 1989; Lange, *Nuclear Free*, pp. 40–42.
46   *NZIR*, Sept.-Oct. 1978, p. 7.
47   Reported in *Auckland Star*, 28 April 1976, quoted in Lodge, 'New Zealand Foreign Policy in 1976', p. 83.
48   *NZFAR*, Jan. 1976, p. 40.

generally) in Southeast Asia and the South Pacific, both diplomatically and to some extent militarily.[49] Whereas Labour had been contemplating the pullout of the New Zealand force from Singapore, this was postponed without date by National. National also declared that it recognised Indonesia as the de facto government of East Timor, and abstained from voting against Indonesia when the issue came before the Fourth Committee of the General Assembly in 1978.[50]

But American isolationism would hardly be a problem for New Zealand if there was no threat. And was there any? The old threats of the 1960s—Vietnam and China—had gone. China was one of the first countries Muldoon visited as Prime Minister. But therein lies a clue, because Muldoon and the Chinese leadership found common cause in their distrust of Soviet ambitions and policies. As Muldoon said before his visit to China, 'all the actions of the Soviet Union in recent times point not to defence but to imperialism and aggression. There is only one power on earth that can resist that aggression and that is the power of the United States, and we must be thankful that . . . there . . . remains in the United States a willingness to be the leader, and indeed ultimately the guardian of the free world.'[51] Muldoon stressed that Soviet missiles could now reach New Zealand and that the Soviet Union could also threaten New Zealand trade routes. Soviet interest in the South Pacific was also a direct threat to New Zealand.

Even a conservative commentator wondered why 'in an era of détente with the Soviet Union, Mr Muldoon had returned to the coldest of Cold War attitudes towards the Russians . . . . Many New Zealanders find Mr Muldoon's preoccupation with the number of Soviet warships in the Indian Ocean almost incomprehensible.'[52] One paper in 1976 reported a decline in Russian naval activity in the Indian Ocean and denials in Washington that the Soviet Union was outpacing America in seapower. Another journalist claimed that New Zealand's Indian Ocean policy was further to the right than that of the United States Congress.[53] Soviet warships had been sighted in the Tasman Sea but it was later admitted that there had been no Russian warships there in the

---

[49] Albinski, 'American Perspectives', p. 142, talked of the 'surrogate' role Australia and New Zealand played for the United States in the region.

[50] 'In New Zealand's dealings with East Timor, the Government has, as necessary, dealt with the authorities that were demonstrably in *de facto* control of the territory . . . now it means the Government of Indonesia.' Acting Minister of Foreign Affairs, Keith Holyoake, *NZFAR*, July-Dec. 1978, pp. 57-58. Both the United States and Indonesia feared that an independent East Timor (a former Portuguese colony) might become a centre of radicalism, a Southeast Asian Cuba.

[51] *NZFAR*, April-June 1976, pp. 10-11; see also *Star Weekender*, 17 April 1976 (Warren Page). Or as one professed Muldoon supporter put it, 'there is a threat both to our free way of life and to our national sovereignty. The communist aim of world domination has never changed—only the methods of attaining that aim . . . .', letter to *Dominion*, 19 May 1976, from Noel Johnston, RNZN retd.

[52] Ian Templeton, *Auckland Star*, 3 June 1976.

[53] *Southland Times*, 9 May 1976; *NZH*, 16 June 1976.

preceding two years.[54] The Soviet Union did approach Tonga but New Zealand knew within days of the Soviet visit that the Tongans would not be signing an agreement with the Russians.[55]

The Americans were indeed rather surprised when the Soviet threat was emphasised most vigorously by New Zealand at the ANZUS Council meeting in 1976.[56] The 1977 ANZUS Council meeting was attended by the United States Deputy Secretary of State (Warren Christopher), not the Secretary, always a sign of diminished American interest—and not therefore necessarily reassuring to the Muldoon government. Christopher declined to say whether Soviet naval strength in the Pacific was greater than in the Indian Ocean or than one year earlier. In respect of the Pacific he said that his government tended not so much to be concerned, as aware of any increased presence of the Soviet Union around the world.[57] Although Talboys still talked of the Soviet threat in 1977 speeches, he admitted that with no Soviet missions and no Soviet navy in the region, the threat had to be kept in perspective.[58]

The extent of National's preoccupations with defence and security was shown through actions as well as words. *Defence Review 1978*, a statement of government policy, stressed that New Zealand's defence effort would be concentrated 'close to home' and would consist primarily of helping to ensure stability in the Southwest Pacific.[59] In a 1984 paper Steve Hoadley noted that in the 1970s New Zealand moved into a new period of alliance relations which he called the 'national independence' period: 'This period found both Britain and the United States withdrawing selectively from forward positions in the Third World, mainly Asia, while New Zealand was reaching out to Asian and South Pacific states more visibly on the basis of New Zealand's particular interests than on the basis of Commonwealth or American ties, although these were never absent.'[60]

This 'reaching out' was not an expensive activity. One observer noted that in respect of defence spending 'the Muldoon Government has . . . not matched threat-oriented rhetoric with defence performance, preferring instead to raise economic arguments to explain under-commitment to defence spending.' In 1977-78 only about 1.8 per cent of GNP was devoted to defence, one of the

54   Dalton West, 'The Soviet Union's Relations with New Zealand', *Round Table*, 278 (April 1980), pp. 202-3. See also Owen Wilkes, 'The Great Russian Scare of 1976', *Monthly Review*, Aug. 1978, pp. 6-8. Citing US sources, Wilkes deduced that on average in 1976 the Soviet Union had 'out of area' [i.e. away from Vladivostok and Petropavlovsk] only two surface combatants. Wilkes also 'guesstimated' maybe four submarines on patrol at any one time.
55   West, 'Soviet Union's Relations with NZ', p. 9.
56   *EP*, 9 Sept. 1976
57   *EP*, 28 July 1977.
58   *ODT*, 22 Sept. 1977. At this time New Zealand was interested in allowing the Soviet Union into its Exclusive Economic Zone, see p. 217.
59   See John Henderson, 'The Burdens of ANZUS', *NZIR*, May/June 1980, pp. 2-3.
60   Steve Hoadley, 'The Future of New Zealand's Alliances', in NZIIA, *New Zealand Foreign Policy: Choices, Challenges and Opportunities*, p. 68.

world's lowest figures. Defence spending as a proportion of government spending fell from nearly 4.7 per cent in 1974 to just under 4.2 per cent in 1977.[61]

One conservative New Zealand commentator, commenting on the record of the Muldoon government, observed that

> If all that matters is trade, then it is clearly permissible to play fast and loose with security issues. Unfortunately too, previous governments [i.e. before 1984] did little to follow up commitments given in successive Defence Reviews to developing the Armed Forces in ways consistent with the changing scene in the Pacific. ANZUS became a substitute for thought, or rather action. No attempt was made to establish defence as a legitimate and proper concern of an independent-minded country. The issues are difficult when there is no obvious threat.[62]

In the case of Australia, a preoccupation with the security of the Australian state and territory had long rivalled, or superseded, concern with the security of the larger entity, be it the Empire or the Western alliance. This concern with national security underpinned Australia's defence decisions in the Second World War and its absolute commitment to securing an alliance with the United States after the war. New Zealand, as we have seen, although it had security interests, articulated these wholly within an alliance framework and had never thought as systematically as Australia about national defence, except possibly in 1938-42. With the end of close Commonwealth and American defence collaboration in the 1970s the time might have been ripe for the development of doctrines of national security. But this did not happen, which is further evidence that neither in the official nor in the popular mind did conventional security concerns loom large.

National's 1978 election plank on foreign relations showed that security—and independence—were expressed in economic as much as in defence terms. It also underscored the way in which Laking 'realism' would evolve from the traditional independence of interest. The initial section, labelled 'Philosophy', stated

> National sees New Zealand as an independent South Pacific nation in an increasingly interdependent world. National will continue to develop a foreign policy designed to:
>
> Stand up for New Zealand's national interests wherever they are challenged;

61 Albinski, 'American Perspectives', p. 141; 'The Expense of Defence', *NZIR*, Jan-Feb. 1979, p. 7. Government spending excludes debt service and miscellaneous investment transactions and is at constant 1977-78 prices. Presumably the advent of National Superannuation payments in 1976 affected the weighting of all other items of government spending.
62 Denis McLean, *New Zealand: Isolation and Foreign Policy*. Sydney, 1990, pp. 16-17.

Fulfil New Zealand's obligations as a responsible member of the international community;

Bearing in mind that foreign policy and trade are inextricably linked, promote the relationships with other countries that will protect existing trade interests and offer new opportunities for expansion of our trade;

Broaden New Zealand's international contacts wherever it will benefit this country to do so.[63]

Cold War tensions, 1978-81

The 1970s saw the 'end of the postwar world', in the view of a number of scholars. The détente in relations between the West on the one hand and China and the Soviet Union on the other had gathered speed: 'the international order under which we lived for a generation or so after 1945 has passed away, irretrievably.' Confrontation had given way to 'dialogue and limited cooperation' in political relations.[64] But in the later 1970s and early 1980s, Cold War tensions increased, particularly after the Vietnamese intervention in Cambodia at the end of 1978 and the Soviet move into Afghanistan late in 1979.[65] These changes revived alliance politics and with them the experience for New Zealand of being a part of a larger whole—in this instance, the Western alliance—in a way which had not been so evident in the mid 1970s. Would New Zealand respond to new alliance pressures in nationalist fashion or can we see a traditional pattern of the alliance partner pursuing its interests within the alliance framework?

The National government's response was traditional. With less pressure on New Zealand than over Korea or Vietnam, it was an even more pronounced version of the traditional conservative mix of rhetorical support and a keen awareness of the need to protect New Zealand interests. The mix was given a particular 'flavour' by personal and ideological differences between Muldoon and President Carter. Confronted with an alliance leader who did not lead—or not in the right direction—Muldoon, like Massey and Doidge before him, did not hesitate to criticise and chastise.

Jimmy Carter, the outsider, elected President at the end of 1976, in the first Presidential election since the Watergate scandal had driven Nixon out, brought an idealism to the White House that had not been seen since the days of Roosevelt.[66] Carter's human rights policies and talk of a nuclear-weapons-

---

[63]   *NZFAR*, July-Dec. 1978, pp. 11–12.
[64]   F. H. Corner, 'Emerging Perspectives in World Politics', *NZFAR*, Aug. 1975, p. 4. See also, for instance, Alastair Buchan, *Change Without War: The Shifting Structures of World Power*. London, 1974.
[65]   The best analysis of these events is Fred Halliday, *The Making of the Second Cold War*. London, 1983. Halliday argues that American foreign policy moved right in the late 1970s because of the revolutionary threat in the third world in places like Angola, Ethiopia and Cambodia. This view is less convincing now than it was in 1983.
[66]   Carter defeated Gerald Ford, who had succeeded Nixon as President in August 1974.

free zone in the Pacific caught the New Zealand government out of step with
Washington, most egregiously so after Muldoon referred to Carter as a
'peanut farmer',[67] but more substantively as well: 'President Carter... talks
about human rights, a moral foreign policy. What does he mean? Is America
going to declare war on every Government that is infringing human rights, and
if not, just how are they going to carry out such a policy?'[68] A projected
meeting between Muldoon and Carter suddenly became difficult to arrange
and was postponed from September to November 1977.[69] Muldoon was
publicly critical of 'trilateralism' and its implication that the United States
would concentrate its attention on Western Europe and Japan, and ignore
other parts of the world, like the southwest Pacific. He was reassured when
this proved not to be the case.[70] Muldoon was concerned that the
Commission's influence in the Carter administration would weaken the
latter's interest in New Zealand's part of the world.[71] Rowling for his part
enjoyed talking, in advance of the 1978 election, of 'some scars left by the
outrageous comments of the Prime Minister and the clear difficulty he had in
arranging a meeting with [Carter]. I believe we can, as a Labour administration, heal up the scars ...'[72]

With the anti-American revolution in Iran, the Vietnamese invasion of
Cambodia, and the Soviet intervention in Afghanistan at the end of 1979,
American policy changed direction. New Zealand found the United States
again taking an interest in its part of the world, and talking of extending
ANZUS into the Indian Ocean. There was even talk of JANZUS—bringing
Japan into ANZUS.[73] Rhetorically at least, New Zealand went along with the
new American line, but there were differences, particularly while Carter was
President, and particularly in respect of trade in the Middle East. Over and
above his personal distaste for Carter, Muldoon demonstrated in charac-

---

67 *Listener*, 15 Oct. 1977.
68 Muldoon, quoted in *EP*, 9 April 1977.
69 *Dominion*, 19 July 1977; see also article in *Listener*, 15 Oct. 1977; Muldoon, *My Way*, pp.
102–4.
70 John Henderson, 'Foreign Policy and the Election', *NZIR*, Sept.-Oct. 1978, p. 23; *Press*, 25
Aug. 1977 (Cedric Mentiplay). Mentiplay quotes a 23 April 1977 address by Muldoon in which he
labelled Carter, Vance and Christopher 'trilateralists'. See also *My Way*, pp. 102–3. The
Trilateral Commission grouped influential individuals from Japan, Western Europe and the
United States, that is from the three dominant capitalist economies, with the goal of promoting
areas of common ground and acceptable patterns of international stability. Muldoon's
reservations about the Commission overlapped with left-wing suspicions of it. There was also a
vein of far right suspicion which believed 'trilateralists' were part of an international Jewish
conspiracy, with agents in both the Kremlin and Wall Street.
71 Henderson, 'Foreign Policy and the Election', p. 23.
72 Rowling interview with Derek Round, *NZIR*, Sept.-Oct. 1977, pp. 4, 9; interview with
writer, 12 Sept. 1989. The election was narrowly won by National.
73 William Tow, 'The JANZUS Option: A Key to Asian/Pacific Security', *Asian Survey*, 18/2
(Dec. 1978), pp. 1221–34; John Henderson, 'The 1980s: A Time for Commitment', *NZIR*, Jan.-
Feb. 1980, p. 6. See also the caution of the Deputy Secretary of Foreign Affairs, Malcolm
Templeton, over the likelihood of such an eventuality, *EP*, 18 May 1981.

teristic fashion the propensity of a New Zealand leader to pursue distinctive interests within the alliance framework.

Carter sought support from other Western nations for sanctions against Iran in 1979. The President of Federated Farmers stated bluntly that New Zealand's farmers would object to the disruption of the newly established lamb trade by an American boycott and was pleased that the United States had agreed that food supplies would be exempt on humanitarian grounds. Eyebrows were raised in Washington when New Zealand re-opened its embassy in Tehran, despite American moves to get all Western countries to break diplomatic relations. Two years later a Wool Board representative claimed that New Zealand's refusal to call for a trade ban during the hostage crisis had worked in New Zealand's favour.[74]

After the Soviet intervention in Afghanistan, the United States had summoned an emergency meeting of the ANZUS Council, at which New Zealand along with Australia gave strong public support to American opposition to the Soviet intervention and to the de facto expansion of ANZUS into the Indian Ocean. The Council, the communiqué read, 'agreed to explore fully the possibilities for enhancing the effectiveness of the treaty partners' military activities in the Indian Ocean, without prejudicing the fulfilment of their respective responsibilities in the treaty area . . . .'[75] Talboys gave a New Zealand gloss on this response in an address arguing that

> most of us would surely want to pitch in and help, in whatever way we can, to avoid the disaster of another world war. I believe . . . that New Zealand can do most to help maintain peace by continuing to act as a reliable ally of the United States, and by working through ANZUS to re-establish confidence in international affairs. If we as a community that tries to uphold Western values, have a contribution to make, we can make it most effectively by working with the one country that has the power to realise the ideals we all share.[76]

What would be involved? New Zealand postponed yet again any decision on withdrawing the force from Singapore.[77] An additional $340 million of long-term defence spending was authorised for replacement combat vehicles for the Army and also a new transport fleet, modernisation of the Orions for the Air Force and frigate refurbishment for the Navy.[78] In April Muldoon told American journalists that the United States could 'count on' New Zealand if fighting broke out in the Persian Gulf. And later in the year Muldoon authorised technical talks at Navy level on the possibility of New Zealand's committing a frigate to an international task force.[79]

[74] *EP*, 1 April 1980; *NZH*, 9 April 1980; *EP*, 14 Sept. 1982.
[75] *NZFAR*, Jan.-March 1980, p. 11.
[76] *NZFAR*, Jan.-March 1980, p. 9.
[77] *EP*, 8 July 1980.
[78] *EP*, 28 Feb. 1980.
[79] *EP*, 22 April, 2 Oct. 1980.

But there was also caution. Rowling's speedy and critical response to the Soviet invasion of Afghanistan allowed him both to emphasise Labour's anti-Communism, its internationalism and its commitment to collective security and also to draw attention to the slowness of the government's response: the Cabinet had not determined its policy until its first post-holiday meeting of the year, late in January (Soviet troops had entered Afghanistan at the end of December), nearly two weeks after Australia had announced a range of retaliatory measures.[80] Mr Sofinski, the Soviet Ambassador, was expelled in February. The government explained that he had been expelled for passing funds to the Socialist Unity Party, but the expulsion did come at a convenient time for a country wishing to make clear its opposition to a range of Soviet activities.[81]

Like the expulsion, the actions New Zealand did take—cutting the Soviet fishing quota, suspending scientific and other exchanges—did not affect New Zealand exports to the Soviet Union. Moreover, the quota cutback, according to fishing industry sources, had been planned before the Afghanistan crisis. Producer interests were again adamant in opposing a trade ban, and Muldoon was quite explicit about it too.[82] Muldoon identified Australian Prime Minister Malcolm Fraser as 'one of President Carter's most active supporters ... who travelled vast distances to drum up support for Carter's policies including, particularly, the Olympic boycott'.[83] Muldoon reacted differently. He was dissatisfied with Carter's crisis management: 'In [respect of the Iran crisis] and in the days following the Soviet invasion of Afghanistan, we were more unhappy with President Carter's habits of making far-reaching decisions without consultation and then expecting his friends and allies to back him up.'[84]

Defence spending did increase at the end of the 1970s, from 1.67 per cent of GNP in 1976-77 to 2.09 per cent in 1979-80. But New Zealand's defence expenditure per capita was still only $114 compared with $272 for Australia and $644 for the United States.[85] When Muldoon talked about helping the Americans in the Gulf, he meant primarily providing naval and air-staging

[80] John Henderson, 'The Burdens of ANZUS', p. 3; interview with Rowling, 12 Sept. 1989. Rowling's response may have been influenced by awareness of the debate within the Labour Party about ANZUS, reinvigorated by the United States' own renewed interest in its ANZUS allies. See *Monthly Review*, March 1980, p. 12; April 1980, pp. 8-9. See also below, p. xx.
[81] Henderson, 'The Burdens of ANZUS', p. 3; Muldoon's account is in *My Way*, pp. 136-7.
[82] *EP*, 28 Feb. 1980; Henderson, 'Burdens of ANZUS', p. 3.
[83] Muldoon, *My Way*, p. 135. The United States lobbied for a boycott of the Olympic Games, which were to be held in Moscow in the northern summer. The contemporaneous debate in New Zealand over political involvement in sports ties with South Africa should be remembered here. See p. 246.
[84] Muldoon, *My Way*, p. 135.
[85] John Turner, 'What Price New Zealand's Security?' *NZIR*, Nov.-Dec. 1981, pp. 14-15. Per cent of GNP figures cited by Turner are from the International Institute for Strategic Studies, *The Military Balance*. London.

facilities and even then recognised that it was more likely that Australia would be used.[86] According to one Washington source, Talboys toned down the 1980 ANZUS communiqué to an agreement to participate in the Indian Ocean 'as resources permit'. The Indian Ocean was of course outside the 'Pacific area' that was the specified operational zone of the ANZUS treaty. In Washington, 'as resources permit' appeared to be a euphemism for 'virtually no involvement', as the best New Zealand could offer was the occasional joint exercise using its Orions.[87] In 1981 a spokesperson for the newly installed Reagan Administration suggested New Zealand should consider replacing rather than refurbishing the naval vessel *Otago*: the government declined. The Minister of Defence, David Thomson, said that New Zealand hoped that the Americans would discount the price of a new frigate. And New Zealand needed to be able to export to pay for one—'we are virtually a retail buyer', he added.[88]

The government went ahead with a contribution to the Sinai Multinational Force assembled to police the Camp David Agreement between Israel and Egypt; it did so in the face of criticism, not just from the left, but from business groups, who contended it might harm trade with Arab countries and Iran and be a breach of the government's 'evenhanded' policy as between Israel and the Palestinians.[89] The government announced a decision to participate in principle at the end of October but there was clearly concern lest new relations in the Middle East be jeopardised: 'we are just starting to set up a network of diplomatic posts, and do not wish to place our new relationships under strain'.[90] The government decided only at the end of November, when the decisions of a number of European countries appeared to have firmed up: 'the decisions by Australia, Britain, France, Italy and the Netherlands to join those who had earlier indicated their readiness to participate do satisfy us that the force will be seen for what it is: a necessary means of maintaining peace in Sinai following Israel's withdrawal'.[91]

The ANZUS debate and national security

American pressure on its South Pacific allies over Afghanistan revived debate in the Labour Party about the merits of non-alignment. A majority of delegates at the Party's 1980 conference voted to withdraw from ANZUS— a more explicit resolution than the 1977 one and the first such resolution

86   *EP*, 22 April 1980.
87   Bruce Wallace, 'Which Way The Alliance?', *NZIR*, Nov.-Dec. 1980, p. 11. The comments are attributed to a 'Washington source'.
88   *NZH*, 13 Jan. 1981.
89   W. J. Barnes, 'Patron-Client Relations within Alliances'. Univ. of Canterbury, M.A. thesis, 1986, p. 159.
90   Talboys, *NZFAR*, Oct.-Dec. 1981, p. 16.
91   Muldoon, *NZFAR*, Oct.-Dec. 1981, p. 39.

to be passed since then.[92] Labour's leadership was still determined to keep New Zealand in ANZUS and as in 1975-78 endeavoured to reconcile the sentiment against nuclear power and in favour of regional rather than global collaboration with ANZUS, rather than using them as a lever against it. Rowling stated the official Labour Party position on ANZUS in June 1980. A Labour government 'would adopt a more independent stand within ANZUS', he said. 'There was absolutely nothing in the treaty that required members to accept visits by vessels or aircraft of other alliance members.' Labour also regarded the Pacific focus of the treaty as crucial, and would ensure that it was maintained: 'the ANZUS treaty was very specific about limiting obligations of alliance members to the Pacific region. The treaty was a commitment to the defence of the Pacific, not to other areas of the world such as the Indian Ocean.'[93] Labour also stressed that it wanted to breathe new life into the relationship, taking it away from purely security preoccupations: 'I'm quite convinced', said Rowling in 1981, 'that the best defence New Zealand can have is a stable and progressive Pacific and Southeast Asian region.'[94]

The Deputy Minister of Finance, Hugh Templeton, a former foreign service officer, contested the anti-ANZUS case. While taking note of the usual ideological and security arguments, he elaborated others: 'rather than dwelling on the traditional arguments for our membership ... the classic military and security arguments ...', he argued,

It is, for example, inconceivable to me—such is the importance the Australians attach to their security relationship with the United States—that we could withdraw from ANZUS and adopt a policy of non-alignment or armed neutrality without doing serious damage to our efforts to establish a closer economic relationship with Australia. In theory, I would agree that the two policies are not conceptually incompatible, but they would be very difficult, if not impossible, to pursue as a matter of practical politics at one and the same time. The point is that a non-aligned or neutral New Zealand would be very differently regarded in Canberra, as well as in Washington. We would also be viewed very differently in the capitals of [other Western, Asian and Pacific] states.[95]

Templeton's presentation suggested, if only by omission, that the argument that the New Zealand needed the alliance because it needed a protector was weakening. He was shifting the case for ANZUS from the traditional

92 New Zealand Labour Party, 64th Annual Conference, April 1980, *Report*, p. 54.
93 Reported in *EP*, 10 June 1980.
94 *NZIR*, Sept.-Oct. 1981, p. 17. At a regional conference in 1981, M. P. Richard Prebble put forward a remit proposing that New Zealand should promote a nuclear- weapons-free zone from within ANZUS, in contrast to a remit urging Labour to withdraw. *EP*, 2 March 1981.
95 Hugh Templeton, 'New Zealand's Defence Policy for the 80s', *NZFAR*, April-June 1980, pp. 6-16. See also Talboys, 'Afghanistan, Indochina and ANZUS: Implications for New Zealand's Foreign Policy', *NZFAR*, Jan.-March 1980, pp. 3-9; 'The United States and New Zealand: Anatomy of an Alliance', *NZIR*, Nov.-Dec. 1980, pp. 2-11.

compound of loyalty and security to a realist argument that New Zealand could not afford, for diplomatic reasons, to leave the alliance.

Others worked from a similar premise—that New Zealand had to be hard-nosed—but reached different conclusions. *Beyond New Zealand*, an international relations text published in 1980, was subtitled, 'The Foreign Policy of a Small State': 'there is a growing recognition that the economic and strategic interests of the large industrialised Western nations ... and the interests of a small isolated island nation do not always coincide.'[96] Bob Edlin, editor of the *National Business Review*, wrote at the beginning of 1981 that while neither major party advocated withdrawal from ANZUS, it was an option 'that was nonetheless worthy at least of examination' in an era of American incompetence (the Tehran hostages rescue mission) and belligerence. Edlin, citing Muldoon's axiom, 'our foreign policy is trade', pointed out that 'as a trading nation we have close and important contact with countries throughout the world and we must be concerned with world problems', and asked that ANZUS like all policies should be subjected to 'constant examination and healthy debate'.[97]

Just over a year later the *NBR* made another contribution to the debate by publishing 'Small is dutiful? The dangers of dependence for small nations where others set the rules', by Jim Clad, Michael Hirschfeld and Marilyn Waring. While Hirschfeld was associated with the Labour Party and Jim Clad was a foreign service officer, later to enter journalism himself, Marilyn Waring was a maverick National M.P. who frequently took dissenting positions on foreign policy and women's issues. The arguments were interesting because, like Templeton's, although to a different end, they used the language of realpolitik. In particular the three writers questioned the worth to New Zealand of having collaborated in the post-1975 ostracism of Vietnam, and noted in contrast New Zealand's non-participation in full trade embargoes of the Soviet Union and Iran and the country's distinctive view of and interest in the Law of the Sea negotiations.[98]

A more traditional perspective on alliances was shown in New Zealand's response to the 1982 Anglo-Argentinian conflict over the Falklands/Malvinas. Muldoon took a strongly pro-British position. New Zealand broke diplomatic relations with Argentina almost immediately, without even awaiting a British request. Some weeks later, while he was in London, Muldoon offered the

96   John Henderson, 'The Foreign Policy of a Small State', in *Beyond New Zealand*. Auckland, 1980, p. 2. *Beyond New Zealand II: Foreign Policy Into the 1990s*, Richard Kennaway and John Henderson, eds, with new material, appeared in 1991.
97   *NBR*, 19 Jan. 1981.
98   As did Lange himself after the breach with the United States in 1985–86: 'countries which trade in many markets simply cannot afford to be too closely identified with any particular power or protector.' *Dominion*, 10 May 1985, report of address to Labour Party Auckland regional conference.

British the use of HMNZS *Canterbury* for deployment in the Indian Ocean to allow them to withdraw one more vessel for combat purposes. While the running on these issues was made by Muldoon, his stance found acquiescence among most National Members of Parliament. Loyalty to the Queen, friendship for Britain and reserve at the very least for African, Asian and Latin ideologies and attitudes were all proclaimed:

> The day the Argentinian Ambassador was sent home, a Cabinet minister worried to me that he and his colleagues might have gone too far. Hard to tell. There didn't seem to be any significant discord (though actual involvement in the war might change that) .... The top leadership of the Government fought in the desert with Monty. Their Britishness is close to them, atavistic instincts stir.[99]

An article by Muldoon in *The Times* was titled 'Why we stand with our mother country'. With it was a drawing by the cartoonist Lurie showing a Prime Minister bare-footed in a flax skirt holding a shepherd's crook with a Union Jack bucket over his arm. Describing himself as a typical New Zealander, Muldoon recalled that his father had served in France and his uncle had landed at Gallipoli and that he had served both in Italy and against Japan. Muldoon described the British Prime Minister Margaret Thatcher as 'one of the finest and straightest politicians I have ever met', while she reciprocated by calling New Zealand 'absolutely magnificent' in their support 'for this country, the Falkland Islanders, for the rule of liberty and the rule of law'.[100]

Muldoon may have been using rhetoric quite deliberately to pursue a specific diplomatic goal. Journalists tried to explain Muldoon's actions in terms of New Zealand interests, usually by asserting that support for Britain would translate into stronger British support for New Zealand in European Community negotiations: 'by quickly lending support to Britain—still a major customer for our primary products—we reinforced a relationship with a country whose help we need at the EEC negotiating table next time we have to fight to maintain our trade with Europe.'[101] His verbal enthusiasm was qualified on the part of others by a great deal of caution, not just from the left, about just how far New Zealand involvement should go:

> there is caucus secrecy, ministerial evasiveness and the Prime Minister's determination not to be drawn on the issue. All this has given rise within New Zealand to unsettling speculation, assumptions and a growing fear that the country

---

[99]　Colin James, *NBR*, 10 May 1982.
[100]　Reports in *EP*, 2 May 1982.
[101]　*NBR*, 12 April 1982. The American intervention in Grenada, October 1983, was supported by New Zealand and justified by reference to the destabilising effect of Cuba in the Caribbean. Subsequent New Zealand responses were cautious, not out of sympathy with the ousted regime, but because of considerations of Commonwealth solidarity.

could find itself involved in a war for which there is little enthusiasm other than support in principle for Britain's stand against Argentina.[102]

Muldoon's loyalism had anachronistic elements, as did the war itself, but the interplay of loyalty and interests was as characteristic of this as of earlier eras.[103] The public caution about anything more than symbolic alignment with Britain was suggestive.

In the transformed world of the 1970s and early 1980s we can identify points of continuity with the earlier patterns of independence in foreign policy. The Commonwealth framework had gone but the traditional interplay of interest and dissent took place against the backdrop first of détente, then of renewed alliance cooperation at the end of the decade. New conceptions of independence were formulated and expressed but not entrenched.

[102]   *EP*, 20 May 1982; also 7 May 1982: 'the great majority of New Zealanders would be concerned if New Zealand's assistance to Britain at this time were to extend to military aid'; and *NBR*, 10 May 1982: 'readers who can think of a host of reasons why we should steer clear of the South Atlantic are invited to challenge our support for Rob and country'.
[103]   Muldoon invoked Savage at the outset of the Second World War: see *EP*, 21 May 1982.

9. A small state in the world economy, 1965-90

As we saw in Chapter 5, the idea of economic independence was expressed primarily within the Commonwealth framework. Labour sought to promote the economic independence of New Zealand within that framework, so as to enhance its ability to maintain full employment policies. National articulated business and farmer interests within the same context. In the later 1950s and early 1960s there was change. That change accelerated in the late 1960s and early 1970s. It was defined most sharply by Britain's successful negotiation of admission to the EEC, which took effect from the beginning of 1973. Politicians and diplomats coped with new realities and scholars analysed.

The new independence

New Zealand's new status in international economic relations, as a small state rather than a Commonwealth member, was underlined on numerous occasions in the late 1960s. Moreover, New Zealand found that its alliances were less meaningful in the world of commerce than in the world of diplomacy and politics.

We can see these patterns in a number of particular instances. Despite the conclusion of the free trade agreement with Australia in 1965, it was clear that the Australian market would not be a substitute for the British market, nor could Australia regard New Zealand in the same light as Britain had, as far as the making of trade policy was concerned. 'You can speak in certain arenas of emotion and warmth and loyalty, and these kind of things; carried into the field of commerce this becomes pretty thin,' said John McEwen, Australian Minister of Trade. 'Australia has a forest products industry,' he went on. 'Australia has a paper industry. It is older than yours .... It is bigger than yours .... it is a matter of supplying a country and industry that has been built on a basis of protection—completely .... It is practically self-sufficient. That is what you have to penetrate. You can rock the boat pretty easily getting into that .... [But] so long as we have patience and commercial understanding about this, it can be done.'[1]

As with Australia, so with the United States: there was no easy transition from political to economic solidarity. Critics had charged throughout the course of the war that New Zealand had either been given butter for guns—or had not: to gain was venal, to miss out incompetent.[2] The government was determined in 1968–69 to show that it could stand up for New Zealand's commercial interests in the United States. Holyoake's visit to the United States in 1968 was also a response to Ambassador Corner's judgement that there was a fund of goodwill to Australia in the United States from which New Zealand also benefited, and that New Zealand's role in Vietnam also put New Zealand in a special category.[3] Holyoake addressed the commercial issues both in public and in private on his rather oddly timed trip (in October 1968, during the run-up to the presidential election in which President Johnson was not even a contender).[4] Holyoake got something—the assurance of some improvement in respect of dairy products when a Tariff Commission reported to the President early in 1969, lamb purchases for the US military commissariat, and a doubling of the cheese quota.[5] In 1969, confronted by the possibility of lamb quotas, Holyoake went back on the offensive and again linked trade access with foreign policy. The public element in this initiative, with Holyoake releasing a letter he wrote to Nixon about the subject in July 1969, seems particularly to have been designed to demonstrate that the government could and would stand up for New Zealand interests.[6] But the effort expended suggested the limits to, rather than the opportunities for, any conversion of alliance 'credits' into commercial benefits.

Experience of Japan, another 'new' market, brought home the same point. In the 1950s Japan had been almost a supplicant, eager to re-establish the

1   *EAR*, March 1967, p. 39; *NZE&T*, 1 April 1967, commented that McEwen's 'dedication to the protection of Australian farmers and manufacturers came through loud and clear'. For further discussion of the New Zealand-Australia Free Trade Agreement (NAFTA), see McKinnon, 'Trading in Difficulties', pp. 163–4.
2   See, for instance, *Critic*, 7 July 1966: the leader of a trade mission to the US reported as saying that military ties with the United States in Asia had helped a great deal; New Zealand might lose goodwill from United States if not in Vietnam, *NZE&T*, 1 Dec. 1966.
3   Corner to Holyoake, 9 June 1968. Ms Papers 1403, 86/3, ATL.
4   See *NZPD*, 358, p. 2887 (6 Nov. 1968); *EAR*, Oct. 1968, pp. 26–27.
5   *EAR*, Nov. 1968, p. 30; Holyoake to Marshall, 6 Jan. 1969, Ms Papers 1814, 512/5, ATL; *Monthly Review*, Nov. 1968, p. 3: 'Muldoon has been telling US that we fully support their policy in Vietnam but we want to be paid—New Zealand has been authorised to compete for the sale of more goods to American military forces in Vietnam and other theatres.'
6   Holyoake wrote that 'New Zealand cannot be expected to play its full part in areas of international cooperation, particularly regional security arrangements to which the United States attaches importance, unless it has the trading opportunities which provide it with the economic means', *EAR*, June 1969, p. 52. The new administration was responsive and Holyoake publicly thanked Nixon and Defence Secretary Melvin Laird on his visit to Washington in September 1969 for their opposition to the Senate amendment proposing embargos or quotas on New Zealand lamb. *EAR*, June 1969, p. 52; Aug. 1969, pp. 54–55; Sept. 1969, p. 15.

commercial relations with all countries that had been sundered and/or restricted by two decades of depression, war and occupation. New Zealand was not crucial to the process from the economic point of view but it did have some political significance, as a Commonwealth member and ally of the United States. It was important for Japan to normalise its relations with such countries, to break down the reservoir of suspicion. With the signing of a trade treaty in 1959, this set of circumstances slowly receded. Through the 1960s, as Japan boomed, its economic importance to New Zealand increased, but New Zealand's importance to it declined. With Japan, New Zealand economic diplomacy first encountered the new world, facing the continuous and unrelenting task of manoeuvering in a bureaucratic and business system in which it enjoyed no advantages of sentiment, knowledge or leverage. It was an outsider, and an impotent one at that: 'it was clear that New Zealand's relations with Japan would never be as "cosy" as with Britain and to develop them would require vigour, sensitivity and imagination.'[7]

The relationship with Britain itself was not as cosy as once it had been—or was remembered to be. In 1966–67 the Wilson government made an abortive bid for EEC membership. In his first announcement Wilson singled out New Zealand as a special case and this was reiterated on subsequent occasions.[8] In April 1969 President de Gaulle unexpectedly resigned. Clearly it would only be a matter of time before the prospect of Britain's entering the Community became a live issue again. As in 1967 (but in contrast to 1961–62), the New Zealand government sought assurances solely in respect of butter, cheese and lamb—and in a sense this meant only the first two, because there was not as yet any Community sheepmeats policy.[9] New Zealand's growing trade relations with the United States and Japan dissuaded the government from offering the Community a special arrangement in the New Zealand market: 'a close and exclusive trading relationship with the EEC ... would militate against our objective of world-wide trade diversification'.[10]

Thus New Zealand accepted that its economic future would lie, not with one partner, but with many. Nonetheless the British seemed to be even more adamant. The change of government in Britain in May 1970 had brought Edward Heath, Macmillan's negotiator of 1961–62 and a committed Europeanist, to the prime ministership. Also committed to Europe was Con O'Neill, the British Foreign Office negotiator, who visited New Zealand in June. He told officials that he was not yet convinced that cheese was a problem and did not want to push proposals on lamb in case it stimulated the introduction of a Community regime for that product. O'Neill's, however,

7   Ann Trotter, 'From Suspicion to Growing Partnership', *NZWA 1957–72*, p. 225; see also further discussion, pp. 217–26.
8   *EAR*, Nov. 1966, p. 17; Feb. 1967, p. 38; July 1967, p. 33.
9   COTP, 6 May 1970, Ms Papers 1403, 398/2, ATL.
10   COTP, 30 June 1970. Ms Papers 1403, 398/2, ATL. See also *NZFAR*, Sept. 1970, p. 23.

was not the only perspective and a subsequent ministerial level meeting with the Commonwealth Secretary, Geoffrey Rippon, in September revealed a considerable measure of agreement between Britain and New Zealand. Cheese stayed in and Rippon accepted that something more than a 'transition to disaster' was needed.[11]

But it was not just the British who had to be convinced: it was also the Europeans. The French Foreign Secretary, Jean de Lipkowski, visited Wellington in January 1971. New Zealand had fought in the war, helped liberate his own country,[12] he said; moreover, it was a stable influence in 'this part of the world'. France 'did not intend to act as an instrument of war against New Zealand'. But, he went on, and it was a big but, France could not accept terms which would threaten the 'political or economic stability of Europe', a euphemism, in such a context, for the Common Agricultural Policy. And he was rigid in defining the transition period as the absolute limit of any special arrangement. From the official record of these talks one can sense the chill in the Cabinet room as de Lipkowski made his icy comments. The French talked about an international dairy agreement but there could be no guarantee that one could be reached.[13] Thus did New Zealand encounter power in international economic relations. Could France, Britain's lesser partner through two world wars, with its unstable and passionate politics, its expertise in folly but not finance, cuisine but not commerce, be in a position to determine New Zealand's future? It seemed so.

In the event the negotiations turned much more on the special relationship between New Zealand and Britain than anything else and in that sense were a reminder of the old world rather than a portent of the new. The proposal finally put forward by the EEC members jointly to Britain on 21 June 1971 allowed for 60 per cent of existing exports in milk equivalent terms at the end of the five-year period, which translated into 75 per cent of existing butter exports and 20 per cent of cheese. The British, with the New Zealanders standing by, managed to increase the five-year figure to 71 per cent milk equivalent, butter only being reduced to 80 per cent of existing volume, but cheese still falling to 20 per cent. The price level guaranteed was to be an average of New Zealand prices on the British market over the four-year period 1969–72. In respect of the post-transition period a review would take place at the end of the third year of the agreement. Although New Zealand made a case on economic grounds, it was the political relationship between Britain and New Zealand that permitted a settlement on these terms. In one crucial respect, therefore, New Zealand was not out in the cold: although the link weakened once Britain was inside the Community, it did not evaporate.[14]

11   COTP, 20 June, 22 Sept. 1970. Ms Papers 1403, 398/2, ATL.
12   Points frequently made both in New Zealand and in Britain.
13   COTP, 28 Jan. 1971, Ms Papers 1403, 399/1, ATL.
14   Henry Lang, 'Economics and Foreign Policy', *NZFAR*, Aug. 1973, pp. 22–23.

Nonetheless, Britain's entry into the Community, culminating in the formal denunciation of the raft of trade agreements with New Zealand dating back to 1932, marked the end of an era.[15]

In 1968 Holyoake had written to one Ambassador, 'our "special" link with Britain has long since gone by the board as far as inter-governmental dealings are concerned .... [and] even if we actively wished to build up a similar relationship with the United States ... would our overtures meet with any genuine response?'[16] At the beginning of 1969 his annual statement on the international scene noted how 'great energy now goes into the building up of tight regional groupings. The superpowers show discomforting signs of retrenchment and renewed isolationism. There is a general disillusionment with the effectiveness of international organisations. The smaller and weaker countries ... find themselves alone and exposed.'[17]

Such comments could have been made about international monetary as well as commercial relations. Britain's devaluation of sterling in November 1967 had raised questions about the security of New Zealand's foreign exchange reserves.[18] And sterling devaluation increased pressure on the dollar, another overvalued currency. Nixon's devaluation of the dollar and introduction of import control in August 1971 were dramatic manifestations of international economic tensions, and also of the extent to which a world of economic blocs—the United States, Europe and Japan—existed alongside the idea of a unified international economy. The settlement on exchange rates reached by the major trading powers at the end of the year was greeted with relief.[19] But the rest of the 1970s brought further evidence of New Zealand's outsider status in the international economy.

Labour and the economy, 1965–75

We saw that in the late 1950s and early 1960s Labour's external economic policies became less ideological. The economic difficulties in the late 1960s made for some reversal of this trend. Interestingly too, as in political relations, the Labour critique, since the war couched in the language of Commonwealth solidarity, was expressed in more purely nationalist terms.

---

15 Termination of Trade Agreements ..., *NZFAR*, Dec. 1972, p. 39.
16 Holyoake to Corner, 10 July 1968. Ms Papers 1403, 86/3, ATL. The letter would have been drafted in the Department of External Affairs.
17 *EAR*, Jan. 1969, p. 8.
18 In July 1968 Britain agreed to guarantee the dollar value of its official reserves; New Zealand for its part (along with other sterling holders) agreed to keep 70 per cent of its official external reserves in sterling. 13 Sept. 1968. Ms Papers 1403, 339/2, ATL. See also *NZEAR*, Jan. 1969, p. 6.
19 See David Calleo, *The Imperious Economy*. Cambridge, Mass., 1982, for a good account of the Nixon initiatives. Both the Prime Minister and the Minister of Finance stressed New Zealand's support for maintaining a global economic system, e.g., 'it is very much in New Zealand's interest that the major trading nations should have an outward looking approach to these problems', Holyoake, *NZFAR*, Dec. 1971, p. 24.

The deflationary measures taken by the government after the 1966 election fostered criticism of the role of the IMF in the formulation of economic policy. The party had become resigned to rather than supportive of New Zealand's membership of the IMF since 1961 and the hard times brought its suspicions of the organisation to the surface again: 'Many people around the country wondered why, shortly after the IMF representatives had visited New Zealand, power charges should go up and the Prime Minister should find it necessary to call on the Managing Director of the IMF when in New York to discuss our balance of payments problems.'[20] At the Labour Party conference in 1968 Kirk ended with an 'impassioned plea': 'Let us remember that the New Zealand Labour party is a New Zealand party, not an IMF party, not a World Bank party, not a submissive party.'[21]

This economic nationalism abated with economic recovery in 1969, but some aspects of it revived in the lead up to the 1972 election and in Labour's first year in office. The decision to establish an overseas shipping line was linked with a fear that foreign investment might become too prominent in New Zealand: the government also established an Overseas Investment Commission. The Minister of Finance, Wallace Rowling, released on 12 January 1973 a statement on overseas investment in which he stressed that investment for speculative purposes would not be welcome; two years later he told a City of London audience that the 25–30 per cent of total company assets in foreign hands was too high 'in relation to our aspiration to be an independent nation, initiating and shaping our economic future'.[22] Labour also set up an export-import bank which was partly designed to encourage trade with centrally planned economies.[23]

Labour was cooler on British entry to the EEC than National. When the possibility of Britain's applying again had been raised in 1967 Nordmeyer had said that British entry would more than any other event cause the dissolution of the Commonwealth.[24] Kirk did not warm to the Conservative Party Prime Minister, Edward Heath, the committed Europeanist, or Carrington, his Foreign Secretary, the Old Etonian. For Kirk, as for Nordmeyer and Nash a decade earlier, the Community was something of a rich men's club, a band of hungry traders. According to Hayward, Kirk believed that Marshall could have tried rather harder than he did for New Zealand. He felt that Marshall and Holyoake had 'valued the good offices of Edward Heath and co.' more highly than New Zealand's future.[25]

There were boundaries to Labour's economic radicalism. Labour had

20 Labour M.P. Ron Bailey, *NZPD*, 350, p. 93 (3 May 1967).
21 Quoted in Hayward, *Diary*, p. 4n.
22 Bassett, *Third Labour Govt*, p. 31; *NZFAR*, Feb. 1975, p. 27.
23 '127 Days', p. 26.
24 *NZPD*, 348, p. 2729 (24 March 1966).
25 Hayward, *Diary*, pp. 6, 10. By the time the Luxembourg agreement was negotiated, the Labour Party in Britain was again opposed to entry.

criticised NAFTA in the 1966 election, but had been more cautious in 1969 and even more so in 1972. Labour had not explicitly opposed membership of the IMF in its 1969 election platform.[26] Further, Labour decided to take New Zealand into the OECD, a decision made in principle by the previous government. Although Kirk tried to give membership an altruistic cast, this was not the main reason for joining. Rather it was done on the grounds that with Britain in the European Community it was important for New Zealand to have some institutional relationship with the major industrial economies, and especially with the Community, in which it was a member on equal terms, not just a supplicant. In respect of the EEC itself, Labour's reservations translated into securing a revision of the price provisions in the protocol, although even that was complicated by the decision of the Labour government in Britain to renegotiate its treaty of accession.[27] At the 1975 Dublin summit, however, the Community's heads of government did agree to regular price reviews, with prices related *inter alia* to the returns to the Community's own farmers, and also envisaged that quotas could remain 'close to effective deliveries in 1974' for the first two post-transition years of 1978–80, while cheese deliveries were not altogether ruled out.[28]

Labour and National attitudes overlapped. Kirk's concerns about shipping, for instance, were not dissimilar to Muldoon's:

> In advising the Government of their intention to sell the Union Company, the P&O Company showed the same lack of consideration that the Conference Lines showed when they gave us two days' notice of their intention to announce the abandonment of their container ship plans, to which New Zealand had committed billions of dollars for facilities. It is not only the suicidal tendencies of its trade unionists that are bringing down the British economy, it is also the insufferable arrogance of many of its industrialists.[29]

Labour and National were also both strong advocates of reform of the international system of trade and payments in particular, which might ensure that the burden of debt and other disadvantages under which third world economies laboured was limited: 'the diffusion of political power in the fifties and sixties is now being matched by a greater diffusion of economic power ... a new economic order will come into being because the old one could not adequately accommodate the interests of the developing countries which have emerged since it was established.'[30] Both supported the post-oil-shock plan

---

[26] See Hugh Templeton, ' "New Era" for the "Happy Isles": the First Six Months of Labour Government Foreign Policy in New Zealand', *Australian Outlook*, 27/2 (Aug. 1973), pp. 160–1. Templeton refers to Labour's 'atavistic antagonism' to international finance but notes that opposition to the IMF did not feature in Labour's 1969 election platform.

[27] *NZFAR*, Nov. 1974, p. 37; *EP*, 6 Nov. 1975.

[28] *EP*, 13 March 1975; *NZFAR*, March 1975, pp. 13–14.

[29] Muldoon, *Young Turk*, pp. 129–30.

[30] Corner, 'Emerging Perspective', p. 6.

for a new international economic order (NIEO). Muldoon indeed argued for many years that the international community had to make a greater effort to meet the economic needs of the third world: 'I've been very critical of many aid programmes which set out to build up the agriculture of the Third World countries while at the same time closing markets to the agricultural products that these programmes would produce. I've argued that theme at the International Monetary Fund for years.'[31] Both parties recognised an overlap between third world economic concerns and New Zealand's own preoccupation about trade access to the developed world.

'Our foreign policy is trade'[32]

Muldoon himself frequently emphasised the importance of economic diplomacy, and of the need for New Zealand to act independently in that sphere: 'On the change of government in 1975 it was obvious that New Zealand had to adopt a different stance in our relationships with our friends, allies and trading partners. We could no longer afford to be a country that said "yes" to everyone and end up with the short end of the stick.'[33]

Economic relations with Britain and the United States were still important but the diplomacy became more predictable. On Muldoon's first overseas visit as Prime Minister in 1976 New Zealand gained an extension of its right to export butter, admittedly in decreasing but still substantial quantities, into the post-transition years of 1978–80.[34] Similar negotiations followed through the rest of the decade, with meat as well as butter coming within the ambit of the talks in later years. Muldoon detailed the negotiation over New Zealand's status in respect of the new Community sheepmeat levy in 1979 in *My Way*. It is evident from this account that Britain continued to support New Zealand inside the Community much as it had done outside it in 1971, although it did not oppose the sheepmeat regime outright as it might have done on an earlier occasion.[35] In respect of New Zealand's beef market in the United States, the commitment of both the Carter and Reagan administrations to multilateralism and free trade preserved New Zealand from the protectionist American beef lobby.[36]

Economic diplomacy with New Zealand's other two significant trade partners, Japan and Australia, traversed newer ground. The economic relationship with Japan in the 1970s was dominated by the 'fish for beef' dispute in 1977–78. In 1978 New Zealand introduced a 200-mile exclusive

---

31 Muldoon in *NZIR*, May-June 1977, p. 8, in interview with John Henderson.
32 Muldoon quoted in *NZIR*, Jan.-Feb. 1980, p. 3, in interview with Derek Round.
33 *NZIR*, Sept.-Oct. 1978, p. 5, in interview with Derek Round.
34 *NZFAR*, April-June 1976, p. 69.
35 Pp. 91–92; see also *NZIR*, Jan.-Feb. 1980, p. 2, Muldoon interview with Derek Round.
36 John Henderson, 'Beefing Up US Barriers', *NZIR*, Jan.-Feb. 1979, pp. 23–24; see also *NZIR*, Sept.-Oct. 1981, p. 14.

economic zone. It was a change which brought fishing more directly within the ambit of the resource economy than before. Foreign countries now had to apply to the New Zealand government to fish within the zone. The application of the Soviet Union, among others, was accepted. With Japan, it was, in Muldoon's eyes, an opportunity to negotiate improved and stable long-term access for New Zealand exports. In May 1977 he told the Japanese that no agreement would be signed with any Japanese fishing organisation until New Zealand could get regular access for farm products on to the Japanese market. The Deputy Secretary of Foreign Affairs, Merwyn Norrish, amplified this strategy even further, suggesting that New Zealand could consider restrictions on Japanese cars, a major breach of New Zealand's traditional commitment to multilateralism: 'It may be objected that restrictions placed on Japanese cars would be discriminatory and in breach of GATT. I no longer believe that is an objection which, if this situation should require it, should prevent us from taking action.'[37]

Diplomatic and more public exchanges followed through 1977 and into 1978. When Muldoon attacked Japan for 'commercial imperialism', he was giving a populist cast to this thinking, one that would have been shared by many Social Credit and probably many Labour voters. The government was in political trouble early in 1978, having lost the Rangitikei seat in a by-election to the Social Credit leader, Bruce Beetham. With the signing at the end of June of an agreement in which the Japanese recognised that 'continuing expansion of meat and dairy products exports, on a stable and secure basis, is a vital element in New Zealand's trading relationships',[38] Muldoon was able to declare a victory and the two countries accordingly signed a fishing agreement. Writing in 1981, Muldoon explained that there were secret clauses in the agreement which provided for increased trade and he claimed in effect that the proof of the pudding—the agreement—was in the eating—the increased trade since 1978: 'we negotiated improved access for our farm products and fish and further tests on our pinus radiata and, in turn, gave the Japanese some fishing quotas for the second half of the year .... There is no doubt that the agreement has enabled us to increase our exports to Japan, and that is what is is all about.'[39] In the case of beef and veal and dairy products, while there was a surge in tonnages shipped to Japan in 1978–79, the growth after that was negligible.[40]

---

[37] *NZFAR*, April-June 1977, p. 19; see also pp. 10–11, 29–30 in the same issue.

[38] Derek Round interview with Muldoon: 'unquestionably the line we took with Japan has been successful', *NZIR*, Sept.-Oct. 1978, p. 5. For texts of agreement, see *NZFAR*, April-June 1978, pp. 12, 13; July-Dec. 1978, pp. 20, 39–42.

[39] *My Way*, p. 123, which can be contrasted with a statement by Tom Larkin, former Ambassador to Japan, at the same time: 'despite tough dealing over access to the Japanese market, New Zealand exports of primary produce are falling and Japan's protectionist policy remains in place', *EP*, 19 May 1981.

[40] Beef and veal, tonnes: 1975, 3122; 1976, 5229; 1977, 5195; 1978, 7788; 1979, 5686; 1980, 3618; 1981, 5580; 1982, 6085; 1983, 7765. Cheese, tonnes: 1975, 16,843; 1976, 18,359; 1977, 18,143; 1978, 22,398; 1979, 26,391; 1980, 22,812; 1981, 22,558; 1982, 24,062; 1983, 22,623.

The Australian-New Zealand economic relationship in these years also underlined the distinctive approach of the Muldoon government. Economic difficulties in Australia had nearly torpedoed NAFTA in 1977. At that time maintaining and enhancing New Zealand's trade access to Australia became a central objective in parts of the New Zealand government, including the Ministry of Foreign Affairs. Talboys gave public recognition to the importance of relations with Australia, particularly in the economic sphere, in 1977 and again in 1978; on this latter occasion he made a six-week visit to Australia and gained a declaration of commitment to closer economic relations from the Australian government. Moving from verbal commitment to action was harder, however. It was really only in 1979, when Australia's Deputy Prime Minister, Doug Anthony, lent his weight to the task of reforming the commercial relationship with New Zealand and providing for totally free trade, that progress began to be made.[41]

However close the affinity of Australians and New Zealanders, New Zealand was, from a commercial point of view, an outsider in the Australian market, as it had been ever since declining to join the Federation at the beginning of the century. A free trade area would not change this: Muldoon had a keen sense himself of the need to protect interests:

I am still preserving an open mind on this question of a change in our domestic relationship. I shall meet Malcolm Fraser and I shall see where we go, but, by contrast to some of the comments, my mind is very open on this thing. I would not express surprise if we find if there is very little we can do. I am sure in specified areas of the economy there is room for greater co-operation but if we are looking at an overall change in the relationship, that I believe is going to be more difficult to bring together.[42]

Journalists thought Muldoon still faced a dilemma two years later: 'Mr Muldoon is understood to have strongly opposed giving any undertaking to abolish import licensing or to rationalise the different export incentive schemes on both sides of the Tasman . . . . Also Mr Muldoon appears to have resisted suggestions that the new CER agreement be signed before the general election later this year.'[43] Muldoon's caution emphasised the similarities between Labour and National over economic relations with Australia. 'There are', Rowling said in 1981, 'questions very much in the minds of New Zealand producers and manufacturers who still have an uneasy feeling that they may be left rather naked in the marketplace if all those restraints or protections which presently exist are suddenly dismantled.'[44]

[41] R. D. Muldoon, *Number 38*. Auckland, 1986, p. 40.
[42] Derek Round, 'Our Foreign Policy Is Trade', *NZIR*, Jan.-Feb. 1980, p. 3, quoted in Jay Alter, 'Mirroring Political and Economic Change . . . The development of CER'. VUW History Dept research paper, 1989, p. 19.
[43] Tony Garnier, *EP*, 19 May 1981 (in a comment on the Muldoon-Anthony talks).
[44] Rowling interview with Bruce Wallace, *NZIR*, Sept.-Oct. 1981, p. 17.

It was the Minister of Industries and Commerce, Hugh Templeton, who made the running on the issue. In March 1982 agreement was reached on the status of both wine and dairy industries under Closer Economic Relations (CER), removing two of the main obstacles to the conclusion of the agreement.[45] Heads of agreement were settled in December 1982, with the formal signing delayed until after the Australian election in March 1983, which returned a Labour government to office.

Economic independence in the 1970s and 1980s was frequently presented in terms of diversification, the necessary break from dependence on one market. This gave the notion of independence the strongly progressive feel that the idea of political independence had had in the 1940s and 1950s; like that, it carried with it an emphasis on greater rather than less involvement in the rest of the world. At the end of 1971 Holyoake had emphasised that 'the search for new markets continues. The process of diversification has in recent years gathered considerable momentum.' Ten years later, Brian Talboys drew attention to the fact that 'one area in which change is occurring, in which we have in fact been far more successful than many people realise, is in diversifying markets and the products we sell in them.' And four years later, the then Minister of Trade and Industry, David Caygill: 'New Zealand has also, in the last two decades, dramatically diversified its range of markets . . . , we export, in total, to 120 countries'.[46]

There was indeed dramatic change. In the later 1970s Australia, Japan and the United States, which had all been 'new' markets for New Zealand in the 1960s, had become traditional markets. Yet paradoxically there appeared at times to be no progress because the moment a goal was accomplished, it became the norm from which a new goal would be measured.[47]

In the 1970s and early 1980s scholars and journalists explored the notion that New Zealand now had a 'foreign policy of trade', and contrasted this in part to the traditional foreign policy of alliances, security and defence. Muldoon, when questioned, usually agreed. In 1977, while denying that trade was 'the "centrepiece" of foreign policy around which diplomatic and even defence aspects of foreign policy became secondary', he explained that Talboys was Minister of both Foreign Affairs and Overseas Trade because 'by far the greatest part of our foreign service effort is in this field of trading relations'. In 1980 he said, 'we are not interested in the normal foreign policy matters to any great extent. We are interested in trade.' And in 1981 he affirmed that was still the case 'apart from specific issues that we get drawn into because of our regional situation'.[48]

[45] *NZFAR*, Jan.-March 1982, p. 35.
[46] *NZFAR*, Dec. 1971, p. 18; July-Sept. 1981, p. 23; Oct.-Dec. 1984, p. 5. Only in the later 1980s did this rhetoric fade—the pattern of New Zealand's trade relations had 'settled', a contrast to the rapid changes of the preceding generation.
[47] The same thing also happened with commodities. Timber, a 'new' export commodity in the 1960s, was a 'traditional' one by the 1980s.
[48] *NZIR*, May-June 1977; p. 7, Jan.-Feb. 1980, p. 3, Sept.-Oct. 1981, p. 13.

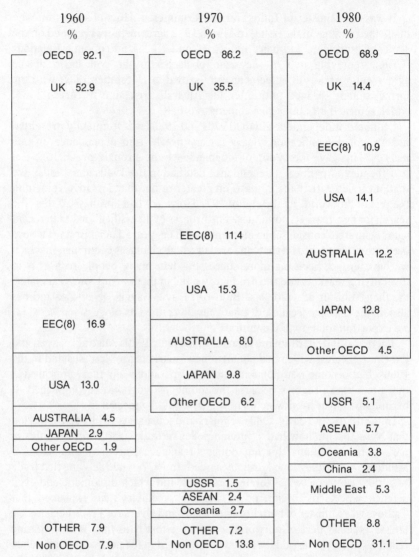

Destinations of New Zealand's exports for the years ended June 1960, 1970, 1980.

John Henderson observed in 1980 that 'New Zealand has been forced to launch an international search for new markets for its agricultural products— to develop what is, in effect, an "agricultural" foreign policy .... New Zealand ... conforms particularly closely to the prediction that small states' foreign policy will relate primarily to economic issues.'[49] Muldoon may have

49   Henderson, 'The Foreign Policy of a Small State', p. 5.

agreed that 'foreign policy is trade' but he was unlikely to have conceived of that as a new departure. His approach to foreign relations was in the tradition, allowing for temperamental differences, of other conservative leaders like Holland and Holyoake. At the core of their concerns in foreign relations was the pursuit of interest. The notion that foreign policy had shifted from a preoccupation with defence to a preoccupation with the economy was partly a misunderstanding. In the 1950s and early 1960s economic relations were not considered part of 'foreign policy'. Trade was no more important in the 1970s than in the 1950s but it was more complex, involving more countries, more negotiations. The stress that Muldoon placed on trade in comparison to other aspects of foreign policy—'we have had far more difficult things in the trade field than this sporting thing'[50]—had parallels in the past too, in the tension between interests and ideals, National and Labour, the need compared with the desire, for a foreign policy.[51]

But Henderson had a point. The world in which that interest had to be pursued had changed, and so in some respects had the pursuit. Had New Zealand's economic foreign policy crossed a line between being the pursuit of interest within an accepted framework and being the pursuit of national interest in a world of competing sovereignties? The picture was not clear. On the one hand the 1970s was an era when the recognition of the profound interdependence of world economies was growing, when the nation-state model was being modified rather than embraced. But New Zealand's own situation was more isolated. Relations with Japan, or even with Australia, did not have the same sense of reciprocity, of shared goals, that the Anglo-New Zealand connection had once possessed. This was even truer in respect of relations with the Middle East.

Energy and the drive for new markets

Interest in the Middle East began at the time of the first oil crisis after the 1973 Arab-Israeli War. It was the quest for resources as much as for markets that put the Middle East on New Zealand's economic map. The oil-price rise after the October War transformed the international economic landscape. It was important for New Zealand to have 'friends in the right places', especially with 'forebodings of a grim winter to come', as the *Evening Post* said in commenting on the government's goodwill mission to the region in February 1974.[52]

Japan, Australia and the United States were all OECD members, all had high living standards, all, even Japan, had developed systems of commerce

[50]   *NZIR*, May-June 1977, p. 7. The 'sporting thing' was the controversy over the New Zealand rugby tour of South Africa in 1976. See below, pp. 242–3.
[51]   See, for instance, above, pp. 112–16.
[52]   *EP*, 29 Jan. 1974.

and finance which made them relatively open to the outside trader. The obstacles were deliberate, not unintentional. The Middle Eastern countries were different. Their commerce and finance were not geared to maintaining efficient distribution systems for foreign goods; their infrastructure of communications and transport was often poor too. There was an affluent consumer market in part of the Middle East—the Gulf—but it was like no other in the world, and the uncertainties about how best to sell in it were as great as with the larger, poorer markets of countries like Iraq, Iran and China.

After the second oil shock in 1979-80, more was heard of the importance of the Middle East. Warren Freer told the government that Iraq's offer of a government-to-government oil deal should not be lightly set aside because of National's support for private enterprise principles. Talboys said that the government had no objections to buying on such a basis.[53] In April 1980 Prince Nawaf, a member of the Saudi royal family, purchased a sheep farm on the Coromandel Peninsula 'with the object of fostering the breeding of leaner grades of sheepmeat preferred in the Middle East', and a few months later the Saudi/New Zealand Capital Corporation (Saudicorp) was established to provide a channel for further Saudi investment in New Zealand. New Zealand was developing a 'special relationship' with Saudi Arabia to head off a potential oil supply crisis. Some of the Middle Eastern countries, Muldoon was reported as saying, were no longer confident about the major powers and wanted to form relationships with smaller countries.[54] In an address in the following year, Talboys noted that

> Over the last few years our biggest export gains have been achieved in the Middle East, the USSR, in the ASEAN countries and in China . . . . Just as encouraging are forecasts which envisage growing demand for food products in countries which will themselves envisage high growth rates—countries like Indonesia, Mexico and Nigeria . . . . Nothing is traditional any more. We are on our own.[55]

The implications had not always been the expected ones. In July 1980 the New Zealand Broadcasting Corporation decided not to screen the controversial *Death of a Princess*, a British television film made about the execution of a member of the Saudi royal family at which Saudi Arabia had protested very strongly. The Corporation said there were 'valid grounds for the claim that the film misrepresented and distorted the values of the way of life it dealt with'. The government welcomed the decision.[56]

---

53   *EP*, 14 March 1980.
54   *NZH*, 9 April 1980. Rowling criticised the Saudicorp agreement as involving an unwarranted breach of New Zealand's foreign investment regulations. In Parliament in May, Muldoon attacked Labour's reaction, pointing out that when the third Labour government was in office, land was sold to British and other European and American buyers. *NZPD*, 429, pp. 66-67 (21 May 1980); *EP*, 22 May 1980. Nothing came of the sheep-breeding plans.
55   *NZFAR*, July-Sept. 1981, pp. 27-28.
56   *NZFAR*, July-Sept. 1980, p. 43.

New Zealand's drive towards energy self-sufficiency, embodied most graphically in the 'think big' campaign of 1981, also underlined the shift away from familiar patterns of international economic relations. 'Much expert opinion', said the Minister of Energy, Bill Birch, in April 1979, reckoned that 'by the middle or late 1980s world demand will have overtaken world supply and at that point New Zealand would need to compete with the industrialised countries of the world . . . . the emphasis must be on security because it may be some years before alternative liquid fuels become cheaper than oil.' One senior official pointed out that the International Energy Agency (IEA) was dominated by the larger oil consumers: could New Zealand, he asked, rely on it to defend its interests?[57]

New Zealand's energy resources would, it was hoped, provide a triple fillip for the country's balance of payments: firstly, the move to energy self-sufficiency would ease the pressure on current account payments; secondly, foreign investment in the industry would provide capital inflow; and thirdly, there might be an export spinoff from the development. Thus both Birch and Muldoon visited Canada in 1982, partly for energy policy reasons: Birch in May had discussions on synthetic fuel production and also on the 'Canadianisation' of the oil industry. In September Muldoon visited Alberta, seeing the methane and ethanol conversion plants of the Alberta Gas Chemicals Coy, an equity partner in the Taranaki methanol project.[58] Birch chaired the annual meeting of the IEA in Paris and also attended an international energy conference in Canberra in May 1983. Was it a war situation? Birch noticed that 'Quite a few people have used the term "resource war" to characterise the new challenge. The result of these discussions can be summarised in one sentence: "The economic miracles of Western Europe and Japan, however impressive, were constructed on foundations more fragile than expected." '[59]

Birch stressed that Australia and New Zealand were equally vulnerable because of their dependence on oil imports. By the time of this meeting oil prices had fallen from their peak but orthodoxy still favoured the view that the relief was only temporary.[60] Birch himself stressed that 'having regard for OECD dependence on raw materials from unstable and vulnerable regions of the world, New Zealand and Australia must develop a cooperative strategic approach to energy supplies to ensure our economic stability, expansion and perhaps even our survival in world affairs'.[61]

The oil shock and the energy crisis seemed to indicate the possibility of

57   *NZFAR*, Jan.-June 1979, p. 23; *NZH*, 9 April 1980. Note that the Australian government at this time had published a major study, 'Australia and the Third World', prepared by a government-organised committee.
58   *NZFAR*, April-June 1982, p. 33; July-Sept. 1982, p. 14.
59   *NZFAR*, April-June 1983, pp. 22-23.
60   *NZFAR*, April-June 1983, p. 24.
61   *NZFAR*, April-June 1983, p. 26.

economic independence becoming identified with a war-style economy, one focused on securing resources rather than on producing and selling. It would be a rather different kind of independence from that usually meant when diversification was talked about and perhaps a little closer to what people were thinking of in the 1930s, though without the Commonwealth framework. But oil prices eased and with them the sense of a crisis over resources.

The triumph of the open economy

The debate over foreign policy in the 1930s was rooted in a connected set of ideas about transforming society generally in which changes in the organisation of the economy were central. In the 1980s the radicalisation and increased influence of the peace movement took place against a backdrop of a precipitous decline in the power of and support for alternative economic thinking. Indeed the fourth Labour government moved New Zealand to the right economically rather than to the left.

National had come into office in 1975 with a commitment to economic liberalisation. The government through its first two terms did maintain a general commitment to liberalisation and to encouraging foreign investment, and both officials and ministers frequently spoke to this effect, particularly when talking to overseas business people.[62]

But by the early 1980s there was pressure to do more, a pressure that stemmed from developments both overseas and at home. The ascendancy of monetarism (at least in theory) in the economic policies of the Reagan administration and the Thatcher government had an important demonstration effect.[63] At home, tax restructuring and the closing of loopholes in 1982 (in particular the Land and Income Tax Amendment Bill No. 2) alienated much National support from the Muldoon government. The right-wing, economically libertarian New Zealand Party flourished.

Problems in the implementation of CER were a sign not just of understandable differences in approach on both sides of the Tasman, but also of Muldoon's increasingly personal management of the New Zealand economy. Muldoon place a moratorium on applications by Australian companies to invest in New Zealand:[64] 'Australia has had major financial penetration of New Zealand since colonisation', said Muldoon. 'The reverse has not been the case.'[65] In a speech in Melbourne in June 1984, just before an

[62] See, for instance, Merwyn Norrish, 'Trade and Investment: the New Zealand Viewpoint', *NZFAR*, July-Dec. 1979, pp. 8–13. Norrish listed economic measures taken by the Muldoon government, 'changes which make the economy more competitive and investment by international firms more attractive'.

[63] In both Britain and the United States new policy directions can be identified in the actions of the previous governments in the late 1970s, the Labour government in Britain and the Carter administration in the United States, but they became particularly associated with Thatcher and Reagan.

[64] *NZFAR*, July-Sept. 1983, p. 32; Oct.-Dec. 1983, p. 31.

[65] *NZFAR*, April-June 1982, p. 12.

election, Muldoon spelt out in detail his view of the problems in the investment relationship between the two countries. He hoped that Australia would liberalise rather than New Zealand restrict, as a way of evening up practice in the two countries. In particular he refuted the Australian charge that the British Lloyd's Bank was seeking back-door entry into the Australian market through its wholly owned New Zealand subsidiary, the National Bank.[66]

What was happening in the Labour Party? Labour had been in a state of flux about its economic policies after its narrow 1978 election defeat. Despite a revival of concern about foreign investment in 1979–80 Labour activists (as distinct from Labour trade unionists) were not deeply preoccupied with economic issues: one commentator argued that the 'radical ferment' that existed at the beginning of the seventies 'evaporated when confronted with the tangible economic problems and political conflict of the mid and late seventies'.[67] Such tendencies facilitated, if only in a negative sense, moves within the party to adopt a more liberal approach to the economy and break with the import-substitution, full-employment strategy that in its fullblown form dated back to Walter Nash and the first Labour government. The clash was dramatised in 1980 when Rowling fired Roger Douglas from the Opposition front bench for writing *There's Got To Be a Better Way*, a reasoned polemic in favour of economic liberalisation.[68]

The change in Labour's economic approach has been detailed by W. Hugh Oliver: 'one of the central features of what would be later called "Rogernomics" i.e. the restructuring of the New Zealand economy, was widely supported within the Labour caucus after 1981'.[69] Oliver has identified the competing ideological tendencies in the party between 1981 and 1984 and the success achieved by Roger Douglas and his allies in securing support for their approach. When Labour took office in the middle of 1984, it gave early evidence of the direction of its economic policy when it ended the moratorium on new Australian investment applications. The devaluation of the dollar at the moment of transfer of power and the floating of the dollar some nine months later confirmed the ideological direction.

We can place the change in policy in New Zealand in an international context. At the beginning of the decade many observers expected the third world and non-traditional markets generally to loom much larger in New

---

[66] *NZFAR*, April-June 1984, pp. 38–40.
[67] Bruce Jesson, 'Formulating a Radical Strategy for the 80s', *Monthly Review*, June 1980, p. 15.
[68] *There's Got To Be a Better Way: A Practical ABC To Solving New Zealand's Major Problems*. Wellington, 1980.
[69] W. Hugh Oliver, 'The Labour Caucus and Economic Policy Formation 1981–1984', in Brian Easton, ed., *The Making of Rogernomics*. Auckland, 1989, p. 35. This is preceded, pp. 31–35, by a discussion of Labour thinking about CER.

Zealand's economic calculations as the decade progressed.[70] But with oil prices past their peak by the end of 1981 economic prospects in the third world waned, a trend reinforced in the case of the Middle East by the Iran-Iraq War. The most dramatic instance was Mexico. An embassy had been opened in Mexico after a visit there by Muldoon in 1980 but by the time the mission was established Mexico's economy had gone from boom to bust.[71] Third- and second-world markets such as Iran, Iraq and the Soviet Union continued to be important to New Zealand but they did not increase in significance to anything like the extent expected at the beginning of the decade.

Insofar as New Zealand trading patterns moved markedly away from the 'four corners' of Europe, Japan, Australia and the United States, it was the newly industrialised economies of Asia that made the difference. The spectacular economic growth on the western rim of the Pacific in the 1980s fuelled dicussion about Asia-Pacific economic relations and New Zealand's place in them as much as the collapse of oil prices dampened talk of expansion into the third world. Indeed it was in the early 1980s that the two conceptions, previously often assimilated into the general category of 'new economic relations', became distinct. Asia/Pacific or the Pacific Basin had quite different ideological overtones from the third world. Whereas one involved some distancing from the community of international capitalism, the other implied a closer embrace. Throughout the 1980s talk about Asia/Pacific was one of the standard ways of expressing a commitment to liberalisation of the New Zealand economy and greater openness to foreign investment and migration. Warren Cooper followed Talboys in being enthusiastic about expanding relations with Asia/Pacific countries.[72] Talk of the Pacific Basin or Asia/Pacific was a lineal descendant of the ideas of 'regional' cooperation fostered by the United States during the Vietnam War era. PBEC, the Pacific Basin Economic Council, and the Pacific Democratic Union of conservative parties in Japan, Canada, Australia, New Zealand and the United States were other expressions of the same set of ideas.

There was continuity between the two main parties in their commitment to increased commercial and financial cooperation with Asia. Derek Davies, editor of the *Far Eastern Economic Review*, described the Labour govern-

[70] See, for instance, Ted Woodfield, 'Marketing in the Middle East', *NZIR*, March-April 1983, pp. 22-23; Dianne Davis, 'New Zealand's Diplomatic Policy: the Need for Review', *NZIR*, July-Aug. 1983, p. 23.
[71] Brian Wearing, 'The Mexican Connection: A Fading Vision', *NZIR*, May-June 1983, pp. 5-7. Trade with Mexico recovered later in the decade.
[72] Interviews with Talboys, Cooper, Nov., Dec. 1989. Both preferred going to Asia to touring European capitals arguing for access. See also Bruce Wallace, 'A Pacific Ocean Community', *NZIR*, Jan.-Feb. 1980, pp. 13-14. Prime Minister Masayoshi Ohira of Japan, a strong advocate of the Pacific Community idea, visited New Zealand briefly at the beginning of 1980.

ment's moves to liberalise approvingly, as bringing it close to Asia.[73] Mike Moore, the Minister for Overseas Trade, was prepared to discuss broadening CER to include Asian countries: 'We have gone', he said, 'from seeing Asia as a source of threat to seeing Asia as a source of opportunity for New Zealand.' He described CER as an 'outward-looking agreement' which should be built on by New Zealand and Australia in the development of their economic relations with Asia.[74]

Economic independence in the 1980s

New Zealand in the 1980s as in the 1970s was trading with—and seeking finance from—Europe, North America and Australia, as well as Asia. New Zealand's economic relations in the 1980s were far more diversified in terms of markets than those of many other OECD countries. Canada did around 75 per cent of its trade with the United States and countries like Ireland and the Netherlands conducted approximately two-thirds of their trade with other members of the European Community. A paper on New Zealand's relationship to a possible yen trading bloc noted that while Japan was an important and growing trading partner for New Zealand, it still only accounted for about 20 per cent of merchandise imports and was very lightly represented on the invisible side. Total receipts from Japan amounted to around 3 per cent of New Zealand's GDP. 'New Zealand', the writer concluded, 'because of our diverse balance of trade, is unlikely to be one of the early joiners of . . . a Pacific Yen currency block.'[75] Nor was it very likely to join any other bloc, in part because none was on offer, but more because multilateralism—the organisation of international trade and payments on an international basis, through negotiations involving all countries simultan-eously—suited New Zealand's circumstances better.

Throughout the 1970s and 1980s, as in preceding decades, New Zealand diplomats had worked on the successive rounds of GATT-sponsored trade liberalisation negotiations. Such trade diplomacy became a central activity of the Ministry of Foreign Affairs, particularly after its amalgamation with the Trade Policy section of the dismantled Department of Trade and Industry and

[73] He said that the market-oriented approach adopted by the government to the economy seemed in Asia an indication that 'New Zealand was joining the world', whereas its foreign policy looked as if it were leaving it. Davies was in New Zealand at the time of the ANZUS crisis, February 1985. When asked whether as a non-Asian country New Zealand was not entitled to take its own point of view on a political issue, Davies replied, 'I beg your pardon, for 20 years your foreign ministers have been telling me how you wanted to be part of the region'. *EP*, 19 Feb. 1985.
[74] *NZFAR*, July-Sept. 1985, pp. 36, 40. See also Maarten Wevers, *Japan: Its Future and New Zealand.* Wellington 1988; Alan Bollard, Frank Holmes, David Kersey and Mary Anne Thompson, *Meeting the East Asia Challenge.* Wellington, 1989.
[75] Peter Nicholls, 'The Role of the Yen in the Pacific Region: New Zealand as a Case Study', paper presented to seminar on 'The impact of deregulation of the Japanese financial market on Asia and the Pacific', Sydney, Nov. 1987.

the formation of the Ministry of External Relations and Trade. The Secretary of the Ministry for most of the 1980s, Merwyn Norrish, was the first person holding that office to have significant experience in the trade policy field.

Both Labour and National supported the multilateral initiative of the Cairns Group, fostered by Australia, an association of predominantly agricultural exporters who wanted to increase the pressure on the Europeans, Americans and Japanese to liberalise their agricultural trade. A meeting of five Southern Hemisphere agricultural producers (Australia, New Zealand, Argentina, Brazil and Uruguay) took place in April 1986 and this was followed by a meeting at Cairns in August 1986 to which a number of other countries with similar interests, including Canada, Chile, Colombia, the Philippines, Thailand and Hungary, also came.[76]

The reality of a small economy in a sometimes benign, but always indifferent, world economy persisted. New Zealand's support for multilateralism and for the Cairns grouping was propelled by its wish to modify the dominance of the major players in the international economic system—the United States, Japan and Europe. There were no satisfactory outcomes in the area which mattered most to New Zealand. And while it was better for New Zealand to be closer to dynamic Asian economies than to troubled African ones, the politics of economic relations with Asia were not easy. Asia was a world in which governments played an important role in economic life. While New Zealand could strive for a more equitable international economic order, and in particular one that catered to its interests, there were many occasions for it to be reminded that it was a small state in the world of economic power.

Economic nationalism did surface in the 1980s. The National Party while in opposition in 1984-90 talked of the need to limit foreign ownership of 'strategic assets' to 25 per cent of equity. And there was certainly popular concern in those years about the alienation of assets, particularly land, to some foreign buyers. A racial element was not difficult to identify: Asian purchases were greeted with much more suspicion than American or Australian. The publication *Foreign Control Watchdog*, produced by the Campaign Against Foreign Control of Aotearoa, provided a radical approach, criticising the role of foreign capital because it was foreign rather than because it was Asian: 'CAFCA is not racist. It does not oppose the people of foreign countries, but the foreign monopolies which are exploiting New Zealanders.'[77]

But it was difficult to conceive of gatekeeping mechanisms being applied in quite the way they were in the 1930s and 1940s because of the extent of New Zealand's integration in world financial markets and its great dependence on overseas sales to finance its imports. In 1938, when exchange and import

---

[76] See, for instance, Merwyn Norrish, 'New Alliances in the World of Multilateral Trade', *NZFAR*, Jan.-March 1988, pp. 7–13, 62–63.

[77] CAFCA statement, n.d.

control was imposed, most New Zealanders never left the country and never needed foreign exchange. While private use of foreign exchange for travel was far from being the most significant component in foreign exchange spending at the end of the 1980s, it was deeply embedded in New Zealand life and would have been very difficult to reduce—but equally odd not to, if foreign exchange were to be rationed.[78] And such a step would pose major difficulties in terms of the attitudes of foreign investors who had become so important in determining the state of the New Zealand economy. As for imports, in the 1930s they included a large direct consumption element which could be curtailed without disrupting the operations of the domestic economy. To do this became much more difficult after the Second World War when imports became predominantly industrial inputs.

Independence may come to be defined in terms of foreign investment, foreign ownership and foreign presence, in districts and in suburbs, rather than in terms of the economic autonomy of the nation state. The independence not of China or India, but of Hawaii, or Alaska, may provide the parallels. American states are of course even less 'independent' than New Zealand. They do not have monetary or tariff autonomy and not much fiscal autonomy either. Nonetheless their citizens, or some of them, are preoccupied with maintaining kinds of economic 'independence'. Their citizens debate questions of state ownership and investment as New Zealand does, they consider the trade-offs between investment and the consequent indebtedness, they worry about their forests, their fisheries and their land, and their ability to ensure that their people are employed and productive.

---

[78] In the year ended March 1939, there were around 56,000 short-term departures from New Zealand; in the year ended March 1986, over 1,000,000; and in the year ended March 1990, 1,646,000 (*New Zealand Official Yearbook*, 1941, p. 40; 1990, p. 153).

10. Kith, kin and southern Africa

Accounts of New Zealand's relations with southern Africa have often focused on the protest movement over sports contacts with South Africa. At the centre of such accounts are the protest movement's heroic efforts to challenge and eventually transform mainstream New Zealand thinking on South African issues, particularly on the ethics of playing South African 'representative' teams for which most (i.e. non-white) South Africans could not be selected. It is a story of good and evil, or at least virtue and folly, in which evil and folly are vanquished. This is partly, and naturally, because most accounts to date have been written by participants, and the protestors have been more articulate about the issue than their adversaries. And it was the protest movement that initiated the often acrimonious debate about relations with South Africa over the three decades from the late 1950s.

When we turn to foreign policy, the picture is necessarily different. Both the second and third Labour governments faced tricky moments over southern African issues, as they attempted to negotiate between majority public opinion on the one hand, and the combined forces of minority public opinion and majority international opinion on the other. And there are some things to say about Labour's internationalism once the southern Africa issue is resolved. But by and large the Labour Party and even the protest movement stayed within the framework of 'loyal' dissent, loyal in this instance to the principles of the multiracial Commonwealth, the evolution of which we discussed in Chapters 4 and 6.

It was interests, both of the kinship and the sporting kind, which kept New Zealand in close, and increasingly controversial, association with the white communities of southern Africa. In the first episode we explore, the No Maori No Tour debate of 1959-60, this controversy was played out primarily within the framework of the independent foreign policy—it entailed domestic ideological debate with limited, certainly not immediate, foreign policy implications. But in 1961 South Africa left the Commonwealth, and ties with white Africa became an increasingly controversial element in foreign relations. For National governments there were two aspects to this, aspects which replicated the pattern we identified in analysing the impact of the Vietnam War: on the one hand, a realist analysis of New Zealand's place in the world and its independence; and on the other, a nationalist response and a nationalist conception of independence—but from the right, not the left.[1] These aspects appear with increasing salience in three episodes: Rhodesia's unilateral declaration of independence in 1965, the New Zealand rugby tour of South Africa in 1976, and the South African rugby tour of New Zealand in 1981.

The nationalism that we can discern on the right over this issue is not of course a new phenomenon. Just as Labour nationalism in the late 1960s inherited left-wing British suspicion of the United States, so right-wing nationalism inherited conservative British suspicion of nationalists, socialists, and rebellious natives. The language of Empire survived in time but moved in space—not from 'Cape to Cairo', but the other way.[2]

First stirrings, 1959-61

It is useful to see the uncertainties and debates of 1959-61, so muted compared with what would come later, although disturbing enough at the time, against the backdrop of the consensus on decolonisation and the new Commonwealth that we examined in Chapter 6. Labour in office, 1957-60, made some new departures. At the United Nations General Assembly session of 1958 the New Zealand delegation for the first time voted for the recurring Indian resolution on the treatment of people of Indian descent in South Africa. Previously New Zealand had argued that such resolutions, however much they embodied commendable ethical principles, were an unwarranted interference in a country's domestic affairs. In the Special Political Committee, it also voted for a resolution critical of South Africa's apartheid policy as a whole.[3]

But on the whole bipartisanship prevailed. And this was hardly surprising when even a British Conservative government was prepared to move forward on Africa. In 1959 Harold Macmillan visited South Africa and told Parliament in Cape Town that 'winds of change' were blowing across the continent. The successful British decolonisation of Africa had become a headline issue, replacing the Mau Mau stories from earlier in the decade. As Nash himself commented: 'During the year the ... African peoples have made increasingly rapid progress towards full national independence and they have displayed a growing sense of their independence and racial solidarity. In my view this advance has been in itself a revolution of extraordinary magnitude ... and one of the most notable features of 1958.'[4]

---

[1] The best discussions of the nationalist radical right *in* New Zealand are by Paul Spoonley: *The Politics of Nostalgia: Racism and the Extreme Right in New Zealand*. Palmerston North, 1987; 'Being British', in Bruce Jesson, Alannah Ryan and Paul Spoonley, *Revival of the Right: New Zealand Politics in the 1980s*. Auckland, 1988, pp. 86-115.

[2] 'Cape (of Good Hope) to Cairo', a common description of the extent of British rule in Africa after the First World War.

[3] See New Zealand statements in *EAR*, Oct. 1958, pp. 21-22, 34-35; *EAR*, Nov. 1959, pp. 33-34, 38-39; see also N84/0034, 0023, NA.

[4] Charles Moore, 'New Zealand's Attitude to South Africa and Its Continuing Membership of the Commonwealth, 1958-1961', VUW History Dept research paper, 1976, p. 10 quoting *EAR*, Jan. 1959, p. 12.

So it was not difficult for the two parties to agree. Labour supported the United Nations operation in the Congo, which succeeded in limiting Soviet influence in the newly independent state. New Zealand shared with Britain and the United States the wish to keep the Soviet Union out of Africa: the American Embassy noted in September 1960 that Nash was concerned lest Soviet action in Africa prove harmful to the United Nations and British interests.[5] In commenting fourteen months later on the Declaration on Colonialism, New Zealand's representative at the United Nations, F. H. Corner, observed that 'the events of the last eighteen months in the central part of the continent have amply illustrated the dangers inherent in international competition and the pressures that can develop when foreign countries are afforded, by the internal weaknesses of a State, an opportunity for pursuing their own ends'.[6]

The prospects seemed better in the British Commonwealth: the promise of a decolonisation which would combine independence with the preservation of essential British, Commonwealth, Western, interests was realised when the largest West African state, Nigeria, moved peacefully to independence in 1960, choosing both to remain within the Commonwealth and to maintain the parliamentary, or Westminster, system of government.

But while the parties agreed on decolonisation there was a potential both for disagreement and for complications in relations with new Commonwealth countries, the African Commonwealth in particular. During 1959 the country's biggest-ever political mobilisation within memory, certainly more substantial than the anti-nuclear movement, arose over the Rugby Union's decision to exclude Maori players from the All Black team to go to South Africa in 1960. The protest attracted an astonishingly wide support: a petition with around 156,000 signatures and citizens' groups in towns and cities up and down the country. The protest seemed to emphasise the moral roots of New Zealand's foreign policy and of the country's view on the world. A memorandum to Nash dated 12 January 1960 noted that

internationally the question is beginning to have repercussions. New Zealand's role in international affairs, particularly her position of moral leadership amongst her Asian neighbours, rests very largely on a reputation for racial equality which is excellent by world standards .... grave concern is being expressed overseas about the realities of this .... the publicity given to the relatively minor incident [re] Dr Bennett in an Auckland hotel .... the decision of the Rugby Union ... will be rightly or wrongly taken as a practical test of New Zealand's reputation for racial equality and tolerance.[7]

5   611.44/9–1060, RG59, USNA.
6   NZ Rep. to UN to Gen. Ass., 22 Nov. 1961, *EAR*, Nov. 1961, p. 34.
7   Dr Bennett, the brother of New Zealand's High Commissioner to Malaya, was refused service in an Auckland hotel because he was a Maori. 12 June 1960, N1324, NA.

The Labour government, and Walter Nash in particular, was caught by surprise. Nash was friendly with Cuth Hogg, the chairman of the Rugby Union. He accepted the Union's view that it was unfair to Maori to expose them to the kind of treatment they might experience if they went to South Africa. It was not a pro-apartheid position, but it was out of touch with the spirit of the time and the mood in the Labour Party. But Nash proved unable to change. McIntosh wrote to Shanahan, then in Ottawa:

> If you were living in New Zealand these days, you would not have had the hardihood to suggest that the Prime Minister might discuss a Rugby tour with the Management Committee of the Rugby Union. I can assure you the country is convulsed and divided on the question of South Africa and the Prime Minister's attitude towards the Rugby Union's decision to exclude Maoris. Mr Nash's attitude is based on the laudable but in my view totally unsound view that the whole question is one for the Rugby Union.[8]

The tour went ahead, and did not create difficulties in foreign policy. The debate ensured that no future Labour government would take such a benign view of sporting relations with South Africa, but did not seem likely to have that effect on National.

In the meantime pressure was building up for South Africa to be expelled from the Commonwealth if it was not prepared to abandon its apartheid policies. How would New Zealand react? In a speech at the United Nations, the New Zealand representative emphasised the close links that existed between South Africa and New Zealand, and stressed that New Zealand would greatly regret the erection of any barrier between South Africa and the rest of the world. At the annual conference of the Methodist Church in November 1959 Maharia Winiata charged the government, on the basis of this statement, with pursuing a policy of not doing anything to antagonise the Union government. He argued that it could only be assumed that this was why the government was averting its eyes from the racial aspects of the football issue.[9]

South Africa's apartheid policies were openly challenged for the first time at the Commonwealth Prime Ministers' Conference in May 1960. Nash commented after the conference that 'perhaps the single issue by which this conference will be remembered was the *apartheid* issue .... Many Prime Ministers, including myself, felt that no good purpose would be served by discussing this issue formally, although it ran counter to the principle of racial equality on which the Commonwealth is founded.'[10] It would be fair to infer from this that Nash hoped to find a solution which did not entail the expulsion

8   McIntosh to Shanahan, 10 March 1960. I am indebted to Malcolm Templeton for this reference.
9   844.46/11-1859. RG59, USNA.
10 *EAR*, May 1960, p. 25.

of South Africa.[11] The more general point to be drawn is that southern Africa issues did not put Labour in the awkward position of being more radical than its friends and allies, as did issues like Laos and Vietnam. Rather Labour faced a problem of being too conservative. It did not take too much imagination to see that problems over southern Africa might be compounded with a National government in office.

Holyoake's initiation into foreign policy as Prime Minister came with the Commonwealth Prime Ministers' meeting in London in March 1961. Holyoake was unhappy about the fact that events had made South Africa's withdrawal unavoidable, although he blamed that as much on Verwoerd as on Nigeria and Ghana.[12] The Afrikaner rather than British complexion of the South African government limited conservative New Zealand sympathy for that country. Indeed much regret was voiced at the fact that South Africa, which had seemingly become 'loyal' with Smuts,[13] had turned out differently:

> Pervading the mystical folklore of New Zealand is a strong loyalty to the Crown.... Such a national attitude makes it difficult for New Zealanders to sympathise with the aspirations of some Commonwealth countries to adopt the form of republican government .... Of all the countries in the Commonwealth the compulsive urge displayed by the Union Government of South Africa to discard the outward symbols of the monarch has roused the greatest interest and the least sympathy.[14]

But conservative attitudes were also evident in the wish to minimise the political and constitutional consequences of South Africa's departure, in the frequent expressions of regret at the cost to the English South Africans and in the murmurings about Afro-Asian dominance of both the Commonwealth and the United Nations.[15]

The Department of External Affairs rejected the notion that South Africa

11 Moore, p. 14.
12 'As the last speaker before adjournment I had urged that members should not be pushed to point which would lead to exclusion of some nine or ten million coloured people of South Africa', Holyoake to Marshall, 15 March 1961, EA 63/1/14/1, MERT. Holyoake added that Macmillan tried to find an acceptable settlement and might have succeeded if it had not been for Verwoerd's intransigence.
13 Smuts, the 'foe turned friend', was the South African Prime Minister during the Second World War. His party lost power to the Nationalists in 1948. One commentator observed that he seemed to New Zealanders to be 'a symbol of the basic solidarity of South Africa with the Commonwealth. His policies had the effect of imbuing the belief that ... there would be no further constitutional demands [from South Africa]', *Round Table*, 203 (June 1961), p. 316.
14 *Round Table*, 203 (June 1961), p. 315.
15 *NZH*, 17 March 1961, said that consciences had been stretched to the limit to accommodate South Africa in recent years, but regretted the loss of moderating influences on the Bantu and Coloured populations and the isolation of the English-speaking whites; in a later editorial, 20 March, the *Herald* referred to the 'possibility of Afro-Asian domination being a little-mentioned but persistent thought arising from the Conference,' while the *Dominion*, 21 March, asserted that 'black Commonwealth leaders needed statesmanship of the highest order if the Commonwealth was to be strengthened by South Africa's departure'.

should enjoy de facto Commonweath status as Ireland had. But in public statements, the New Zealand approach was coloured by sorrow rather than anger, and tended to reiterate the distinction between English and Afrikaner. The Nationalist government, it was pointed out at the United Nations, 'has never commanded the votes of appreciably more than half of the white voters in general elections .... It is still today solidly opposed by over one million people of British descent as well as by many Afrikaans speaking citizens.'[16]

South Africa's departure from the Commonwealth transformed the structure of New Zealand's relations with the white communities of the continent. Relations with southern Africa were no longer accommodated within the 'old' Commonwealth framework and New Zealand's interests in maintaining those relations, in whatever form, were now likely to elicit countervailing pressure or hostility from fellow Commonwealth members— or both.

Rhodesia

Despite all the clatter and clamour, the Rhodesian natives in fifty years' time will probably have more land of their own than the unfortunate natives of New Zealand.[17]

Commonwealth conferences through the 1960s were dominated by the Rhodesia issue, which reached a climax in 1965–66 in the aftermath of Rhodesia's unilateral declaration of independence. In 1962 Holyoake had told the General Assembly that the UN role in decolonisation, from New Zealand's point of view, was 'to ensure that the forces making for international change are resolved in an orderly and peaceful manner .... the inclination is to call for extreme measures to dispose of the [colonial] problem immediately.... This, however, is to step right outside the United Nations framework.'[18]

When the Federation of Rhodesia and Nyasaland broke up in the early 1960s, it became clear that the British and the self-governing white minority in Southern Rhodesia[19] disagreed on the future of that country, in particular on the condition that it show progress towards majority rule before becoming independent. New Zealand's formal stance was the same as Britain's: that majority rule was the goal but that it was not Britain's obligation to implement it, a position which contrasted with that of some of the African Common-

16 *EAR*, Oct. 1961, pp. 54–55.
17 H. B. Vogel, *A Maori Maid*. London, 1898, pp. 7–8.
18 *EAR*, Sept. 1962, p. 51, address to the General Assembly.
19 Given the change of name at independence in 1980 from Rhodesia to Zimbabwe, it seems appropriate to use 'Rhodesia' as a synonym for the white community and the white government of what was formally the British self-governing colony of Southern Rhodesia, even after the unilateral declaration of independence in 1965: Northern Rhodesia became independent as Zambia in 1964.

wealth states, who argued that Britain did have a duty to introduce majority rule, by force if necessary. Yet even this relatively cautious position made many in New Zealand unhappy.

For many conservative New Zealanders, Rhodesia, though distant to the eye, was close to the heart. The white minority population was almost entirely of British origin, not Afrikaner and British, as in South Africa. Throughout the whole of the Rhodesia crisis many New Zealanders in prominent positions expressed sympathy with the white Rhodesians and it was evident by its actions or rather lack of them that the National government was sensitive to this opinion, which was particularly strong in rural New Zealand, not least in some parts of the country where the Social Credit League was mounting a strong challenge in the 1966 election. The *Daily News*, Taranaki, was perhaps the most pro-Rhodesian paper: it defended the white Rhodesians as 'loyal Britons who believe that Britain has stabbed them in the back. Eighty years of effort will be dust and ashes if the African takes over.'[20] The *Daily Post* asked, 'would Rhodesia go the way of the Congo or not?'; the *Dominion* argued that it was all too easy to lose sight of the 'legitimate claims of the white Rhodesians and to ignore their plight' and also drew the analogy with the Congo.[21] The Mayor of Dargaville wrote to Holyoake that it would be a 'terrible thing for New Zealand to be a party to such inhuman treatment of white settlers by handing the country over to Communist inspired trouble makers. Contrary to reports the 4 million Africans are supporting Premier Smith and his Government.'[22]

Numbers of New Zealanders had relatives among the white population, sons or daughters, maybe cousins. Throughout the crisis the newspapers would intermittently feature 'letters from Rhodesia': Rhodesian residents wrote back to their families, who made their letters available to the local papers. These letters would always be given some prominence, the reliability of their accounts thereby attested, as it was implicitly by the fact that the correspondents were people with New Zealand connections. The letters always defended the Smith government and claimed that everyone in Rhodesia, black and white, was behind the government.

A New Zealand-Rhodesian Society was established early in 1966. The Chairman was S. Green, the Mayor of Dargaville, the Vice-Chairman, a National Party candidate in the forthcoming election. The not particularly sympathetic *Monthly Review*, describing the inaugural meeting, noted that 'easily the most colourful figure was a bearded Commander Ryan, who placed himself as not from Rhodesia, "really a Kenya man". In his booming voice he

20 *Daily News*, 12 Oct. 1965. EA245/8/3, MERT.
21 *Daily Post*, 2 Nov. 1965; *Dominion*, 28 Oct. 1965; *Auckland Star*, 13 Oct. 1965, was critical of Ian Smith, the rebel Rhodesian leader, but elicited a host of pro-Smith letters. All on EA245/8/3, MERT.
22 12 Oct. 1965. EA245/8/3, MERT.

told of weekly phone calls to Keith Holyoake. "He agrees with pretty near all I say, but trouble is he doesn't do anything." '[23] There was plenty of pro-Rhodesian sentiment in the National Party. Even in the government there was a great deal of sympathy. When Holyoake wrote to Smith urging him not to declare independence, he referred to the fact that New Zealanders had 'nothing but admiration for the European inhabitants of Rhodesia who have by their own special skills and industry established a prosperous and highly developed society'.[24] Tom Macdonald, the High Commissioner in London and former Minister of Defence and External Affairs, talked of the sympathy and understanding New Zealanders had for the 'European farmers in Rhodesia'.[25]

The existence within New Zealand of a 'substantial body of opinion which supports the policies and objectives of the Smith regime'[26] plainly influenced government policy. When the newly established Commonwealth Secretariat organised a meeting of Commonwealth leaders in Lagos in January 1966, New Zealand, like Australia, interpreted it in part as an effort to bludgeon Britain into a radical policy (although Holyoake was not as dogmatic about this as Menzies). Holyoake refused to attend the meeting himself or to send a senior Cabinet Minister, despite requests from the Nigerian Prime Minister and from Harold Wilson himself. New Zealand, enjoying a one-year term on the Security Council, cast a sole vote against a resolution before the Security Council in May seeking the intensification of further measures against the Smith regime: the United States and Britain had both abstained rather than face the attacks that would be made on them if they voted against (there were enough abstentions to assure the motion's defeat):

one assessment of our general attitude seems to be simply that we are 'pro-British'—and this seems to be rather taken for granted as it was when we voted on the Suez question . . . . In answer to many questions as to why we had broken ranks we have given a three point answer: (a) from the outset we had favoured neither a Security Council meeting nor further action (b) expediency might have favoured abstention but New Zealand could not fail to oppose a resolution providing for resort to force, especially when avenues to a peaceful settlement were being destroyed (c) vote also cast against African methods in confronting the Council about which we felt strongly.[27]

After the September 1966 London Commonwealth Conference, one of the bitterest in the association's history, Holyoake was particularly exercised by the emergence of an Afro-Asian caucus—notices calling meetings had

23 *Monthly Review*, March 1966, p. 6.
24 5 Oct. 1965, EA245/8/3, MERT.
25 11 Oct. 1965, EA245/8/3, MERT.
26 DEA guidance survey for posts, 6 Dec. 1965, EA245/8/3, MERT.
27 NZ Mission to the UN to DEA, Wellington, 25 May 1966, EA245/8/3, MERT.

appeared on the conference notice board side by side with the official notices.[28] A split was averted at the conference, but only just.

Ronald Algie, the former Speaker of the House and Cabinet Minister, described Rhodesia as a 'Crown Colony, ruled like New Zealand in the early days, by people from London. New Zealanders used to hate the London Government and wanted independence. The same thing pertained to Rhodesia. It wanted to manage its own affairs.'[29]

Nonetheless, the government did not follow the advice of its 'friends' like Commander Ryan over the Rhodesia issue. It followed British government policy, which was to deny any 'aid or comfort' to the rebel regime, but to refuse to use force to implement its commitment to 'no independence before majority rule'—NIBMAR. In some respects New Zealand was laggard compared with Britain: New Zealand did not impose full sanctions against Rhodesia at the time of the unilateral declaration of independence as Britain had. But nor did the government make any attempt to align itself with the Smith regime. The government was not principled about this. It is more accurate to say that, as with the sporting issue in later years, too vigorous a pursuit of the Rhodesian cause would have tended to isolate New Zealand from its friends as much as from those with whom it felt it had less in common. The government's determination to keep its involvement to a minimum was also a factor in its response, or lack of it. Kinship was the only interest 'aligning' New Zealand with Rhodesia. Over Rhodesia a major crisis was avoided, because while New Zealand sentiment was involved, New Zealand interests were less plainly so. But the response was nationalist in all but name. As one observer put it: 'The left has triumphed. New Zealand has at last an independent foreign policy. African delegates denounce our voting record at the United Nations .... Keith Holyoake has spoken out against the use of force to settle international disuputes .... It is Ian Smith's Rhodesia that has brought the Government round to seeing that the humanitarian Left was advising it wisely.'[30]

Internationalism under stress

Rhodesia was part of a wider series of developments which fostered National disillusion with the international order. It was National, rather than Labour, which dissented.

Remembering Suez, many were pleased to see Nasser get a bloody nose in

[28] Holyoake's anger was not paired with any equivalent disapproval of the confidential briefings that Australia, New Zealand, Canada—and the United States—had received from the British government throughout the course of the crisis. See EA245/8/3, MERT, *passim*.
[29] M. P. K. Sorrenson, *New Zealand and the Rhodesia Crisis: The Lessons of History*. Auckland, 1968, p. 1, quoting *NZH*, 17 Oct. 1967. Sorrenson, a historian of race relations, presented the liberal, anti-colonialist argument.
[30] *Dispute*, Nov. 1966, p. 23.

the Six Day war of June 1967 between Israel and its Arab neighbours. The war contributed, as Suez had in its time, to a mood of disaffection with the United Nations and the Commonwealth. The Secretary of External Affairs questioned the continued worth to New Zealand of both institutions in a public address in 1967.[31] In *New Zealand Foreign Policy in Retrospect*, Bruce Brown traced the course of New Zealand disillusionment with the United Nations in the mid 1960s, a by-product in effect of the loss of Western influence in the organisation, although it was presented in more subtle fashion: 'New Zealand has argued that it presses the role of the United Nations too far to suppose that it is the function of the international community not only to react collectively to acts of aggression but more, to reach out to right political wrongs, to seek to redress regional grievances.'[32] Brown described the strategy of the Africans and their allies on issues like apartheid in South Africa, Rhodesia, South-west Africa (Nambia) and the Portuguese territories as being to pass resolutions in the General Assembly by large majorities, which, even if they might in practice be ignored, 'create a climate of opinion . . . exert moral and political pressure particularly on Western governments who tend to be more susceptible to this approach and whose actions may be decisive.'[33]

The same outlook led to changed attitudes to the Commonwealth, which had been the scene of bitter arguments between the Afro-Asian members and the 'old Commonwealth' in 1964 and 1965 as well as in 1966. Many observers predicted the breakup of the association after the 1966 London meeting and indeed it was another two and a half years before the heads of government met again. Brown again records, if not the disillusionment, then certainly the unhappiness: 'They did not wish to permit the Commonwealth conferences to turn themselves into an examination of the domestic policies of its members, yet they had to accommodate themselves to some extent to the vehemence of African-led protest since, in moral terms, they did not wish to appear to defend policies of racial predominance.'[34] This was an issue in sporting matters too:

Nowhere did the isolation of many New Zealanders show more starkly than in their bewildered reactions to developments which accurately reflect a world of growing racial conflict . . . . The New Zealand Olympic Association wondering why such a fuss broke out over South Africa participation in the Mexico Olympics; the amateur athletics authorities accepting an invitation to take part in South Africa's 'all white' consolation games; the Rugby Union in 1966 caving in only to Governmental pressure—all of these were pointers to isolation from what is, in many contexts, now the main stream of international opinion.[35]

31 *EAR*, Feb. 1968, p. 30.
32 Bruce Brown, *New Zealand Foreign Policy in Retrospect*. Wellington, 1970, p. 38.
33 Brown, *Retrospect*, p. 38.
34 Brown, *Retrospect*, p. 42.
35 Brown, *Retrospect*, p. 43. The Mexico Olympics were held in 1968: the Rugby Union 'caved in' to a strongly worded suggestion from Holyoake that it not send a team to South Africa in 1967 from which Maori players would be excluded.

On the economic front both the Dairy Board and the Chamber of Commerce campaigned in 1967 for closer relations with South Africa.[36] In June 1969 the South African Minister of External Affairs visited New Zealand and in July 1969 the NZIIA held a one-day seminar on New Zealand-South African cooperation in an era of British withdrawal from the Indian Ocean. In 1972 Marshall, now Prime Minister, argued that it was better to build bridges with South Africa than walls. Twice in 1972 the government denied rumours that it was contemplating or had embarked on some kind of alliance with South Africa.[37]

While African issues weakened internationalism on the right, they reinforced it in the Labour Party. The third world was popular with Labour in the 1960s and 1970s. The Cold War was seen as a conservative construct which may have had something to do with 1940s and 1950s Europe but had nothing to do with 1960s and 1970s Asia—or Africa. The debate about the Vietnam War had fostered the third-world, anti-colonial orientation of Labour internationalism.

It was sport rather than kinship that increasingly directed this attention towards southern Africa. The 1970 All Black tour of South Africa, which had included three Maori and one Pacific Islands player, had been opposed, paradoxically it seemed to some, by the same coalition which had argued 'No Maori No Tour' in 1960. The issue, said M.P. for Northern Maori, Matiu Rata, was not 'whether or not Maoris should be included in any team', but 'whether or not we, as a nation with an enviable reputation in race relations can afford to have anything to do with [South Africa].'[38] A student group, Halt All Racist Tours (HART), was formed, as its name implied, specifically to sunder all sporting ties with the apartheid regime in South Africa. Scholars explored the international implications of the issue, as they had Rhodesia.[39] But for most of the New Zealand public, the prospect of a return South African rugby tour in 1973 was enticing. South Africa was New Zealand's premier rival in the contest for world rugby supremacy: it was not an easy contest to forgo.

The relationship between protestors and Labour over the prospective tour was uneasy. In 1972 polls suggested that 80 per cent of the population supported the tour and Labour did not commit itself to cancelling it, although it plainly was less than sympathetic and it wanted the government to take a stronger stand against apartheid in the United Nations, particularly by increasing its grant to the United Nations Trust Fund on Southern Africa. But

---

36   *New Zealand Commerce*, 16 Oct., 15 Dec. 1967.
37   *NZFAR*, March 1972, p. 27; June 1972, p. 78; Nov. 1972, p. 54.
38   *EP*, 8 April 1968, quoted in *Monthly Review*, May 1968, p. 10. See also Richard Thompson, 'Race, Kinship and Policy: Africa and New Zealand', *NZWA 1957–72*, pp. 113, 117.
39   See, for example, Ken Keith, *International Implications of Race Relations in New Zealand*. Wellington, 1972.

apart from saying that it would not hold an official reception for the South African team should it come, Labour was careful to say that it would not interfere in the tour, nor did it commit itself to vote for contentious resolutions introduced into the General Assembly that would have had the effect of putting the United Nations on a war footing *vis à vis* South Africa. Once in government, Kirk skilfully manoeuvred a cancellation of the tour, trying to take the country with him to the greatest extent possible, stressing the likelihood of domestic disruption and the impact on the Christchurch Commonwealth Games as much as the anti-apartheid argument. Kirk announced the 'conditional postponement' of the tour on 10 April 1973: 'the Government is ready to accept and welcome a team when one condition has been fulfilled and that condition is that the South African team should be, and should be seen to be, a genuine merit-based team.'[40]

With the tour issue out of the way, Kirk's enthusiasm for the Commonwealth, and the forum it provided for close relations with third world countries, could flourish. He attended the Ottawa Commonwealth Conference in August 1973. With Whitlam he urged the need for strong measures to resolve the Rhodesian problem. The British tried to isolate the Tanzanian leader, Julius Nyerere; Kirk reportedly said, 'we can and must express the solidarity we feel with President Nyerere and our other African colleagues'. Kirk's stance helped ensure that both 'old' and 'new' Commonwealth took a united stand on the issue with Britain.[41] In Jakarta Kirk recalled Fraser's support for Indonesian independence. Kirk visited Bangladesh and India, which said something about his priorities: he had been a warm supporter of Bangladeshi independence, having become involved in 1971, as Chairman of the Socialist International. When the democratically elected left-wing leader Salvador Allende was overthrown in Chile by the military, he was 'sick at heart'. When the Ministry of Foreign Affairs put up a proposal for recognition of the new government, Kirk wrote a 'NO' across the submission in five-inch-high letters.[42]

Kirk relished the January 1974 Commonwealth Games and the opportunity to meet visiting Commonwealth leaders; he welcomed Nyerere, the first African leader to visit the country. With the tour postponed, Kirk was able to make strong speeches about racism and underdevelopment without laying himself open to charges of hypocrisy: for instance, he compared the status and situation of Africans in South Africa with that of Aboriginals in Australia.[43]

The controversy over the 1973 tour did demonstrate that relations with

---

40 *NZFAR*, April 1973, p. 22, see also pp. 23–28.
41 MacLeod, 'New Foreign Policy', pp. 296–7.
42 Hayward, *Diary*, p. 173.
43 Hayward, *Diary*, p. 208 (Jan. 1974); see also p. 175, strong speech by Kirk on South Africa, 16 Oct. 1973. Bassett, *Third Labour Government*, p. 39, comments that the caucus quickly realised in 1973 that 'on matters of race, Kirk was the most radical in Caucus, bar none'.

South Africa were a minefield for Labour. But it was a domestic minefield. National's position was the reverse. It was about to learn the hard way that it was easy, even with one's 'friends', to get out on a limb in respect of South Africa. There were no prizes in Commonwealth diplomacy for getting into bed with apartheid, or for seeming to.

Muldoon and the first Commonwealth crisis

Kirk's successor, Rowling, thought the Kirk government had become too preoccupied with the third world. But it was Muldoon who exploited the unease and hostility which some of Labour's decisions and attitudes had elicited. The imminence of an election, plus plans for an All Black tour of South Africa in 1976, had combined to keep relations with Africa a highly political issue in 1975. The memory of the cancellation of the 1973 Springbok tour had not faded and National calculated on a strong measure of public sympathy for a stand which challenged the government's stance on sporting ties with South Africa, and its general political stance on decolonisation of the continent. The division in the community between the protest groups planning to stop the 1976 tour and the Opposition backing the Rugby Union in its determination to proceed with it, demonstrated that Kirk's 1973 decision had not produced or been grounded in any consensus. Consistent with the stand it had taken in 1973 the Rowling government said that it would not stop the tour but would try to dissuade the Rugby Union from going ahead with it. The Opposition successfully moved the issue away from the matter of support for or opposition to white South Africa and on to the more congenial and advantageous ground of the freedom of New Zealanders to travel.[44]

The conduct of General Idi Amin of Uganda, and of other African leaders was both attacked and identified as representative of Africa generally. Abraham Ordia, the President of the Supreme Council of Sport for Africa, described the Muldoon government as the arch-enemy of the Council. National M.P.s and others responded in kind. Many leaders of the New Zealand anti-apartheid movement met with intense hostility, even hatred, from some, incomprehension from others.

In the debate about apartheid in the UN Special Political Committee, the New Zealand representative detailed aspects of the country's opposition to apartheid, including its support for a sports boycott, but pointed out that while the government made every endeavour to discourage sports players from visiting South Africa, 'it will not go to the extent of restricting the freedom of New Zealanders to travel where they wish overseas', a right enshrined in article 13 of the Universal Declaration of Human Rights.[45] It

44   See exchanges in Parliament reported in *NZFAR*, May 1975, p. 88; June 1975, p. 69; July 1975, p. 70.
45   *NZFAR*, Oct. 1975, p. 52.

was, however, the National Party that held the initiative on this issue in 1975. In its 1975 election manifesto it did not have a section specifically on international relations but it did have one entitled 'Freedom, sports and human rights'. While addressing issues of individual freedom in New Zealand, it also talked about relations with South Africa:

> the National Party does not support apartheid or communism or any other form of political extremism. But we *do* respect the rights of other nations to deal with their own internal problems in their own way .... We also believe each individual should be free to follow his own conscience, without having someone else's morality forced on him. This means that we believe that every New Zealander should be free to have contact or play sport with, anyone in the world .... if the Rugby Union wishes to invite the Springboks to New Zealand next winter, we will make them welcome.[46]

Through the months leading up to the New Zealand rugby team's departure for South Africa in June 1976 the Muldoon government defended its position of non-interference on the grounds of sporting rights and the freedom of New Zealanders to travel and rejected very firmly any notion that the decision had foreign policy dimensions or that New Zealand supported apartheid. 'Sportsmen had the same rights as any other New Zealanders and the Government intends to uphold them', Talboys wrote in reply to criticism from the President of the Supreme Council for Sport in Africa. 'There will be no more political interference in sport. This does not mean we condone racial discrimination in South Africa or anywhere else.'[47]

Diplomatic pressure on the government mounted after the team left for South Africa, with the Organisation of African Unity calling for its members to boycott the Montreal Olympics in protest at New Zealand's participation. The New Zealand position was not helped either by the outbreak of racial violence in South Africa, particularly in the city of Soweto, on the eve of the All Blacks' arrival in that country. Twelve African countries decided in the end to boycott the Games. Statements that the countries concerned were of no sporting significance did not hold water only two years after an African and a New Zealander had vied for the Commonwealth 1500 metres record at Christchurch. The African boycott took some of the excitement from the track competitions.

The 1976 tour was a diplomatic disaster unprecedented in the country's history. The government admitted that 'Because the All Blacks had gone to South Africa—and gone just after the Soweto riots—it was widely believed that we were in favour of apartheid, and of apartheid in sport. Some people even seemed to think that this Government is racist in its outlook and actions.'[48] Not even Canada, Australia or Britain were firmly on New

---

46 1975 National Party manifesto.
47 *NZFAR*, March 1976, p. 41.
48 Minister of State, Keith Holyoake, commenting on responses from delegations at the United Nations, *NZFAR*, Oct.-Dec. 1976, p. 16.

Zealand's side. Holyoake was stark in his view of the diplomatic consequences of the government's policy:

> Most African nations have made it clear that they will not compete against New Zealand in any field as long as [it] maintains sporting contacts with South Africa . . . . they could destroy the [1978 Commonwealth] Games. If they decide not to take part, the issue is almost certain to arise at the Commonwealth Heads of Government meeting in London next June . . . . Most New Zealanders believe that politics should be kept out of sport. This Government is strongly opposed to political interference in sporting affairs and we are doing all we can to stop it. But we have to be realistic . . . . [49]

Ministers and officials were on the lookout for hopeful signs that public opinion would permit them to adhere to both the anti-apartheid policy and to their support for freedom in sport: 'in a changing climate of public opinion the majority of New Zealanders are now opposed to further sporting contacts with South Africa and it is my belief that this attitude will be reflected in the decisions of the sports bodies.'[50]

Nonetheless, confronted with criticism of New Zealand from Africa and Africans, much National Party opinion reacted in characteristic terms. Thus in a Commonwealth Day address in 1977 Internal Affairs Minister Alan Highet alluded to the fact that while New Zealanders might feel that apartheid was abhorrent, 'perhaps we can never feel in the way Africans feel the true nature of the angry disgust which is felt by those who are the subject of this foul discrimination . . . . I readily admit that from time to time I have felt both annoyed and frustrated by the response of Africans to our sincere efforts to respect their deeply felt concerns without denying to our people rights which are important to them . . . .'[51]

The persuasion had to continue, both from within and without. At the 1977 Commonwealth Heads of Government meeting an agreement of sorts was reached: a form of words which allowed both Africans and the New Zealand Prime Minister to claim victory for their respective positions. The Gleneagles Agreement, as it was known, committed, *inter alia*, all member countries to accept as an 'urgent duty' of each of their governments 'vigorously to combat the evil of apartheid by witholding any form of support for, and by taking every practical step to discourage contact or competition by their nationals with sporting organisations, teams or sportsmen from South Africa . . . .'[52] A further section acknowledged that it was 'for each Government to determine in accordance with its laws the methods by which it might best discharge these commitments. But they recognised that the effective fulfilment of their

49 *NZFAR*, Oct.-Dec. 1976, pp. 15-16.
50 *NZFAR*, Oct.-Dec. 1976, p. 14.
51 *NZFAR*, Jan.-March 1977, p. 31.
52 *NZFAR*, July-Sept. 1977, p. 13.

commitments was essential to the harmonious development of Common-wealth sport hereafter.' Muldoon took responsiblity for the 'in accordance with its laws' caveat.[53]

The government's commitment at Gleneagles brought the Labour and National positions together. Labour was not as radical as the anti-apartheid movement, even though it was sympathetic to the cause. In July 1976 Rowling emphasised that Labour 'would not have physically intervened to stop the ill-fated rugby tour. However we would have made sure our opposition was well understood by the Rugby Union and the world.' As Prime Minister, Rowling had opposed moves to impose a trade ban on South Africa or to exclude that country from the United Nations General Assembly.[54] Rowling emphasised that the sports issue had distorted the Commonwealth association—he compared the 1975 Kingston meeting with the 1977 London one, stressing the latter's domination by the issue of sports relations with South Africa—'the mess that New Zealand had in fact created . . . .'[55]

At the time, Gleneagles was widely seen as a solution. The government continued to reassure their own constituency: 'in countries that know us better I would think that no damage has been done whatever', as Muldoon said in answer to a question about the impact of the controversy. It also tried to persuade.[56] Talboys gave a series of addresses directed at least in part at members of his own party. Some of what he said sat uneasily with many National Party supporters, especially when he talked about the handicap suffered by the West in Africa from its association with South Africa and Rhodesia.[57] But the international reaction to the 1976 tour had been a scorching experience for National, and realism was the order of the day. The government did prove it could discourage minor sporting codes from touring South Africa or from inviting South African teams to New Zealand. The issue did not feature in the 1978 election: interviews with party leaders in the middle of 1978 did not even mention it.[58] Public opinion probably had shifted after the 1976 tour: in April 1976, before the tour, 56 per cent favoured it, 21.8 per cent opposed and 22.2 per cent were undecided.

The 1981 tour and the second Commonwealth crisis

Asked at the beginning of 1980 what he thought would be a significant pattern

---

[53] Muldoon, *Muldoon*. Wellington, 1977, pp. 206-7.
[54] John Henderson, 'Labour's Foreign Policy: a Moral Perspective', *NZIR*, Sept.-Oct. 1977, p. 8.
[55] Henderson, 'Labour's Foreign Policy: a Moral Perspective', p. 5.
[56] Henderson, 'An Exclusive Interview with the Prime Minister', *NZIR*, May-June 1977, p. 7.
[57] Stuart McMillan, *Press*, 12 Sept. 1977; McMillan also commented, *Press*, 20 April 1977, on 'old' Commonwealth attitudes to the crisis.
[58] Except for Tony Kunowski of the Values Party, who noted that the government had 'succeeded in extricating themselves from positions that they created in the first instance, like the issue of sporting contacts with South Africa, particularly the Gleneagles Agreement' (*NZIR*, Sept.-Oct. 1978, p. 11).

in politics in the decade about to start, Sir Guy Powles punted for 'the decade of the third world'.[59] He took exception to Muldoon's 'foreign policy is trade' argument. Over the next two years differences over what was essentially a third world issue, relations with South Africa, again both divided the country and precipitated a crisis in New Zealand's relations with the Commonwealth.

A South African rugby team was scheduled to visit New Zealand in the winter of 1981. Would the government's view of its responsibility to discourage the tour be sufficient to stop it—in effect, to get the New Zealand Rugby Football Union to stop it? In September 1980 the Union announced that it was inviting a merit-selected South African team; if it came it would be the first Springbok tour since 1965.

The government was quick to condemn the Union's decision.[60] Talboys continued to persuade: in an address entitled 'Living in the Real World' early in 1981 he recalled a time

> when to us Persia was a land of magic carpets; the Arabian peninsula was a backdrop for raids by romantic Bedouin warriors ... Afghanistan was up the Khyber Pass from British India; Black Africa was mysterious and perhaps a little frightening but quiescent under the British, the French and the Belgians; and Asia was a vast overpopulated place somewhere up north, colourful but a bit sinister.[61]

And in another address late in the same year he argued that New Zealanders had to 'set aside some of the stereotypes our generation acquired in the Western Desert and elsewhere and build partnerships beyond the ethnic and cultural confines of the anglophone Anglo-Saxon ... heritage'.[62]

But the government refused to do more than persuade—it made it clear that it had no intention of prohibiting a South African team from entering the country. For those attached to their sport, the local imperative was more powerful than the international one. In July 1980 polls showed 50 per cent approved of the expected tour of New Zealand, despite the fact that much media opinion was now hostile to any formal or substantive breach of the Gleneagles Agreement. The Prime Minister read correctly the minds of many country and some town and city New Zealanders: in making a final appeal to the Rugby Union not to bring a South African team to New Zealand, he talked of 'cemeteries in Europe in which the New Zealand and South African soldiers lay buried alongside each other: the silver fern next to the springbok'.[63]

By this time opinion was balanced on a knife edge: in May 1981 41 per cent

---

59 *EP*, 19 Jan. 1980.
60 'I must say at once that I am quite astonished that in more than four pages of statements not a single mention has been made of the Gleneagles Agreement ...', Talboys to the NZRFU, *NZFAR*, July-Sept. 1980, p. 33.
61 *NZFAR*, Jan.-March 1981, p. 3.
62 *NZFAR*, Jan.-March 1981, p. 9.
63 *NZFAR*, July-Sept. 1981, p. 20.

of the electorate were in favour of the tour and 43 per cent opposed. But elections are contested electorate by electorate and in many seats with strong pro-tour sentiment the government was being challenged not by Labour but by Social Credit. Social Credit was not in favour of the tour—but neither was the government, formally. Was it not possible that voters might desert National for Social Credit if the tour was stopped?

The government's dilemma was compounded by the growing evidence that it faced a major crisis over foreign policy. The Commonwealth agreed to transfer the forthcoming meeting of the Commonwealth Finance Ministers in Auckland to Nassau in the Bahamas. It was a direct challenge to Muldoon and he boycotted the meeting. There was also the ominous possibility of censure at the Commonwealth Heads of Government meeting in Melbourne in early October 1981. *The Times* (London) published an article by Muldoon in which he made it clear that his loyalties lay with the 'old' not the 'new' Commonwealth; of the latter he expressed his opinion in uncharacteristic understatement: 'if some of our Commonwealth partners are finding it difficult to do in 20 years what Britain did in perhaps that number of centuries, we should at least be patient. If the rule of law becomes an impediment to be ignored in the interest of the achievment of the goal, then we should chide, but preferably not slap.'[64] Muldoon was emphasising a gulf in values, of ideology and of sentiment. The only Commonwealth countries mentioned by name in the address and not criticised were Canada, Britain and Australia. The Commonwealth was conceived of in historical, progressive terms which also threw emphasis on Britain: 'the spreading of the Westminster parliamentary tradition and the values that have been established in Britain over many centuries'. The failure of Africans to criticise the United States and Britain to the degree they criticised New Zealand was a bone of contention. And so was their interpretation of the Gleneagles Agreement—a failing for which Muldoon attributed some of the responsibility to the Commonwealth Secretary-General, Sonny Ramphal: 'he knows better than anyone else what the true interpretation is, and it is my view that he should have been more diligent in explaining that'.[65]

But this did not address the fundamental foreign policy issue—a diplomatic crisis in New Zealand's Commonwealth relations. A government opposed to apartheid found itself discussing the possibility of the end of the Commonwealth. When asked during the tour whether there was any possibility of New Zealand either being asked to leave the Commonwealth or leaving voluntarily, Muldoon had not rejected the question out of hand as being too fanciful even to consider: 'I think there would be a revulsion of feeling against the Commonwealth in Australia, Britain and to some extent Canada'. If it did happen, 'it would be the beginning of the end of the Commonwealth. I would think politi-

---

[64] *The Times*, 29 July 1981, reprinted in *NZFAR*, July-Sept. 1981, p. 43.
[65] Interview with Bruce Wallace, *NZIR*, Sept.-Oct. 1981, p. 43. In the aftermath of Gleneagles, Muldoon had been very complimentary about Ramphal's role. Muldoon, *Muldoon*, pp. 207-8.

cal forces in the old Commonwealth would lead in that direction.'[66] But could Muldoon be so sure? Certainly no Commonwealth government, not even Thatcher's, was welcoming the prospect of the issue arising at Melbourne.[67] And what sort of a political outcome would it be if only Britain supported New Zealand? Would New Zealand become the boy in the playground who calls on his friends to support him, only to discover that they think his adversaries are in the right? Would a tantrum follow?

The South African team arrived in the last week of July and left in the last week of September. Massive civil disruption took place throughout the course of the tour on the occasion of all the matches, at cities and towns everywhere as well as at the match venues. The second match, at Hamilton, was cancelled after demonstrators invaded and occupied the ground. The police stance towards the demonstrators hardened after Hamilton: protest leaders for their part were aware that public opinion might be alienated by excessive violence; moreover the very size of the demonstrations, in five figures in the bigger towns, increased their responsibilities. Demonstrations took on the quality of ritual standoffs between protestors and police. No further games were cancelled because of demonstrator action although one was called off in advance because police did not consider they could make the ground secure. Only at the last match, in Auckland, did protest become violent.

Public opinion did shift during the tour—maybe the protest leaders' analysis was correct. By the end of the tour 54 per cent of those polled thought the Springboks should not have come, up 11 per cent from May. Possibly only this shift in public opinion stopped the foreign policy crisis deepening. At the Melbourne Commonwealth meeting, Muldoon reiterated the official New Zealand interpretation of Gleneagles. He was not challenged: African leaders and others were impressed by the scale and sincerity of the protest in New Zealand and took that rather than the government's position as the true measure of New Zealand's hostility to apartheid. It was a more subtle and perhaps therefore more powerful, humiliation, than that meted out in 1976. In 1982 New Zealand stood for election to the Security Council and failed: most African countries opposed its candidature.[68]

---

66 Interview with Bruce Wallace, *NZIR*, Sept.-Oct. 1981, p. 15. When asked a similar question in 1977, Muldoon had responded that he 'wouldn't dignify that kind of thing with an answer' (Henderson interview, *NZIR*, May-June 1977, p. 7).

67 The awkwardness between Muldoon and Australian Prime Minister Malcolm Fraser, the latter's commitment to Commonwealth cooperation, and the fact that he was hosting the meeting, did not help New Zealand either. In 1982 Muldoon praised Britain as the one country that had stood by New Zealand unequivocally over the Gleneagles Agreement (*The Times*, 20 May 1982, quoted in *EP*, 21 May 1982).

68 Malcolm McKinnon, 'Impasse or Turning Point: New Zealand and the 1981 Springbok Tour', *South Africa International*, 13/1 (July 1982), pp. 23–24. Nyerere stated that he did not think that any population represented at the meeting had shown such determination against, or opposition to, sporting links with South Africa as had New Zealand. Bryce Harland, *On Our Own: New Zealand in the Emerging Tripolar World*. Wellington, 1992, p. 67.

Again as in 1976 Labour was closer to the spirit of New Zealand support for the multiracial Commonwealth and the international anti-apartheid movement: 'We wouldn't have to alter New Zealand's attitude to the Commonwealth because the people of New Zealand have a very strong attitude towards it. I think the difficulty is that our association . . . has been put at risk by some very irresponsible actions . . . in particular by the Prime Minister.'[69] Labour presented itself as the party of the status quo in respect of the Commonwealth, casting National as the party of unwelcome change and disruption. The anti-apartheid movement did not have either the will or the capacity to impose a more powerful direction on New Zealand policy, for instance in the direction of a trade boycott or support for the armed struggle in southern Africa. In the 1981 election some urban seats shifted to Labour and some rural to National —an accurate reflection of the political fall-out of the tour.

The two crises over sporting relations with South Africa showed that nationalism could inform the idea of independence from the right as well as from the left, and for equally ideological reasons. National's attacks on African states, heads of governments and sporting organisations had a nationalist feel—these were the bullies, New Zealand was the victim. The attacks on organisations in New Zealand such as HART were not so different from the 1930s attacks by conservatives on disloyal Labour, except that it was the nation, not the Empire, that was at risk from without and within.

What would have happened if New Zealand had had its association with the Commonwealth suspended? National would undoubtedly have claimed that the issue was solely one of sport, that New Zealand was as opposed to apartheid as anyone, that while it might be temporarily out of step with its Commonwealth partners, it certainly was not in step with anyone else. And it would have claimed the nationalist ground from its opponents—the pattern of argument, in fact, used, just four years later, by a Labour government over the nuclear ships visit crisis.

Conclusion

The change of government in 1984 brought of course a change of stance on southern African issues. The South Africans closed their consulate in Wellington in anticipation of receiving their marching orders from the new government. New Zealand's first embassy on the African continent was established in Harare, capital of the now independent state of Zimbabwe, formerly Rhodesia. The first High Commissioner was Chris Laidlaw, a former All Black who had toured South Africa but later become an articulate opponent of contact with that country's apartheid regime. The Rugby Union accepted the much more rigid position of the new government on sporting contacts: the 1985 'Cavalier' tour to South Africa was an unofficial one and

69 Bruce Wallace interview with Rowling, *NZIR*, Sept.-Oct. 1981, p. 18.

its participants were penalised, if not very severely, for their participation.

In terms of foreign relations the new policy had all the hallmarks of orthodoxy. At a stroke the new government had removed all the contention between New Zealand and fellow Commonwealth members over its relations with South Africa. Within New Zealand demonstrations ended. Without the tour issue to mobilise opinion and to foster wider debate, Africa sank below the horizon. Labour had no interest in developing its position on South Africa—it was enough that its stance was acceptable to the rest of the Commonwealth. When African countries decided to boycott the 1986 Edinburgh Commonwealth Games in protest at British sporting contacts with South Africa, there was no discussion in New Zealand about the worth of joining in the boycott, and no lead from the government about it.[70] In his memoir on the ANZUS crisis Lange made a number of passing comments about Commonwealth leaders and the third world generally that suggest a big distance between his outlook and that of the Labour Party during the Kirk government; his account of Commonwealth Heads of Government meetings was cynical and dismissive.[71] And the government moved only slowly to introduce full trade sanctions against South Africa.

The public position was similar. The public was informed about apartheid, which was a classic liberal issue; by that I mean an issue which addressed the ethical stances of people with whom New Zealanders could identify—the white regime in South Africa, and the support that regime received from the United States, Britain and New Zealand. There was much less interest in, or ability to comprehend, intra-African issues that were just as important to Africans themselves—the prospects for democracy in black Africa, the debt crisis, even famine (except when it was dramatised and sentimentalised by the Western media).

A more general point can be made here about the fate of Labour internationalism. That internationalism had revolved around a number of major causes—anti-Fascism, anti-colonialism, anti-militarism. As victory in the Second World War had ended active anti-Fascism, so the completion of the process of decolonisation weakened the anti-colonial cause. The issues were still there, as preoccupation with the third world, with a new international economic order, suggested. But they had become much less clear, more diffuse. We saw how central the Commonwealth was to both progressive and conservative New Zealand views of the world in the 1950s. By the 1980s it no longer played that role, both because it had been so divided over South Africa, but also because there was not the same clear sense of moving forward, certainly not in a fashion immediately recognisable to the New Zealand inheritors of the British tradition of concern for the liberation of oppressed

---

[70] Nor for that matter much evidence of public concern about or identification with the African position.
[71] Lange, *Nuclear Free*, pp. 168–70, 194.

peoples. Yet New Zealand was involved in the world, through trade, travel and communications, more than ever before.

The record of the fourth Labour government's Africa policy confirmed that Africa was a problem in foreign relations for the National rather than for the Labour Party. Labour policy on Africa put it in line with international opinion. National's 'independence' did not. Nationalist language was rarely used by conservatives in talking about New Zealand foreign policy. Yet the language of conservative thinking about Suez, about southern Africa, about the third world generally, came close: 'By taking a stand on the sporting issue, Mr Muldoon has brought his own brand of independence into New Zealand foreign policy.'[72] Under a slightly different set of circumstances this could have become the dominant language and reality of New Zealand's foreign relations, that of a small isolated country, somewhat out of step with the international community of which it was putatively a member, radically hostile to the liberal temper of the international community as a whole, its population suspicious of, insular in attitude towards, the rest of the world, a country like Catholic Ireland, Salazarist Portugal, Francoist Spain. As it was, we saw something which stopped short of that and was rather the play of an 'independent', but not progressive, interest in foreign policy. National's—or Muldoon's—stance on southern Africa was not a colonial relic but a perfectly comprehensible element in the pattern of contemporary New Zealand foreign relations.

For diplomats the experience was formative. It was the diplomats rather than New Zealand as a whole who had had to live in Talboys's 'real world'. As with the contemporaneous economic diplomacy, diplomats learnt hard lessons in the play of power in international relations.

---

72 John Henderson, 'Muldoon: New Zealand and the World', *NZIR*, May-June 1977, p. 10.

11. Power and independence in the Pacific

It is appropriate in the study of New Zealand external relations since the 1960s to separate out New Zealand relations with the Pacific[1] as well as its relations with the African Commonwealth. In the case of Africa the separate treatment is justified because the issue created difficulties for National rather than Labour and brought into focus right-wing rather than left-wing nationalism. In respect of the Pacific, it might be thought that the reason for separate treatment is that New Zealand has a special role there, and also that the country has in recent decades acquired a Pacific identity. Both of these notions will be scrutinised rather than taken for granted. The starting point of this discussion is different. In its relations with most of the world, New Zealand lacks power. In the Pacific, it has it. The size of the country's economy in relationship to the Pacific, its importance in Pacific trade, as a source of aid and as a destination for migrants, its defence, political and educational relationships, the readiness with which it could collaborate with Australia on Pacific issues, not to mention more distant states like the United States and Britain, all meant that power was an inescapable issue in New Zealand-Pacific relations.

It should be evident at this point that this is an important distinction for our discussion of independence in foreign policy. The main argument of this book is that the idea of independence in New Zealand has not traditionally been about power, or the wresting of it. It has been about the articulation of interest within an accepted framework, an accepted distribution of power; and it has been about dissent, also within that framework. Until the 1980s, New Zealand applied to the conception of independence in the Pacific exactly the same kind of pattern that had characterised its view of its own independence. There were

---

[1]   It should be noted at this point that Pacific is used in this discussion to refer to the island states and communities to New Zealand's north, stretching from New Guinea to Pitcairn, in other words what is also called the 'South Pacific'. New Zealand usage confines the word 'Pacific' in this fashion, reserving the terms 'Asia-Pacific', 'Pacific Rim' or 'Pacific Basin' for the larger region encompassing most of the Pacific Ocean's littoral. Within the island arc New Zealand's attention is focused on the island groups from Fiji in the west to the Cooks in the east. 'The Islands', a term in common use in New Zealand, is not favoured by Pacific countries themselves.

accepted kinds of independence, and there were unaccepted kinds. The former obscured power relations, the latter brought them to the surface. Independence could not be associated with radical or revolutionary socialist change—there would be no Congos, no Vietnams. Independence would be associated with a newly enhanced ability on the part of the Pacific peoples to speak up on their own behalf, instead of requiring the metropolitan powers to do so for them—in this respect the South Pacific Forum was exactly analogous with the Commonwealth and of course was initially composed exclusively of former British territories, Australia and New Zealand included. And there was a progressive side to the independence: in the new world, economic and social issues, not politics and the military, were to be at the centre of affairs. Even by comparison with Australia and Britain New Zealand was seen as more enlightened, more liberal, in the Pacific. We also see this idea of independence in the diplomatic alignments of New Zealand and Pacific countries *vis à vis* the rest of the world and in the rhetoric of Pacific identity. The Pacific was a place where it was easy to feel good about New Zealand's role.

This model encountered a significant challenge only in 1987, the year of the Libyan 'incursion' and the Fiji coups. Since then, New Zealanders have talked less freely about the Pacific, less readily assumed an identity of interests and values between New Zealand and the various Pacific countries.

Decolonisation and stability

Independence was not an immediate issue in the Pacific in the postwar period even though it was foreshadowed in the case of Samoa. Samoa's independence in 1962 came at a time when the drive to decolonisation was becoming universal. The new Afro-Asian majority in the United Nations saw no value in colonialism at all and this outlook became significant in United Nations agencies and committees. The end of colonialism was the cry, the 1960 United Nations Declaration on Colonialism the charter.[2]

The transplanting of the ideas behind New Zealand's independent foreign policy into policy towards the Pacific can be neatly identified with Western Samoan independence in 1962, not least because one of the chapters in *New Zealand's External Relations*, which we examined at the end of Chapter 6, dealt with New Zealand's role in the region.

New Zealand was already committed to Samoan independence and was not averse to independence generally, on either ideological or pragmatic grounds, as were all the other Pacific administering powers. But independence meant to New Zealand something different from its meaning in Africa and Asia. It was drawn from the New Zealand, not the anti-colonialist, nationalist, lexicon and had all the connotations with which we have become familiar.

[2] See J. V. Scott, 'Getting Off the Colonial Hook', in *NZWA 1957-72*, pp. 123-6.

Western Samoan internal self-government, achieved in 1959, met with universal approval: it had the support of the Opposition and the editorial columns of the daily press[3] as well as of the government. This unanimity did not mean that New Zealand was simply happy to get Samoa off its hands—or at least to see a major step towards that outcome. It also indicated that the transition was not expected to raise any concerns about the future political complexion of an independent Samoa: the future governors of the country were expected to be both well-disposed towards New Zealand and also in full control of their country. They would be drawn from the traditional leadership families of Upolo and Savai'i.

National organised a plebiscite in Western Samoa to conform to the United Nations wish that the trust territory conduct an act of self-determination before it became independent. Sir Guy Powles, still High Commissioner in Apia, told Wellington that the view that it would be an expression of anti-colonialism and nationalism was not realised: 'for one who was looking for the usual symptoms of repressed nationalism considered appropriate to such occasions, the results must have been extremely disappointing'.[4] Uniquely in the annals of decolonisation, the Samoan population voted against a one-person one-vote system, opting instead for a matai system of representation despite New Zealand and United Nations pressure for universal suffrage.[5]

The pattern set by Samoan independence remained for New Zealand governments the favoured one. Interestingly almost all Pacific states became independent during the time in office of National governments.[6] But it would be difficult to identify any respect in which Labour might have handled the transition differently, or taken any different initiatives in respect of states which New Zealand did not administer.

New Zealand's support for independence for Pacific countries was widely believed in New Zealand to be less unqualified, more enthusiastic than was the case with other metropolitan powers and this in turn was seen to be linked to the quality of New Zealand's own race relations. In reporting on the factors ensuring the willingness of the international community to relieve New Zealand of the obligation to report on Cook Islands, 'first, and of key importance', it was stated, 'was the widespread belief that New Zealand's record in the related field of race relations was a reliable guide to the sincerity of its intentions in decolonisation'.[7]

New Zealand had pushed ahead with free association with Cook Islands. And after Cook Islands came Niue. In these cases it had consulted the United

3   *Dominion*, 30 Sept. 1959; *EP*, 2 Oct. 1959, N1722/0433, NA.
4   Annex to AB61/21, 1 June 1961, EA 63/1/14/1, MERT.
5   See Mary Boyd, *Decolonisation*, p. 21. The matai were those of chiefly status—matai suffrage enfranchised only a minority of the adult Samoan population.
6   The exceptions were Niue—self-government, 1974, and Papua New Guinea—fully independent of Australia, 1975.
7   *AJHR*, 1966, A. 2, p. 56.

Nations, although other colonial powers, notably Britain, would have preferred that it had not, and it was not actually obliged to, as it was with respect to Samoa, a trust territory.[8] Such an initiative was part of New Zealand's self-image: 'the South Pacific region of the future will not need "administering powers" so much as powers who are prepared to work with new nationalist movements and with local administrations increasingly responsible to the island peoples. New Zealand's own colonial past and her liberal tradition of friendship for emergent peoples—together of course with her deep involvement in the region—fit her to play this role.'[9]

Labour and National had supported independence for Samoa on the assumption it would be achieved consensually and benignly, in sharp contrast with the transition in Africa, and parts of Asia. It was also expected that the newly independent country, and any others in the region, would remain aligned: 'the Pacific will remain Pacific in every sense of the word. We do not wish to import what may be called "Congo situations" into the dependent territories there, nor to sow seed beds for possible cold-war clashes.'[10] There would have been no enthusiasm for Sukarno's prophecy in 1965 that the people 'to our east in Oceania must be given a chance to become masters in their own homes and manage their own affairs . . . . do not be shocked if a time comes when the Pacific Ocean explodes, rebels and the peoples set up their own independent countries.'[11] 'We have a direct national interest as a South Pacific power', said Holyoake in 1963, 'in doing all we can to ensure that within our own region nationalism is diverted into constructive channels, that the tensions and dangers of racialism are averted, and that the search of the island peoples for economic progress is assisted through genuine cooperative endeavour.'[12]

Despite such comments, the notion of New Zealand at the centre of, or leading, a Pacific community was little articulated in the 1960s and New Zealand's decolonisation model, the transfer of power in Samoa and Cook Islands, remained just that, a model. New Zealand did not in the 1960s bear the primary responsibility for maintaining stability in the region. This was still a responsibility of the British, south of the equator, and the United States, to the north. Where New Zealand became involved, it was in supporting the British.[13] In the early 1960s the British hoped to draw New Zealand into a

8   Scott, 'Getting Off the Colonial Hook', p. 133.
9   F. H. Corner, 'New Zealand and the South Pacific', in *NZER*, p. 149.
10   P. K. Edmonds, in the general debate on the report of the Trusteeship Council in the Fourth Committee, *EAR*, Oct. 1961, p. 29.
11   Extract from an address by Sukarno, *EAR*, April 1965, p. 31.
12   Holyoake, 'New Zealand's External Relations in a Changing World', *EAR*, Aug. 1963, p. 23.
13   For example, in April 1961 HMNZS *Pukaki* was sent to the then Gilbert and Ellice Islands because of possible disturbance arising out of an industrial dispute on Ocean Island. It was not required because the dispute was settled before the vessel arrived. Holyoake explained that 'the purpose of *Pukaki*'s mission was to serve as a deterrent against disorders which might have resulted in bloodshed' (*EAR*, April 1961, pp. 23, 24).

greater sense of responsibility towards the region. The New Zealanders learnt that Lord Selkirk, the Commissioner-General for the British territories in Southeast Asia and United Kingdom Commissioner for Singapore, was concerned about the problem of maintaining internal security in the Pacific Islands. There were difficulties in the existing plan to bring troops in from Singapore. He assumed this was of interest to Australia and New Zealand as well as to the United Kingdom and that while the former two had never given any commitment to assist in maintaining internal security in the British territories, it was quite possible that the British might seek such assistance if an emergency actually arose. Under such circumstances it would help if New Zealand had representation in Fiji. But the Holyoake government was careful to circumscribe its response for fear that it could find itself over-burdened— or just burdened. It was pointed out in talks with the British that 'successive New Zealand governments had been unwilling to enter into specific commitments re such a situation and there was no basis for planning how help could be given. Moreover seemed unlikely that government at present would consider representation.'[14] External Affairs officials connived at getting the British to put pressure on their own ministers: 'whether we like it or not we simply have to accept responsibility in Fiji because of the declining British interest in the area and the fact that our own interests in the Pacific are becoming of increasing significance .... My own personal feeling is that you should encourage them to press us officially on the matter.'[15] But Holyoake declined, as might have been expected. As one official commented, 'It had to be recognised that any British suggestion that New Zealand and Australia ought to play a larger role in security problems in the Pacific could not help but increase the fears Ministers (and others) in New Zealand already had about a British "scuttle" in the Pacific.'[16]

Independence and stability

But the British could not be kept in the Pacific for ever: 'Britain is in a leaving mood', as one foreign service officer put it in 1969, and 'New Zealand's own interests and those of its friends are very much involved. Although we look beyond the South Pacific to discern any threat to our own security, the stability and welfare of the islands must, in the longer term, be of increasing importance to us.'[17]

In the Pacific 1970 was a key year for independence. Although Cook Islands had achieved self-government in association with New Zealand in

14 Extract from memo to London, talks on Fiji in Wellington with a British official, 12 March 1963. EA62/45/1, MERT.
15 McIntosh to White, 23 May 1963. EA62/45/1, MERT.
16 Jermyn (NZ High Commission, London) to Craw, 30 Aug. 1963. EA62/45/1, MERT.
17 *EAR*, May 1969, p. 7.

1965 and small, phospate-rich Nauru had become independent in 1968,[18] it was the independence of Tonga and Fiji from Britain in 1970 that gave a new feel to Pacific politics. Even when they were British-protected state and colony respectively, New Zealand had had close defence and commercial ties with both. It was natural that New Zealand would see itself bound to accept some responsibility for the two newly independent states: 'We have, over the years acknowledged our mutual defence interests by helping in Tonga and Fiji—who, in turn, have freely helped us in two major wars and later in skirmishes—and by ensuring that our lines of communication through the Pacific remain open. The stability and well-ordered progress of the Islands is, therefore, the key to any development of what other interests New Zealand may have, commercial or political.'[19]

The notion that there was a 'Pacific Way' of independence, that there were no fundamental differences, and therefore no fundamental political issues between New Zealand and the Pacific states became central. In answer to a question about the possibility of a South Pacific Forum in 1971 Holyoake had replied 'the New Zealand government has, as usual, taken the lead and has indicated our willingness to assist [South Pacific governments] in any way which they would find helpful.'[20] The South Pacific Forum was very important both in registering the reality of an independent Pacific and also in providing a diplomatic means of fostering stability in the region. Initially it was composed entirely of Commonwealth members and so was de facto a regional Commonwealth organisation. Holyoake and the Ministry of Foreign Affairs were concerned that the Commonwealth was forgetting about the Pacific, because the issues elsewhere, such as southern Africa, were more compelling, more immediate.

The rhetoric of South Pacific Year did not talk about power.[21] The assumption was that problems could be worked out, values reconciled, within the existing framework, even though the Pacific states were less powerful than New Zealand or any of their other neighbours. This would be the Pacific Way. Although a token respect was paid to the notion that New Zealand could learn from the Pacific, the language was for the most part the language of 'responsibility', of meeting educational and other aid challenges.

The establishment of the Forum and the independence of Fiji and Tonga meant that Labour in office did not have an agenda for the Pacific distinct from National's. The rhetoric was a little different but not the reality. Even Niue's attainment of self-government in free association with New Zealand in 1974 was essentially fulfilling the plans of the previous government. The opposition

[18] For Nauru, see Barrie Macdonald, *In Pursuit of the Sacred Trust: Trusteeship and Independence in Nauru*. Wellington, 1988.
[19] Duncan McIntyre, Minister of Island Affairs, *NZFAR*, Jan. 1971, p. 13.
[20] *NZFAR*, March 1971, p. 14.
[21] 'New Zealand in the South Pacific', *NZFAR*, Jan. 1971, pp. 3-8.

to French nuclear-weapons testing and the campaign for a South Pacific nuclear-weapons-free zone discussed in Chapter 8 did, however, suggest a different conception of stability.

Through the later 1970s and up till 1987 the pattern of independence and stability held good: on the one hand a belief, and to some extent an accurate one, that relations among the Pacific states and between them and New Zealand, Australia and other outside powers were consensual and stable; on the other hand, at the margin, issues of power, of gatekeeping, that were handled without difficulty until the first Fiji coup.

Whereas in the 1960s the 'stabiliser' role had belonged to Britain, in the 1970s and 1980s New Zealand governments would point out to European countries and the United States the valuable role it played, along with Australia, in the South Pacific. For instance, a European parliamentary delegation reported on the 'economic and strategic importance of New Zealand in the South Pacific, where the Community is linked to certain countries though the Rome Convention ...'.[22]

In an address late in 1981 Talboys addressed the issue of relations with the region in similar terms: 'it is where we are most able to play a special role in both political and economic affairs. It is also a region which is attracting increased attention from countries outside the Pacific.'[23] Provided the island states did not align themselves with unwelcome outside powers there was a certain acceptance that the political style would be different. None of the voting systems in Samoa, Tonga, or Fiji was fully democratic but this was accepted as part of the Pacific Way.

In contrast, instability could come from within New Zealand and if it did, was dealt with swiftly. When in July 1977 the crew of the New Zealand ship *Ngahere*, in port in Suva, went on strike in sympathy with Fiji waterfront workers, Muldoon made clear to Mara, the Prime Minister, his opposition to the New Zealanders' actions: 'I am aware from private communications with the Prime Minister of Fiji, and from his public statements, how deeply is resented in Fiji what is considered to be interference in their internal affairs by the nationals of other countries, particularly those [with] which [they] enjoy the closest and most friendly relations.'[24]

In 1977 and 1978 three states experienced some instability: Fiji, Nauru and Cook Islands. In the first two instances the status quo ante was eventually restored: in Fiji with Mara's sweeping victory in the September 1977 elections; and in Nauru with the eventual return of Hammar de Roburt to the presidency in May 1978, after two rivals had proved successively unable to maintain themselves in power.[25] New Zealand was most directly involved in

22   *NZFAR*, Jan.-March 1981, p. 38.
23   *NZFAR*, Oct.-Dec. 1981, p. 15.
24   *NZFAR*, July-Sept. 1977, p. 47.
25   *NZFAR*, Jan.-March 1978, p. 39.

the disturbances in Cook Islands because of the constitutional link between the two countries. A serious dispute about the legality of certain practices in connection with the election, which cast doubts on its outcome, led the Prime Minister to conclude on the basis of reports received that the 'social fabric of the Cook Islands could well be subjected to strong pressure'.[26] Muldoon explained that the Cook Islands police were worried about their ability to maintain law and order, which in turn raised the possibility of New Zealand involvement. The new government under Dr Tom Davis accepted police assistance from New Zealand: 'It would have been unthinkable for us to refuse to respond to a request for assistance from the Cook Islands Government in a situation in which life might be in danger.'[27]

But the main concern was always outside powers, in particular the Soviet Union, later Libya, especially in respect of Vanuatu, the former New Hebrides, which became independent in 1980. It was a new kind of independence because it was partly the result of a nationalist movement which, unlike the Samoan movement, developed and achieved its objective in a contested political climate.[28] The 1981 Forum discussed Solomon Islands concern that the Soviet Union intended to proceed with a marine survey institute in Solomon Islands and Vanuatu waters contrary to the expressed stand of the Solomon Islands government. The Forum supported Solomon Islands opposition to the Soviet plan and praised its decision not to offer the Soviet vessel assistance and facilities. The Forum further welcomed the alternative offer made by New Zealand, Australia and the United States to undertake a geophysical and oceanographic survey and research programme in the region.[29] The Secretary of Foreign Affairs stressed in 1984:

It will continue to be of overriding importance for New Zealand that the South Pacific generally should remain western-oriented .... to avoid the development of conditions of political or economic instability which the Soviet Union or some other unfriendly or opportunistic power could exploit [and] to ensure that the western powers themselves (I am thinking particularly of France, the United States and Japan) are responsive to South Pacific concerns.[30]

In an address on defence of the Pacific and Indian Ocean area the Minister of Defence, David Thomson, concluded by looking at the aims and achievements of the Mutual Assistance programmes in defence that New Zealand ran with Fiji, Tonga and Papua New Guinea. In May 1984 senior officials from the New Zealand Ministries of Foreign Affairs and Defence visited Niue, Fiji, Tonga, Western Samoa and Cook Islands in May for

26 *NZFAR*, July-Dec. 1978, p. 51.
27 *NZFAR*, July-Dec. 1978, p. 52.
28 For further discussion, see below, p. 269.
29 *NZFAR*, July-Sept. 1981, p. 61.
30 *NZFAR*, April-June 1984. p. 12.

discussions on defence and security issues, including the role of a Ready Reaction Force.

On the French territory of New Caledonia Muldoon noted in 1982 that 'the South Pacific Forum at its last meeting took a positive view of the reforms the French Government is introducing. My opinion is that these reforms must be allowed time to work through. Should, however, the French government change course and seek to interrupt the political process that is now evolving, New Zealand and most other countries would take a rather a different view. Happily there are no signs of this taking place . . . .'[31] This caution reflected a preoccupation with the 'radical' nature of the Kanak nationalist movement in New Caledonia and in particular its putative links with Libya and the Soviet Union through Vanuatu, which established diplomatic relations with Cuba in 1983.

The change of government in 1984 did not make a big difference in this area of policy. Indeed a case can be made for saying that because of its differences with the United States, the fourth Labour government went to some effort to emphasise the common interests it had with other Western powers in the Pacific. The nuclear-weapons-free-zone agreement reached in August 1984 was a 'soft agreement': it committed countries to do what all did anyway—to refrain from manufacturing, storing, or using nuclear weapons. At the same Forum Lange, along with other leaders, opposed the pressure from Prime Minister Walter Lini of Vanuatu to have New Caledonia returned to the United Nations list of territories to be decolonised.[32] The plan for a Ready Reaction Force, proposed in the 1983 Defence Review, was carried on by the Labour government. While its role in the South Pacific was unclear, observers from varying perspectives agreed that it could allow New Zealand to participate in military actions as far afield as Southeast Asia or Korea.[33] At the time of the ANZUS crisis in February 1985 Lange stressed that New Zealand was committed 'and will continue to act as a stabilising influence in the South Pacific. Maintenance of an appropriate level of conventional forces is part of that commitment.'[34]

Lange accused the Soviet Union of having 'a long-term aim of subversion in the South Pacific and of using fishing agreements with impoverished island nations as a means of doing that'. He was concerned about Soviet penetration of the South Pacific in the light of diplomatic moves between Vanuatu and the Soviet Union to allow fishing in the island state's economic zone, as well as to provide port and aircraft landing facilities.[35] Libya's actions, in particular its

31   *NZFAR*, July-Sept. 1982, p. 12.
32   *Press*, 1 Sept. 1984.
33   See, *inter alia*, James Rolfe, 'Securing the South Pacific', *NZIR*, Nov.-Dec. 1985, pp. 16-18; Owen Wilkes, 'Gurkhas of the South Pacific', *New Outlook*, Sept.-Oct. 1984, pp. 32-35. Rolfe was a serving army officer, Wilkes a peace activist.
34   *EP*, 7 Feb. 1985.
35   *EP*, 7 July 1986.

interest in the Kanak nationalist movement in New Caledonia and its plans to open a mission in Vanuatu, met with stronger responses. Lange met Australian Foreign Minister Hayden at Ohakea Air Force base on 1 May: Hayden had left Canberra at 3 a.m. to attend the meeting. Australian defence analysts claimed that the Libyan attempt to gain a foothold in the South Pacific posed the 'first real threat' to regional security since the Second World War. The Americans also publicly warned the Libyans off and Libyan plans, if they could be so characterised, did not proceed further. It was a demonstration of the way power, not usually visible, did inform Pacific relations.[36]

Independence and interest

We have discussed independence in the Pacific in terms of ideological limits to the kind of nationalism, of independence, that was tolerated. What about that other kind of independence characteristic of New Zealand, the independence of interest? When the power relationship is reversed, we see the notion of interest from the other side. It was not just that the Pacific states could articulate their interests—within the agreed framework of independence, so too could New Zealand. New Zealand was in other words in the situation that it had placed Britain—being needed more than it needed. Indeed the relationship was probably more unequal between New Zealand and the Pacific countries than it had been between New Zealand and Britain. Were there ways in which the interplay of interests rested, as it did between Britain and New Zealand, on a recognition of interdependence? Or was it more like the situation in which New Zealand found itself from the late 1960s, an outsider in the world of the 'great commercial and political powers'?

We can see the pattern of interest manifest in a number of ways. At a broad level New Zealand thinking saw the Pacific countries, even those whose people enjoyed New Zealand citizenship, as 'overseas', outside the New Zealand frame of reference. The New Zealand press, radio, later television, did not treat Pacific audiences as domestic audiences or Pacific news as domestic news. They were spoken to, but they did not speak back, or not so that New Zealanders could hear them: this was very much like the situation of a colony such as New Zealand had been in relation to England, or London.

From this perspective, independence, or for that matter any status short of full integration, was a way by which the dominant power could limit its moral and economic responsibility to the people in the subordinate community.

---

[36] *EP*, 1 May, 2 May, 1987; *Sunday Times*, 3 May 1987. The displeasure with Vanuatu dated back at least to its opening of diplomatic relations with Cuba in 1983 as well as being aroused by more recent Libyan overtures and activities: for instance, at a Pacific Peace Forum in the Libyan capital in April 1987, the Libyan leader, Colonel Gaddafi, called for Pacific islands to join an anti-imperialist front. Representatives of Australian Aboriginal groups attended: Maori groups were invited but did not go. Note that New Zealand had expelled a Soviet diplomat, for unrelated reasons, a week before the Hayden-Lange meeting.

New Zealand's 'independence' had been in the interests of Britain as much as of New Zealand, and indeed had arguably been encouraged by the former more than sought after by the latter. So independence for the Pacific, from this point of view, was a New Zealand interest, as well as a Pacific one. And New Zealand found, just as Britain had, that the dependent communities saw things differently, thought in terms of a political community and shared objectives, just as New Zealand had done with Britain.[37]

And, as was the case between New Zealand and Britain, New Zealand and Pacific interests were not completely antithetical. New Zealand's interest in Pacific stability was itself an 'interest' which moderated more strident domestic concerns, and the presence of populations of Pacific origin in New Zealand also influenced the formulation of New Zealand policy. Further, as some scholars have argued, at least in respect of the 'migration-aid-remittance' economies such as Cook Islands, there was a certain stability, that is, a congruence of interests, in the ties between New Zealand and the dependent communities.[38]

Interest was central in the Pacific policies of Labour as well as National, despite the former's idealism. Even during Kirk's prime ministership we can see the play of interest when the question of a Pacific shipping line arose. A New Zealand/Pacific Islands shipping conference was held at Waitangi at the end of October 1973. New Zealand labour and business interests were represented along with both the New Zealand and Pacific governments. The debate demonstrated the extent to which sectional New Zealand interests could have different perspectives from that of the New Zealand government, with its emphasis on political friendship with the Pacific countries. The government wanted to help with the establishment of a shipping line but the interests of the labour movement meant that it could not contemplate limiting costs by using cheap Pacific labour. New Zealand unions were concerned at the effect of any Pacific initiative in shipping on seafarers' wages and conditions of employment.[39]

One conflict of interest came to the fore in 1974–75, the regulation of immigration. Recession meant that business demand for migrant labour slackened. As unemployment grew, albeit slowly, pressures increased, for both economic and racial reasons, for migration from the Pacific to be curtailed. In its 1975 manifesto National did not directly allude to the issue of Pacific immigration but its likely approach could be inferred from its statement that selection criteria for immigration would be based on family

---

[37]   Brian Talboys, Minister of Foreign Affairs, 1975–81, commented on how surprised he was to find that Pacific leaders thought of New Zealand as 'one of them'. Interview, 8 Dec. 1989.
[38]   I. G. Bertram and R. F. Watters, 'The Mirab Economy in South Pacific Microstates', *Pacific Viewpoint* 26/3, pp. 497–519 (1985). See also *Pacific Viewpoint*, 27/2 (1986), pp. 47–59, for further comment by Bertram and Watters.
[39]   *NZFAR*, Oct. 1973, p. 10.

links with New Zealanders and also from the stress it placed on lawbreaking immigrants. Immigrants who committed serious breaches of the law could be deported, while 'the Courts will be encouraged to make appropriate use of the present provisions relating to deportation, which will be reviewed and strengthened if necessary. National will, in addition, give the Minister of Immigration discretion to deport any person, who, within two years of his arrival, is convicted of an offence punishable by a term of imprisonment.'[40] The attention given to the issue indicated National priorities in this area and the party's judgement of the links in people's minds between Pacific immigration and crime. In the new year the National government made work permit agreements with Fiji, Samoa and Tonga which in effect restricted immigration from those countries and adjusted it to the demand for labour in New Zealand. At the same time the immigration regulations were policed more rigorously, a policy which created a great deal of dissatisfaction in the Pacific when the police apprehended some individuals overstaying permits by visiting homes at unsocial hours, for instance early in the morning. The government might have taken the flak if it had only been domestic—migration restriction was popular, especially in Auckland. But the impact on the Pacific itself was another matter: 'I would be less than frank if I were to deny that there are some areas of strain in Samoan-New Zealand relations .... The immigration issue has generated a measure of ill-feeling in some island countries.'[41] One reporter noted that from within the region 'it is clear that New Zealand's economic problems and attitudes towards Polynesian immigrants has produced a backlash .... Criticism has even resulted in members of a New Zealand delegation to a conference on ways to assist the South Pacific held in Australia recently, in the face of critical questions, dissociating themselves from government policy.'[42]

At the beginning of 1977 Talboys—not Muldoon on this occasion—made an extensive three-week visit to the region, going to Cook Islands, Niue, Tonga, Samoa and Fiji, the 'first comprehensive visit by a New Zealand Minister responsible for New Zealand's relations with the region'.[43] It was not just immigration that was causing difficulties: so too was the way that the new government had backed off the previous government's support for a South Pacific nuclear-weapons-free zone.

The broad purpose of Talboys's trip was made clear in a speech he made to the Fiji Press Club on 28 January: 'I want personally to reaffirm my Government's and New Zealand's continuing commitment to work with the

---

40 National Party manifesto, 1975.
41 Tupuola Efi, Prime Minister of Western Samoa, on a visit to New Zealand in July 1976. For general discussion of the episode, see Mary Boyd, 'Australia, New Zealand and the Pacific', in Ralph Hayburn, ed., *Foreign Policy School 1978: Australia and New Zealand Relations*. Dunedin, 1978, pp. 40–41.
42 Tony Garnier, *EP*, 22 Sept. 1976.
43 *NZFAR*, Jan.-March 1977, pp. 52–64.

countries of the South Pacific with their governments and peoples—to advance the common interests of us all.'[44] On his return Talboys commented in relation to the overstayer episode that 'no one disguised the fact that it had left scars. The whole issue had been a difficult one for all concerned and there will be a general sense of relief when it is finally resolved by the steps that the Government is now taking.'[45] And Muldoon, in Australia in March 1977 said 'the South Pacific countries need our special aid to help them solve their development problems within the context of their own economies, to become self-sufficient, and to increasingly look upon us as friends who back their words with deeds. If *we do not*, others who do not share our philosophies *will*.'[46]

The overstayer episode demonstrated the power of domestically driven or domestically fostered concerns to collide with Pacific interests: its resolution gave evidence of the countervailing forces at work on both sides. On the one hand, Pacific governments had little leverage; on the other, the New Zealand government did have a stake, an interest, in good relations with the Pacific countries. Like the Commonwealth, the Pacific remained one of Muldoon's 'domains' throughout his prime ministership. He attended all the annual meetings of the South Pacific Forum that took place while he was Prime Minister. He made a point of becoming friendly with Pacific leaders and had some successes.[47] Muldoon frequently criticised third world governments, and disparaged Labour for its idealism about them, but his stance towards the Pacific after the overstayer episode was always positive.

Immigration control was not of course abandoned after 1976, nor were other forms of gatekeeping. In two later episodes in the time of the Muldoon government, the matter of language achievement tests and of Western Samoan citizenship rights, the government acted swiftly to protect what it saw as New Zealand interests. Citizenship difficulties arose with Samoa following the Privy Council decision handed down in July 1982 that all Samoans born between 1924 and 1949 were British subjects and therefore New Zealand citizens. After a series of discussions between the two governments a protocol was signed in August which arrived at a compromise by granting any Western Samoans resident in New Zealand at the time, or acquiring permanent residence status subsequently, the right to acquire citizenship on application: New Zealand legislation was then passed which overturned the Privy Council decision.[48]

44   *NZFAR*, Jan.-March 1977, p. 54.
45   *NZFAR*, Jan.-March 1977, p. 63.
46   *NZFAR*, Jan.-March 1977, p. 22.
47   Muldoon, *My Way*, pp. 110-20, discusses the Pacific, and cites his close friendship with Tupuola Efi (p. 118).
48   *NZFAR*, July-Sept. 1982, pp. 24-25; Oct.-Dec. 1982, pp. 5-11 (McLay address on issue). For the language achievement tests issue, see *NZFAR*, April-June 1980, p. 49, Jan.-March 1981, pp. 19-20.

Nor did Labour's immigration policy vary significantly from National's. It is true that in 1975 Labour resisted pressure to clamp down on immigrants as National did subsequently. But it did this partly because it believed that immigration restriction had harmful effects on the Pacific economies which might only lead to increased aid pressure on New Zealand. It had no intention of lifting immigration controls altogether. Indeed Labour sent several hundred workers back to the Pacific and produced plans a few weeks before the election to curb Pacific immigration.[49] And although Lange might have said in the first months of his prime ministership that his government would emphasise the South Pacific context of New Zealand diplomacy ('We live in the South Pacific, and that is where our interests lie'),[50] it proceeded cautiously too—and when it did not, regretted it. In 1987 visa-free arrangements were introduced with a number of countries, including Fiji, Western Samoa and Tonga. But the large numbers who appeared to be arriving in New Zealand from those countries with the intention of staying longer than the prescribed three-month period led the government to cancel the new arrangements after only a matter of weeks.

In respect of trade there was not a great deal to choose between the two parties either. Both initiated and/or supported preferential trade arrangements and both tended to refrain from directly tackling New Zealand interest groups, for instance tomato growers.[51] Initiatives such as the PIIDS (started 1976), the Forum Line (1978) and SPARTECA (1980) raised the profile of problems as much as solved them.[52] The Forum Line required subsidisation, as Kirk had expected.[53] At the Forum meeting in 1983 it was recorded that SPARTECA was 'generally working well, although there were a number of areas where continuing assistance was necessary for Forum Island countries to take full advantage of the various provisions of the agreement.'[54]

In June 1982 the Director of the Fiji Economic Development Board visited New Zealand and had talks with official and business interests including the

---

[49] Barrie Macdonald, 'Pacific Immigration and the Politicians', *Comment*, (new series) 3 (1977), pp. 11-14.

[50] *NZFAR*, Oct.-Dec. 1984, p. 7.

[51] Increases in clothing and other imports from the Pacific from the late 1980s reflected a general liberalisation of New Zealand's tariff policy, not a specific variation in respect of the Pacific.

[52] PIIDS, Pacific Islands Industrial Development Scheme; SPARTECA, the South Pacific Regional Trade and Economic Agreement. For the early years of PIIDS, see Boyd, 'New Zealand, Australia and the Pacific', p. 41; for SPARTECA, see *NZFAR*, July-Sept. 1980, pp. 46-48.

[53] Malcolm Templeton, *NZFAR*, July-Sept. 1983, p. 45; New Zealand gave $2.841 million to the Forum Line in 1982 plus $3.8 million for a vessel, while there was also a $5.2 million subsidy for the Cook Islands-Niue service. By 1984 the Forum Line's trade and financial situation were improving, partly because of the financial contributions pledged by governments at the 13th Forum, but also because of a loan from the European Investment Bank for the purchase of containers. *NZFAR*, April-June 1984, p. 5.

[54] *NZFAR*, July-Sept. 1983, p. 41.

Manufacturers' Federation and the Auckland Chamber of Commerce. Fiji had established the EDB in 1981 in part to promote investment and export-oriented industries in Fiji.[55] The New Zealand High Commissioner to Fiji, Lindsay Watt, argued that SPARTECA had worked well for Fiji and that trade in non-sugar exports to New Zealand had expanded. He went on to say that

> from time to time it is put to New Zealand that SPARTECA isn't free enough, that Fiji cannot compete, that the 'rules of origin' requiring 50 per cent Fijian (or New Zealand) content should be relaxed. Well, I don't accept that. We are more than happy to look at particular cases, or particular anomalies that arise. But as a general rule, SPARTECA was not designed to turn Fiji into a pipeline for cheap goods from Asia or elsewhere. I would suggest that it rather was put in place to allow Fiji to use its own brainpower and its own resources to make products for a secure New Zealand market.[56]

Watt's idea was of two private-sector export-oriented economies relating to each other: in this case, that is, as distinct presumably from other parts of the Pacific, a commercial rather than a government-to-government relationship. The implication was that in this fashion Fiji would escape from under-development. When trade agreements did not work, even before 1984 the tendency was to emphasise free-market rather than structural solutions, as befitted a parsimonious metropolitan power:

> The important thing will be that each country will be exporting to the other the products it makes best and most efficiently, and which make best use of its indigenous resources. It is hard to judge now what these products will be. Sugar and tourism ... forestry too, presumably. The rest will have to await the dictates and demands of the marketplace .... what we are really aiming for, in my view, is an easy and wide-ranging and completely equal commercial and financial relationship. I am sure that, like the development of Fiji, the New Zealand-Fiji relationship must depend on the ability and enthusiasm of the private sector. I also imagine, that as the Fiji economy moves forward in the next 20 years the non-reciprocal nature of SPARTECA will become increasingly anachronistic.[57]

For some Pacific states trade was not the issue—aid was. When Samoa became independent in 1962, the stress was on a soon-to-be-attained self-reliance: 'the aim of any scheme of assistance will be to help Western Samoa to become self-reliant as quickly as possible'.[58] Great hopes were still held of aid in the early 1970s. The third Labour government was receptive to the lobbying for increased aid to address third-world problems. The pressure for

55 *NZFAR*, April-June 1982, p. 48.
56 *NZFAR*, July-Sept. 1983, p. 42. Later in the 1980s, Fiji did become a 'pipeline'.
57 *NZFAR*, July-Sept. 1983, p. 43.
58 *EAR*, Oct. 1961, p. 8.

the government to increase New Zealand's aid vote stemmed ultimately from reflection on the workings of the international economic order as well as the moral imperative that in an earlier era found its predominant expression in missionary work. In an address to the United Nations Association in April 1973 Kirk brought both these themes together: 'the fact that a vast gap exists between the rich nations and the poor nations and that it is widening not narrowing, is one of the great international issues—perhaps the greatest—of our time .... read the records of recent United Nations or Commonwealth trade or economic conferences to discover the mood and feeling that is there.'[59]

Kirk went on to announce that the government had decided to increase the proportion of GNP allocated to aid, with a target of the 0.7 per cent of GNP for official development assistance, while it also intended to encourage a goal of 1 per cent of GNP in total resource transfers. The immediate implications were substantial: an increase in the aid vote to $27.4 million, compared with $19.4 million in 1972-71 (0.36 per cent of GNP), with the aim of reaching $41 million in 1974-75 (0.5 per cent of GNP) and with the 0.7 per cent target in mind ($62 million). In August 1975 an Aid Advisory Committee was established, a recognition of the continuing political commitment of the government to its aid goals or at least its recognition of the importance of the issue to many of its supporters. In Labour's last year, aid had reached 0.55 per cent of GNP.

These were large increases, large sums compared with what had gone before. Kirk had entered the caveat of dependence on 'availability of resources and the GNP performance' but the mood of the statement was optimistic and forward-looking. It was thus consistent with both the buoyancy in the economy in 1973 and the enthusiasm of Labour supporters at seeing their ideas, objectives and election promises become policy, as Kirk recognised:

> What I have just said represents a major policy decision by this Government, a decision of great significance in both foreign and domestic economic policy terms .... New Zealand can afford to give more aid. If we are serious about trying to create a just world economic order, if we mean it when we talk about improving the living standards of our neighbours, the programme I have outlined is a minimum contribution from this country.[60]

Aid was to go predominantly, to the Pacific: 'New Zealanders', said Kirk, 'will see the importance of an emphasis on helping out with problems on our own doorstep.'[61] Muldoon too saw merit in directing aid at the South Pacific:

59 *NZFAR*, April 1973, p. 12.
60 *NZFAR*, April 1973, p. 11.
61 *NZFAR*, Oct. 1973, p. 4.

'I've taken the view that this is an area where we can do things that other countries can't do. We're getting the best value for the taxpayer's dollar that we spend in aid in that area.' But National was much more sceptical about aid than Labour. And recession made a difference too. In National's first year aid was cut back to 0.44 per cent of GNP and in 1979–81 stood at only 0.27 per cent.[62]

That the drive for aid by the third Labour government had a 'bubble' quality was suggested by the limited aid efforts of the fourth Labour government. Prosperity, not idealism, appeared to be the key. The ideals in the fourth Labour government in respect of the South Pacific were not so different from those of the third. But the economic circumstances were different and the political support that underpinned the anti-nuclear policy, with its limited financial implications, did not mobilise over aid to the same extent. By 1989 only three OECD countries had lower aid levels than New Zealand—Austria, Ireland and the United States. In 1990 New Zealand was second to bottom of those OECD countries that provided development assistance.[63]

The interplay of interest between the Pacific states and New Zealand bore many points of comparison with the unequal interplay of interest between New Zealand and Britain. In both cases the inequality was buttressed by a certain stability—neither New Zealand, nor the Pacific states, despite dissatisfaction with the pattern of the relationship, were dissatisfied enough, or had a clear enough sense of alternatives, to want to demolish or radically transform the structure.

Alignments with Pacific states: how radical?

We now turn to look at two ways in which New Zealand ties with the Pacific were used to underpin the notion of independence in *New Zealand* foreign policy. The first, to be discussed in this section, is the way in which New Zealand and Pacific countries aligned, often against the major powers. The second is the rhetoric of New Zealand's Pacific identity—which will be examined in the next and penultimate section.

The most striking and persistent alignment was that against the French, in respect of both nuclear testing and decolonisation. We have considered attitudes to French nuclear testing in our discussion of New Zealand nationalism and foreign policy in Chapter 8. French colonialism was another issue which united Pacific states with Australia and New Zealand. In 1980 New Zealand, even with a conservative government in office, was prepared to take on the cause of independence in the New Hebrides and subsequently New Caledonia. This was partly an expression of preoccupation with stability, as we have seen.

62   David McCraw, 'Kirk to Muldoon', pp. 648–9.
63   *Dominion*, 2 Feb. 1990; 12 July 1991.

Pre-independence difficulties in the Anglo-French territory of the New Hebrides became particularly pronounced in the first months of 1980. There were separatist movements on Espiritu Santo in the north and Tanna in the south. There were also political differences between the francophone and anglophone populations about representation in the future independent state. The New Hebrides had been an Anglo-French condominium, in which the Francophones dominated the government, elected with a two-thirds majority in the National Assembly in November 1979. New Zealand's involvement at this stage was peripheral: authority rested with the French and British governments and some of the difficulties stemmed in fact from their inability to concert their policies. Nonetheless in response to disturbances and to a British government statement, Talboys expressed at the beginning of June New Zealand's strong support for an independent New Hebrides and for the 'democratically elected' government, as it was carefully described in the statement, of New Zealand-educated Father Walter Lini and the Vanuaku Pati. Mr Talboys also wrote to Lini himself, expressing New Zealand's strong support for his government and for the emergence of an independent New Hebrides on 30 July, the date agreed to by the colonial powers.[64] Ironically, New Zealand clashed, as we have seen, with Vanuatu more than with any other state in the Pacific in the 1980s until the first Fiji coup.[65]

The independence of New Caledonia was a popular cause in New Zealand, even amongst the Pakeha population, who might have been expected to identify with the the population of French origin, the Caldoches, rather than with the indigenous Melanesians. But anti-French sentiment seems to have been stronger, although it did not so directly influence policy because of concern about Libya and the Soviet Union.

Alignments were established in respect of other issues too. The failure of the United States to ratify the Law of the Sea opened up a breach between it and the Forum states, including Australia and New Zealand. The United States did not recognise that highly migratory species—basically tuna—could be 'owned' as a resource by a country through whose waters they happened to pass, so the Americans were not prepared to recognise royalty agreements entered into between the government of such a country and fishing companies operating in its waters.[66]

The American stance was a major issue at the 1982 Forum. A lengthy resolution seeking a change in the American position was agreed on.[67] The resolution noted that the United States itself had asserted rights over billfish, another highly migratory species, within its fisheries zone. Muldoon himself in an earlier comment in June had expressed the hope that 'the present

---

[64] *NZFAR*, April-June 1980, pp. 47–48.
[65] See above, pp. 259–61.
[66] *NZFAR*, April-June 1982, p. 11.
[67] *NZFAR*, July-Sept. 1982, pp. 22–23.

American administration, or one of its successors, will take the enlightened view that the fishery resources of the Pacific should be recognised as the property of the island states which otherwise have so little'.

The tuna issue did have a political dimension, as Cooper noted in an address to an American audience. The Pacific island states, he pointed out, 'are sympathetic to western interests and ideals ... but they do wonder about American attitudes':

> The refusal of the American administration to sign the Law of the Sea convention has caused Polynesian and Micronesian people to ponder why pressure from multinationals interested in mining the seabed is successful. They seek recognition by deep-water fishing nations, including the United States, that they have the right to exploit the living resources of their own 200-mile economic zones. The most important of these are tuna. A recognition of the rights of these countries to exploit tuna resources is essential to the maintenance of goodwill.[68]

At the opening of the Law of the Sea convention for signing in December 1982 the New Zealand representative referred obliquely to the American position when he noted that the small Pacific states would 'only obtain the full benefit of their exclusive economic zones if other more powerful states are prepared to respect their international obligations in this regard'.[69] This issue was not fully resolved until the late 1980s.

The nuclear-waste issue was another on which the Pacific states and New Zealand found common ground. Talks were held with Japanese officials in August 1980 about plans for 'experimental' dumping of low-level radioactive waste in the north-western Pacific, 900 kilometres south-east of Tokyo. The Japanese were not seeking permission, they were offering reassurances about what they intended to do anyway. The 1981 Forum, unconvinced, issued a strong statement calling on Japan and the United States to 'store and dump their nuclear waste in their home countries rather than storing or dumping them in the Pacific'.[70] While not a major diplomatic issue at this time, it had the potential to become one, as environmental issues became increasingly sensitive and the pressures from countries like Japan and the United States became stronger. As with the Law of the Sea, this was a new kind of politics.

While on colonial and economic issues National and Labour took similar positions in the Pacific, Labour was more radical over the South Pacific nuclear-weapons-free zone. This was for New Zealand essentially an alliance issue, as we saw in our analysis of the 1974–75 debate about the zone. But Labour's pursuit of it did owe something to its belief that it was a Pacific issue as well as a wider expression of New Zealand's own anti-nuclear policy.

68   *NZFAR*, Oct.-Dec. 1982, p. 22.
69   *NZFAR*, Oct.-Dec. 1982, p. 58.
70   *NZFAR*, July-Sept. 1981, p. 61.

The signing of the Treaty of Rarotonga in 1986 was for New Zealand an act of solidarity with its smaller neighbours and of demarcation from the metropolitan nuclear powers, the United States, France and Britain, none of which would adhere to the treaty protocols when invited by the signatory states. Labour Cabinet Minister Helen Clark argued, unavailingly, that the United States should 'look at what is happening in the South Pacific with a benign inference that it is a corner of stability .... an area where it does not have to engage in direct controversy with the Soviet Union'.[71]

But can we deduce from this catalogue of instances of cooperation between Pacific countries and New Zealand that there is a radical 'Pacific' dimension to New Zealand's foreign policy? Probably not. We can in fact fit both the anti-French and the Law of the Sea and allied issues into the traditional idea of independence in foreign policy.

The position of New Zealand governments on colonial issues in particular was plainly not as radical as that of some Pacific states, notably Vanuatu. Neither the Muldoon, nor even the Lange government supported Vanuatu positions on New Caledonian independence. Both opposed proposals to seat Kanak (Melanesian) nationalist representatives at Forum meetings. Both saw independence in terms of self-determination for the New Caledonian population as a whole, rather than solely for Kanaks. As for the nuclear-weapons-free zone, by the early 1980s the notion almost had 'motherhood' status: 'New Zealand, together with other members of the South Pacific Forum, had subscribed to the idea of a nuclear weapons free zone as long ago as 1976 .... New Zealand and Australia should argue at the South Pacific Forum for the need to take a further step to realise this idea.'[72] It was notable too that Vanuatu did not sign the Treaty of Rarotonga because it was too limited an agreement—there was a boundary, in other words, on the left as well as the right.

The other New Zealand stances towards the Pacific, such as fishing and Law of the Sea issues, which account for its radical 'feel', are clearly classic interest-driven policies. The clashes with the United States over tuna, over the Law of the Sea, over nuclear waste, fit exactly into the pattern of New Zealand foreign relations we have come to expect and can be set alongside the protracted disputes in the nineteenth and early twentieth century about subsidised shipping and the American monopoly on the Honolulu/California routes, the contests about cable routes and the 1930s squabbles about mid-Pacific islands.[73]

---

71 Carolyn Stephenson, 'Interview with Helen Clark', *Bulletin of Concerned Asian Scholars*, 18/ 2 (April-June 1986), p. 86 (interview conducted Aug. 1985).
72 Ruth Richardson, *NZPD*, 453, p. 2452 (15 Sept. 1983).
73 See above, p. 50.

Independence and a Pacific identity: the rhetoric

... the freedom of thought possessed by people who had not themselves conquered those wretched foreign lands, but had it done for them by their forbears, and now took leave to make liberal thought the mode.[74]

It is with these elements in the pattern of New Zealand-Pacific relations in mind that it is most useful to look at the rhetoric of New Zealand in the Pacific, the way in which Pacific policy has been interpreted in terms of a new identity, in some instances given a radical gloss, and also in terms of an independence which is seen in evolutionary and progressive terms. So New Zealand has 'at last' become an independent Pacific power, has 'at last' acquired a Pacific identity. The present writer prefers to see the language used by New Zealanders to describe New Zealand-Pacific relations as a language of informal empire, the obverse of the language of independence in foreign policy used until the 1960s. The idea of a new Pacific identity in this respect becomes simply another device for framing the power relationship, much as Portugal once referred to itself as a Luso-African society, Spain as Ibero-American, Britain as maritime, France as committed to a *mission civilisatrice* in its overseas territories. The evidence of new identity overlooks the roots of New Zealand attitudes to the Pacific in nineteenth-century British colonial thinking about the region.

The argument that New Zealand's own identity was changing and that this underlined the change in foreign policy had two components. One was that New Zealand was losing its colonial character and becoming itself a 'Pacific nation'. This was essentially an argument about the identity of the population of European origin. Corner suggested in 1961 that 'just as the process by which New Zealanders lost touch with their own area contributed to the loss of our national self-confidence and sense of national identity, so a re-discovery of our role in the South Pacific will contribute to the process by which we are regaining our national confidence and re-discovering our unique identity as New Zealanders'.[75] The other related argument was that New Zealand, by confronting the Maori issue at home, and by opening its doors to migration from the Pacific, was changing its identity because the composition of its population was changing. Taken at its fullest extent Corner's advocacy would have involved fundamentally changing New Zealand identity—he recommended, for instance, unrestricted immigration from all Polynesian countries. For Corner this was what identity was about—'the renaissance of the Maori people is making New Zealand the chief country of Polynesia and is restoring our moral right to take a leading part in its affairs'.[76] As one politician

---

[74] Thomas Mann, *Joseph and His Brothers*, trans. H. T. Lowe-Porter. Harmondsworth, 1978, p. 560.
[75] Corner, 'New Zealand and the South Pacific', p. 132.
[76] Corner, 'New Zealand and the South Pacific, p. 150.

put it nearly a decade later, 'It has taken many years for us to realise that we are also South Pacific Islanders: that our home is here, much of our ancestry is here, and our future most definitely lies in this area.'[77]

Sometimes the two arguments were combined, that is, it would be argued that white New Zealanders had become more aware of, more attuned to the Pacific because of the immigration from Pacific countries. In addressing a UNESCO conference in Indonesia at the end of 1973, in a speech which departed from the prepared text, Kirk pointed out that

> a conference like this is invaluable to a country like my own because it is held in a country that is one of the richest in art and culture .... We have created wealth but we do not yet have the culture .... The New Zealand style was for a long time a European style, somewhat awkwardly adapted to the change of skies and atmosphere. The Polynesian part of our heritage worked steadily to transform the perceptions of the new arrivals, for the influence of the land and its setting could not be denied. But for a century or more that older heritage, that Polynesian heritage, was not generally recognised. Nor indeed were its links with and throughout the South Pacific, this archipelago [and beyond] .... Our eyes are open. We see ourselves as a society whose attitudes bear the imprint of our Pacific and Polynesian environment.[78]

And similarly, two decades later: 'Pakeha New Zealanders now look out on the world from our toehold in the South Pacific more confident than ever before of who we are and where we stand. The increasingly palpable presence among us of those who have joined us from our neighbouring islands in the Pacific is one valuable and continuous reminder that the Pacific is our home.'[79]

The present writer is sceptical both of the claim that Pakeha have changed their identity in this way and that New Zealand foreign policy has a distinctively Pacific orientation. It is true that the kind of 'kinship' politics that Muldoon and to some extent Lange, and other Labour politicians like Prebble and Moore, have practised *vis à vis* the Pacific does represent something new in New Zealand Pacific policies. It certainly influences the concentration of the aid vote on the 'nearest neighbours'—that part of the Pacific including Kiribati and Tuvalu, Fiji, Tonga, Samoa and Cook Islands.

But it would be difficult to argue that a *Pacific* identity governed New Zealanders' approach, or that of their government, to the region as a whole. Public attitudes are easier to discern. In 1983 the Nuclear Free and Independent Pacific conference faced major difficulties in staying united because of a difference in emphasis between those for whom the important

77 Duncan McIntyre, *NZFAR*, Jan. 1971, pp. 9–15.
78 *NZFAR*, Jan. 1974, pp. 24–25.
79 Peter Simpson, *Metro*, June 1990, p. 115. And another, similar, comment by Lange, *NZFAR*, Oct.-Dec. 1987, p. 9.

issue was indigenous rights and those for whom it was the anti-nuclear campaign. White New Zealanders and Pacific Islanders had different identities, rooted in different historical circumstances and experiences. In 1985 Witi Ihimaera spoke movingly at the Otago Foreign Policy School of the need for New Zealand-Aotearoa to recognise its 'descent' from the Pacific and to reach out to Hawaii, Tahiti, Samoa, Tonga—the Polynesian family. To him this was the starting point for any truly independent New Zealand foreign policy, because it would be an independence that would reach back before Pakeha colonisation had taken the country in a different direction. Kinship was the necessary basis for policy.[80]

Ihimaera was calling for change. Institutional change did not occur. Nor were there sufficient Maori and/or Pacific Island senior policymakers for it to occur. And the public had not shifted to a Pacific identity either. Whereas 54 per cent of New Zealanders polled in 1985 were prepared for New Zealand to commit armed forces in the event of an attack on Britain, only 42 per cent were prepared to make the same commitment in respect of Cook Islands, Niue and Tokelau and only 36 per cent in respect of an independent South Pacific country.[81] It seems that in the 1980s, for white New Zealand at least, the Pacific was not just 'overseas'—in some respects it was further away than Britain.

The same difference manifested itself in 1990-91. At no stage during the 1990 sesquicentennial celebrations was it officially proposed that New Zealand invite other Pacific countries to play some special role in the celebrations, as might befit other 'members of a family'. It was the inaction, the silence, that was revealing. In contrast a year later at the silver jubilee celebrations of the Maori Queen, Dame Arikinui Te Atairangikaahu, representatives of Pacific countries were accorded pride of place:

> Let me first of all extend a personal greeting to my special guests from afar. From those fragrant lands of our own antiquity scattered like gleaming pearls across the [Pacific]. Malietoa Tanumafili, Head of State from Western Samoa, Samoa silasila, bountiful, beautiful, vast and venerable; Queen Haialevalu Mata'aho of the gracious truly friendly isles of Tonga; Prime Minister Ratu Sir Kamisese Mara and Adi Lady Lala of Fiji, country of many islands and many blessings; Pomare Ari'i of Tahiti, where the scented breezes drift above a dancing sea; Kekaulike Kawananakoa, from faraway Hawaii; remote yet close to my heart; Geoffrey Henry, Prime Minister of the Cook Islands, dainty jewels upon an endless ocean; President Dowiyogo, of that tiny island treasure, Nauru of rich natural resources; Pa Ariki of Rarotonga, a

---

80 Witi Ihimaera, 'New Zealand as a Pacific Nation', *New Directions*, pp. 122-37; see also Ihimaera, 'The Long Dark Tea-Time of the South', in Ramesh Thakur, ed., *The South Pacific: Problems, Issues and Prospects*. London, 1991, pp. 133-44.

81 *Defence and Security: What New Zealanders Want*. Annex, p. 20. Another contrast: 74 per cent of Pacific Islanders thought New Zealand should make a 'great deal of effort' to be on good terms with the United States, compared with 65 per cent of Pakeha and 44 per cent of Maori (p. 41).

special blossom on our family tree; and to my distinguished guests from Aotearoa. Tena kotou. So often in these last twenty-five years we have been guests in your countries and enjoyed your generous hospitality. Thank you for being with us on this special day.[82]

The Ministry of External Relations and Trade played an important part in arranging these visits. But the Pakeha majority were not involved. Their Pacific identity is as Anglo-Celtic, not Polynesian, Pacific Islanders, an identity they had possessed for some time. A change had occurred—the same change that occurred in respect of New Zealand foreign relations generally. In the 1960s New Zealand external relations ceased to be primarily mediated through Britain. In the case of the Pacific, that meant to some extent inheriting Britain's role. New Zealand assumed an old identity rather than forged a new one.

The impact of the Fiji coups

The Fiji coups in 1987, more than any other event, transformed the framework of New Zealand-Pacific relations. The coups brought to the surface the differences between Pacific and New Zealand political cultures. They made it clear that power was an element in Pacific politics and they shattered the notion of a 'Pacific Way', at least the meaning that had attached to that phrase in New Zealand. They made it less plausible for New Zealand to talk about its Pacific identity as a synonym for an identity and outlook shared with the Pacific states.

The divergence in response to the coups between Pacific leaders on the one hand and Australian and New Zealand leaders on the other was very marked. From the governments of the other Pacific countries, all in the hands of populations of indigenous origin, it was the silence that spoke loudly: in the case of New Zealand and Australia, white liberal sympathies were engaged on the side of civil liberties and the Indian population, were angered by the offence done to democratic procedures. Lange himself was characteristically vigorous and articulate in his defence of Indian/human rights. The main exception to this was opinion in the Maori community, which had some general sympathy for the position of the indigenous Fijians, and in some instances expressed strong support for the aims of the coup leaders.[83]

The coups made the power relations operating within Pacific states manifest. What about New Zealand and Australia? Would they show the mailed fist beneath the velvet glove? Would they intervene to protect democracy? Intervention was bad, democracy was good—that was the

---

[82] *Nga Kauwae*, May/June 1991.
[83] Roderic Alley, 'The 1987 Military Coups in Fiji: The Regional Implications', paper presented to the NZ Political Studies Association Conference, May 1989. A parallel with New Zealand government attitudes to New Caledonia can be discerned.

theory. What happened when it broke down? There was a certain irony in liberal public opinion confronting an issue which had preoccupied the British and the Americans before them—did the means justify the ends?

New Zealand and Australia did not intervene. Liberal sentiment played a part—there was a recognition of the ethical perils of military intervention, however noble the cause. But there were practical considerations too. New Zealand in particular had very limited ability to respond to the coups militarily, even had it considered such a course of action. This was not just a matter of the limited logistical capability to deploy substantial force at a distance. It was a recognition that Fiji was not Grenada or even the Falklands —Viti Levu alone, the main island, was a terrain of rugged country, extending the distance from Napier to Wanganui and with a half million population. And the Fiji army, well-trained—by New Zealand—did not have a tradition of capitulation.[84]

Moreover, while liberalism might have grieved at the practical consequence—the coups were not reversed—realpolitik coped. Stability was still a goal. For all that the Fiji coup toppled a constituted government, it did not enhance the influence of an undesirable outside power as had events in Vanuatu. The newly elected Labour government in Fiji had taken an anti-nuclear stance parallel to New Zealand's, much to the chagrin of the United States; the coup leaders reversed this.[85] But the restoration of United States influence, despite the tensions between Wellington and Washington over New Zealand's anti-nuclear policy, was not regarded in the same light as an extension of Libyan or Soviet influence. And a preparedness to deal with the post-coup regimes acknowledged also the opportunities that were otherwise left open to French diplomacy in the region.[86]

In the aftermath of the Fiji coups some of the rhetoric on the Pacific became more cautious, particularly in government, where the difficulties involved in promoting values and ideologies more popular in New Zealand than in the Pacific were evident.[87] Policy shifted along the spectrum from dissent to interest. The peace movement was disappointed at the decision of the fourth Labour government to sign a frigate contract with Australia in August 1989 and a review of Pacific policy was promised as a way of demonstrating that the government would not allow policy to be militarised by the back door. From such a perspective a 'Pacific' policy and a 'peace' policy should be insepar-able. But the review did not make radical recommendations. Instead it stressed that 'New Zealand policy towards the region should be guided by

---

84 *Dominion*, 10 April 1992, has discussion of the issue of deploying New Zealand forces in Fiji after the first coup.
85 Ramesh Thakur, 'Nuclear Issues in the South Pacific', in *The South Pacific: Emerging Security Issues and US Policy*. Washington, 1990, p. 48.
86 This point is discussed in Alley, 'The 1987 Military Coups in Fiji', p. 18.
87 See, for example, Minister of Foreign Affairs, Russell Marshall, 'A South Pacific Role for New Zealand', *NZERR*, Jan.-March 1989, pp. 11-17, especially pp. 14-16.

clear and explicit considerations of national interest . . . . New Zealand should [respond constructively to the needs of Pacific Island countries] not just out of a sense of altruism or moral obligation . . . but because it is in our interests to do so.'[88] Perhaps equally revealingly, the most specific of the review's sixty-two recommendations were that ministerial contact with Fiji be restored and RNZAF surveillance flights from Fiji be resumed.[89] As one perceptive commentator on Pacific affairs put it, New Zealand and Australian responses to the coups 'indicated a preference [for] the habits and practices of established national interest diplomacy. No longer unique, the South Pacific was now yet another arena of external relations in which the use of force, calculations of immediate state interest and the use of security intelligence provided an immediate backdrop of assessment.'[90]

The 1987 coups challenged existing notions of relations in the Pacific just as the ANZUS crisis in 1985 challenged relations across it. The diplomacy and politics of aid, trade, aid, migration, kinship and interdependence were not altogether displaced, but conflicts were exposed to view, as were the different meanings that attached to the idea of independence. The task of building a true Pacific community was proving complex. A language of common identity could not always explain, and might indeed obscure, the nature of New Zealand-Pacific relations.

[88] Report of the South Pacific Policy Review Group, *Towards a Pacific Island Community*. Wellington, 1990, pp. 4–5.
[89] *Towards a Pacific Island Community*, pp. 241–2. The review rejected however the resumption of military cooperation in advance of the restoration of parliamentary government.
[90] Alley, 'The 1987 Military Coups In Fiji', p. 15.

12. The ANZUS crisis and independence in New Zealand foreign policy

For many, independence in foreign policy in the 1980s became synonymous with the anti-nuclear policy; even more than in the past, therefore, the word acquired opaque qualities, used so often and in so rhetorical, even ritualistic— our ... 'nuclear-free-and-independent-foreign-policy'—a fashion, that its particular meaning and historical context were obscured. In this final chapter we want to examine the meaning of independence in relation to the anti-nuclear policy. The Labour Party took office in 1984 committed to keeping nuclear weapons and nuclear power out of New Zealand, a commitment which in due course brought it into collision with the United States and other allies. Not only, however, did the Labour government refuse to modify its policy; in 1990 the National Party adopted the same anti-nuclear stance. By that time 'independence' in New Zealand foreign policy had become virtually synonymous with the anti-nuclear policy.

What kind of independence was this? This episode, more than any other, not excepting the exchange crisis in 1939, made explicit the role of power in New Zealand's foreign relations (as distinct from those of the Pacific states). We look first at the course of the crisis, then analyse the Labour government's policies, the anti-nuclear movement, and public opinion generally.

The course of the crisis

Afghanistan did not become a second Vietnam for the United States: indeed quite the reverse, it became a Vietnam, an unwinnable war, for the Soviet Union, with the United States and its allies able to witness the discomfiture of the rival superpower. To understand the 1984–86 crisis in relations between New Zealand and its allies, particularly the United States, we need rather to keep in mind other developments. The early 1980s were characterised in both Europe and the United States by a surge of anti-nuclear sentiment that provided the essential context for the New Zealand movement in its early years. The intensification of Cold War tensions, particularly in the aftermath of the Soviet intervention in Afghanistan, and American disillusion with détente formed an important backdrop; so too did the election of Ronald Reagan to the presidency of the United States, with his determination to achieve superiority in nuclear weapons over the Soviet Union, at the end of 1980. Very quickly, the early 1980s movement acquired a greater significance than the 1950s and early 1960s disarmament movement. In the United States it fixed on the nuclear-freeze proposal, in Europe on opposition to the deployment of Cruise missiles by NATO.[1]

We have seen that there was an active anti-nuclear movement in New Zealand in the 1970s. And if Labour had won the 1981 election—and it did receive more of the popular vote than National—there would have been an alliance crisis, as there was in fact in 1984. But those three years made a big difference to the locus of the anti-nuclear and peace movements in New Zealand life and politics. The New Zealand movement was responsive to the increased activity overseas, while at home a particular trigger remained the visits of American nuclear-powered vessels to local ports: at such times public opinion on the issue became both vocal and polarised. In March 1981 Devonport in Auckland, the site of a navy base, declared itself nuclear-free; a year later another three local authorities had followed suit.[2] On the eve of Anzac Day 1982, the Catholic bishops issued a very strong statement of opposition to nuclear weapons and to any defence that relied on them. On 29 April, Labour M.P. Richard Prebble introduced into Parliament a Nuclear Free Zone (New Zealand) bill. Prebble had introduced such a bill in 1976: this time he dropped the provision banning nuclear-powered vessels in an attempt to secure National Party support for the measure—unsuccessfully.[3] At the Labour Party's annual conference in May, against the backdrop of another visit by *Truxtun*, Rowling declared that 'nuclear weapons will not be allowed into New Zealand ports under a Labour government, and that's the message'.[4] Prebble's modification of his bill, and Rowling's stress on weapons rather than ships testified to a shift in public concerns, one linked to increased Cold War tensions. Fear of nuclear war as much as of nuclear disaster preoccupied the public mind in the early 1980s in contrast to the more explicitly environmental concerns of the 1970s: 'the concern currently taking greater hold throughout the country is not, as the Minister of Foreign Affairs, Mr Cooper, might have us think, confined to paranoic freaks and the like. It is more a genuine and growing fear on the part of ordinary people of what could

[1] The first big demonstration in Germany took place in late 1981. For one discussion of the impact of the movement, see Andrei Markovits, 'Americanism and Anti-Americanism in Germany: Some Thoughts on a Controversial Topic'. Paper presented to the 1983 Europeanists Conference, Washington DC, Oct. 1983. Markovits noted that sentiment against missile deployment in Germany could not, judging from public opinion polls, be equated with anti-Americanism; *EP*, 17 May 1982, referred to the 'swelling tide of anti-nuclear sentiment'.

[2] Jennifer Hellen, *New Outlook*, Oct.-Nov. 1983, pp. 16–21.

[3] *NZPD*, 443, pp. 654, 658 (29 April 1982).

[4] *EP*, 12 May 1982.

happen.'[5] When the *Texas* visited in 1983, letters to one metropolitan paper ran 2:1 in favour of port visits.[6] But by September 1983 another thirty-seven local authorities had declared themselves nuclear-free.[7]

More than in the 1970s, anti-nuclear sentiment informed and popularised critiques of ANZUS. The Australian election in March 1983 probably helped: some opinion in the Australian Labor Party wanted a change and as a result of Australian pressure there was a 'review' of ANZUS in 1983. In August 1983 Jack Hunn, who had publicised his views about non-alignment in 1968, wrote again in the *Listener* questioning the worth of ANZUS. A revised edition of the 1977 publication, *Alternatives to ANZUS*, was published, with an introduction by Roderic Alley. That introduction made it clear that it was the preoccupation with nuclear weapons that was at the heart of the 'ANZUS debate': 'This publication is intended as part of the continuing debate that New Zeaand faces in a world of colossal and burgeoning armaments yet declining real security. An appropriate focus for New Zealand involves this country's membership within the ANZUS treaty arrangement, originally negotiated in 1951.'[8]

We have seen that changing formulations of interest affected government thinking about ANZUS. The ideological defence increased in salience, suggesting that the interest arguments were perceived to be less convincing. The introduction to *Defence Review 1983* stressed that 'defence policies arise out of the deepest assumptions and principles on which society is built . . . . as between today's contending ideologies we are not neutral . . . . The basic stance of New Zealand—a Western country committed to the democratic way of ordering our lives and to the maintenance of active linkages with the major centres of influence in the United States, Europe and Asia—has not altered.' The senior levels of the Ministry of Foreign Affairs were committed to ANZUS and the ideological assumptions that underpinned it: 'those of us who prefer American to Soviet influence in the world depend on the American nuclear arsenal—the world being the way it is—to keep that influence predominant.'[9] And the Minister a year later said, 'I don't see how New Zealand can be evenhanded as between the Soviet Union and the United States. We are a democracy, we have an independent judiciary, we have a free press, we are one of the free societies in the world. We have these things in common with Australia, the United States, and other Western countries. We share with all of them a common interest in preserving our way of life and resisting the expansion of Soviet influence.'[10]

5   *EP*, 30 April 1982.
6   *EP*, 10 Aug. 1983.
7   Hellen, *New Outlook*, p. 16.
8   Roderic Alley, 'The Alternatives to ANZUS: A Commentary' in Roderic Alley, ed., *Alternatives to ANZUS*. Rvsd edition, Auckland, 1984, p. 1.
9   Secretary of Foreign Affairs, Merwyn Norrish, *NZFAR*, April-June 1983, p. 60.
10   *NZFAR*, April-June 1984, p. 8.

The frequency with which ideological arguments were advanced contrasted with the limited force of the arguments grounded in interest. As in the mid 1970s, protection from the Soviet Navy was one: 'there is full recognition that from Cam Ranh Bay in Vietnam to the Indian Ocean a Soviet fleet of great proportion exists.' But for those in the anti-nuclear movement another 'interest' was more potent: New Zealand was threatened by the nuclear weapons of its ally, not by the navy of a distant adversary.[11]

The Labour Party leadership nonetheless still wanted, as in the 1970s, to reconcile anti-nuclearism and ANZUS, rather than using one to demolish the other. David Lange, leader of the party in succession to Rowling from February 1983, made a number of efforts to soften the party's nuclear ban. The new Australian Labor government had adopted a policy of accepting the passage of nuclear-powered ships through any South Pacific nuclear-weapons-free zone that might be established. Lange floated the idea that the party policy should be changed to allow nuclear-propelled warships into the country and the nuclear-weapons-free zone, believing it should be possible 'to distinguish the need to guard against the immediate dangers of nuclear reactors, and our wish to counter the threat posed by political decisions to build, deploy and threaten the use of nuclear weapons'.[12]

The only immediate result of the Lange initiative, which had overlooked the environmental origins of the anti-nuclear movement, was to bring down the wrath of the party activists. The strength of party feeling on the issue was clear. Opening the party's Auckland regional conference in May 1983, the President, Jim Anderton, said that 'a nuclear free Pacific must mean exactly that. No nuclear powered or nuclear armed warships must have New Zealand ports as a base, no matter what flag they fly.' According to the *Herald* reporter, conference delegates greeted Anderton's reaffirmation 'with cheers and prolonged applause'.[13]

In February 1984 Lange visited the United States and had talks with officials at a time when he was still exploring the possibility of steering the party away from what might be a confrontation with the United States if it won the forthcoming election. Despite conference votes in 1982 and 1983 in favour of unilateral withdrawal from alliances with nuclear powers, the Labour leadership continued to be committed to ANZUS: Labour entered the election campaign in 1984 with a commitment not to pull out of the alliance, but to renegotiate it on an anti-nuclear basis. Rowling, now the party's foreign affairs spokesperson, argued that if the Americans found themselves 'unable to

---

11   Minister of Foreign Affairs, Warren Cooper, *NZFAR*, Oct.-Dec. 1982, p. 21. For questioning comment on the Soviet threat, see Andrew Mack, 'Is There a Soviet Threat?', *Peace Dossier*, 3 (July 1982, repr. May 1983), Vietnam Associates for Peace Studies; Walden Bello, Peter Hayes and Lyuba Zarsky, 'The Nuclear Peril in the Pacific', paper presented to the Alternatives to ANZUS Conference. Wellington, June 1984.
12   Lange, *Nuclear Free*, p. 33.
13   *NZH*, 14 May 1983.

accept some of our basic requirements, such as our stance on the nuclear issue, it would be they not us who would be frustrating an agreement for progress and peace'.[14]

The election was precipitated unexpectedly after National M.P. Marilyn Waring had refused to vote against anti-nuclear legislation introduced by the Labour Party (the government had a parliamentary majority of only one). While anti-nuclear sentiment was not widespread in the National Party, anti-nuclear stances had been adopted by two other parties besides Labour: Social Credit and the New Zealand Party. Both were more conservative than Labour. The 'Beyond ANZUS' conference held during the election campaign demonstrated the range and the extent of the challenge to foreign policy orthodoxy, with more than 600 delegates attending.[15]

The transition period after Labour's election victory in July 1984 brought its own drama, with uncomfortable Americans and Australians attending the ANZUS Council meeting in Wellington with outgoing Foreign Affairs Minister Warren Cooper, while the newly elected Labour government proclaimed both its determination to implement an anti-nuclear policy and to retain the alliance.

The South Pacific Forum, meeting in Tuvalu at the end of August, reached agreement on promoting the nuclear-weapons-free zone, despite the different emphases of the Australian and New Zealand Labour governments, New Zealand's determination to ban nuclear warships from its ports giving its policy a more radical edge than Australia's.[16] The September 1984 Labour Party conference again called for New Zealand to withdraw from alliances with nuclear powers, but Lange reaffirmed the government's decision to stay in ANZUS. In October, New Zealand hosted TRIAD 84, an ANZUS exercise, the largest peacetime one to date in New Zealand.[17]

Crisis erupted in the new year.[18] At the end of January the United States announced that New Zealand had declined a request to receive a visit from the USS *Buchanan*, on the grounds that it could carry nuclear weapons. There is a strong supposition that the Americans expected the request to be accepted.[19]

[14] Quoted in *Alternatives to ANZUS*, v. 2, pp. 18–19.
[15] Christine Dann, 'Introduction', in Barbara Harford, ed., *Beyond ANZUS: Alternatives for Australia, New Zealand and the Pacific*. Auckland, 1984, p. 3.
[16] See press coverage, 25 Aug.–1 Sept. 1984; *NZFAR*, July–Sept. 1984, pp. 36–38.
[17] Dann, p. 4.
[18] The most thorough near-contemporary and informed accounts of these and related issues are found in Stuart McMillan, *Neither Confirm Nor Deny*. Wellington, 1987 and Roderic Alley, 'ANZUS and the Nuclear Issue', in Jonathan Boston and Martin Holland, *The Fourth Labour Government: Radical Politics in New Zealand*. Auckland, 1987, esp. pp. 202–6.
[19] The *Buchanan* had visited Auckland, to almost no protest, in 1979. For an account of the diplomacy preceding the fall out in February, see Kevin Clements, *Back From The Brink*, pp. 131–5. It is not possible to establish from Lange's own account, *Nuclear Free*, pp. 79–80, what the United States administration could reasonably have expected to be the response to a request to allow a naval vessel to visit New Zealand.

It is probable that some of the Cabinet at least wanted to find a way of reconciling American wishes with the anti-nuclear policy. But sentiment in the party and in the peace movement was a powerful influence on caucus and on the government: 10,000 demonstrated in Auckland within two days of the news of the possible *Buchanan* visit.[20]

A crisis that had arisen in large part because one party, New Zealand, did not believe in power in foreign policy, now became an open conflict with the other party, the United States, which did. The United States severed all intelligence and military ties with New Zealand immediately. Officers on courses in the United States suddenly found themselves on the way home; regular diplomatic consultations in Washington ended abruptly—New Zealand's access to the State Department was limited to the middle ranks of Department officers; access to the White House and the Pentagon (Defence Department) ceased. New Zealand's decisions were not put in any kind of local perspective; they were challenges to American policy and were handled according to the book. The Navy in particular was determined not to countenance the New Zealand decision, and it found allies in the Pentagon and the State Department. Many in the administration felt bitter with Lange and had a sense of betrayal—which is perhaps understandable when Lange himself wrote retrospectively of the pre-*Buchanan* period, 'My advisers and I had one goal in common. We wanted to see an American vessel in a New Zealand port.'[21]

The United States wanted to ensure that 'New Zealanditis' did not become contagious. It feared that New Zealand's stand could 'refuel the anti-nuclear movement in western Europe where West German, British, Dutch and Belgian activists are trying to bar the continued deployment of United States medium-range Cruise and Pershing II missiles'.[22]

Australia's response to the crisis followed a similar pattern to that of the United States, except that New Zealand was more important to Australia than it was to the United States, and this moderated the force of its response. Initially though, there was emotion and ill-feeling at the official level, which was not unconnected with the difficulties that Australian Prime Minister Bob Hawke faced at the time over American missile testing in the Tasman Sea. However, Hawke made publicly clear to Lange at the end of January what the government already knew, that Australia would be upset if New Zealand took its anti-nuclear policy to the point of a breach with the United States. It was clear in Hawke's eyes that it was New Zealand, not the United States, which had to compromise. Hawke's (coincidental) visit to Washington early in

20 *New Zealand Times*, 2 March 1986 (*sic*); Clements says 15,000.
21 Lange, *Nuclear Free*, p. 80.
22 *Time*, 18 Feb. 1985; see also *EP*, 12 Oct. 1984, 'Domino fear in ANZUS collapse'; and comments by Marilyn Waring, quoting confidential sources within the Reagan Administration and Congress, *EP*, 7 Aug. 1985: 'The strongest possible representations were made to the Administration by the West German, British and Japanese Governments to make an example of New Zealand.'

February underlined the differences between the Australian and New Zealand positions. At the same time Australia made it clear, and New Zealand welcomed this, that the trans-Tasman link would not be affected by the dispute between New Zealand and the United States if at all possible.[23]

At no point did it prove possible to re-establish the previous alliance relationship. The United States would not budge on its 'neither confirm nor deny' policy. New Zealand would not abandon its anti-nuclear stance. The New Zealand government continued, however, to formulate its positions as one concerned solely with the matter of nuclear weapons, not with the alliance as a whole. The Prime Minister again resisted calls from a Labour Party conference to adopt a non-aligned stance and withdraw from ANZUS. The government did indicate that it would introduce legislation to make New Zealand nuclear free. Clause 9 of the bill said that the Prime Minister might grant approval for warship access only 'if he is satisfied that the warships will not be carrying any nuclear explosive devices upon their entry into the internal waters of New Zealand'.[24] The United States refused to discuss the bill, but Pentagon and State Department officials were quoted as saying, 'if the legislation proceeds our defence obligations will be effectively terminated'.[25] Hearings were held on the bill through 1986, and it became law in June 1987. A Public Advisory Committee on Disarmament and Arms Control was established to advise the Prime Minister, *inter alia*, on the implementation of the Act, but responsibility for decisions rested with the Prime Minister.[26]

Lange and the American Secretary of State George Shultz met at Manila in July 1986, but agreed to part as 'friends, not allies'.[27] In 1989 Lange suggested in a speech at Yale University that New Zealand should formally withdraw from ANZUS as its membership in the alliance was now notional. The idea was firmly rejected by his Cabinet colleagues. Three months later Lange resigned and was replaced as Prime Minister by Geoffrey Palmer. Late in 1989 New Zealand opposed a UN General Assembly resolution deploring United States military intervention in Panama and the overthrow of its leader, Manuel Noriega.[28] On 1 March 1990, Mike Moore, Minister of Foreign Affairs and Overseas Trade, met James Baker, Secretary of State in the Bush Administration, the first such high-level contact since the Manila meeting. 'I don't think it makes very good sense to continue a ban on high level contacts

---

23 See, for instance, the strong statement by Foreign Minister Bill Hayden, *EP*, 14 Feb. 1985 and report from Canberra, *EP*, 6 March 1985: 'Hawke is unlikely to accede to growing Opposition demands to take a hard line with Mr Lange over New Zealand's refusal to allow visits by nuclear-capable American warships'. See also *EP*, 14 Aug. 1986, 'New Zealand-Australia military link holding fast'.
24 Michael Pugh, *The ANZUS Crisis, Nuclear Visiting and Deterrence*. Cambridge, 1989, p. 145.
25 Clements, *Back From the Brink*, pp. 143-4.
26 *EP*, 26 Nov., 11 Dec. 1985.
27 All countries that were neither allies nor enemies were friends in the eyes of the United States.
28 *NZEAR*, Oct.-Dec. 1989, pp. 58-59; *Dominion*, 2 March 1990.

other than military intelligence', Baker had averred during a Senate hearing the previous day.[29] Concerned that its support for the repeal of the anti-nuclear legislation might affect its performance in the coming election, National committed itself later in March to unqualified support for the anti-nuclear policy.

Before concluding this outline it is useful to assess the influence of a number of factors which either coloured or set boundaries to the dispute. Firstly, personality played a significant part in exacerbating the dispute. The atmosphere between Lange and most of the senior Americans involved in the episode, including George Shultz, was not good. Many of the Americans took a personal dislike to Lange and had no interest in moderating the Administration's stance while he remained in charge. Some of the acerbity with which the conflict was flavoured can be attributed to this element.[30]

Secondly, the dispute looks titanic viewed through the New Zealand end of the telescope, a view station in which differences between small and larger ally had always been insignificant. Viewed through the lens of another ally (or for that matter the United States itself), it presents a different picture. We can see many parallels between New Zealand and other alliance members in the 1980s. Spain had a hotly contested referendum on NATO membership in 1988; Iceland was, and long had been, a member of NATO but with no military installations of its own; Greece faced major controversy over American bases; Ireland retained in the 1980s its combination of neutrality with ideological alignment with the Western alliance: historically it had viewed British rule in Northern Ireland much as New Zealand did the American nuclear-armed ships, but could do less about it. France continued to abjure NATO defence cooperation while maintaining political cooperation, as it had since 1966. Germany and Japan, with their powerful peace movements, provided other parallels with New Zealand. The attitude of Norway and Denmark to nuclear-weapons visits was cautious.[31]

Thirdly, while the United States reacted harshly, it did set clear boundaries to the 'punishment' that New Zealand was to receive.[32] Ironically, by taking action in the sphere of military cooperation, it both harmed the constituency in New Zealand most committed to cooperation with the United States, namely the defence establishment, and also rendered it less able to perform the tasks which the United States ostensibly claimed were important to it: 'American reprisals ... reduce American and allied regional capabilities'.[33]

[29] *NZEAR*, Jan.-Feb. 1990, p. 4.
[30] McMillan, *Neither Confirm Nor Deny*, p. 113, is excellent on this.
[31] McMillan, *Neither Confirm Nor Deny*, pp. 65-67, looks at Norway, Iceland and Japan.
[32] Maybe taking *Time*'s observation to heart: 'Since Lange has the general support of 70 per cent of his countrymen, the United States might have a lot to lose by trying to turn the screws too tightly' (18 Feb. 1985).
[33] Henry Albinski, 'United States Security Interests and the New Zealand/ANZUS Problem'. Submission to United States House of Representatives Subcommittee on East Asia and the Pacific, April 1986, pp. 4-5.

The New Zealand foreign service, in some parts of which there was strong support for participation in the alliance, also suffered from the freeze on high-level contacts with the Americans and the effect this had on relations with other allies, in particular the Australians—the British and the Canadian governments allowed a greater flow of information to New Zealand, at least informally. Further, the United States did not impose trade sanctions on New Zealand. Although some of the more hawkish elements in the Administration and in Congress talked in such terms, it never became policy.[34]

These 'mitigating circumstances' are important, and certainly give the dispute a limited character from the United States perspective. But in terms of our discussion they are not decisive. New Zealand's conception of independence had been so intermingled with ideas of collaboration, with membership in a wider community of nations, that what might have been a limited clash for another country had major ramifications. It was also true both that New Zealand had gone significantly further than any other United States ally and that the United States had no strategic or economic incentive to take special care with New Zealand: it could act decisively and know that it would not suffer any consequences.

This then is the outline of the crisis. We now want to analyse the components of the New Zealand position, and of New Zealand opinion. We will use the familiar categories of dissent and interest, and will also consider the role of realism and nationalism in the dispute; we will derive from this exercise a conclusion about the meaning—or meanings—of independence in foreign policy at the end of the 1980s.

Dissent

While the conflict revealed a world of power, the government expended considerable energy in rejecting the radical label, both in word and deed. The pattern of dissent that triggered the crisis had strong moderate as well as more radical origins and it was the former that meant the government could adhere to the policy, despite the challenge to the United States, without suffering electoral damage.

The notion that the anti-nuclear policy was a pro-Soviet policy had some

[34]   Hugh Nevill, 'No retaliation, no help', *EP*, 7 Feb. 1985; 'Senator moves for trade curbs on New Zealand', *Press*, 8 Feb. 1985; 'US threats to trade seen as scare-mongering', *Press*, 9 Feb. 1985; 'Hit New Zealand economy, Reagan advised', *EP*, 20 Jan. 1989: this last refers to revelations in Lehmann, *Command of the Sea*. Navy Secretary Lehmann collaborated with Defence Secretary Caspar Weinberger in putting proposals forward for economic sanctions against New Zealand in late 1986, after New Zealand had passed its anti-nuclear legislation but they were, according to Lehmann, denounced at an interdepartmental meeting as 'needlessly provocative'; 'Rowling recalls row with Cheney', *Dominion Sunday Times*, 26 March 1989: Rowling on Congressman Cheney's determination to proceed with trade ban legislation but also a subsequent assurance that the legislation would not proceed: 'I will put it into one end of the churn, I won't seek any co-sponsors and it won't come out the other end.'

currency at the time of the crisis, but it was mostly a matter of rhetoric on the part of critics of the policy. 'This socialist Government', said one letter to the editor at the peak of the crisis in February 1985, had to explain why it took such pains to 'antagonise the USA, Australia, South Africa, trusted traditional old friends and at the same time ignore the cruelties, inhumanities and territorial ambitions of Soviet Russia.'[35] For Jim Sprott, leader of Peace Through Security, which organised a petition seeking a referendum on the government's anti-nuclear stance, the peace movement was the result of Soviet subversion, in New Zealand and worldwide.[36]

National Party politicians stressed during the crisis the ideological dimensions of the dispute, with Muldoon charging that Lange had been anti-American ever since he had been refused a visa by the United States because he worked for an Auckland law firm one of whose clients was the Communist Party, with M.P. Norman Jones claiming the government was playing into the hands of the Soviet Union.[37] 'I am saddened', said Sue Wood, President of the National Party, 'that those nations congratulating us now are the Soviet Union, the People's Republic of China, and Vanuatu. Where are our friends? Where are our allies? .... The ANZUS Treaty is not only the pivot of the New Zealand defence system, it is also an expression of unity with Australia, the United States and the western world.'[38] One article late in 1985 portrayed National's Deputy Leader, Jim Bolger, 'stumping' National Party branches painting a picture of a gleeful Kremlin rubbing its hands over the ANZUS row.[39]

Some Americans responded in similar fashion. Secretary of State George Shultz, while telling Congress that the United States did not intend to over-react and turn New Zealand from an ally into an enemy, stressed that 'with the Soviet presence in Vietnam ... and the extension of their influence ... in Cambodia, the Soviet presence in that part of the world has grown very greatly'.[40] The American Ambassador, H. Monroe Browne, located the alliance within the framework of the Second World War and America's own abandonment of isolationism—'we recognised that if freedom was not defended where it was already under attack ... then what remained of freedom thereafter would, at best, be limited in its range and duration, and hollow in its meaning'. Monroe Browne went on to explain how the failure of the Soviet Union to cooperate after the war and its ability to frustrate the workings of the United Nations meant that the 'United States and other Free World countries established a series of alliances for mutual security, spanning

---

35 *EP*, 13 Feb. 1985.
36 *EP*, 14 March 1985.
37 *NZPD*, reported in *EP*, 13 March 1985.
38 *EP*, 14 Feb. 1985.
39 *New Outlook*, Nov.-Dec. 1985, p. 36.
40 *EP*, 21 Feb. 1985.

much of the globe'.[41] For some of the right-wing think tanks in Washington such as the Heritage Foundation, and also within the Administration, the New Zealand government was simply 'soft on Communism': speeches by the President of the FOL, Jim Knox, in Eastern Europe were seen as possible indicators of the government's own stance, as was Lange's attitude to the Vietnam War.[42]

But the Labour government was not a left-wing government—indeed it was more right-wing than any Labour government in the country's history. Just to be sure, it made a point of distancing itself from the Soviet Union. Again there were precedents from the past. Rowling had always stressed Labour's anti-Soviet credentials: 'we don't want them in our part of the world in any shape or form, nuclear or otherwise, and the whole purpose of the nuclear weapons free zone is to keep everyone out of our particular region.'[43] Labour did not want Soviet nuclear-powered vessels replacing American ones: that was not the issue at all, Rowling said on one occasion. In December 1984 Labour turned down an application by Aeroflot for landing rights in New Zealand to service Soviet fishing vessels.[44] During the ANZUS crisis, Lange called the Soviet Ambassador to his office to tell him that the official Soviet news agency had misrepresented New Zealand's position in its dispute with the United States. Lange was reported as saying that New Zealand was an 'unshakable member of the western alliance and that our policies are not directed at any of our traditional friends'.[45] In his own account of the nuclear ships crisis, Lange stressed the fact that his government had no intention of leaving the Western alliance and had no wish to be confused with Nicaragua or Cuba.[46] Nor did he want New Zealand mixed up with Iran or Libya. If alignment with the Kremlin was impossible, membership of the non-aligned movement was also far-fetched. As we have seen, this was a government which paid less, not more, attention to the third world than its Labour predecessors. And it followed a domestic economic policy that linked it more, not less, firmly to the world of international capitalism.

The New Zealand government continually emphasised that the country was 'anti-nuclear not anti-American'. Lange stressed the limited nature of Labour's challenge after the Labour Party conference in September 1984 and again during the crisis in February 1985.[47] During the crisis and after, far from

---

41 *Listener*, 30 March 1985.
42 Richard Griffin, 'You're out of the ball game', *Listener*, 4 May 1985.
43 Interview with Bruce Wallace, *NZIR*, Sept.-Oct. 1981, p. 16.
44 *NZFAR*, Oct.-Dec. 1984, p. 32.
45 *EP*, 23 Feb. 1985.
46 Lange, *Nuclear Free*, p. 96.
47 'The Labour Party is not anti-American. I am not anti-American. The Government is not anti-American. Our policy is not anti-American.' *EP*, 11 Sept. 1984. Later statements by Lange in Roderic Alley, ed., *Disarmament and Security*. Wellington, 1985, p. 6; *NZFAR*, Jan.-March 1985, p. 5; Lange, *Nuclear Free*, p. 96.

taking the further step of terminating American installations on New Zealand soil that might conceivably infringe the anti-nuclear policy (such as the Deep Freeze operation in Christchurch and the Black Birch observatory in Marlborough), the government defended their utility and in the case of Deep Freeze argued that the decision of the United States not to relocate the installation was a vindication of government policy.[48]

The government pursued a pro-Western policy in the South Pacific, especially, as we have seen, with respect to Libyan influence.[49] In Southeast Asia it stressed the continuity of its policy with that of the National Party and its common interests with Australia, the United States and the ASEAN countries themselves. The government postponed any immediate action on withdrawing the battalion from Singapore (although withdrawal had been envisaged by the third Labour government) nor did it demonstrate any wish to adopt aspects of the radical agenda for Southeast Asia—criticism of Indonesian activities in East Timor or West Papua for instance, or recognition of the Vietnamese-backed Heng Samrin government in Cambodia. And while the Lange government supported the new Aquino government in the Philippines, this aligned it with, not against, the United States.

We now consider the nature of the dissent itself. The anti-nuclear movement had, as had all such movements since the 1950s, an important international dimension, particularly with movements in other English-speaking countries. The visit of Australian-based Helen Caldicott in 1983 was a major event in the peace activities of that year, whilst the Greenham Common women's protest against Cruise missile deployments in Britain had a high profile in New Zealand. Both of these connections draw attention to the important overlaps between the women's movement and the peace movement.[50]

By the mid 1980s anti-nuclear sentiment in New Zealand elicited support right across the political spectrum, not just from those who rejected ANZUS. Polling in 1986 showed that only 29 per cent of Labour voters thought New Zealand was safer outside ANZUS than in;[51] 57 per cent of Labour supporters polled favoured New Zealand's staying in ANZUS.[52] But in the same poll, 69 per cent of New Zealanders wanted to ban nuclear-powered ships, nuclear-

[48]   Albinski, 'United States Security Interests and New Zealand', p. 2: Albinski noted that the Lange government had not demanded assurances that foreign military aircraft reveal their armament: 'Were such a requirement applied, the Antarctic-related operation Deep Freeze would be jeopardised'; see also Ramesh Thakur, 'Creation of the Nuclear-Free New Zealand Myth', *Asian Survey*, 29/10 (Oct. 1989), pp. 933–4, where he notes PACDAC concern about the possibility that the Black Birch installation may contravene the anti-nuclear policy.
[49]   See Chapter 11.
[50]   For comment about women and the peace movement, see 'Inside the Peace Movement', *New Zealand Times*, 2 March 1986.
[51]   *Defence and Security: What New Zealanders Want*, Annex, pp. 65–66 (the equivalent figure for National Party supporters was 5 per cent).
[52]   *Defence and Security: What New Zealanders Want*, Annex, pp. 61–62.

weapon-armed ships or both, in other words wanted a policy which was in conflict with the United States 'neither confirm nor deny' policy and therefore with United States interpretation of the obligations of alliance membership.[53] To many people anti-nuclearism was not grounded in radical preoccupations about indigenous peoples or American imperialism. There had been non-radical elements in the peace movement since the 1950s, as we have seen. In his study of the movement, *Back from the Brink*, Kevin Clements noted in conclusion that 'it will be difficult to maintain the solidity of the anti-nuclear position as sections of the peace movement tackle racism, sexism, anti-colonialism, development for liberation, and social justice at home and abroad. It is clear already that some people whose motivation is primarily anti-nuclear feel uncomfortable about more general social movements and are dropping out of active involvement in the movement.'[54] Lange stressed on a number of occasions that anti-nuclear sentiment spread far beyond the activist peace movement which gave it birth.[55]

Popular identification with Australia and Britain was so strong that it clearly embraced many of those who were also sympathetic to the anti-nuclear policy. The 1985 survey of public opinion on defence and security showed 63 per cent of New Zealanders were prepared to use armed force if requested by Australia and 54 per cent if requested by Britain in the event of an attack on Australian or British territory respectively.[56] A 1984 poll showed that 79 per cent of New Zealanders identified Australia as a country they had a lot in common with, while 62 per cent of Australians accorded the equivalent status to the United States (the United States registered 14 per cent on the New Zealand poll and New Zealand 37 per cent on the Australian poll).[57] Further, in 1986 71 per cent of those polled supported New Zealand membership of ANZUS. During the 1991 Gulf War polls suggested that 80 per cent supported the newly elected National government's decision to provide non-combat support to the anti-Iraq coalition in which Britain played a prominent role.[58]

Anti-nuclear sentiment had always found supporters outside the left—for instance, among farmers[59] and businesswomen's groups, who had little ideological affinity with the more radical approach of many in the peace

---

[53]   Poll figures in *Defence and Security: What New Zealanders Want*, Annex, pp. 70–71. The three categories broke down as 3 per cent, 28 per cent and 38 per cent respectively.
[54]   Clements, *Back from the Brink*, p. 122. See also *New Outlook*, Sept.-Oct. 1983, pp. 33–34, report on the Vanuatu Nuclear Free and Independent Pacific conference including discussion of divisions in the New Zealand delegation between Pakeha and radical Maori.
[55]   And which he criticises, Lange, *Nuclear Free*, pp. 150–2.
[56]   Annex, p. 20.
[57]   Campbell, *Social Base of Australian and NZ Security Policy*, p. 82.
[58]   *Age* (Melbourne), 4 Dec. 1990, quoted in Richard D. Fisher, Jr., 'How to Reinvigorate America's Alliance with Australia and New Zealand', *Asian Studies Center Backgrounder*, 114 (15 July 1991), p. 5.
[59]   At its conference in April 1991 Federated Farmers endorsed anti-nuclearism on environmental grounds.

movement. The extent to which at least a muted anti-nuclearism had become an orthodoxy rather than the prerogative of the peace movement had been evident in the Muldoon government's own assertion that New Zealand itself was not a nuclear power and not a member of an alliance calling for a reflex commitment.[60] Newspapers recognised this too: 'the force of left-wing thinking on the American ships issue has been given democratic impetus by genuine nuclear fears in this country.'[61] The parallels with the anti-tour movement are instructive. Public opinion, much of it from the public-sector middle class, could be mobilised against the tour and in favour of the anti-apartheid cause, but the same momentum could not be maintained for a campaign against racism in New Zealand. The peace movement had some of the characteristics of the anti-tour movement (and also the anti-Vietnam War movement before that, although students seem to have been much more active there), in particular with its strong roots in the middle class including a segment of the church-going population, as well as in the working class and left wing—indeed as in the 1950s, many in the peace movement were keen to stress that it was not dominated by the left.[62] The peace movement was a classic single-issue campaign for many of those involved. While on the one hand this could from a left point of view be seen as useful leverage to open up the matrix of attitudes and practices that encouraged people to accept and tolerate capitalist hegemony, the reverse was always possible too. Without firm roots in the left, the anti-nuclear movement might become only symbolically radical, and indeed because so satisfyingly so, might make the task of radicalising New Zealanders and New Zealand politics even harder.

Most observers have understandably puzzled over the association in the record of the fourth Labour government of a 'radical' policy like anti-nuclearism with its markedly right-wing economic policy. The eager adoption of anti-nuclearism by the otherwise right-wing New Zealand Party of 1983–84 is equally problematic. Some writers have seen the two positions as inconsistent.[63] Others have identified both policies as 'radical' without positing any more consistent relationship between them.[64] Jack Vowles, in a

60 Joseph Camilleri, *ANZUS: Australia's Predicament in the Nuclear Age*. Melbourne, 1987, p. 131.
61 *EP*, 2 Feb. 1985.
62 Clements, *Back from the Brink*, p. 122. 'Despite the radical rhetoric of meetings like Beyond ANZUS the New Zealand peace movement is not dominated by the left or communist elements'; *EP*, 30 July 1986, 'Accusations that the anti-nuclear movement was communist-inspired were "wild, untrue" and lacking proof': Larry Ross, secretary of the New Zealand Nuclear Free Zone Committee in reply to charges by Air Vice-Marshall I. G. Morrison (retd).
63 Clements, *Back from the Brink*, p. 189. Clements writes, 'there are few indications . . . that the current Labour government wishes to shift from anti-nuclearism to a more pro-active foreign or defence policy. Given the generally conservative preferences of the New Zealand public and politicians (the anti-nuclear policy is anomalous), and profound economic problems affecting the country . . . .' Parenthesis in original.
64 See, for instance, Jonathan Boston and Martin Holland, 'The Fourth Labour Government: Transforming the Political Agenda', in Boston and Holland, *The Fourth Labour Government*, p. 9.

cover story on the New Zealand Party in *New Outlook*, identified its anti-nuclear position as one that was likely to appeal to liberals and those on the left, rather than being central to its own ideology—'opposition to ANZUS', he commented, 'has been one of the major progressive causes for over 10 years'. In a study on voting in the 1987 election, Vowles deduced that anti-nuclearism was as important in influencing voters to vote Labour as was Rogernomics, but did not enquire into the relationship between the two: the implicit assumption was that they were contraries.[65] But anti-nuclearism and opposition to ANZUS were not the same. In his *Quiet Revolution*, Colin James talked of the 'sense of self-confidence common to both the anti-nuclear and the economic people'—they fitted together well. He saw the espousal of anti-nuclearism as confirming the radicalism of the economic policies of the New Zealand Party and of the fourth Labour government rather than suggesting any conservatism in the anti-nuclear issue. James argued that Robert Jones, leader of the New Zealand Party, was even more explicit than the Labour government in seeing the anti-nuclear policy as an expression of independence. James seemed to feel that his readers would not necessarily accept a family relationship between right-wing economics and left-wing anti-nuclearism but argued himself that there was, using the unifying idea of 'independence'.[66]

Jones also disparaged the Soviet threat, and this brings us to a third significant dimension of *conservative* anti-nuclearism—anti-militarism. Conservatism in New Zealand has been so characterised by pro-military attitudes, especially in this century, that it has been difficult to identify the existence of an anti-militarist conservatism. Yet there have been precedents enough—the scrapping of compulsory military service by a conservative government in 1930, and travelling in place as well as time, conservative suspicion of taxation and standing armies, doctrines which flourished in mid-nineteenth century Britain and in the United States up to Pearl Harbor at least. We will come back to this in our discussion of interest.

Security and parsimony

Was New Zealand insecure, threatened, in the mid 1980s? The Labour government did not think so: 'I didn't consider we were in danger. Cam Ranh Bay was closer to Paris than it was to Wellington. The war in Vietnam was

[65] Jack Vowles, 'The New Right', *New Outlook*, March-April 1984, pp. 12–16; 'Rogernomics and antinuclearism': paper presented to the 1989 NZPSA Conference.

[66] James, *Quiet Revolution*, p. 174 and see also discussion, pp. 174–6. Clearly this is a notion of independence with shorter historical antecedents than the conception formulated in this study. It is essentially a description of the anti-Muldoonist coalition. James's notion took on more substance for this writer observing the coalitions of left civil libertarians and free marketeers which toppled the Communist regimes in Eastern Europe in 1989–90 and which had identifiable parallels with the configuration of the early years of the opposition to the *ancien régime* in France, 1788–91. The question of the nature of the radicalism and its relationship to capitalism is still begged.

over but the dominoes of Southeast Asia had not . . . fallen. The island states of the South Pacific were unlikely to subject themselves to Marxist teachings while the Christianity of the missionaries still flourished.'[67] And later: 'The whole point about New Zealand's case was that it rested on an analysis of New Zealand's unique strategic situation'[68]—which was a different situation from Australia's: whereas Australia looked to the United States for an alliance, New Zealand looked to Australia. This simple fact was at the core of the different evaluations of ANZUS in the two countries.[69]

Such an outlook made for differences with Pacific and Asian governments too. Michael Somare in Papua New Guinea, and Tom Davis in the Cook Islands were both outspoken about their concerns, while George Shultz's visit to Fiji on the way home from talks with the Australians in February 1985 gave evidence of that country's position.[70] Discreetly, but unequivocally, Asian leaders like Lee Kuan Yew of Singapore and Yashuhiro Nakasone of Japan made their concern known that New Zealand was weakening the Western alliance—and in particular the American position in the western Pacific.[71] But the United States reaction to New Zealand demonstrated, if Asian and Pacific leaders had not already known, that the Reagan Administration meant the United States to remain a Pacific Ocean power.

Did public opinion agree with Lange? Polls varied in their findings, partly probably because the questions varied, but overall it would seem that around two thirds of the population did not believe there was a threat, certainly not from the 'traditional' sources—the Soviet Union and/or Asia. A 1984 poll found 58.6 per cent disagreed with the notion that any country was likely to threaten New Zealand, compared with 33.4 per cent who agreed. A 1985 poll which asked whether New Zealand was 'unlikely to ever be attacked' found that 47.1 per cent disagreed. But this poll may have been affected by the tension with the United States. Certainly when asked a year later which, if any, countries posed a military threat to New Zealand over the next fifteen years,

---

67 Lange, *Nuclear Free*, p. 40.
68 Lange, *Nuclear Free*, p. 110.
69 Andrew Mack, 'Denuclearisation in Australia and New Zealand: Issues and Prospects', *Australian Outlook*, 43/3 (Dec. 1989), p. 24. One submission to the Defence Committee of Enquiry, 1986, not from a peace activist, asked, 'What value is there for New Zealand in fighting wars for other nations? Geographic isolation and smallness has its disadvantages. From a defence point of view it has advantages which we should capitalise on.' For one peace group's attitude to defence, see, 'Forces Marshal for Just Defence,' *New Zealand Times*, 9 Feb. 1986.
70 *Dominion*, 24 Aug. 1984; *Press*, 29 Aug. 1984 (Davis); *Dominion*, 5 Sept. 1984 (Davis); *Dominion*, 17 June 1985 (Fiji). At the 1986 Forum meeting there were differences between Lange and Lini over expanding the role of the Forum, and with the Fiji Labour Party leader, Timoci Bavadra, over weakening the proposed nuclear-weapons-free zone treaty, *Dominion*, 11 Aug. 1986; *EP*, 12 Aug. 1986.
71 See, for instance, *EP*, 25 Feb., 6 March 1985; *NBR*, 22 April 1985: 'Indirect ASEAN pressure on New Zealand', but note also an element in the Asian reaction of 'nothing to do with us'.

although 31 per cent chose the Soviet Union, 14 per cent named the United States, and 13 per cent France.[72]

Despite this lack of any belief in a traditional threat a majority of New Zealanders continued to support ANZUS because it represented a familiar and acceptable alignment in the broadest diplomatic and political sense, not because it was necessary for the country's security. In the 1985 Defence Committee of Enquiry poll, 44 per cent wanted New Zealand to stay in ANZUS but without ship visits, a larger proportion than either those who were prepared to accept ship visits or do without ANZUS.[73] While observers regularly identified this as a contradiction—which, if membership of ANZUS be seen as requiring the assent of Australia and the United States as well as New Zealand, it was—it was also quite consistent with a model of New Zealand foreign relations in which interests are pursued and dissent articulated within a wider framework, be it the Commonwealth or ANZUS.

We turn now to that other persistent 'interest'—parsimony in general and caution about military spending in particular. The National governments in the postwar era were always public supporters of the need for a strong defence and for cooperation with allies. National suppported Peter Fraser in introducing compulsory military training in 1949 and vigorously opposed Labour's cancellation of it in 1958. National reintroduced selective service in 1961 and opposed its termination by Labour in 1972. And National remained loyal to Anzac Day and what it represented to many of the Second World War generation far longer than many in the Labour Party.

Yet there was more rhetoric than substance to this support for a strong defence. Selective service in 1961 was not the same as compulsory military training and New Zealand did not send conscripted soldiers to Vietnam as did Australia and the United States. The Muldoon government did not reintroduce selective service at all (though nor for that matter did either of New Zealand's ANZUS allies have conscription by that time) and military spending remained a low priority throughout that government's term of office.

So it was not surprising that a new generation of conservative politicians and observers, confronted with a debate about nuclear weapons, could take a much more sceptical stance in relation to defence issues than their predecessors. One commentator wrote in March 1984 that the New Zealand

---

[72] Campbell, *Social Basis of Australian and NZ Security Policy*, pp. 85–86. In comparison, in the last-mentioned poll, Indonesia, Japan and 'Southeast Asia' were each only specified by 3 per cent of respondents.

[73] Annex, pp. 76–76a. 37 per cent would have accepted ship visits, 13 per cent would have abandoned ANZUS; see also Tony Garnier, *EP*, 26 Aug. 1986, 'when it comes to peacetime defence, it seems that New Zealanders want to have their cake and eat it too.' See also Camilleri, *ANZUS: Australia's Predicament in the Nuclear Age*, p. 134: 'There is reason to think that the very high level of support for ANZUS [in NZ] represented not so much endorsement of a military alliance as attachment to a political relationship with strong sentimental and cultural connotations.'

Party's policy on military spending was consistent with traditional conservative hostility to high public spending and with the party's stance as a libertarian, not an authoritarian, right-wing party.[74] Robert Jones claimed he was achieving extraordinary results persuading the New Zealand public that spending even one cent on military activity was a 'disgraceful indictment on all of us'.[75] The New Zealand Party and subsequent right-wing politicians like Roger Douglas all used a language of waste in talking about defence spending, exactly like English eighteenth-century parliamentary reformers.

These same patterns recurred during the 1988–89 debate over plans to buy new frigates in conjunction with the Australians. The momentum of the anti-frigate campaign was maintained by the peace movement and was strongest in the Labour Party. But public opinion polls demonstrated that opposition to the frigates reached far beyond the ranks of peace movement activists. This opposition seems to have been a matter of interest rather than ideology and in particular a belief that the frigates cost too much and that there were better uses for the money. Both Roger Douglas, architect of Labour's rightwards economic revolution, and Hugh Fletcher, one of the country's most prominent businessmen, spoke out against the frigate purchase. Derek Quigley, whom Muldoon had fired from Cabinet in 1982, produced a report in 1989 which, although it endorsed the frigate purchase, recommended a more than 10 per cent cut in the total defence spending.[76] Holland and Holyoake, not Fraser and Kirk, were forebears of this kind of thinking.[77] It also had parallels, perhaps ironic ones, in the value accorded defence spending and the dislike of federal taxes in American state and local politics.

The defence of ANZUS: tradition and realism

Those who defended the importance of maintaining ties with the United States and other allies, even if at the 'cost' of having nuclear weapons or nuclear-powered vessels in New Zealand ports, can be characterised in two main ways. They overlapped in practice but had distinct origins. On the one hand there were those who held to that belief in New Zealand as a part of a wider whole that was so central to earlier formulations of independence in foreign

74 Jerome Elkind, *New Zealand Times*, 18 March 1984 (see also Stephen Levine's comparison of the NZP to Thomas Jefferson, noting the NZP was not a party steeped in militarism, *New Zealand Times*, 8 Jan. 1984). I would not go along with Elkind's analysis altogether: maybe 'authoritarianism' has been offloaded from the army on to the police, an argument supported by polls which show that (as the defence forces have had a lower and lower profile) the police are held in very high esteem.

75 *NZH*, 10 March 1984.

76 *Dominion*, 10 Oct. 1988; *Dominion Sunday Times*, 29 Jan. 1989; *EP*, 2 March 1989.

77 For the pros and cons of the frigates see *NZIR*, March-April 1989, pp. 2–19; for discussion after the event of the anti-frigate campaign and the public attitudes involved, see *Peacelink*, 77 (Nov. 1989), pp. 7–13; for the official position, see *NZERR*, July-Sept. 1989, pp. 14–17, statement by Prime Minister Geoffrey Palmer: a substantial portion of it addressed the question of the affordability of the frigates and the expected benefits for New Zealand industry.

policy. Others argued in terms of power politics, echoing therefore the Laking formulation of the late 1960s and Hugh Templeton's argument in 1980. We will call these two currents of opinion ANZUS traditionalism and ANZUS realism.

ANZUS traditionalists were like many in the anti-nuclear movement in assuming a close solidarity between New Zealand and Australia, the UK, the US and Canada. But unlike the anti-nuclear movement they believed that this solidarity should be expressed through the maintenance of a close political and security cooperation at the government-to-government level. This reflected a different evaluation of New Zealand's interests, but also a certain degree of institutional habit. For both the armed forces and the diplomats, the alliance, the participation with Britain, the United States, Canada and Australia, was a defining element in their profession. The peer group, the grouping of like-minded diplomats or soldiers, was important to them. Their numbers were small—they became habituated very quickly to the range of contact that was possible.

It was revealing that the group from which the conservatives felt excluded was not just ANZUS, although that was the only formal alliance of which New Zealand was a member—it included Britain and Canada as well as Australia and the United States. Other countries ran well down the list. The extent to which alliance arguments were grounded in sentiment rather than interest was evident in the frequent references to Britain as a party to the ANZUS dispute. When the Dominion (itself a revealing adjective) President of the RSA announced the demise of ANZUS in 1991, he went on to argue for 'a renegotiated alliance to take us into the 21st century, not just involving the original ANZUS partners, but with the U.K. as well and possibly with other nations concerned with ensuring the integrity of the Pacific region'.[78] For Warren Cooper, Minister of Defence in the Bolger government, one of the costs of the ANZUS dispute was the relegation of New Zealand to the 'minor league', along with countries like Papua New Guinea.[79] The idea of participating in global security, alongside the United States and the United Kingdom, still had some appeal:

We ... intend to make the most of our own limited defence capacity by maintaining the most effective defence cooperation possible with Australia, the United States and the United Kingdom. These are countries with which New Zealand has had a long tradition of useful cooperation. It's patently obvious that the interests of small countries like New Zealand lie in the direction of collective security. So yes, we are rejoining the Western camp, and we're doing it on our terms.[80]

---

[78]   *RSA Review*, 56/6, 6 Dec. 1991.
[79]   Comments on *Morning Report*, Radio New Zealand, 9 Oct. 1991.
[80]   Minister of Foreign Affairs, Don McKinnon, *NZERR*, Jan.-March 1991, p. 5.

As this last comment suggests, the traditional and the realist defences of ANZUS did overlap. Realists after 1985 followed Hugh Templeton rather than Bob Edlin in stressing the diplomatic costs to New Zealand of the quarrel with the United States: its diplomacy had been made more complicated and demanding, it had been deprived of that easy entree to the 'corridors of power' in Washington and other capitals it had enjoyed in the past.

In July 1985 covert French agents blew up the Greenpeace vessel, *Rainbow Warrior*, in Auckland harbour. France admitted culpability only when Auckland police identified those responsible and their affiliation with the French government. The bombing itself seemed testimony to the powerlessness of New Zealand, the small Pacific country. Even though the French government—eventually—acknowledged its guilt, neither the United States nor Great Britain chose to chastise it as they had other governments for acts of state-sponsored violence (for instance, the killing of a British police officer by Libyan Embassy staff in London in April 1986).[81] And French pressure on New Zealand trade effectively prevented New Zealand putting the apprehended French agents on trial.[82]

The severance of defence ties with the United States placed a greater focus on the defence relationship with Australia. *Defence Review 1987* argued that defence cooperation with Australia was now central to New Zealand's security.[83] Quite apart from the controversy that arose over one of the consequences of this evaluation, the proposal to buy new frigates in conjuction with an Australian frigate-building programme, the demise of ANZUS revealed again to policymakers the realities of power in even this international relationship. In his study of the impact of the ANZUS dispute on New Zealand's armed forces, Peter Jennings predicted that Australia might prove to be 'a harder taskmaster to New Zealand than ever was the United States'.[84] Lange himself observed in respect of the negotiations over the frigates: 'They had us over a barrel. Having put so much of the government's credibility into the defence relationship with Australia, we had to pay the asking price.'[85]

In the late 1960s Laking had advised a doctrine of realism in foreign policy at a time when New Zealand had faced a sharply diminished interest in its part of the world and its concerns on the part of its traditional allies. The ties with allies had remained more intimate in the 1970s than had perhaps been expected and it was with the Africans and the Arabs that the realities of power

81 Michael King, *Death of the Rainbow Warrior*. Auckland, 1986, p. 194.
82 Lange, *Nuclear Free*, p. 124.
83 Clements, *Back From the Brink*, pp. 165-6, 168-74.
84 Peter Jennings, *The Armed Forces of New Zealand and the ANZUS Split: Costs and Consequences*. Wellington, 1988. Quoted phrase is cited in review of Jennings by Ramesh Thakur, *NZIR*, Nov.-Dec. 1988, p. 24.
85 Lange, *Nuclear Free*, p. 167. On the other hand, Australian Defence Minister Kim Beazley's zeal for the frigate programme increased New Zealand's leverage.

were most evident. In 1985 New Zealand's *own* actions precipitated a crisis that drew attention to how dismissive long-standing friends and allies could be of New Zealand's concerns, should they so choose. It is doubtful whether New Zealand diplomats relished the fact that it should be they, and not the anti-nuclear public, who experienced this dismissiveness so directly.

Nationalism

If defenders of ANZUS were thrust by events into the world of realpolitik, what of the supporters of the anti-nuclear policy? Was the ANZUS crisis New Zealand's war of independence, was the key task of Labour to produce an independent foreign policy, one which 'tells the world that our decisions will be made in Wellington, not in Washington, London, nor Canberra'?[86] Was David Lange a New Zealand George Washington, counselling against entangling alliances? For Ewan Jamieson, New Zealand was 'at odds with its past'.[87] For Denis McLean the issue was 'Isolation and Foreign Policy'.[88] 'It would not be the least of the ironies of the present ANZUS disagreement', said one American commentator, 'if it resulted in New Zealand adopting an attitude to foreign relations similar to that of the United States in the 1930s; not as a reaction to the policies of the decadent European powers but as a reaction to the policies of the originator and erstwhile chief spokesman for isolationism, the United States.'[89]

Certainly nationalism was an element in the picture. America's 'bullying tactics', as they were seen, in February 1985, were the despair of the Opposition and almost certainly helped the government. Of more than 2000 letters received in the Prime Minister's office in the first days of the crisis, over 90 per cent supported the government's anti-nuclear stand, and although some were 'form' letters, these were not in a majority.[90] A McNair/*Dominion* poll released in mid February showed that support for banning nuclear weapons from New Zealand, which had previously stood at over 70 per cent, was down to 56 per cent, 'with clear indications that this would erode further if New Zealand were to be excluded from ANZUS or if our trade were to be adversely affected'. But a Heylen/*Eyewitness News* poll showed that 73 per cent approved of the government's policy of banning nuclear weapons from entering the country. The difference between the two polls suggests the extent to which nationalism played a part in the movements of opinion during the crisis. One of the directors of the Heylen polling organisation pointed out that

86 Rowling quoted in Alley, 'Alternatives to ANZUS', p. 18.
87 Ewan Jamieson, *Friend or Ally? New Zealand at Odds with its Past*. Sydney, 1990.
88 Denis McLean, *New Zealand: Isolation and Foreign Policy*.
89 Ronald H. Spector, 'The Origins of ANZUS: New Zealand American Relations in Happier Times' in *New Directions*, p. 49. Quote is preceded by a longer discussion of American isolationism.
90 *EP*, 6 Feb. 1985.

their poll asked about government policy, while the McNair poll asked for opinions on the issues themselves: 'the questions were different and I expect this would probably account for the difference. People are tending to support more strongly the Government's policy rather than make an opinion on the issue.'[91] Sir John Marshall said that the United States could without any real disadvantage have quietly accepted New Zealand's policy while it lasted and stayed out of ports. 'Instead it has adopted a high-handed, uncompromising attitude which has antagonised many New Zealanders who in other respects are pro-American.'[92]

The crisis produced the first indication of what was admittedly only a notional disloyalty on the part of the armed forces to the constituted government since the Colonels' revolt in 1938: 'One way they had of showing their annoyance with the government was to leak stories to the news media complaining about reductions in military efficiency or falling morale among the armed forces. Reports filtered back to me of defence attachés overseas who spoke disparagingly of the government and its policy. Senior officers in unguarded moments on the cocktail circuit uttered words of bitter condemnation of the government's conduct.'[93] Many diplomats felt the same way—as has been noted, it was ironically they who suffered from the United States freeze on high-level contacts, on intelligence-sharing. What had once been loyalty becomes at the stroke of an electoral outcome, 'collaboration'. What had once been seditious becomes respectable. It was a familiar memory or experience in any country with a revolutionary or radical episode in its past or recent history. It was not familiar to New Zealanders.

The *Rainbow Warrior* episode also elicited a nationalist reaction and Lange's popularity increased in the aftermath of the dispute.[94] Even the British were not immune. When the British Foreign Secetary Geoffrey Howe chastised the government in 1987, the *Christchurch Star* responded that 'at best Sir Geoffrey's remarks were thinly veiled threats that New Zealand could suffer in trade terms .... At worst ... a remarkably unsophisticated attempt to sway New Zealand voters away from the Government .... This country is no longer the blindly patriotic South Sea outpost it once was. There is now an independence and a sense of nationality that make his clumsy attempt at influencing New Zealand's affairs deeply offensive.'[95]

This writer is convinced that the 'nuclear free and independent foreign

---

91   *EP*, 19 Feb. 1985; see also *Dominion*, 18 Feb. 1985; Tom Scott, 'ANZUS debate still bowling along', *EP*, 23 Feb. 1985.
92   Quoted in Colin James, 'Not So Brave New World, *NBR*, 22 Aug. 1986.
93   Lange, *Nuclear Free*, p. 68.
94   Michael Pugh, 'New Zealand, a Nuclear-Free Model', *World Today*, 42/3 (March 1986), p. 41.
95   *Christchurch Star*, 1 May 1987. It is interesting to note that even in writing in such nationalistic fashion, the *Star* expected—and rightly I think—that its readers would understand that 'patriotic' referred to loyalty to Britain, not to New Zealand.

policy', as articulated in the Labour Party at least, is a nationalist phenomenon and therefore different in kind, not just degree, from the ideas of independence which we have explored through the rest of this book.

Was the new outlook the culmination of a long-term development? One view is that 'the policies pursued by the Labour government since 1984, while controversial in many respects, have the great merit of issuing from an assumption of independent nationhood, finally freed from the constraints of a colonial legacy. New Zealand's nuclear-free policy is perhaps the most striking symbol of this achievement.'[96] The present writer takes a different approach. As in the 1960s, it is important to keep in mind the British origins of New Zealand nationalism, of both left and right. In 1990, as in 1968 or 1969, New Zealand nationalism did not involve a challenge to the British character of New Zealand life. The conflict with Britain over the anti-nuclear policy was intermittent and not central: there was no public outcry, for instance, at Britain's refusal to send the royal yacht *Britannia* to accompany the Queen on her visit to New Zealand in 1990, on the grounds that it would be breaching Britain's 'neither confirm nor deny' policy.[97] Indeed impressionistic evidence suggests that some of the 'British' elements in post-colonial New Zealand such as the Crown and the flag are seen by a wide spectrum of opinion as 'national' symbols.[98]

For Labour, independence had certainly become a creed, something to be defended rather than to be attained, and this too drew attention to continuity with that past when Labour spokespeople defended the importance of maintaining the British orientation of New Zealand foreign policy. 'We have created a new tradition over the past few years', said Mike Moore, then Prime Minister, talking about foreign policy just before the 1990 election.[99] The foreign policy section of Labour's 'Aims and Values' exercise in 1991 was called 'Towards an Independent Foreign Policy', but what it described had a conservative rather than a radical feel: 'Labour believes that our nuclear free and independent foreign policy is an excellent starting point to meet the challenges posed by the dramatic changes the world has undergone.'[100]

If the 'new tradition' is more 'tradition' than 'new' it is nonetheless clearly about power in a way that other and earlier ideas of independence were not. How then did this nationalism come out of the interplay of dissent and interest which we analysed earlier in this chapter? At Waitangi Day celebrations in

96   Peter Simpson, *Metro*, June 1990, p. 114.
97   Incident cited in Lange, *Nuclear Free*, pp. 7-9.
98   See for instance *EP* poll, 5 March 1992, which showed around 70 per cent support both for the Crown and the flag. Respondents were self-selected. In another sphere: New Zealand is the only country outside the British Isles in which the British soap opera, *Coronation Street*, is shown on prime time television—and is one of only three in which it is shown at all.
99   *NZIR*, Nov.-Dec. 1990, p. 7.
100   'Labour: Aims and Values 1991. First Report of the Policy Renewal Process'. New Zealand Labour Party, 1991, p. 31.

Washington DC in 1991, Professor Keith Jackson commented that 'it is the ANZUS controversy which perhaps more than any other single factor had proved to be the catalyst for the emergence of a deeply held sense of New Zealand independence .... the nuclear ships visits controversy has become part of New Zealand's sense of national identity.'[101] The notion of a catalyst is a valuable one. Attitudes before the crisis broke, and even thereafter, bore many hallmarks of the ideas about foreign policy which we have identified as characteristic of New Zealand in 1960 and before and after that time. 'Out there' was a world which would and could understand and accept New Zealand's actions, even if it did not fully welcome them. That is the feeling which had been integral to the meaning of independence in the history of New Zealand policy. Nationalism became significant when New Zealand was thwarted, when the rejection occurred, rather than before. The ANZUS crisis elicited, was not caused by, a nationalist response from the New Zealand public. And this is as one would expect. Nationalism is partly about power and February 1985 was a moment when power was felt. The nationalism and the older elements in the pattern of independence in foreign policy now coexist, just as those older elements and loyalism once coexisted.

It is never easy to discern what the future might hold. Power now informs the notion of independence, but the assumptions and practices of the older patterns will persist. As one historian of Japan has put it, 'the international task of the 1990s requires national adjustments to a world in which power will be differently and more interdependently shared than before. Lacking both recent precedent and national inclination, few countries are making that adjustment gracefully.'[102] New Zealand is in a curious situation. Its history meant that its notion of independence has been largely free of notions of state power. At a time when the world as a whole has for the first time a real opportunity to realise the promise of the League of Nations Covenant and the United Nations Charter, New Zealand has experienced more directly than in its past the reality of power in the world's affairs. It has every reason to support the development of an international order in which state power is moderated, not untrammelled.

---

[101] Keith Jackson, 'New Zealand in 1991: A Nation Is as a Nation Does', *NZIR*, July-Aug. 1991, p. 27.
[102] Carol Gluck, 'Anatomies of the New Japan', *TLS*, 5 July 1991, p. 24.

Bibliography

PUBLISHED SOURCES: BOOKS AND ARTICLES

Airey, Willis. 'Siegfried after 50 years', *Political Science*, 6/2 (Sept. 1954).

Albinski, Henry. 'American Perspectives on the ANZUS Alliance', *Australian Outlook*, 32/2 (Aug. 1978).

Alley, Roderic. 'The Alternatives to ANZUS: A Commentary', in Roderic Alley, ed., *Alternatives to ANZUS*, rvsd edition, Auckland, 1984.

Alley, Roderic. 'ANZUS and the Nuclear Issue', in Jonathan Boston and Martin Holland, *The Fourth Labour Government: Radical Politics in New Zealand*. Auckland, 1987.

Alley, Roderic. ' "The Awesome Glow in the Sky": New Zealand and Disarmament', in *NZWA 1957-72*.

Alley, Roderic, ed. *Disarmament and Security*. Wellington, 1985.

Alomes, Stephen. *A Nation At Last? The Changing Character of Australian Nationalism 1880-1988*. North Ryde, NSW, 1988.

Alves, Dora. *Anti-Nuclear Attitudes in Australia and New Zealand*. Washington, 1985.

Anderson, Benedict. *Imagined Communities*. London, 1983.

Andrews, E. P. *Isolationism and Appeasement in Australia 1935-1939*. Canberra, 1970.

Baker, Paul. *King and Country Call: New Zealanders, Conscription and the Great War*. Auckland, 1988.

Ball, Desmond, ed. *The Anzac Connection*. North Sydney, NSW, 1985.

Barrowman, Rachel. *A Popular Vision: The Arts and the Left in New Zealand, 1930-1950*. Wellington, 1991.

Bassett, Michael. *Confrontation '51*. Wellington, 1972.

Bassett, Michael. *The Third Labour Government*. Palmerston North, 1976.

Bassett, Michael and Robert Nola, eds. *New Zealand and Southeast Asia*. Auckland, 1966.

Beaglehole, J. C. 'International and Commonwealth Relations', in Horace Belshaw, ed., *New Zealand*, Berkeley, 1947.

Beeby, C. *The Antarctic Treaty*, Wellington, 1972.

Bennett, Bruce. *New Zealand's Moral Foreign Policy 1935-1939: The Promotion of Collective Security Through the League of Nations*. Wellington, 1988.

Bercovitch, Jacob, ed. *ANZUS in Crisis*. London, 1989.

Bertram, I. G. and R. F. Watters. 'The Mirab Economy in South Pacific Microstates', *Pacific Viewpoint* 26/3 (1985).

Boyd, Mary. 'Australia, New Zealand and the Pacific', in Ralph Hayburn, ed., *Foreign Policy School 1978: Australia and New Zealand Relations*. Dunedin, 1978.

Boyd, Mary. *Decolonisation: New Zealand and the Practice of Trusteeship*. Wellington, 1987.

Brands, H. W., Jr., 'From ANZUS to SEATO: US Strategic Policy Towards Australia and New Zealand, 1952-54', *International History Review*, 9/2 (May 1987)

Brown, Bruce. *New Zealand Foreign Policy in Retrospect*. Wellington, 1970.

Brown, Bruce. *The Rise of New Zealand Labour*. Wellington, 1962.

Brown, Bruce, ed. *Asia and the Pacific in the 1970s: The Roles of the United States, Australia and New Zealand*. Wellington, 1971.

Burnett, Alan. *The A-NZ-US Triangle*. Canberra, 1988.

Buchan, Alistair. *Change Without War: The Shifting Structures of World Power*. London, 1974.

Buszynski, Leszek. 'SEATO: Why it Survived Until 1977 and Why It Was Abolished', *JSEAS*, 12/2 (Sept. 1981).

Cairns, Jim. *Living With Asia*. Melbourne, 1965.

Calleo, David. *The Imperious Economy*. Cambridge, Mass., 1982.

Camilleri, Joseph. *ANZUS: Australia's Predicament in the Nuclear Age*. Melbourne, 1987.

Campbell, David. *The Social Base of Australian and New Zealand Security Policy*. Canberra, 1989.

Ceadel, Martin. *Pacifism in Britain 1914-1945: The Defining of a Faith*. Oxford, 1980.

Chase, Eugene P. 'Peter Fraser at San Francisco', *Political Science*, 11/1 (March 1959).

Chin, Kin Wah. *The Defence of Malaysia and Singapore: The Transformation of a Security System 1957-1971*. Cambridge, 1983.

Clements, Kevin. *Back From the Brink: The Creation of a Nuclear-Free New Zealand*. Wellington, 1988.

Committee on Vietnam. *Intervention in Vietnam*. Wellington, 1965.

Condliffe, J. B. *New Zealand in the Making*. London, 1930.

Corner, F. H. 'Emerging Perspectives in World Politics', *NZFAR*, Aug. 1975.

Corner, F. H. 'New Zealand and the South Pacific', in *NZER*.

Cowan, James. *Travel in New Zealand: The Island Dominion*. Chch, 1926.

Cowie, Donald. 'The Empire Through New Zealand Eyes', *Political Quarterly* (Oct. 1938).

Cumberland, Kenneth. 'New Zealand and the Post-War World', *Agenda*, 3 (1944).

Cunninghame, R. R. 'Foreign Policy and Political Alignments', in *NZER*.

Curthoys, Ann and John Merritt, eds. *Australia's First Cold War: 1945-1953*. v. 1. *Society and Culture*. North Sydney, NSW, 1984.

Curthoys, Ann and John Merritt, eds. *Better Dead than Red: Australia's First Cold War: 1945-1959*, v. 2. North Sydney, NSW, 1986.

Dalziel, Raewyn. *Julius Vogel. Business Politician*. Auckland, 1986.

Dann, Christine. 'Introduction', in Barbara Harford, ed., *Beyond ANZUS: Alternatives for Australia, New Zealand and the Pacific*. Auckland, 1984.

Davidson, J. W. *Samoa mo Samoa*. Melbourne, 1967.

Davies, Diane. 'New Zealand's Diplomatic Policy: the Need for Review', *NZIR*, July-Aug. 1983.

Day, Douglas. *The Great Betrayal—Britain, Australia and the Onset of the Pacific War*. North Ryde, NSW, 1988.

Deschampsneufs, Henry. 'Role of the Southern Dominions in South-East Asia', *New Commonwealth*, June 1952.

Dingman, Roger. 'The Diplomacy of Dependency: The Philippines and Peacemaking with Japan, 1945-1952', *JSEAS*, 17/2 (Sept. 1986).

Dingman, Roger. 'John Foster Dulles and the Creation of the Southeast Asia Treaty Organisation in 1954', *International History Review*, 11/3 (Aug. 1989).

Dorling, Philip. *The Origins of the ANZUS Treaty: A Reconsideration*. Bedford Park, SA, 1990.

Downie Stewart, William. 'New Zealand's Pacific Trade and Tariff', *Pacific Affairs*, 4 (1931).

Eagles, Jim and Colin James, *The Making of a New Zealand Prime Minister*. Wellington, 1973.

Fairburn, A. R. D. 'Literature and the Arts' in Horace Belshaw, ed., *New Zealand*. Berkeley, 1947.

Fairburn, Miles. 'New Zealand and Australasian Federation 1883–1901: Another View', *NZJH*, 4/2 (Oct. 1970).

Fisher, Richard D., Jr. 'How to Reinvigorate America's Alliance with Australia and New Zealand', *Asian Studies Center Backgrounder*, 114 (15 July 1991).

Gardner, Richard N. *Sterling Dollar Diplomacy in Current Perspective*. New York, 1980.

Gold, Hyam, ed. *New Directions in New Zealand Foreign Policy*. Auckland, 1986.

Gordon, Bernard K. *New Zealand Becomes a Pacific Power*. Chicago, 1960.

Grebenshchikov, E. 'ANZUS: The Labyrinths and Deadlocks of the Bloc Policy'. *Far Eastern Affairs*, no. 2, 1985.

Gustafson, Barry. *From the Cradle to the Grave*. Auckland, 1986.

Guthrie-Smith, H. *Tutira: The Story of a New Zealand Sheep Station*. 4th ed., Wellington, 1969.

Haast, H. F. von and G. H. Scholefield. 'New Zealand and the Pacific', *Pacific Affairs*, 3 (1930).

Halliday, Fred. *The Making of the Second Cold War*. London, 1983.

Hamer, David. *John Morley: Liberal Intellectual in Politics*. London, 1968.

Harland, Bryce. 'New Zealand, the United States and Asia: The Background to the ANZUS Treaty', in Peter Munz, ed., *The Feel of Truth*, Wellington, 1969.

Harland, Bryce. *On Our Own: New Zealand in the Emerging Tripolar World*, Wellington, 1992.

Hayward, Margaret. *Diary of the Kirk Years*. Wellington, 1981.

Henderson, Alan. *The Quest for Efficiency: The Origins of the State Services Commission*. Wellington, 1990.

Henderson, John. 'The 1980s: A Time for Commitment', *NZIR*, Jan.-Feb. 1980.

Henderson, John. 'Beefing Up US Barriers', *NZIR*, Jan.-Feb. 1979.

Henderson, John. 'The Burdens of ANZUS', *NZIR*, May-June 1980.

Henderson, John. 'Foreign Policy and the Election', *NZIR*, Sept.-Oct. 1978.

Henderson, John. 'The Foreign Policy of a Small State', in J. Henderson, R. Kennaway and K. Jackson, *Beyond New Zealand*.

Henderson, John. 'Labour's Foreign Policy: a Moral Perspective', *NZIR*, Sept.-Oct. 1977.

Henderson, John. 'Muldoon: New Zealand and the World', *NZIR*, May-June 1977.

Henderson, J., R. Kennaway and K. Jackson. *Beyond New Zealand*. Auckland, 1980.

Hirschmann, Albert O. *Exit, Voice and Loyalty*. Cambridge, Mass., 1970.

Hoadley, Steve. 'The Future of New Zealand's Alliances', in NZIIA, *New Zealand Foreign Policy: Choices, Challenges and Opportunities*, Wellington, 1984.

Holland, R. F. *Britain and the Commonwealth Alliance*. London, 1981.

Holyoake, K. J. 'New Zealand's External Relations in a Changing World', *EAR*, Aug. 1963.

Howard, Michael. 'Lonely Antipodes', *Round Table*, 245 (Jan. 1972).

Ihimaera, Witi. 'The Long Dark Tea-Time of the South', in Ramesh Thakur, ed., *The South Pacific: Problems, Issues and Prospects*, London, 1991.

Ihimaera, Witi. 'New Zealand as a Pacific Nation', in Hyam Gold, ed., *New Directions in New Zealand Foreign Policy*.

Jackson, Keith. ' "Because It's There . . .": A Consideration of the Decision to Commit NZ Troops to Malaysia beyond 1971', *JSEAS*, 2/1 (March 1971).

Jackson, Keith. 'New Zealand in 1991: A Nation Is as a Nation Does', *NZIR*, July-Aug. 1991.

Jackson, Keith. 'New Zealand and Southeast Asia', *Journal of Commonwealth Political Studies*, 9/1 (1971).

James, Colin. *The Quiet Revolution*. Wellington, 1986.

Jamieson, Ewan. *Friend or Ally? New Zealand at Odds with its Past*. Sydney, 1990.

Jennings, Peter. *The Armed Forces of New Zealand: the ANZUS Split: Costs and Consequences*. Wellington, 1988.

Jesson, Bruce. *Behind the Mirror Glass: The Growth of Wealth and Power in New Zealand in the Eighties*. Auckland, 1987.

Keith, Ken. *International Implications of Race Relations in New Zealand*. Wellington, 1972.

Kendle, John. 'The Round Table Movement: Lionel Curtis and the Formation of the New Zealand Groups in 1910', *NZJH*, 1/1 (April 1967).

Kennaway, Richard. 'Foreign Policy', in Ray Goldstein & Roderic Alley, eds., *Labour in Power. Promise and Performance*. Wellington, 1975.

Kennaway, Richard. *New Zealand Foreign Policy 1951-1971*. Wellington, 1972.

Kennaway, Richard and John Henderson, eds. *Beyond New Zealand II: Foreign Policy into the 1990s*. Auckland, 1991.

King, Michael. *Death of the Rainbow Warrior*. Auckland, 1986.

King, Michael. *Te Puea*. Auckland, 1977.

Kirk, Norman. *New Zealand and its Neighbours*. Wellington, 1971.

Kolko, Gabriel. *Vietnam: Anatomy of a War*. New York, 1985.

Laking, George. 'International Problems Confronting New Zealand in the 1970s', in NZIIA, *Foreign Policy in the 1970s*, Wellington, 1970.

Lang, Henry. 'Economics and Foreign Policy', *NZFAR*, Aug. 1973.

Lange, David. 'New Zealand: Changing Directions', *Round Table*, 291 (1984).

Lange, David. *Nuclear Free: The New Zealand Way*. Wellington, 1990.

Larkin, T. C., ed. *New Zealand's External Relations*. Wellington, 1962.

Levine, Stephen. *The New Zealand Political System*. Sydney, 1979.

Levine, Stephen. 'ANZUS: the American View', *NZIR*, May-June 1977.

Levine, Stephen. 'Public Opinion and the ANZUS Treaty', *NZIR*, May-June 1976.

Lissington, M. P. *New Zealand and Japan 1900-1941*. Wellington, 1972.

Lissington, M. P. *New Zealand and the United States 1840-1944*. Wellington, 1972.

Lodge, Juliet. *New Zealand and the European Community*. London, 1988.

Lodge, Juliet. 'New Zealand Foreign Policy in 1976', *Australian Outlook*, 31/1 (April 1977).

Lough, N. V. 'New Zealand's External Economic Relations', in *NZER*.

Mabon, David. 'Elusive Agreements: The Pacific Pact Proposals of 1949-1951', *Pacific Historical Review*, 57/2 (May 1988).

McCraw, David. 'The Demanding Alliance: New Zealand and the Escalation of the Vietnam War', *Australian Journal of Politics and History*, 34/3 (1988).

McCraw, David. 'From Kirk to Muldoon: Change and Continuity in New Zealand's Foreign-Policy Priorities', *Pacific Affairs*, 55/4 (Winter 1982-83).

McCraw, David. 'New Zealand and the Baltic States: Principle versus Pragmatism in Foreign Policy', *Australian Outlook*, 35/2 (Aug. 1981).

McCraw, David. 'Reluctant Ally: New Zealand's Entry into the Vietnam War', *NZJH*, 15/1 (April 1981).

Macdonald, Barrie. 'Pacific Immigration and the Politicians', *Comment*, (new series) 3 (1977).

Macdonald, Barrie. *In Pursuit of the Sacred Trust: Trusteeship and Independence in Nauru.* Wellington, 1988.

McGibbon, Ian. 'The Australian-New Zealand Defence Relationship Since 1901', *Revue Internationale d'Histoire Militaire*, 72 (1990).

McGibbon, Ian. *Blue-Water Rationale: The Naval Defence of New Zealand 1914-1942.* Wellington, 1981.

McGibbon, Ian. 'New Zealand's Intervention in the Korean War, June-July 1950', *International History Review*, 11/1 (May 1989).

McIntosh, A. D. 'Administration of an Independent Foreign Policy', in *NZER.*

McIntosh, A. D. *et al. New Zealand In World Affairs*, v. 1, *1945-1957.* Wellington, 1977.

McIntosh, A. D. 'Origins of the Department of External Affairs and the Formulation of an Independent Foreign Policy', in *NZWA 1945-57.*

McIntyre, David. 'The Future of the New Zealand System of Alliances', *Landfall*, 21/4 (Dec. 1967).

McIntyre, David. 'Peter Fraser's Commonwealth', in *NZWA 1945-57.*

McIntyre, W. David. 'Labour Experience in Foreign Policy', in Hyam Gold, ed., *New Directions in New Zealand Foreign Policy.*

McIntyre, W. David. *New Zealand Prepares for War.* Christchurch, 1988.

Mack, Andrew. 'Denuclearisation in Australia and New Zealand: Issues and Prospects', *Australian Outlook*, 43/3 (Dec. 1989).

Mack, Andrew. 'Is There a Soviet Threat?' *Peace Dossier* (a publication of the Victorian Association for Peace Studies), 3 (July 1982).

McKinley, Michael. 'Labour, Lange and Logic: An Analysis of New Zealand's ANZUS Policy', *Australian Outlook*, 39/3 (Dec. 1985).

McKinnon, Malcolm. 'Equality of Sacrifice: Anglo-New Zealand Relations and the War Economy, 1939-1945', *JICH*, 12/3 (May 1984).

McKinnon, Malcolm. 'Impasse or Turning Point: New Zealand and the 1981 Springbok Tour', *South Africa International*, 13/1 (July 1982).

McKinnon, Malcolm. 'The New World of the Dollar' in Malcolm McKinnon, ed., *The American Connection.* Wellington, 1988.

McKinnon, Malcolm. 'Trading in Difficulties', in *NZWA 1957-72.*

McKinnon, Malcolm, ed. *New Zealand in World Affairs*, v. 2, *1957-1972.* Wellington, 1991.

McLean, David. 'ANZUS Origins: A Reassessment', *Australian Historical Studies*, 24/94 (April 1990).

McLean, Denis. *New Zealand: Isolation and Foreign Policy.* Sydney, 1990.

MacLeod, Alexander. 'Foreign Commitments in Dispute', *Round Table*, 237 (Jan. 1970).

MacLeod, Alexander. 'The New Foreign Policy in Australia and New Zealand: The Record of the Labour Governments', *Round Table*, 255 (July 1974).

MacLeod, Alexander. 'New Zealand, Britain and the Commonwealth'. *Round Table*, 244 (Oct. 1971)

McLeod, John. *Myth and Reality.* Auckland, 1986.

McLuskie, Rob. *The Great Debate: New Zealand, Britain and the EEC, the Shaping of Attitudes.* Wellington, 1986.

McMillan, Stuart. *Neither Confirm Nor Deny.* Wellington, 1987.

Mansergh, Nicholas. *Survey of British Commonwealth Affairs: Problems of External Policy, 1931-1939.* London, 1952.

Marshall, Sir John. *Memoirs.* v. 1. Auckland, 1983.

Marshall, Sir John. *Memoirs.* v. 2. Auckland, 1989.

Mediansky, F. A. 'Australia's Security and the American Alliance', *Australian Outlook*, 37/1 (April, 1983).

Mediansky, F. A. 'ANZUS in Crisis', *Australian Quarterly*, 57/1 and 2 (Autumn-Winter 1985).

Miller, J. D. B. *Survey of Commonwealth Affairs, 1952-1969*. London, 1974.

Milner, I. F. *New Zealand's Interests and Policies in the Far East*. Vancouver, 1939.

Mitchell, Austin. *Politics and People in New Zealand*. Christchurch, 1969.

Monk, W. F. 'New Zealand Faces North', *Pacific Affairs*, 26/3 (Sept. 1953).

Muldoon, R. D. *Muldoon*. Wellington, 1977.

Muldoon, R. D. *My Way*. Auckland, 1981.

Muldoon, R. D. *Number 38*. Auckland, 1986.

Muldoon, R. D. *The Rise and Fall of a Young Turk*. Wellington, 1974.

Mullins, Ralph. 'New Zealand's Defence Policy', *NZFAR*, July 1972.

Munz, Peter. 'A Personal Memoir', in Peter Munz, ed., *The Feel of Truth: Essays in New Zealand and Pacific History presented to F. L. W. Wood and J. C. Beaglehole*. Wellington, 1969.

Nash, Walter. 'New Zealand and the Commonwealth', *United Empire*, 28/ns 1 (Jan. 1937).

New Zealand Institute of International Affairs. *New Zealand Foreign Policy: Choices, Challenges and Opportunities*. NZIIA 50th Anniversary Conference. Wellington, 1984.

New Zealand Institute of International Affairs. *New Zealand Foreign Policy with Special Reference to South-East Asia* (Report of an NZIIA Study Group). Wellington, 1968.

New Zealand Institute of International Affairs. *Security in the Pacific*. Wellington, 1946.

Norrish, Merwyn. 'New Alliances in the World of Multilateral Trade', *NZFAR*, Jan.-March 1988.

Norrish, Merwyn. 'Trade and Investment: the New Zealand Viewpoint', *NZFAR*, July-Dec. 1979.

O'Farrell, P. J. *Harry Holland, Militant Socialist*. Canberra, 1964.

Oka, Takashi. 'Stability in Asia', *Foreign Affairs*, 63/3 (1985).

Oliver, W. H. 'Moralism and Foreign Policy', *Landfall*, 19/4 (Dec. 1965).

Oliver, W. Hugh. 'The Labour Caucus and Economic Policy Formation 1981-1984', in Brian Easton, ed., *The Making of Rogernomics*. Auckland, 1989.

Olssen, Erik. *John A. Lee*. Dunedin, 1977.

Olssen, Erik. 'The Origins of ANZUS Reconsidered', *Historical and Political Studies*, 1/2 (Dec. 1970).

Orange, Claudia. 'An Exercise in Maori Autonomy: The Rise and Demise of the Maori War Effort Organisation', *NZJH*, 20/2 (April 1987).

Ovendale, Ritchie. *Appeasement and the English Speaking World—Britain, the United States, the Dominions and the Policy of Appeasement 1937-1939*. Cardiff, 1975.

Page, Warren and Brian Lockstone. *Landslide '72*. Dunedin, 1973.

Parker, Michael. *The SIS*. Palmerston North, 1979.

Pearson, Mark. *Paper Tiger*. Wellington, 1988.

Pemberton, Gregory. *All The Way: Australia's Road to Vietnam*. Sydney, 1987.

Phillips, Jock, '75 years Since Gallipoli', in David Green, ed., *Towards 1990*. Wellington, 1990.

Pimlott, Ben. *Labour and the Left*. Cambridge, 1971.

Pugh, Michael. *The ANZUS Crisis, Nuclear Visiting and Deterrence*. Cambridge, 1989.

Pugh, Michael. 'New Zealand. A Nuclear-Free Model', *World Today*, 42/3 (March 1986).

Rabel, Roberto. 'New Zealand and the United States in the Early Cold War Era, 1945-1949', *Australasian Journal of American Studies*, 7/2 (Dec. 1988).

Rabel, Roberto. 'Vietnam and the Collapse of the Foreign Policy Consensus', in *NZWA 1957-72*.

Rabel, Roberto. 'The Vietnam Antiwar Movement in New Zealand', *Peace & Change*, 17/1 (Jan. 1992).

Ravenhill, John, ed. *No Longer an American Lake*. Sydney, 1989.

Reese, Trevor. 'The Australia-New Zealand Agreement, 1944, and the United States', *JCPS*, 4/1 (March 1966).

Ricketts, Rita. 'Old Friends, New Friends: Cooperation or Competition?' in *NZWA 1957-72*.

Roberts, Nigel. 'Foreign Affairs: The Legend and Legacy of Norman Kirk', *Islands*, 3/4 (Dec. 1974).

Rolfe, James. 'Securing the South Pacific', *NZIR*, Nov.-Dec. 1985.

Ross, Angus. *New Zealand Aspirations in the Pacific in the Nineteenth Century*. Oxford, 1964.

Ross, Angus, ed. *New Zealand's Record in the Pacific Islands in the Twentieth Century*. Wellington, 1969.

Ross, Angus. 'Reluctant Dominion or Dutiful Daughter? New Zealand and the Commonwealth in the Inter-War Years', *JCPS*, 10/1 (March 1972).

Royal Society of New Zealand, *Report of the Ad Hoc Committee on the Omega Navigation System*. Wellington, 1968.

Salmond, John. 'New Zealand and the New Hebrides' in Peter Munz, ed., *The Feel of Truth*. Wellington, 1969.

Scott, Dick. *Years of the Pooh-bah: A Cook Islands History*. Auckland, 1991.

Scott, J. V. 'Getting Off the Colonial Hook', in *NZWA 1957-72*.

Siegfried, André. *Democracy in New Zealand*. 2nd ed., with an introduction by David Hamer, Wellington, 1982.

Simpson, Tony. *A Vision Betrayed*. Auckland, 1984.

Sinclair, Keith. *A Destiny Apart*. Wellington, 1986.

Sinclair, Keith. 'Fruit Fly, Fireblight and Powdery Scab: Australia-New Zealand Trade Relations 1919-1939', *JICH*, 1/1 (Oct. 1972).

Sinclair, Keith. 'New Zealand's Future Foreign Policy', *Political Science* 18/2 (Sept. 1966).

Sinclair, Keith. 'New Zealand's Metamorphosis', *International Journal*, 29/3 (1974).

Sinclair, Keith. *Walter Nash*. Auckland, 1976.

Sinclair, Keith, ed. *Tasman Relations*. Auckland, 1987.

Smith, T. R. *South Pacific Commission*. Wellington, 1972.

Socknat, Thomas, J. *Witness Against War: Pacifism in Canada 1900-1945*. Toronto, 1987.

Sorrenson, M. P. K. *New Zealand and the Rhodesia Crisis: The Lessons of History*. Auckland, 1968.

Spector, Ronald H. 'The Origins of ANZUS: New Zealand American Relations in Happier Times', in Hyam Gold, ed., *New Directions in New Zealand Foreign Policy*.

Spender, Percy. *Exercises in Diplomacy: The ANZUS Treaty and the Colombo Plan*. Sydney, 1969.

Spoonley, Paul. 'Being British', in Bruce Jesson, Alannah Ryan and Paul Spoonley, *Revival of the Right: New Zealand Politics in the 1980s*, Auckland, 1988.

Spoonley, Paul. *The Politics of Nostalgia: Racism and the Extreme Right in New Zealand*. Palmerston North, 1987.

Starke, J. G. *The ANZUS Treaty Alliance*. Melbourne, 1965.

Stephenson, Carolyn. 'Interview with Helen Clark', *Bulletin of Concerned Asian Scholars*, 18/2 (April-June 1986).

Sutch, W. B. *Recent Economic Changes in New Zealand*. Auckland, 1936.

Taylor, Don. 'A World of Their Own', *Listener* (UK), 5 April 1956.

Taylor, Nancy M. *The New Zealand People at War: The Home Front*. Wellington, 1986.

Taylor, Richard. *Against the Bomb*. Oxford, 1988.

Taylor, R. Alister, ed. *Peace Power and Politics in Asia*. Wellington, 1969.

Templeton, Hugh. ' "New Era" for the "Happy Isles": the First Six Months of Labour Government Foreign Policy in New Zealand', *Australian Outlook*, 27/2 (Aug. 1973).

Templeton, Hugh. 'New Zealand and Africa', *EAR*, Jan. 1967.

Templeton, Hugh. 'New Zealand's Defence Policies for the 80s', *NZFAR*, April-June 1980.

Templeton, Ian and Keith Eunson. *Election '69*. Wellington, 1969.

Templeton, Malcolm. *Defence and Security: What New Zealand Needs*. Wellington, 1986.

Templeton, Malcolm. 'Moving on from Suez', in *NZWA 1957-72*.

Templeton, Malcolm. *Top Hats Are Not Being Taken*. Wellington, 1989.

Thakur, Ramesh. 'Creation of the Nuclear-Free New Zealand Myth', *Asian Survey*, 29/10 (Oct. 1989).

Thakur, Ramesh. 'A Dispute of Many Colours: France, New Zealand and the "Rainbow Warrior" Affair', *World Today*, 47/12 (Dec. 1986).

Thakur, Ramesh. *In Defence of New Zealand: Foreign Policy Choices in the Nuclear Age*. Boulder, Colo., 1986.

Thakur, Ramesh. 'Nuclear Issues in the South Pacific', in *The South Pacific: Emerging Security Issues and U.S. Policy*. Washington, 1990.

Thakur, Ramesh and Hyam Gold. 'The Politics of a New Economic Relationship: Negotiating Free Trade Between Australia and New Zealand', *Australian Outlook*, 37/2 (Aug. 1983).

Thompson, Richard. 'Race, Kinship and Policy: Africa and New Zealand', in *NZWA 1957-72*.

Thomson, Warren, June Gregg and Doug Craig (Defence Alternatives Study Group). *Old Myths or New Options? The New Zealand Security Debate after the Nuclear Ships Ban*. Chch, 1988.

Tow, William. 'The ANZUS Dispute: Testing US Extended Deterrence in Alliance Politics', *Political Science Quarterly*, 104/1 (Spring 1989).

Tow, William. 'The JANZUS Option: a Key to Asian/Pacific Security', *Asian Survey*, 18/2 (Dec. 1978).

Trotter, Ann. 'From Suspicion to Growing Partnership: New Zealand and Japan', in *NZWA 1957-72*.

Trotter, Ann. *New Zealand and Japan 1945-1952: The Occupation and the Peace Treaty*. London, 1990.

Trotter, Ann. 'New Zealand in World Affairs: Sir Carl Berendsen in Washington 1944-1952', *International History Review*, 12/3 (Aug. 1990).

Trotter, Ann. 'Personality in Politics: Sir Carl Berendsen', *NZJH*, 20/2 (Nov. 1986).

Turner, John. 'What Price New Zealand's Security?' *NZIR*, Nov.-Dec. 1981.

Vowles, Jack. 'The New Right', *New Outlook*, March-April 1984.

Wallace, Bruce. 'A Pacific Ocean Community', *NZIR*, Jan.-Feb. 1980.

Wallace, Bruce. 'Which Way The Alliance?', *NZIR*, Nov-Dec 1980.

Wearing, Brian. 'The Mexican Connection: A Fading Vision', *NZIR*, May-June 1983.

West, Dalton. 'The Soviet Union's Relations with New Zealand', *Round Table*, 278 (April 1980).

Wight, Martin. 'The Balance of Power', in *Survey of International Affairs, 1939–1946: The World in March 1939*, Royal Institute of International Affairs, London, 1952.

Wilkes, Owen. *Demonstrations Against the American Military Presence in New Zealand*. Wellington, 1973.

Wilkes, Owen. 'Gurkhas of the South Pacific', *New Outlook*, Sept.-Oct. 1984.

Wilson, J. V. 'NZ's Participation in International Organisations', in *NZER*.

Wood, F. L. W. 'The Anzac Dilemma', *International Affairs*, 29/2 (April 1953).

Wood, F. L. W. *New Zealand and the Big Powers: Can a Small Nation Have a Mind of Its Own?* (NZ National Party, Sir Sidney Holland Memorial Lecture). Wellington, 1967.

Wood, F. L. W. 'NZ and Southeast Asia', *Far Eastern Survey*, Feb. 1956.

Wood, F. L. W. *The New Zealand People At War: Political and External Affairs*. Wellington, 1958.

Wood, F. L. W. *New Zealand in the World*. Wellington, 1940.

Wood, F. L. W. *This New Zealand*. Hamilton, 1952.

Wood, F. L. W. 'Why did New Zealand not join the Australian Commonwealth in 1900–1901?' *NZJH*, 2/2 (Oct. 1968).

Woodfield, Ted. 'Marketing in the Middle East', *NZIR*, March-April 1983.

NEWSPAPERS AND PERIODICALS

New Zealand Herald
Auckland Star
Evening Post
Dominion
Press
Otago Daily Times

A number of other newspapers are occasionally cited; these are usually derived from a secondary source, for instance a clipping on an official file.

GOVERNMENT OF NEW ZEALAND PUBLICATIONS

New Zealand Parliamentary Debates
Appendices to the Journals of the House of Representatives
Defence Committee of Enquiry, *Defence And Security: What New Zealanders Want*. Wellington, 1986.
Defence Review—(with year of publication)
Documents Relating to New Zealand's Participation in the Second World War. 3 vols. Wellington, 1949, 1951, 1963.
Documents in New Zealand's External Relations, ed. Robin Kay: v. 1: *The Australia-New Zealand Agreement 1944*. Wellington, 1972; v. 2: *The Surrender and Occupation of Japan*. Wellington, 1982; v. 3: *The ANZUS Pact and the Treaty of Peace with Japan*. Wellington, 1986.
External Affairs Review (1951–68); *New Zealand External Affairs Review* (1969); *New Zealand Foreign Affairs Review* (1970–88); *New Zealand External Relations Review* (1988–); monthly, to March 1976 inclusive, thereafter quarterly, except July-Dec. 1978, Jan. -June 1979 and July-Dec. 1979, when twice-yearly.

Encyclopaedia of New Zealand. ed. A. H. McLintock, 3 vols., Wellington, 1966.
New Zealand Official Yearbook.
New Zealand Foreign Policy: Statements and Documents. Wellington, 1972.
Report of the South Pacific Policy Review Group. *Towards a Pacific Island Community.*
 Wellington, 1990.

GOVERNMENT OF THE UNITED STATES PUBLICATIONS

Foreign Relations of the United States, 1950, v. 6, *East Asia and the Pacific*. Washington,
 1976.
Foreign Relations of the United States, 1951, v. 6, *East Asia and the Pacific*. Washington,
 1977.

MONTHLY AND OTHER JOURNALS (dates denote periods for which journals were
 frequently consulted)

Associated Chambers of Commerce. *Annual Report* (1935-45)
Australasian Insurance and Banking Record (1935-60)
Dispute (1965-67)
Here and Now (1949-57)
National Business Review (1980-87)
New Zealand Commerce (1955-66)
New Zealand Economist and Taxpayer (1960-70)
New Zealand International Review (1976-)
New Zealand Labour Party. *Report of Annual Conference* (1966-)
New Zealand Monthly Review (1960-80)
New Outlook (1983-86)
Round Table (1935-75)
Tomorrow (1934-40)

WEEKLY, MONTHLY AND OTHER PERIODICALS OCCASIONALLY CONSULTED

Foreign Control Watchdog
Comment
Craccum
Critic
Landfall
Metro
New Zealand Listener
New Zealand Manufacturer
Nga Kauwae
Pacific Affairs
Peacelink
RSA Review
Salient
Weekly News

UNPUBLISHED SOURCES

National Archives, Wellington

Selected files were consulted in the following series:

Nash Papers
WAII-21, War History Narratives, Second World War
EA series, official records of the Prime Minister's Department and the Department of
    External Affairs
T series, official records of the Treasury

Ministry of External Relations and Trade, Wellington

A. D. McIntosh Papers (selected items)
Official records of the Ministry, especially 63/1/14/1 (Airmail Bulletin), 245/8/3
    (Rhodesia), 478/4/6 (Vietnam).

Alexander Turnbull Library, Wellington

Ms Papers 1403. Papers of Rt. Hon. Sir John Marshall
Ms Papers 1624. Papers of Rt. Hon. S. G. H. Holland
Ms Papers 1814. Papers of Rt. Hon. Sir Keith Holyoake

Victoria University of Wellington

Papers of Sir Carl Berendsen. Autobiography ms, vs. 1, 2

National Archives, Washington DC

RG43, records of the National Advisory Council
RG59, records of the Department of State
In both instances records pertaining to New Zealand for the period to 1960 (for RG59)
    and the 1950s (for RG43) were consulted.

National Records Center, Suitland, Md.

RG169, records of the Mutual Aid (Lend-Lease) administration
Records pertaining to New Zealand were consulted.

Harry S Truman Library, Independence, Mo.

Harry S Truman Papers, Official File

Public Record Office, London

CAB 128, v. 19
CAB 129, vs. 45
Records pertaining to Pacific defence, 1951.

UNPUBLISHED SOURCES: THESES, CONFERENCE PAPERS AND RESEARCH PAPERS

Albinski, Henry. 'United States Security Interests and the New Zealand/ANZUS Problem.' Submission to United States House of Representatives Subcommittee on East Asia and the Pacific, April 1986.

Alley, Roderic. 'The 1987 Military Coups in Fiji: the Regional Implications.' Paper presented to the New Zealand Political Studies Association Conference, Wellington, 1989.

Angus, Barbara. 'Public Opinion in New Zealand Towards Japan 1939-1945.' WAII-21/19a, NA.

Alter, Jay. 'Mirroring Political and Economic Change . . . The development of CER.' VUW History Dept research paper, 1989.

Ansell, Graham. 'New Zealand and Australia.' Paper given to the 1970 Otago Foreign Policy School, Dept of Univ. Extension, Univ. of Otago, 1970.

Ashby, Mike. 'Under Southern Skies: Sources of New Zealand Foreign Policy, 1943-1957.' VUW, Ph. D. thesis, 1989.

Attwell, Peter. ' "The Cheering Never Stopped": The Royal Tour of New Zealand 1953-1954.' VUW History Dept research paper, 1989.

Attwood, B. M. 'Apostles of Peace: the New Zealand League of Nations Union.' Univ. of Auckland, M.A. thesis, 1979.

Barnes, W. J. 'Patron-Client Relations within Alliances.' Univ. of Canterbury, M.A. thesis, 1986.

Beaglehole, J. C. 'The Development of New Zealand Nationality.' VUW History Dept, c. 1955.

Bolitho, David. 'The Development of Anti-Communism in New Zealand Politics.' VUW History Dept research paper, 1976.

Carter, D. S. 'The Attitude of the New Zealand Communist Party to Foreign Affairs, 1930-1941.' Univ. of Auckland, M.Phil. thesis, 1981.

Dalton, Hugh. 'Diary', v. 5. London School of Economics and Political Science.

Dowman, Ian. 'N.Z., the U.S. and "United Action": A Study of N.Z.-U.S. Relations April-June 1954.' VUW History Dept research paper, 1985.

Eaddy, Rob. 'New Zealand and the Korean War: the First Year.' Univ. of Otago, M.A. thesis, 1983.

Enright, P. T. 'The First Labour Government and the Rise of Cultural Nationalism 1936-1949.' Univ. of Otago, Postgraduate Diploma, 1979.

Galvin, M. Noelle. 'New Zealand and the U.N. Partition of Palestine, 1947-49.' Univ. of Canterbury, M.A. thesis, 1982.

Gershenfeld, Roman. 'The Holyoake and Nash Visits to the USSR.' VUW History Dept Honours essay, 1989.

Gershenfeld, Roman. 'The Russo-Finnish War and the New Zealand Press.' VUW History Dept. Honours essay, 1989.

Green, Michael. 'New Zealand and the Malayan Emergency.' VUW History Dept research paper, 1969.

Kember, James. 'The Establishment of the New Zealand Mission in Washington.' VUW History Dept research paper, 1971.

Kirchner, Stephen. 'New Zealand Security Policy Under Labour 1984-1981.' ANU Political Science Honours research paper, 1989.

Kohn, E. P. 'Internationalism, Imperialism and Insecurity: The Effect of the United States on New Zealand's International Outlook in the Early 1920s.' M.A. thesis, VUW, 1991.

Knox, Sara. 'Something is happening in Asia.' VUW History Dept. Honours essay, 1989.

McCraw, D. J. 'Objectives and Priorities in New Zealand's Foreign Policy in Asia 1949–75: A Study of the Issue of the Recognition of the People's Republic of China and of Security Policies in South-East Asia.' Univ. of Otago, Ph.D. thesis, 1978.

McGibbon, Ian. *New Zealand and the Korean War*, v. 1. Forthcoming, Auckland, 1993.

McKenzie, J. W. 'New Zealand and Czechoslovakia'. VUW History Dept research paper, 1969.

McKinnon, Malcolm. 'The Impact of War: Anglo-New Zealand Economic Diplomacy 1939–1954.' VUW, Ph.D. thesis, 1981.

McKinnon, W. S. 'New Zealand Military Involvement in Vietnam'. Memoir by the Chief of the General Staff, 1965–67, in possession of author.

Markovits, Andrei. 'Americanism and Anti-Americanism in Germany: Some Thoughts on a Controversial Topic.' Paper presented to the 1983 Europeanists Conference, Washington D.C., Oct. 1983.

Mellor, J. 'New Zealand and the Formation of Israel 1947–49.' VUW History Dept. research paper, 1976.

Monk, W. F. 'New Zealand and the United States' (Paper A), 30 April 1953. EA58/9/ 1, MERT.

Monteith, P. A. 'New Zealand and the Czechoslovak Crisis.' Univ. of Auckland, M.A. thesis, 1980.

Moore, Charles. 'New Zealand's Attitude to South Africa and Its Continuing Membership of the Commonwealth, 1958–1961.' VUW History Dept research paper, 1976.

Moriarty, Kevin. 'A Historical Survey of the Foreign Policy of the New Zealand Waterside Workers' Union 1945–1951.' VUW History Dept research paper, 1976.

New Zealand Labour Party. 'Labour: Aims and Values 1991. First Report of the Policy Renewal Process.' Wellington, 1991.

Nicholls, Peter. 'The Role of the Yen in the Pacific Region: New Zealand as a Case Study.' Paper presented to seminar on 'The impact of deregulation of the Japanese financial market on Asia and the Pacific', Sydney, Nov. 1987.

Oliver, Robin. 'Ideology, the Slump and the New Zealand Labour Party: A Study of the Ideology of the NZ Labour Party in the 1930s.' Univ. of Auckland, M.A. thesis, 1981.

O'Shea, J. D. 'New Zealand and the Italo-Ethiopian Dispute.' WA-II 21, NA.

Pratt, N. D. 'The New Zealand Government's Attitude to Appeasement Policies.' VUW History Dept. research paper, 1969.

Rabel, Roberto. 'Between War and Peace: The New Zealand Experience in Trieste, May–June 1945.' Paper presented to the New Zealand Historical Association Conference, Feb. 1987.

Ritchie, C. D. 'New Zealand's Palestine Policy.' Univ. of Auckland, M.A. thesis, 1986.

Sewell, Keith. 'N.Z. Perceptions of European Affairs, 1945–49: An Examination of Parliamentary Opinion.' VUW History Dept research paper, 1976.

Skudder, Susan. ' "Bringing It Home": New Zealand Responses to the Spanish Civil War, 1936–1939.' Univ. of Waikato, Ph.D. thesis, 1986.

Swafford, Glenn. 'The Opposition to New Zealand's Involvement in the Korean War.' VUW Hist. Dept. research paper, 1982.

Templeton, Malcolm. 'Ties of Blood and Empire: New Zealand's Involvement in Middle East Defence and the Suez Crisis, 1947–1957.' MERT, 1988.

Tweddle, Grant. 'The U.S. Military Presence in New Zealand.' Univ. of Canterbury, M.A. thesis, 1983.

Wilson, F. O. 'New Zealand's Attitude to the Spanish Civil War.' VUW History Dept. research paper, 1969.

Witheford, H. 'The Labour Party and War', part ii. WA-II 21/45c, NA.

Witheford, H. 'Samoa, the War and Trusteeship'. WAII-21/22a, NA.

INTERVIEWS (conducted between August and December 1989)

Bill Hindmarsh & Colonel H. J. G. Low (both involved in the New Zealand Party)
Sir Wallace Rowling
Rt. Hon. David Lange
Hon. Warren Cooper
Rt. Hon. Brian Talboys

Election victories and officeholders, 1935–90

Abbreviations

PM	Prime Minister
MEA/MFA	Minister of External/Foreign Affairs
MF	Minister of Finance
LO	Leader of the Opposition
SEA/SFA	Secretary of External/Foreign Affairs

Year	Election victory[1]	PM	MEA/ MFA	MF	LO	SEA/ SFA
1935	Labour	Michael Joseph Savage		Walter Nash	George Forbes	
1936					Adam Hamilton	
1937						
1938	Labour (Oct.)					
1939						
1940		Peter Fraser[2]			Sidney Holland	
1941						
1942						
1943	Labour (Sept.)		Peter Fraser[3]			A. D. McIntosh
1944						
1945						
1946	Labour					
1947						
1948						
1949	National	Sidney Holland	Frederick Doidge	Sidney Holland	Peter Fraser	
1950					Walter Nash[4]	
1951	National (Sept.)		Clifton Webb			
1952						
1953						
1954	National		Tom Macdonald	Jack Watts		
1955						
1956						

316

Year	Election victory[1]	PM	MEA/ MFA	MF	LO	SEA/ SFA
1957		Keith Holyoake[5]				
	Labour	Walter Nash	Walter Nash	Arnold Nordmeyer	Keith Holyoake	
1958						
1959						
1960	National	Keith Holyoake	Keith Holyoake	Harry Lake	Walter Nash	
1961						
1962						
1963	National				Arnold Nordmeyer	
1964						
1965					Norman Kirk	
1966	National					G. R. Laking
1967				Robert Muldoon		
1968						
1969	National					
1970						
1971						
1972		John Marshall	Keith Holyoake			
	Labour	Norman Kirk	Norman Kirk	Bill Rowling	John Marshall	
1973						F. H. Corner
1974		Bill Rowling[6]	Bill Rowling	Bob Tizard	Robert Muldoon	
1975		Robert Muldoon	Brian Talboys	Robert Muldoon	Bill Rowling	
1976						
1977						
1978	National					
1979						
1980						M. Norrish
1981	National		Warren Cooper			
1982					David Lange	
1983						
1984	Labour (July)	David Lange	Frank O'Flynn	Roger Douglas	Robert Muldoon James McLay	
1985						
1986					Jim Bolger	

Year	Election victory[1]	PM	MEA/ MFA	MF	LO	SEA/ SFA
1987	Labour (Sept)		Russell Marshall			
1988			Russell Marshall and Mike Moore[7]	David Caygill		
						G. K. Ansell
1989		Geoffrey Palmer				
1990		Mike Moore	Mike Moore			
	National (Oct.)	Jim Bolger	Don McKinnon	Ruth Richardson	Mike Moore	

1   Month indicated if not November
2   Savage died in office, 27 March 1940.
3   Department of External Affairs established in 1943, renamed Ministry of Foreign Affairs, 1 Jan. 1970.
4   Fraser died 12 Dec. 1950, Nash was elected leader of the Labour Party, 17 Jan. 1951.
5   Holland retired because of ill health in September, two months before the election
6   Kirk died in office, 31 Aug. 1974.
7   Ministry of External Relations and Trade established, 1 Dec. 1988.

Index